INTERNATIONAL MEDIA LIABILITY

Civil Liability in the Information Age

INTERNATIONAL MEDIA LIABILITY

Civil Liability in the Information Age

Editor

Christian Campbell

PUBLISHED UNDER THE AUSPICES
OF THE CENTER FOR INTERNATIONAL LEGAL STUDIES
Salzburg, Austria

JOHN WILEY & SONS
Chichester • New York • Weinheim • Brisbane • Singapore • Toronto

Published in 1997 by   John Wiley & Sons Ltd,
                           Baffins Lane, Chichester,
                           West Sussex, PO19 1UD, England

                           National   01243 779 777
                           International (+44) 1243 779 777

                           e-mail (for orders and customer enquiries): cs-books@wiley.co.uk
                           Visit our Home Page on http://www.wiley.co.uk
                                     or http://www.wiley.com

Other Wiley Editorial Offices

John Wiley & Sons Inc., 65 Third Avenue,
New York, NY 10158–0012, USA

WILEY–VCH Verlag GmbH, Pappelallee 3,
D-69469 Weinheim, Germany

Jacaranda Wiley Ltd, 33 Park Road, Milton,
Queensland 4064, Australia

John Wiley & Sons (Asia) Pte Ltd, 2 Clementi Loop #02–01,
Jin Xing Distripark, Singapore 129809

John Wiley & Sons (Canada) Ltd, 22 Worcester Road,
Rexdale, Ontario M9W 1L1, Canada

Library of Congress Cataloging-in-Publication Data
International media liability / editor, Christian Campbell.
       p.   cm.
    "Published under the auspices of the Center for International
Legal Studies, Salzburg, Austria."
    Includes index.
    ISBN 0–471–96578–2
    1. Mass media—Law and legislation.   2. Libel and slander.
3. Press law—Criminal provisions.   I. Campbell, Christian T.
II. Center for International Legal Studies.
K4240.I56   1997   97–28574
346.03'4—dc21   CIP

British Library Cataloguing Publication Data
A catalogue record for this book is available from the British Library

ISBN 0–471–96578–2

Typeset in New Baskerville and Franklin Gothic by the Center for International Legal Studies,
Salzburg, Austria

Printed and bound in Great Britain by Bookcraft (Bath) Ltd, Midsomer Norton, Somerset
This book is printed on acid-free paper responsibly manufactured from sustainable forestation,
for which at least two trees are planted for each one used for paper production.

Contents

Contents

Contents

WILLIAM AKEL, Simpson Grierson, Auckland, New Zealand

PETER L. BARTLETT, Minter Ellison, Melbourne, Australia

KATHIE D. CLARET, Archibald Andersen, Neuilly-sur-Seine, France

JAVIER CREMADES, López Lozano, Cremades & Sánchez Pintado, Madrid, Spain

W.J.H.T. DUPONT, Molengraaff Instituut Privaatrecht, Universiteit Utrecht, Utrecht, The Netherlands

TIM J. EDWARD, Maclay Murray & Spens, Edinburgh, Scotland

GILL GRASSIE, Maclay Murray & Spens, Edinburgh, Scotland

MASAO HORIBE, Hitotsubashi University, Faculty of Law, Tokyo, Japan

DIETER HUBER, Constitutional Service of the Federal Chancellery, Vienna, Austria

E.J.M. JEUNINK, Molengraaff Instituut Privaatrecht, Universiteit Utrecht, Utrecht, The Netherlands

ROGER D. MCCONCHIE, Ladner Downs, Vancouver, Canada

JOHN MIDDLETON, Hitotsubashi University, Faculty of Law, Tokyo, Japan

MATTHIAS PRINZ, Prinz Neidhardt Engelschall, Hamburg, Germany

LAURENT ROUZEAU, Archibald Andersen, Neuilly-sur-Seine, France

C.J.M. VAN BERKEL, Molengraaff Instituut Privaatrecht, Universiteit Utrecht, Utrecht, The Netherlands

TRACEY J. WALKER, Simpson Grierson, Auckland, New Zealand

ALAN WILLIAMS, Denton Hall, London, England

AUSTRALIA

Peter L. Bartlett
Minter Ellison
P.O. Box 769G
Melbourne VIC 3001
Australia
Tel: (613) 9229 2000
Fax: (613) 9229 2666

CANADA

Roger D. McConchie
Ladner Downs
1200 Waterfront Centre
200 Burrard Street
P.O. Box 48600
Vancouver V7X 1T2
Canada
Tel: (604) 687 5744
Fax: (604) 687 1415

ENGLAND AND WALES

Alan Williams
Denton Hall
Five Chancery Lane
Clifford's Inn
London EC4A 1BU
England
Tel: (171) 242 1212
Fax: (171) 404 0087 or 320 6161

FRANCE

Kathie D. Claret and Laurent Rouzeau
Archibald Andersen
41, rue Ybry
92576 Neuilly-sur-Seine cedex
France
Tel: (331) 5561 1010
Fax: (331) 5561 1515

GERMANY

Matthias Prinz
Prinz Neidhardt Engelschall
Tesdorpfstr. 16
20148 Hamburg 13
Germany
Tel: (40) 443 066
Fax: (40) 410 6714

JAPAN

Masao Horibe and John Middleton
Hitotsubashi University
Faculty of Law
Kunitachi
Tokyo 186
Japan
Tel: (81 425) 72 1101
Fax: (81 425) 74 7704

THE NETHERLANDS

W.J.H.T. Dupont, C.J.M. van Berkel
and E.J.M. Jeunink
Molengraaff Instituut Privaatrecht
Universiteit Utrecht
Nobelstraat 2A
3512 EN Utrecht
The Netherlands
Tel: (3130) 253 7153
Fax: (3130) 253 7203

NEW ZEALAND

William Akel and Tracey J. Walker
Simpson Grierson
92–96 Albert Street
Private Bag 92518
Wellesley Street
Auckland
New Zealand
Tel: (649) 358 2222
Fax: (649) 307 0331

SCOTLAND

Gill Grassie and Tim J. Edward
Maclay Murray & Spens
3 Glenfinlas Street
Edinburgh EH3 6AQ
Scotland
Tel: (131) 226 5196
Fax: (131) 226 3174 or 225 9610

SPAIN

Javier Cremades
López Lozano, Cremades & Sánchez Pintado
Guzman El Bueno, 21
28015 Madrid
Spain
Tel: (341) 549 8080
Fax: (341) 549 8280

UNITED STATES

Dieter Huber
Constitutional Service of the
  Federal Chancellery
Ballhausplatz 4
1010 Vienna
Austria
Tel: (431) 53 1150
Fax: (431) 53 1152 823

Tables

Cases

Legislation

International Instruments

Australia

Chapter 1
Australia

Peter L. Bartlett
Minter Ellison
Melbourne, Australia

Introduction

The Australian approach to the role of the media in society, and the **1.1**
extent of its legal rights and obligations, is based on a unique blend of
conventions and laws. It is an idiosyncratic jurisdiction, which does not
mirror the approach taken in any other one country.

   The freedoms that the media enjoy, as well as the legal mechanisms
that restrain it and impose certain civil liabilities on it, are derived from
a number of sources including:

(1) The Common Law;
(2) The legislation of the Federal Parliament;
(3) The legislation of the various State Parliaments;
(4) The Australian Federal Constitution; and
(5) To a lesser extent, principles of international law.

The Australian Constitution impacts on the operations of media organi-   **1.2**
sations to the extent that it includes specific rights considered necessary
for the effective operation of the Australian Federal system. One relevant
example is the right to transmit communications nationally, which is
derived from the provision that trade, commerce and intercourse among
the states shall be absolutely free.[1] More recently it has been held that the
Australian Constitution also provides an implied right of free speech in
relation to political discussion. However, to a large degree, the rights and
obligations of the media in Australia are determined by Federal and State
Parliaments and the Common Law (as enunciated by the courts).

   Much of Australian media law has been developed by the courts
articulating the Common Law, but both the Federal and State Parliaments

---

1. Constitution Act 1900 (Cth), s 92; see also *Miller v TCN Channel Nine Pty Ltd.* (1986) 161 CLR 55.

can change or modify the Common Law by introducing legislation. Federal Parliament can legislate on all matters in relation to which the Australian Constitution has conferred powers on it. All remaining powers are left to State or Territory Parliaments. There are six states and two territories in Australia, each being separate legal jurisdictions.

The result of these different sources of law is that one of the greatest difficulties when assessing media law in Australia is the lack of uniformity between the different jurisdictions. For example, any national broadcaster or print media organisation is subject to eight regimes of defamation law. In some areas of the media, there is, in addition to state legislation, federal legislation impacting on the conduct of business. One area that is uniform is those laws governing radio and television, which are embodied in federal legislation.

For those laws that are determined by Common Law, the ultimate decision-making body is the Australian High Court. Appeals can be made from decisions of the highest court in each jurisdiction to the High Court.

Australian judges do not make law as parliaments do when they legislate. Instead, judges apply established, but not rigid, principles to the facts in each particular case.

Three broad areas have been covered in the following overview of media liability law in Australia. The discussion concentrates on civil rather than criminal liability and the overall perspective is the "regulation of communications".

The areas dealt with cover:

(1) Protection of reputation, including analysis of Australian defamation law and passing off;
(2) Protection of information, which includes consideration of privacy laws which operate in Australia; and
(3) Protection of the public interest which looks at the action of breach of confidence and prohibited speech legislation.

Defamation

1.3   The Australian Constitution does not recognise any express right of free speech. Unlike the United States with its Bill of Rights, or the United Kingdom with its Westminster system, the founders of the Australian Constitution decided that the processes of democracy would serve as the principal safeguards for the rights and freedoms on which a healthy, effective media depends.

While some specific rights have been explicitly recognised in the Australian Constitution, such as that of trade and commerce between States, the Australian approach has resulted in the High Court, the highest appellate court in Australia, having an important role in the interpretation of and enunciation of legal rights, freedoms and obligations. Recent Australian High Court decisions, discussed below, have held that the Australian Constitution contains a limited right of free speech. This is significant for the media and the operation of defamation laws across the country, however, the full extent of that significance is still a point of conjecture.

Defamation regime

Any defamation laws, by their nature, pose a threat to free speech. But as Australia has no national defamation law, the extent of that threat will depend on the State jurisdiction in which an action is brought, as well as the practical and political realities that impact on whether a particular plaintiff decides whether or not to sue. The defamation laws operating in the eight separate State jurisdictions have a number of fundamental differences. One difference is the source from which the law is derived. The law is either based on the Common Law, or a code or, as in the case of New South Wales, a hybrid of both legislation and the Common Law. Further fundamental differences also exist in the definitions of what constitutes defamation, the elements of the defences and even the available remedies. **1.4**

Sources of Defamation Law

In Victoria, South Australia, Western Australia, the Northern Territory and the Australian Capital Territory, defamation law is derived from the Common Law, with certain legislative modifications. In Queensland and Tasmania, defamation law is wholly codified. There has also been an adoption of a code in Western Australia; however, it is primarily limited to criminal defamation. Defamation law in New South Wales operated pursuant to a code until 1974, when the State Parliament passed the Defamation Act 1974 (NSW). That legislation returns some areas of defamation law to the purview of the Common Law, while making other elements subject to specific provisions of the Act itself. **1.5**

The lack of uniformity in Australian defamation law presents increasing difficulties in the developing communications era, where evermore sophisticated technology makes a mockery of State and Territory borders. Various moves throughout legal and governmental circles over the last 20 years towards achieving defamation uniformity have met with little practical success.

The most recent opportunity to frame the basis for uniform defamation legislation came with the inquiry held by the New South Wales Law Reform Commission in 1994. However, the Commission's Report,[2] released in September 1995, and discussed below, makes a number of recommendations for defamation reform which do not tackle various stances currently taken in other States. In seeking to achieve a more workable and effective defamation law for New South Wales, the recommendations in the Report may, if implemented, steer that State even further away from uniformity with the other jurisdictions.

Elements of the defamation action

1.6 The plaintiff in a defamation action must establish the elements of the cause of action; that the defendant published material concerning him or her that was defamatory of him or her. If these elements are established, and no defence operates, the publisher (that is, the person who or entity which "published" the material) will be held civilly liable.

Libel and slander

1.7 The Common Law distinguishes between libel and slander. Generally, libel is defamatory matter that is published in a permanent form, such as that which occurs in the print media. Defamatory material is categorised as slander if it is in more transient form, and generally is published to the ears rather than the eyes. Libel is actionable without proof of actual financial loss, whereas slander generally requires such proof. The basis for this distinction is founded on the assumption that some damage will necessarily flow from publication in permanent form, and that oral statements do less harm than written ones.

The distinction between libel and slander has been abolished in Queensland, Tasmania and the ACT.[3] This is also effectively the case in New South Wales where slander is actionable without proof of special damage. While the distinction has not been abolished in other jurisdictions, its effect has been limited by the Broadcasting Services Act 1992 (Cth) (picking up a provision in the former Broadcasting Act 1942 (Cth)), which deems radio and television broadcasts to be publications in permanent form.[4] This legislative provision recognises both the weakness of

---

2. "Defamation", New South Wales Law Reform Commission, Report number 75, Sydney 1995.

3. Criminal Code (QLD), s 368; Defamation Act 1957 (Tas), ss 6 and 9(1); ACT Defamation Act 1901 (NSW), s 3(2).

4. Broadcasting Services Act 1992 (Cth), s 206.

the assumptions on which the distinction between libel and slander is founded and the power and reach of the electronic media.

What is defamatory

In determining whether material is defamatory, an assessment of what is   **1.8**
meant by the material, or what imputations are conveyed by it, must be made. Whether that meaning or imputation falls within the definition of what is defamatory must then be considered. The judge decides whether material is capable of bearing a defamatory meaning. If it is so capable, the next question is one of fact: whether the material does in fact convey a defamatory meaning. This is a question for the jury if there is one. Most actions for defamation in Australia are heard before a judge and jury. The exception is the Australian Capital Territory, where actions are normally heard by a judge sitting alone.

Classical English judicial definitions of defamatory meaning continue to have an influence on the assessment of what is defamatory in modern Australian cases. These include:

(1) A publication that is calculated to injure the reputation of another by exposing him to hatred, contempt or ridicule;[5]

(2) A statement that would tend to lower the plaintiff in the estimation of right-thinking members of society generally;[6] and

(3) Material that tends to make people shun and avoid the plaintiff.[7]

The framing of the test in terms of "hatred, contempt, or ridicule" has   **1.9**
been criticised as too narrow and has been generally supplanted or at least enhanced by the "lowering estimation" test. This test also encompasses such imputations as a person being disloyal, rude, hypocritical, ungrateful, selfish, mean or a bad sport.

The "shun and avoid" test extends the categories of what may be classified as defamatory to encompass material that has a tendency to exclude the plaintiff from society, rather than simply injuring his or her reputation.[8] The courts have positively applied this test to allegations of insanity, disease or rape.[9]

---

5. *Parmiter* v *Coupland* (1840) 151 ER 340, 342 (Baron Parke).

6. *Sim* v *Stretch* [1936] 2 All ER 1237, 1240 (Lord Atkin).

7. *Youssoupoff* v *Metro-Goldwyn-Mayer* (1934) 50 TLR 58, 587 (Lord Justice Slesser).

8. *Sungravure Pty Ltd.* v *Middle East Airlines Airliban SAL* (1975–76) 134 CLR 1, 24 (Mason J).

9. *Dawson Bloodstock Agency Pty Ltd.* v *Mirror Newspapers Ltd.* [1979] 1 NSWLR 16; *Boyd* v *Mirror Newspapers Ltd.* [1980] 2 NSWLR 449.

Each of the three tests — "hatred, contempt and ridicule", "lowering estimation" and "shun and avoid" — with their different emphases and outcomes, contribute to the definition of what is defamatory; an imputation can be held to be defamatory if it satisfies any one of the tests. This was illustrated in *Boyd* v *Mirror Newspapers Ltd.*,[10] where a rugby player brought proceedings following an article published in the sporting pages of the *Sydney Daily Mirror*. The player complained that the article conveyed the following imputations:

(1) That he was so fat and slow that he could not properly play in his position in first grade rugby league football;

(2) That he was so fat as to appear ridiculous as he came on to the field; and

(3) That he had so allowed his physical condition to degenerate that he was a hopeless player.

1.10 The Court in that case held that the first imputation was not capable of defaming the plaintiff, as the description of "fat and slow", even if used to describe a rugby player, would not tend to make people shun and avoid the player, nor did it present him as ridiculous. However, the Court did hold that the second imputation was capable of defaming the plaintiff, because to say of someone that he appeared to be ridiculous, without any suggestion of fault on his part, could still be defamatory. The defendant actually conceded that the third imputation was capable of defaming the rugby player. It certainly satisfied the "lowering estimation" test and perhaps, in the Australian context, where fit sporting heroes are held up for national acclaim, could also satisfy the "hatred, contempt and ridicule" test.

The code, which applies in Queensland and Tasmania, abandons the Common Law reliance on a person's reputation being disparaged. It treats as defamatory any:

". . . imputation concerning any person, or any member of his family, whether living or dead, by which the reputation of that person is likely to be injured, or by which he is likely to be injured in his profession or trade, or by which other persons are likely to be induced to shun or avoid or ridicule or despise him".[11]

1.11 There are a number of features common to both the code and Common Law definitions of defamatory material:

(1) The plaintiff does not need to prove that the imputation was untrue;

(2) The fact that an allegation is untrue does not necessarily make it defamatory;

---

10. [1980] 2 NSWLR 449.

11. Criminal Code (QLD), s 366; Defamation Act 1957 (Tas), s 5.

(3) The fact that a plaintiff is annoyed, or has his or her feelings hurt by the publication of private, personal or confidential information does not make the material defamatory; and

(4) It is sufficient if the material has a tendency to defame the plaintiff; he or she does not need to prove that those who read, saw or heard the material actually responded in the manner contemplated by the tests.

A number of Australian cases illustrate how it may be defamatory to **1.12** display a plaintiff in a ridiculous light, notwithstanding that the material may not in fact disparage the plaintiff's reputation. In one case, a photograph had been published of a rugby league player and other team members having a shower after a game.[12] The plaintiff complained that the full frontal photograph appeared to expose his penis, making him a laughing stock. Damages of A$350,000 were awarded by the jury at trial; however, these damages where subsequently reduced on appeal. The court at first instance held that the photograph was capable of exposing him to ridicule, and was therefore capable of defaming him. This finding was not displaced on appeal. Further cases have distinguished between merely exposing someone to good-natured humour and actually deriding the person using humour as the vehicle.[13] The context of a humorous statement can be vital.

There are few reported cases of defamation actions that have arisen from a cartoon or caricature in Australia. However, it is possible that serious imputations of fact may lie visibly beneath the humorous surface, making a cartoon or caricature actionable in defamation.

A cartoon published by Australian *Penthouse* in 1993 featured a well-known female television news reader seated at a news desk, naked from the waist down. The cartoon was captioned "News Flash". A defamation action was threatened and the cartoon was withdrawn from publication and a public apology extended. It was arguable that the cartoon treated the newsreader as a sex object, implied she was promiscuous and certainly exposed her to ridicule.

What the defendant intended to convey is generally irrelevant.[14] However, Hunt J in the Supreme Court of New South Wales has taken the view that, for the resolution of some issues, it may be relevant to consider what the ordinary listener, reader or viewer would have understood the publisher's intention to be, from what was published.[15] For instance, where a statement

---

12. *Ettingshausen* v *Australian Consolidated Press Limited* (1991) 23 NSWLR 443.

13. *Emerson* v *Grimsby Times & Telegraph Co. Limited* (1926) 42 TLR 238.

14. *E Hulton & Co.* v *Jones* [1910] AC 20.

15. *Hepburn* v *TCN Channel Nine Pty Ltd.* [1983] 2 NSWLR 664, 667; *Baltinos* v *Foreign Language Publications Pty Ltd.* (1986) 6 NSWLR 85, 90.

is made or written in jest, the fact that the publisher intended the statement as a joke is of itself no defence to an action for defamation unless the statement was understood by those to whom it was published as having been intended as such.

The "right-thinking" members of Lord Atkin's test have been recast in Australian cases as "the ordinary citizen of fair average intelligence"[16] or "ordinary decent folk in the community"[17] or "hypothetical referees".[18]

Australian law has adopted the principle established in English cases that material is not defamatory merely on the basis that a particular sector of the community would find it so.[19] Glass JA in the New South Wales Court of Appeal has held that it is enough that "an appreciable section of the community" would interpret the statement as defamatory.[20]

Publication

1.13 The size of the audience to whom defamatory material is published does not matter, but the audience must be greater than simply the person whom the publication concerns.

Newspapers, television (particularly current affairs programmes) and radio are the most common vehicles for the publication of defamatory material. Books, magazines, posters and hand bills, paintings, the lyrics of songs and theatrical performances may all communicate defamatory material. Essentially, "publication" for the purposes of defamation law may occur by whatever means humans use to communicate with each other.

The code definitions of publication are comprehensive. The Queensland Code refers to the speaking or making of words or sounds, the making of signs, signals or gestures, or the public exhibition, or at least the showing of the defamatory matter, to any other person than the person defamed.[21]

The Tasmanian Code defines publication to have a very similar scope. While there is no specific reference to publication by signs, signals or gestures, there is reference to communication "in any other manner".[22]

---

16. *Slatyer v Daily Telegraph* (1908) 6 CLR 1, 7 (Griffith J).

17. *Gardiner v John Fairfax & Sons Pty Ltd.* (1942) 42 SR (NSW) 171, 172 (Jordan CJ); *Consolidated Trust Co. Ltd. v Browne* (1948) 49 SR (NSW) 86, 88 (Jordan CJ).

18. *Readers' Digest Services Pty Ltd. v Lamb* (1982) 150 CLR 500, 506 (Brennan J).

19. *Tolley v JS Fry & Sons Ltd.* [1930] 1 KB 467, 479 (Greer LJ) (Court of Appeal).

20. *Middle East Airlines Airliban SAL v Sungravure Pty Ltd.* [1974] 1 NSWLR 323, 340 (Glass JA); *Hepburn v TCN Channel Nine Pty Ltd.* [1983] 2 NSWLR 682, 693–694 (Glass JA).

21. Criminal Code (Qld), s 369.

22. Defamation Act (Tas), s 7(B).

The irrelevance of the publisher's intentions contributes to the application of strict liability for publication.[23] In imposing strict liability, however, a distinction is drawn between primary and secondary publishers. In the case of a newspaper article, for example, the primary publishers are constituted by the journalist who wrote the article, the editor and sub-editor involved in its preparation and presentation, the proprietor of the newspaper and even the printers. This chain of liability can also begin with a letter to the editor, or a statement made by an interviewee. Strict liability for publication applies to this group.

Secondary publishers are those who play a lesser, more mechanical, role in the distribution of defamatory matter such as booksellers and newsagents. Secondary publishers are still liable for publication, but may be able to rely on the defence of "innocent dissemination".[24] To do so, they must prove that they did not know or had no reason to know or suspect that the material they distributed contained defamatory matter.

Publication takes place in each instance where the material is read, seen or heard by a person other than the person defamed. Many newspapers and magazines and a number of radio and television programmes are circulated or broadcast throughout Australia. A person who claims to have been defamed by such a publication brings a single action, but can plead a separate cause of action for each state or territory where the publication took place. It is possible that such a plaintiff could achieve different results regarding the publication in different jurisdictions.

One case brought in the Australian Capital Territory[25] concerned an interview in a Canberra television studio in an edition of a television programme, *This Day Tonight*, which was broadcast in the Australian Capital Territory, New South Wales and Victoria. The plaintiff succeeded in the actions in some jurisdictions but not others. A defence operated in New South Wales regarding one of the pleaded imputations, whereas no defence applied in Victoria or the Australian Capital Territory.

Each person who repeats or republishes defamatory material will be held liable to the same extent as the original publisher whether or not they endorse the statement,[26] unless a particular defence operates to protect them, such as qualified privilege. To plead the defence of justification (or truth), a defendant must establish the truth of the defamatory imputation. To show merely that the statement was made

---

23. *E Hulton & Co. v Jones* [1910] AC 20.

24. *Emmens v Pottle* (1885) 16 QBD 354, 357 (Lord Esher MR), and 358 (Bowen LJ); *Goldsmith v Sperrings Limited* [1977] 1 WLR 478, 486–488 (Lord Denning MR).

25. *Gorton v Australian Broadcasting Commission and Walsh* (1973) 22 FLR 181.

26. *McCauley v John Fairfax & Sons Limited* (1933) 34 SR (NSW) 339, 341–342 (James J).

by the person quoted, or that the particular rumour referred to was in fact circulating, are irrelevant "truths", and as such insufficient to establish the defence.

Identification

1.14　To succeed in a defamation action the plaintiff must establish that the publication concerned him or her, that is, that he or she was the person defamed. "Person" in this context refers to legal personality, so that an organisation with legal personality, such as a trade union or a company, may sue in defamation. References to an address or occupation, physical characteristics, mannerisms or social habits may be sufficient to identify someone, notwithstanding that the publisher may not have intended to identify that person. The test to be applied is whether the material is such that people who are acquainted with the plaintiff would be led to reasonably believe in the circumstances that he or she was the person to whom the publication referred.[27] Similarly, a fictional work may still defame a person if it could reasonably be understood to refer to that person.[28]

A publication that was intended to refer to a particular person, which is defamatory but true of that person, may also defame another person who bears the same name, or who is in some other way similarly identified. In one Australian case a witness had given evidence to a public inquiry into allegations of corruption in the Victorian Police Force. A witness in the inquiry had stated that "First Constable Lee of the Motor Registration Branch" had accepted a bribe. A journalist reported the witness as having said that "Detective Lee" had accepted a bribe. There were in fact three officers in the police force operating in Victoria all named Lee, being the Constable in the Motor Registration Branch, and two other detectives. The two detectives successfully sued the newspaper.[29]

The Detective Lee case illustrates the importance of describing the person referred to with sufficient particularity so as to minimise the material's ability to be read as referring to someone else.

A group of people cannot be defamed as a group. Further, an individual may not sue regarding defamatory material concerning a group or body unless the material may reasonably be understood to refer to that particular person.[30] A corporation does not have a "personal reputation" and

---

27. *David Syme & Co. Limited v Canavan* (1918) 25 CLR 234, 238 (Isaacs J).

28. *E Hulton & Co. v Jones* [1910] AC 20.

29. *Lee v Wilson* (1934) 51 CLR 276, 283–286 (Starke J), 295 (Dixon J), and 299 (Evatt and McTiernan JJ).

30. *David Syme & Co. Limited v Canavan* (1918) 25 CLR 234, 238 (Isaacs J).

therefore can only sue over allegations relating to its business operations, such as whether it conducts its business competently or honestly.[31]

An allegation about a deceased person is actionable only if it defames a living person.

Defamation on-line

A difficulty with any analysis of the legal issues involved in defamation   **1.15**
on-line in Australia, and internationally, is the current lack of judicial consideration of the issues. In determining what civil liability service providers, authors and media organisations may face for any defamation on-line, principles are largely determined by drawing analogies with existing defamation principles.

In Australia there has only been one decision specifically related to defamation on-line. *Rindos* v *Hardwick*[32] was a case brought by an anthropologist employed as a university lecturer in Western Australia. The plaintiff complained that he had been defamed on a science anthropology bulletin board on the Internet. The plaintiff made out his claim and was awarded A $40,000 damages.

The case was undefended, so unfortunately the analysis of the legal issues involved with defamation on-line was limited. However, *Rindos* v *Hardwick* clearly recognised that a communication on an electronic bulletin board will be treated as publication for the purposes of defamation.

In *Rindos* v *Hardwick* the defendant was the author of the original defamatory message. What is presently undecided by the courts in Australia is the extent to which service providers or system operators may be held responsible for defamation on-line. In this regard Australian courts will be looking closely at decisions that have been handed down in the United States.[33]

The Australian judiciary will need to refer back to the traditional categories of primary publishers (*i.e.*, broadcasters or newspaper publishers), secondary publishers (*i.e.*, booksellers or newsagents) and facility providers (*i.e.*, telephone companies), and determine which of these categories best describes this new group of media players. The extent of liability that they face should be based on this categorisation.

---

31. *Bargold Pty Ltd.* v *Mirror Newspapers Limited* [1981] 1 NSWLR 9; *National Union of General and Municipal Workers* v *Gillian* [1946] KB 81.

32. Unreported, Ipp J., Western Australian Supreme Court, 31 March 1994.

33. See, *e.g.*, *Cubby Inc.* v *CompuServe Inc.* 776 F. Supp. 135 (SDNY 1991), *Stratton Oakmont Inc.* v *Prodigy Services Co.* 1995 WL 323710 (NY. Sup Ct 1995) and *Religious Technology Centre* v *Netcom Online Communication Services* 1995 WL 707167 (ND. Cal 1995).

Australian media players already involved (or considering becoming involved) in the on-line world are carefully monitoring international developments in the law of defamation on-line. Of particular interest and concern are the United States cases involving on-line communications service providers CompuServe,[34] Prodigy[35] and Netcom.[36]

The global nature of on-line communications means that jurisdiction is another area that raises significant legal issues when considering liability for defamation.

Defamatory material originates in one jurisdiction but it may be available to anyone in the world who has network access to the particular site on which the material appears. Applying the established principles of defamation actions in Australia, the defamatory material would be found to have been published in every single country where there is computer access to the particular site.

This means that parties in one country could be held liable for defamation appearing in another country that has quite a different defamation regime. Internationally, the degree to which countries protect their citizens against defamation and the level of damages awarded in defamation actions varies greatly.

This creates a further problem of enforcement. In many cases the identity of a publisher of defamatory material will be anonymous and untraceable. Furthermore, even if the person was identifiable in the on-line world, he or she may be anywhere in the real world, making any legislation impracticable, considering the very real difficulties of enforcement.

Defences

1.16   Australian defamation law recognises the public interest in free speech in some circumstances, so that certain defences operate to protect a publisher who has defamed a plaintiff. Those defences include:

    (1)   Justification (or "truth");
    (2)   Absolute privilege;
    (3)   Qualified privilege;
    (4)   Fair comment;
    (5)   Innocent publication;
    (6)   Consent; and
    (7)   Triviality.

---

34. *Cubby Inc.* v *CompuServe Inc.* 776 F. Supp. 135 (SDNY 1991).

35. *Stratton Oakmont Inc.* v *Prodigy Services Co.* 1995 WL 323710 (NY. Sup Ct 1995).

36. *Religious Technology Centre* v *Netcom Online Communication Services* 1995 WL 707167 (ND. Cal 1995).

The operation and availability of these defences vary between Australian **1.17** jurisdictions. A further defence arising out of a constitutional implied right of free speech in relation to political matters has also recently been enunciated by the High Court and is also discussed below.

Justification

The operation of defamation law is such that a defamatory publication is **1.18** presumed to be false. The defendant therefore carries the burden of proving the publication was true (or of establishing another defence). This clearly puts the plaintiff at an advantage (compared with the operation of the law of injurious falsehood, discussed below).

Truth alone is a complete defence to a defamation action in Victoria, South Australia, Western Australia and the Northern Territory. However, to be protected by this defence in New South Wales, Queensland, Tasmania and the Australian Capital Territory, a defendant must go further than simply establishing that the defamatory imputations were true. The defendant must also show that the material was published for the "public benefit",[37] or that it relates to a matter of "public interest".[38] These additional elements introduce a measure of privacy protection in those jurisdictions. It is not sufficient that the public would be curious to read, see or hear the publication. The defendant must show that the publication is for the benefit of the public, or that it is in the interests of the public.

The timing of a publication is relevant. Past transgressions that the media revives may be true, but not justifiable, if the courts do not regard the publication of those transgressions as having been done in the public interest or for the public benefit.[39]

The burden of establishing the defence of justification has great practical significance for the media. A media organisation must be able to prove the truth of a publication by evidence that is admissible in court. Information obtained from secondary sources will generally be inadmissible as hearsay. This puts pressure on journalists who have undertaken to a source that his or her identity will not be disclosed (see below under discussion of breach of confidence for an overview of the position regarding disclosure of journalists' sources). These difficulties of proof clearly have the potential to have somewhat of a "chilling effect" on the way the media reports true publications as well as false ones.

---

37. Criminal Code (QLD), s 376; Defamation Act 1957 (TAS), s 15; and in the ACT, the Defamation Act 1901 (NSW), s 6.

38. Defamation Act 1974 (NSW), s 15.

39. *Rofe v Smith's Newspapers Ltd.* (1925) 25 SR (NSW) 4, 21–22 (Street ACJ).

Absolute privilege

1.19 Statements made in the course of proceedings in Parliament, in court, or in certain tribunals, and documents presented in these proceedings or published under their authority are accorded absolute privilege. The rationale for this defence is that, in these situations, free communication is considered so vital to the interests of society that a person's interest in protecting his or her reputation is displaced. The motive of the speaker or writer, or the accuracy of their statement is irrelevant. As this defence is directed towards upholding the institutions of the Parliament and the courts, the same absolute protection does not extend to any republication of those statements.

Qualified privilege

1.20 The circumstances in which qualified privilege subsists varies, depending on the Australian jurisdiction. This defence encompasses a variety of activities that are all protected on public policy grounds. Generally, the defence of qualified privilege serves to protect publications that are:

(1) Made in the performance of a duty or to protect an interest;
(2) Made in reply to an attack;
(3) Fair and accurate reports of certain proceedings;
(4) Extracts from certain documents; or
(5) Official notices.

1.21 The fundamental distinction between absolute and qualified privilege is that absolute privilege provides protection regardless of the publisher's motive for publication, whereas proof that the publisher was motivated by malice will defeat a defence of qualified privilege. In this context, malice means an improper motive such as spite or ill will, or where there is no honest belief in the truth of the material.

Corresponding duty and interest

1.22 At Common Law, a communication attracts qualified privilege if the person making the communication has a legal, social or moral duty or interest to make that communication to the person to whom it is made, and the person who receives the communication has a corresponding duty or interest to receive it. This reciprocity is an essential element which has limited the applicability of this form of qualified privilege to the media.[40]

---

40. *Arnold* v *The King-Emperor* (1914) 30 TLR 462, 468; *Morosi* v *Mirror Newspapers Ltd.* [1977] 2 NSWLR 749.

Publication to the public at large has generally been held to be too wide for the necessary reciprocity to subsist; however, recent developments in the High Court have potentially expanded this defence quite significantly, where the material complained of constitutes "political discussion".

In *Theophanous* v *Herald & Weekly Times*,[41] the majority said:

> "Common law qualified privilege must now be viewed in the light of the implied constitutional freedom. That does not necessitate a review of its essential feature, namely, publication on an occasion of qualified privilege or of the Common Law requirement that publication be without malice. It does, however, require some consideration of the notion of reciprocal interest and duty. The public at large has an interest in the discussion of political matter such that each and every person has an interest, of the kind contemplated by the Common Law, in communicating his or her views on those matters and each and every person has an interest, in receiving information on those matters. It is an interest which exists at all times, it is not confined to situations where it is publicly anticipated that a federal election will be called. It follows that the discussion of political matters is an occasion of qualified privilege."

1.23 See below for further discussion of the expansion of qualified privilege in relation to political discussion and the implied constitutional right to freedom of speech.

The Common Law defence of "duty and interest" applies in all jurisdictions except Queensland and Tasmania; however, in New South Wales both the Common Law defence and a statutory defence are available.[42]

Right of reply

1.24 The Australian law recognises that a person who has been publicly criticised is entitled to defend himself or herself by a counter-attack that defames the original critic. The reply must be relevant and reasonably proportionate to the original criticism and must be published to substantially the same audience. For example, the editor of a newspaper is entitled to respond to a public attack on the newspaper's reputation. This form of qualified privilege will also be granted to the media when it provides a person who has been publicly criticised with the opportunity to respond.

---

41. (1994) 182 CLR 104.

42. Defamation Act 1974 (NSW), s 20(1)(c) and s 22.

Fair and accurate reports of certain proceedings

1.25 Qualified privilege will exist where a publication is a fair and accurate report of certain proceedings that are outlined below. The policy justification for qualified privilege attaching to such reports is based on the right of the public to attend public proceedings and also to inform themselves of what occurred there, irrespective of their ability to attend. The value to the media in being able to have access to these reports cannot be underestimated.

Not all Australian jurisdictions have the same rules regarding fair and accurate reports of proceedings and the Common Law position has been overshadowed by specific legislative enactments broadening the scope of this form of qualified privilege in most States.[43] These specific statutory enactments are not so broad as to completely supplant the Common Law. In Queensland, Tasmania and Western Australia the Common Law defence of fair and accurate reporting is not available.

1.26 **Fair and accurate report** A report will be fair and accurate where it "substantially records what was said and done".[44] This gives considerable scope for abridgement, paraphrasing or modification. However, the report cannot be said to be fair and accurate if it substantially alters the impression a reader would receive or misrepresents a material fact. Consequently, a publication that quotes a suggestion that is defamatory, such as during cross-examination in court, which does not contain the witness's denial will misrepresent that the witness could not or did not refute the claim.[45]

It is immaterial that the statements recorded in the publication were irrelevant to the issues being litigated (or debated) or that the statements themselves are factually untrue.[46] The reason for this is that what has been recorded is no different from what a member of the public could have heard had they attended the particular proceeding.

1.27 **Proceedings** At Common Law, fair reports of judicial proceedings, parliamentary proceedings and public meetings may all attract qualified privilege.

    (1) *Judicial Proceedings* — The privilege afforded to fair and accurate reports of judicial proceedings are invariably defined in legislation,

---

43. *E.g.*, Wrongs Act 1958 (Vic), s 3A(1) in relation to parliamentary proceedings and s 3A(2) in relation to court proceedings.

44. *Waterhouse* v *Broadcasting Station 2GB Pty Ltd.* (1985) 1 NSWLR 58, 62–3 (Hunt J).

45. See, *e.g.*, *Thompson* v *Truth and Sportsman Ltd.* (1933) 34 SR (NSW) 21.

46. *Waterhouse* v *Broadcasting Station 2GB Pty Ltd.* (1985) 1 NSWLR 58, 62–3 (Hunt J).

which may even grant absolute privilege.[47] The judicial proceedings must have been conducted in open court, in the sense that the public had a right to be admitted.

In addition, publication must not constitute a contempt.

For example, publication of evidence found to be inadmissible by a trial judge, or parts of a proceeding protected by a suppression or pseudonym order cannot be published. Affidavits and pleadings that may be part of the court record are not protected unless they have been read out or tendered in open court.[48]

Reports of a foreign country's[49] judicial proceedings do not necessarily attract privilege at Common Law.[50] A defendant must prove that the foreign court proceedings are of significant local concern.

The proceedings of quasi-judicial proceedings may also be protected at Common Law if such publication meets the policy objectives of qualified privilege. This is becoming increasingly important in Australia as quasi-judicial tribunals have proliferated in recent years. However, where the public is barred from attending the proceedings, it would seem that this justification is undermined. So a defendant would have to establish that the public has a genuine interest in knowing the outcome of the proceedings. Specific statutory provisions often confer privilege on the reports of commissions and tribunals.[51]

(2) *Parliamentary Proceedings* — Fair and accurate reports of parliamentary proceedings or debate or proceedings of both State and Federal parliamentary committees are accorded qualified privilege at Common Law. At the federal level the Parliamentary Privileges Act 1987 (Cth) provides a statutory statement of privilege.[52]

(3) *Public Meetings* — In Australia the Common Law does not afford privilege to the proceedings of public meetings, local council meetings or other local bodies. However, in all jurisdictions except Victoria

---

47. See, *e.g.*, Wrongs Act 1958 (Vic), s 4 in relation to publication in Victoria of Victorian court proceedings.

48. *Gobbart v West Australian Newspapers* [1968] WAR 113.

49. *Bunker v James and Downland Publications Ltd.* (1981) SASR 286 rejected the argument that state judicial proceedings are not "foreign" to other states. One can look on this as arising from the federal nature of Australia.

50. NSW is the only jurisdiction where foreign proceedings do automatically attract privilege: Defamation Act 1974 (NSW), s 24, Sch 2, cll 1, 2(5).

51. See, *e.g.*, Equal Opportunity Tribunal hearings: Defamation Act 1974 (NSW), s 24, Sch 2, cl 2(12) and proceedings before the Independent Commission Against Corruption: Defamation Act 1974 (NSW), s 24, Sch 2, cl 2(18).

52. Parliamentary Privileges Act 1987 (Cth), s 10(1).

and the Australian Capital Territory, public meetings are privileged by virtue of statute,[53] as are local (municipal) council meetings in all jurisdictions.[54]

(4) *Extracts from Certain Documents* — Excerpts from parliamentary papers, public records and public notices may also amount to fair and accurate reports and attract qualified privilege. Statutory protection is afforded to a copy of the whole, or extracts from, any paper published by order or under the authority of Parliament.

Extracts from records to which the public has access, and that are maintained pursuant to statutory authority, are also afforded qualified privilege. Once again, as with all instances of qualified privilege of fair and accurate reports, this is subject to the material being published without malice and the extract actually being fair and accurate.

(5) *Official Notices* — Most jurisdictions in Australia grant statutory privilege to notices or reports issued for public information by a state or the federal government. A distinction must be carefully maintained between official notices, which are protected, and mere publicity circulars or media releases that keep parliamentary members in the public eye, which are not protected.

Unlike other sources of information, there is considerably less latitude to paraphrase official notices and the reporting must be much closer to the actual notice.[55]

1.28 **Loss of qualified privilege** The protection of the defence of qualified privilege may be lost if the privilege is abused. A defendant may not take advantage of the occasion to make statements that it does not believe to be true, or makes out of spite or for some other improper purpose. The malice of a journalist may also be imputed to his or her employer. To establish malice in this context, it is not sufficient to show that the defendant published an unreasonable, unfair or even untrue statement. The plaintiff must also establish that the defendant published the statement either knowing that it was false, or without having an honest

---

53. Defamation Act 1974 (NSW), s 24, Sch 2, paragraph 2(9); Wrongs Act 1936 (SA), s 7(1)(a); Criminal Code (Qld), s 374(7); Criminal Code (WA), s 354(7); Defamation Act 1957 (Tas), s 13(1)(h); Defamation Act (NT), s 6(1)(a).

54. Wrongs Act 1946 (SA), s 7(1)(b); Criminal Code (Qld), s 374(6); Criminal Code (WA), s 354(6); Defamation Act 1957 (Tas), s 13(1)(g); ACT: Defamation (Amendment) Act 1909 (NSW) (in relation to newspaper reports only), s 5(h); Wrongs Act 1958 (Vic), s 5 (in relation to newspaper reports only; re municipal councils except where neither the public nor reporters are admitted); Defamation Act (NT), s 6(1)(b); Defamation Act 1974 (NSW), indirectly through s 24(2) and schedule 2, paragraph 2(a).

55. See, *e.g.*, *Campbell* v *Associated Newspaper Ltd.* (1948) 48 SR (NSW) 301; *John Fairfax & Sons Ltd.* v *Hook* (1983) 47 ALR 477.

belief in its truth. This would include a consideration of whether the defendant published recklessly as to whether the matter was true or false, or failed to inquire as to its truth.[56] This analysis could also involve considering whether the publisher had some other improper motive for publishing the material, having published for a dominant purpose other than those purposes for which the privilege is given.[57]

Fair comment

Fair comment is the defence most frequently used by media organisations **1.29** in response to a defamation action. This defence most commonly arises in relation to the treatment of current affairs, sports coverage and entertainment and the criticism of literature, art and theatre. The defence is based on freedom of speech considerations.[58] Essentially, this defence allows expressions of opinion on matters of public interest to be shielded from defamation liability. It must be proven by the defendant that the comments were published as a fair comment on a matter of public interest.

Comment and statements of fact

A comment is "something which is or can reasonably be inferred to be a **1.30** deduction, inference, conclusion, criticism, judgment, remark, observation, etc.".[59] Only comments recognisable as such are afforded protection. No protection is given to statements presented as facts concerning or describing the subject.[60]

The comment is examined in the context of the whole of the published material; however, if statements of fact and statements of opinion are intermingled there is a risk that the reader will get the impression that the whole report consists of assertions of fact.[61] Similarly, the form of expression is not determinative. Introducing statements with phrases such as "it appears to me", or "in my opinion" will not necessarily mean that the listener or reader will realise the comments are statements of opinion rather than fact.

Where the facts on which the comment is based are not stated or indicated, courts are likely to find that which is purportedly comment is

---

56. *Sinclair* v *Bjelke-Petersen* [1984] 1 QdR 484.

57. *Horrocks* v *Lowe* [1975] AC 135 at 149–150 per Lord Diplock (with whom Lords Wilberforce, Hodson and Kilbrandon agreed).

58. *Slim* v *Daily Telegraph* [1968] 2 QB 157, 170 (Lord Denning MR).

59. *Clarke* v *Norton* (1910) VLR 494, 499 (Cussen J).

60. *Broadway Approvals Ltd.* v *Odhams Press Ltd.* [1964] 2 QB 683; Defamation Act 1974 (NSW), s 35.

61. *Hunt* v *Star Newspaper Co. Ltd.* [1908] 2 KB 309, 319–20 (Fletcher Moulton LJ).

in reality an assertion of fact.[62] The rationale for this is that the publisher has not given sufficient information for the public to assess the weight of the comment and make up their own minds.

The facts supporting the comment must also be true or protected by absolute privilege. Invention, misdescription or a misquotation of facts on which the opinion is based may all cause the defence of fair comment to fail.

The comment must be fair in the sense of being honestly held.[63] *Obiter dicta* in *Purvan v North Queensland Newspapers Co. Ltd.*[64] indicated that the Australian High Court will follow *Telnikoff v Matusevitch*,[65] which held that the test for fair comment is objective, that is, whether any fair-minded person could honestly express that opinion on the proven facts. The burden of proof of establishing this rests with the defendant. However, even though the comment may satisfy the objective test, the defence can be defeated if the plaintiff proves the defendant was actuated by express malice. It is a matter of contention whether malice will defeat the defence of fair comment in all jurisdictions. In regard to the code jurisdictions, it appears reasonably clear that malice is not a factor to be considered.[66]

Matter of public interest

1.31   For fair comment to apply, the comment must be on a matter of public interest. The "public interest" is such an amorphous concept that it would be expected that it is impossible to formulate an authoritative definition as to its scope. This indeed is borne out by judicial decisions.[67]

An indication of the scope of "public interest" can, however, be ascertained from the cases where it has been successfully argued. The concept includes aspects of public concern such as public administration, government affairs, the administration of justice and the public affairs of professionals, corporations and institutions. Commentary and criticism of plays, books, films and other works in the public purview also fall within the definition.

Public interest does not usually extend to private affairs of people, so comment in this regard will not be protected by this defence. The defence does not protect the criticism of the private affairs of public figures.[68]

---

62. See, *e.g.*, *Myerson v Smith's Weekly Publishing Co. Ltd.* (1924) 24 SR (NSW) 20, 26 (Ferguson J).

63. *Lloyd v David Syme & Co. Ltd.* (1985) 3 NSWLR 728.

64. (1994) 68 ALJR 1.

65. [1992] 2 AC 343.

66. Criminal Code (Qld), s 375; Defamation Act 1957 (Tas), s 14(1)(a); Criminal Code (WA), s 355, and *Defamation Ordinance* 1938 (NT), s 6 A. *Cawley v Australian Consolidated Press Ltd.* [1981] 1 NSWLR 225.

67. *London Artists v Littler* [1969] 2 All ER 193, 198, (Lord Denning).

68. *Mulch v Sleeman* (1929) 29 SR (NSW) 125, 137 (Ferguson J).

Innocent publication

As has been discussed above, the state of the mind of the publisher is **1.32** generally irrelevant when considering whether there has been an actionable defamation. It has been held that a publisher was liable for defamation where the publisher had no knowledge and could not readily find out the facts from which the defamatory inference was drawn.[69] In such a case the publisher clearly had no intention to defame. The possibility of inadvertently defaming an unknown person remains a real risk for media organisations.[70]

As a consequence, New South Wales and Tasmanian legislatures have introduced a procedure whereby an offer of amends may be made where the publisher took reasonable care in publication, did not intend any defamatory comment and did not know of the facts that made the statements defamatory.[71] If the offer is accepted then the publisher must publish a correction and an apology. On publication the person defamed is barred from ever instituting litigation in regard to the defamation. If the offer is not accepted then it is a mitigating factor that the defendant was willing to publish a correction and apology.

Consent

Consent is clearly a defence to defamation at Common Law. However, it **1.33** is necessary to prove not only that the person had notice of the publication but that they actually authorised it.

Triviality

Triviality is not a Common Law defence to defamation *per se*. However, **1.34** if the published material contains only a mild sting, it is more likely the Court will hold that it did not adversely affect the reputation of the person, and therefore was not defamatory.

In New South Wales, Queensland, Tasmania and the Australian Capital Territory, a defence exists that gives consideration to the circumstances surrounding publication as well as the nature of the publication. NSW, Queensland, Tasmania and the ACT have a defence that the publication was not likely to injure the person defamed, although in all but New South Wales, this is limited to oral publication.[72]

---

69. *Cassidy* v *Daily Mirror Newspapers Ltd.* [1929] 2 KB 331.

70. See, *e.g.*, *E Hulton & Co.* v *Jones* [1910] AC 20 and *Lee* v *Wilson* (1934) 51 CLR 276 for examples of just such liability arising.

71. Defamation Act 1974 (NSW), ss 36–45; Defamation Act 1957 (Tas), s 17.

72. *Defamation Law of Queensland* 1889, s 20; Defamation Act 1957 (Tas), s 9(2); ACT: Defamation Act 1901 (NSW), s 4; Defamation Act 1974 (NSW), s 13.

Free speech and political discussion

1.35 In Australian defamation cases, judges have often been asked to follow the line of United States cases that began with *New York Times* v *Sullivan*,[73] and recognise a public figure defence. The invitation has never been taken up.

Australian Law Reform Commissions have also considered the merits of adopting a public figure defence but have declined to recommend its introduction.[74]

Despite judicial and legislative reluctance to adopt a public figure defence, the Australian High Court decision in *Theophanous* v *Herald & Weekly Times Ltd.*[75] has ushered through the back door a defence that some commentators have referred to as a form of public figure defence.[76]

The Australian Constitution does not expressly protect "freedom of speech", unlike the position, for example, in the United States. However, what was confirmed in *Theophanous* was:

(1) The existence of an implied constitutionally guaranteed freedom of speech in relation to political communications; and
(2) That discussion of political matters is an occasion of qualified privilege.

1.36 In 1997, the High Court will hear the State and Australian Governments' submissions to review and overturn the *Theophanous* principles.

Implied freedom of speech guaranteed by Australian Constitution

1.37 The implied freedom of speech recognised in *Theophanous* is applicable in relation to political discussion. It was stated in that case:

> "The concept [of political discussion]. . . includes discussion of the political views and public conduct of persons who are engaged in activities that have become the subject of political debate, e.g., trade union leaders, Aboriginal political leaders and economic commentators."[77]

---

73. (1964) 376 United States 254.

74. *Defamation*, New South Wales Law Reform Commission, DP 32, Sydney 1995, Chapter 10 and *Defamation*, New South Wales Law Reform Commission, Report number 75, Sydney 1995, Chapter 5. At Para 5.22 it was concluded by the Commission that the public figure defence appears to contribute to problems of lengthy and costly proceedings and would hinder effective adjudication of the issue of truth.

75. (1994) 124 ARL 1 ("Theophanous"). See also *Stephens* v *Western Australia Newspapers Ltd.* (1994) 125 ALR 80.

76. Deamer, "Don't Jump for Joy" (1994), 26 *Gazette of Law and Journalism* 3.

77. *Theophanous*, 14 (Mason CJ, Toohey and Gaudron JJ) — 3 of the majority of 4 in *Theophanous*.

It was held that where material falls within the scope of the implied 1.38 freedom, there exists a constitutional defence to a claim that the material is defamatory. For a publisher to successfully rely on this free speech defence, in addition to the requirement that the published material is "political discussion", it is necessary for the publisher to establish that it:

(1) Did not know the material was false;
(2) Did not publish recklessly, that is, not caring whether the material was true or false; and
(3) Did not publish unreasonably.

Although it is not yet clear exactly what will be required to satisfy these 1.39 elements, the burden on a media defendant to prove that a publication was "reasonable in the circumstances" is likely to be a heavy one. In effect, the defendant will be required to produce evidence of a nature that would negate any finding of malice.

Since *Theophanous* there have been a number of cases in which attempts have been made to plead the free speech defence.[78]

Lovell v *Hancock*[79] concerned passages of a book that allege that a police officer was involved in a conspiracy to pervert the course of justice by fabricating evidence and falsifying a confession. The court took a broad interpretation of "political discussion" and allowed the free speech defence to go forward. The concept of "public affairs" was treated as interchangeable with "political discussion".

However, it is probably not correct to categorise this new freedom of speech defence in Australia as a public figure defence. The reason for this is that, although the defence will often apply where the plaintiff is a public figure, the determining factor remains whether the material is in fact political discussion. The application of the defence is referable to the subject matter of discussion rather than the position of the person who issues proceedings.

Qualified privilege and political discussion

In *Theophanous* it was said that the Common Law "duty-interest" defence of 1.40 qualified privilege must now be viewed in light of the implied constitutional

---

78. In both *Williams* v *John Fairfax & Sons*, Supreme Court of New South Wales, 24 October 1994, which concerned severe criticism of a Magistrate in the conduct of his office, and *Kime* v *Moody*, Supreme Court of New South Wales, 15 December 1994, which involved a local government councillor, the free speech defence was allowed to go forward.

79. Supreme Court of Western Australia, 4 April 1995.

freedom. The majority in that case decided that the discussion of political matters is an occasion of qualified privilege. It was stated:

> "The public at large has an interest in the discussion of political matters such that each and every person has an interest, of the kind contemplated by the Common Law, in communicating his or her views on those matters and each and every person has an interest in receiving information on those matters".[80]

1.41 This widened considerably the previously accepted view in Australia of the required reciprocal interest and duty for qualified privilege. This is a particularly important development for the media, as traditionally, due to the wide circulation that the mass media has, the public at large was seen as too wide a group to have the necessary interest in receiving material. Of course, what was not altered is the ability of the qualified privilege defence to be defeated if the plaintiff establishes malice.

The recognition of instant reciprocity established by the discussion of a political matter was discussed in a number of cases prior to *Theophanous*. It appears reasonable to conclude that all voters have a corresponding interest and duty to discuss political matters and so it is not surprising that discussion of political matters was found to be an occasion of qualified privilege.

The "political discussion" qualified privilege defence has received judicial interpretation recently. In *Harte* v *Wren*,[81] the plaintiff, a police officer, had been accused of corrupt activities. Contrary to the view of what constitutes "political discussion" which was taken in *Lovell* v *Hancock*,[82] the judge rejected the defendant's defence that the publication was made on an occasion of qualified privilege. The judge took a more conservative view of the *Theophanous* decision and held that discussion of political matter must involve politicians or candidates for political office.[83]

A different view of the scope of the political discussion qualified privilege was taken in *Sporting Shooters Association (Vic)* v *Gun Control Australia*.[84] Judge Shelton in that case was of the view that discussion of gun control was discussion of political matter.

The judge did not accept that it was necessary to consider whether the material was published reasonably, recklessly or whether the defendant was aware of its falsity. The view was taken that these considerations were

---

80. (1994) 124 ARL 1, 143, 25–26.

81. Supreme Court of the Northern Territory, 19 January 1995.

82. Supreme Court of Western Australian, 4 April 1995, 147.

83. The decision in *Harte* v *Wren* should not be followed. It is contrary to the views on the concept of political discussion expressed in *Theophanous* by Mason CJ, Toohey and Gaudron JJ.

84. County Court of Victoria, 2 March 1995.

only relevant to the separate defence founded on a constitutionally guaranteed implied freedom of political discussion. The result of this is that the newly recognised qualified privilege defence is considerably wider than the defence based on an implied freedom of political discussion and less burdensome for a defendant. The decision is on appeal.

It will be some time before the exact scope and content of the freedom of political speech defences are determined. In the meantime, the developments provide an interesting area of debate for academics, challenging questions for the judiciary and a nightmare for pre-publication legal advisors.

Remedies for defamation

Damages

The aim of a person instituting a defamation action is both to vindicate **1.42** and to be compensated for harm suffered to their reputation and feelings. However, it is also clear that the quantum of damage "is more a solatium rather than a monetary recompense for harm measurable in money".[85] In most defamation actions damage is presumed on proof of the action.

As most defamation actions are heard before a jury, it is the jury that determines the lump sum award of damages. In fixing the sum that will compensate for harmed reputation the tribunal of fact may consider any actual pecuniary loss suffered, injury to reputation and injury to feelings.[86] Any excessive or inadequate award of damages may be appealed and set aside by an appellate court. Awards in personal injury cases may be used as a guide by the appellate court in assessing whether the defamation awards are excessive.[87]

Amounts classified as actual pecuniary loss include any measurable financial loss such as loss of employment by reason of the defamatory statement. Injury to personal feelings and health takes into account any psychological, emotional or physical impact of the remarks on the plaintiff. Usually the amount that can be identified as measurable actual loss is minimal, while quantifying the injury to reputation and feelings is notoriously difficult.

Other factors which are relevant in determining the quantum of damages are whether the defendant has published a retraction or apology (a mitigating factor) that the plaintiff already had a bad reputation,

---

85. See, *e.g.*, *Uren* v *John Fairfax & Sons Ltd.* (1967) 117 CLR 118, 150 (Windeyer J).

86. *McCarey* v *Associated Newspapers Ltd.* (number 2) [1965] 2 QB 86, 104 (Pearson LJ).

87. *Carson* v *John Fairfax & Sons Ltd.* (1992–1993) 178 CLR 44.

the nature of the defamatory matter and the circumstances in which it was published, including the coverage and medium of publication.

If the defendant's actions are particularly reprehensible then either aggravated or punitive damages may be awarded as part of the compensatory damages. Aggravated damages are appropriate where the injury has been increased after publication by improper conduct. Lord Reid in *Broome* v *Cassell & Co. Ltd.* suggested that such a situation would arise where the defendant:

> ". . . behaved in a high-handed, malicious, insulting or oppressive manner in committing the tort or he or his counsel may at the trial have aggravated the injury by what they there said".[88]

1.43 In all jurisdictions except New South Wales,[89] punitive (or exemplary damages) are available where it is proved the defendant has been particularly high-handed, insolent, vindictive or malicious or in some way contemptuous of the rights of the defamed person. The focus in awarding punitive damages is not on compensating the plaintiff but rather on punishing the defendant.

Injunctions

1.44 Injunctions may be sought either after issue of proceedings and before the beginning of the trial or as a final order after the plaintiff has been successful. In the latter case an injunction will only be granted where there is a real likelihood that the defendant will repeat the defamatory publication.

The courts are disinclined to grant injunctions, particularly where they determine that damages would be an adequate remedy. The most likely situation where an application for an injunction would be successful is in the case of interim injunctions, which only have effect for a very short time, such as overnight, until hearing of the full interlocutory injunction application.

In the case of *ex parte* injunctions, this disinclination is founded on the general danger in an adversarial system of determining an issue without giving the defendant an opportunity to present its arguments or defences. Interlocutory injunctions (maintaining the *status quo* until the final hearing) are not frequently awarded in defamation actions. The courts recognise that by the time the proceedings have been adjudicated the material will have lost its newsworthy value. Consequently, a court will not

---

88. [1972] AC 1027, 1085.

89. Defamation Act 1974 (NSW), s 46(3).

order an interlocutory injunction if there is any room for doubt that the material is defamatory or a sustainable ground of defence exists.[90]

Case illustration — awards

What follows is a list of cases indicating the type of awards that have been   **1.45** given in Australia in defamation actions. It is clear from consideration of the examples provided that there is a large degree of variance in the quantum of damages awarded between the different jurisdictions within Australia. Generally, juries decide the quantum of damages. A number of jury verdicts have subsequently been set aside or reduced on appeal. It is also worth noting that many actions are settled out of court, often on confidential terms.

(1) *Hartley* v *Nationwide News Pty Ltd.*,[91] making an award of A $935,000, was recently set aside by the New South Wales Court of Appeal[92] and a new trial on the question of damages was ordered. The plaintiff, a licensed migration agent, brought an action in regard to an article published in the *Fairfield Advance*, a suburban newspaper with a circulation of approximately 43,000. Mr. Hartley argued that the article carried the imputation that he acted illegally and dishonestly in his conduct as a migration agent.

(2) *Nugawela* v *Crampton & the Royal Australian College of General Practitioners* (1996) awarded A $600,000 plus A $86,770 interest. In this case, the New South Wales court awarded damages to a doctor defamed in a letter sent to only 22 people. It was found that the letter carried a number of defamatory imputations including that the plaintiff was prepared to make false claims to secure support for a medical informatics association and thereby enhance his standing among professional colleagues.

(3) *Carson* v *John Fairfax & Ors*[93] resulted in an award of A $600,000. The New South Wales Court of Appeal set aside this verdict and ordered a new trial on damages.[94] The decision to hold a new trial on damages was unsuccessfully appealed to the Australian High Court. On a retrial on damages, the plaintiff was awarded A $1.3-million.[95] This case concerned two articles published in the *Sydney Morning*

---

90. *Stocker* v *McElhinney* (number 2) (1961) 79 WN (NSW) 541.

91. Unreported, NSWSC, 13 September 1995.

92. Unreported, NSW Court of Appeal, 15 March 1996.

93. (1993) 178 CLR 44.

94. (1991) 24 NSWLR 259.

95. (1994) 34 NSWLR 72.

Herald regarding Mr. Carson, a prominent commercial solicitor. The imputations said to arise out of the articles included that the plaintiff had attempted to intimidate a medical practitioner and conspired to evade service of criminal proceedings.

(4) *Andrews & Co.* v *John Fairfax & Sons*[96] awarded A $480,000. The New South Wales Court of Appeal held that a failure to make enquiries from the proper sources before publishing, as well as the fact that the defendant failed to make out the defence of contextual truth, was relevant to the jury's assessment of whether an award of aggravated damages was appropriate. However, it set aside this damages verdict and ordered a new trial on damages. The matter settled prior to an appeal being heard in the Australian High Court.

(5) *Perkins* v *New South Wales Aboriginal Land Council* (1996) made an award of A $470,000. The plaintiff, a former director of the Office of Aboriginal Affairs, sued over two media releases, an announcement, a letter to the then Premier and a memorandum to all Aboriginal land councils and Aboriginal communities in New South Wales. The publications attacked the plaintiff over administration of the funding for the land councils in New South Wales.

(6) *Singleton* v *Ffrench*[97] involved an award of A $450,000. The New South Wales Court of Appeal set aside this verdict and ordered a new trial on all issues[98] but the matter settled before the new trial.

(7) *Ettingshausen* v *Australian Consolidated Press*[99] awarded A $350,000. The New South Wales Court of Appeal set aside this verdict and ordered a new trial on damages.[100] Damages were reduced on appeal to A $100,000. This case concerned a photograph of the plaintiff, a rugby league player, which was published in *HQ* magazine. The photograph was of the plaintiff having a shower after a game. The plaintiff complained that the full frontal photograph appeared to expose his penis. The court held that the photograph was capable of exposing the plaintiff to ridicule.

(8) *Makim* v *John Fairfax & Sons Ltd.* (1990), resulting in an award of A $300,000 plus A $65,000 interest, settled before an appeal was heard by the New South Wales Court of Appeal. The plaintiff had sued in relation to two articles published by the defendant in the *Sydney Morning Herald* and the *Sun Herald* newspapers. Each article

---

96. (1980) 2 NSWLR 225.

97. (1986) 5 NSWLR 425.

98. (1986) 5 NSWLR 425.

99. (1991) 23 NSWLR 44.

100. Unreported, NSW Court of Appeal, 13 October 1993.

alleged that the plaintiff (described as the sister of the Duchess of York) had separated from her husband and that she had been engaged in an adulterous relationship with an Argentinean polo player. The imputation complained of was that such a relationship was contrary to the moral obligations of her marriage.

(9) *Comalco* v *ABC*.[101] The Federal Court reduced the A $295,000 award to A $100,000 after which the matter settled prior to the appeal being heard by the Australian High Court. This case concerned interviews with third parties that were broadcast by the defendant, the Australian Broadcasting Corporation. The interviewees made a series of allegations against the plaintiff.

(10) *Chakravarti* v *Advertiser Newspapers Ltd.*[102] awarding A $268,000, is being appealed on the verdict. This case concerned articles appearing in the *Adelaide Advertiser* regarding evidence given to a Royal Commission into the collapse of the State Bank of South Australia. Reference in the articles was made to the plaintiff who was peremptorily dismissed from his position as Chief General Manager of a computer and office supply company.

(11) *Coyne* v *Citizen Finance*.[103] The West Australia Supreme Court reduced the A $150,000 verdict to A $50,000,[104] but the Australian High Court reinstated the original verdict. This case concerned a public notice Citizen Finance had placed in *The West Australian* newspaper. The notice imputed that Coyne had misrepresented his involvement with Citizen Finance in a joint venture land development and fraudulently incurred debts on its behalf.

It should be noted that in publications since 1 January 1995, judges, rather **1.46** than juries, assess damages in defamation cases in New South Wales.[105] This is likely to impact on the level of damages awarded in that State.

Of further significance is that New South Wales legislation now provides that in determining the quantum of damages, the judge in a defamation matter must consider the general range of damages for non-economic loss in personal injury awards in New South Wales. At Common Law, there is still some controversy as to the appropriateness of drawing comparisons between defamation and personal injury awards.[106]

---

101. (1985) 64 ACTR 1.

102. (1995) 181 LSJS 218.

103. (1991) 172 CLR 211.

104. [1990] WAR 333.

105. Defamation Act 1974 (NSW), s 7A.

106. See *Coyne* v *Citizen Finance Limited* (1991) 172 CLR 211, *Carson* v *John Fairfax & Sons Ltd.* (1993) 178 CLR 44 and *Ettinghausens* v *Australian Consolidated Press Ltd.*

New South Wales Law Reform Commission

1.47 In September 1995, the New South Wales Law Reform Commission released its report on defamation. A Bill has been introduced into the New South Wales Parliament to adopt the recommendations of the Commission.

The report states that the recommendations made are an attempt to achieve the best possible defamation law for New South Wales. Unfortunately, if adopted, the recommendations would move New South Wales even further away from uniformity with the other States.

Declaration of falsity

1.48 The New South Wales Law Reform Commission noted that damages awards often come years after the publication and are given little publicity or no publicity at all if a settlement is confidential. The Commission questioned whether in fact monetary damages are an adequate vindication of the plaintiff's reputation.

In light of this concern, the Commission recommended the remedy of a declaration of falsity.

Such a remedy would:

(1) Only be available if sought by the plaintiff within four weeks of publication;
(2) Be in the court's discretion to grant, with no jury role;
(3) Bar a plaintiff from seeking general damages in New South Wales but not damages for economic loss; and
(4) Allow a successful plaintiff to recover an order for indemnity costs.

1.49 The Commission stated that the declaration of falsity has the advantage that a defendant is forced to litigate the issue of truth or concede it.

Although at first glance the declaration may seem attractive to media defendants, as the plaintiff must prove falsity, the plaintiff could simply deny the truth of the allegations, effectively leaving the defendant to prove that they were true.

Of some concern for media organisations is the fact that a publisher cannot rely on the defences of qualified privilege, fair comment, contextual truth or the implied freedom of speech defence.

Correction

1.50 The New South Wales Law Reform Commission recommended that where a defendant publishes a prompt correction in terms agreed to by the plaintiff, the publisher will have a complete defence.

However, the correction must be "adequate" (that is, in the plaintiff's opinion). Often a plaintiff will seek the publication of a correction that goes too far, and to which the media organisation is unlikely to agree. The test of what is an adequate correction should be objectively, rather than subjectively, assessed. The plaintiff could still seek damages for economic loss.

Limitation period

1.51 The New South Wales Law Reform Commission also recommended that the limitation period for defamation actions should be reduced to one year from the date of publication.

Injurious falsehood

1.52 This tortious action is similar to the old actions of slander of goods and slander of title. It has been expanded in Australia to encompass any kind of falsehood that adversely affects a prospective advantage, whether or not of a trading or commercial nature.[107]

Injurious falsehood consists of the publication to a third person of either oral or written false statements concerning a person or his or her trade or property, which is calculated to induce others not to deal with that person. In practice, this tort is rarely used. There is a degree of overlap with defamation actions and the burden on the plaintiff of proving falsity, special damage and malice has diminished the role of the action.

Elements of the action

1.53 There are three basic elements that a plaintiff must make out to succeed in an action for injurious falsehood. He or she must prove that:

(1) The statement is false;
(2) The statement was published maliciously; and
(3) The plaintiff has sustained actual pecuniary damage as a result of the statement.[108]

---

107. John Fleming, *The Law of Torts* (1982), 710.

108. *Ratcliffe v Evans* [1892] QB 524 at 527–8.

Falsity

1.54 Unlike defamation, in an action for injurious falsehood there is a positive burden on the plaintiff to establish that the statement in issue is untrue. It is not enough to show that a person has made an adverse comparison with a competitor's goods or services, nor made a truthful disparagement of another's goods or services. Trade puffing, comparisons and exaggerations are recognised as being a normal part of everyday commerce.[109] These statements are more likely to be characterised as a "trader's puff" rather than a false statement.

> "The courts are reluctant to go into the question of whether one product is better than another. However, a factual assertion will be actionable as an injurious falsehood if the statement can be shown to be untrue".[110]

Malice

1.55 A plaintiff must show that the material was published maliciously. Malice means that material was published with the aim of injuring the plaintiff or was published with some other dishonest or improper motive. Malice is presumed if, at the time of publication, the defendant knew the statement was untrue and likely to injure the plaintiff.

While recklessness will not automatically amount to malice, a defendant will also be liable if he or she knew that the statement was likely to injure the plaintiff and still made the statement, not caring whether it was true or false. Malice may also be proved where there is an intention to injure without just cause or excuse.

Damage

1.56 A plaintiff must have suffered "special" damage as a direct and natural result of the publication of the material to make out the action. "Special" damage is actual pecuniary loss or damage, which includes loss of business. This tort provides no remedy for hurt feelings. It has been commented that ". . . the insistence on special damage has seriously impaired the usefulness of this action".[111]

---

109. However, there are other restrictions under the Trade Practices Act 1974 (Cth).

110. Trindade and Cane, *The Law of Torts in Australia* (1985), 154.

111. Fleming, *The Law of Torts* (1992), 712.

Remedies

The remedies available for injurious falsehood are injunctions restrain- **1.57**
ing the publication of the statement, and damages. Damages are limited
to the actual pecuniary loss or damage sustained. No damages are available for hurt feelings. It appears that under this rubric injunctions are
more easily obtained than in defamation proceedings.[112] However, in one
case it was held that where freedom of speech and the liberty of the press
are involved, the rules covering injunctions in defamation proceedings
cannot be avoided simply by framing an action in injurious falsehood.[113]

Injurious falsehood and defamation

While the action for injurious falsehood has many similarities to a defa- **1.58**
mation action, there are important differences. Defamation focuses on
and protects a person's interest in their personal reputation, whereas
injurious falsehood protects a person's interest in the continuing value of
his or her business, products or property.

Unlike defamation (where the falsity of a defamatory statement is
presumed) a plaintiff in an injurious falsehood action must prove that the
statement made was actually false. In defamation, damage is presumed on
proof of the publication of defamatory material. In comparison, in
injurious falsehood, damage is an essential element that the plaintiff
must make out. Finally, in an action for injurious falsehood the plaintiff must prove malice. In defamation this burden is only imposed on a
plaintiff once a defendant has raised a defence of qualified privilege or
fair comment.

The usefulness of injurious falsehood as a means of protecting business and trading reputation is diminished in those Australian
jurisdictions that operate under a defamation code. In the code states,
the statutory definition of defamatory matter includes statements that are
likely to injure a person in his or her profession or trade. There has also
been a suggestion that at least one of the Common Law definitions of
defamatory matter does not depend on damage to a plaintiff's reputation
and focuses on the injury to trade and business.[114] The inclusion of
business reputation in the code states and its possible expansion at
Common Law may render the tort of injurious falsehood redundant.

---

112. Trindade & Cane, *The Law of Torts in Australia* (1985), 157.

113. *Swimsure (Laboratories) Pty Ltd.* v *Mc Donald* [1979] 2 NSWLR 796, 800–1 (Hunt J).

114. *Sungrauvre Pty Ltd.* v *Middle East Airlines Airliban SAL* (1975) 134 CLR 1, 23–24 (Mason J).

Protecting personality

1.59 Media organisations sometimes use the effective marketing tool of "character merchandising" whereby goods and services are marketed by taking advantage of an association with a real or fictional person, character, group or organisation. However, the media must be wary as the use of this promotional tool without the particular identity's knowledge or permission may attract civil liability as a result of laws that operate to protect personality.

Internationally, each jurisdiction provides a different level and approach to the protection of personality. In Australia, personality is protected through the recently expanded tort of passing off which is supplemented by protection provided by section 52 of the Trade Practices Act 1974 (Cth) ("TPA"), which prohibits misleading or deceptive conduct in trade or commerce.

Passing off

1.60 The Australian courts, recognising the commercial reality behind character merchandising, have taken a flexible approach to the scope of the tort of passing off. In Australia, the tort provides protection for real or fictional characters whose name, likeness or image is used to enhance sales of goods or services without their consent. However, in *Moorgate Tobacco* v *Philip Morris*,[115] the High Court of Australia expressly rejected the adoption of a more general tort based on unfair competition.

It was an Australian court, in *Henderson* v *Radio Corporation*,[116] which concerned dancers whose images were used on a record cover, which first established that character merchandising deserved special treatment within the tort of passing off. It did so by removing the requirement that the plaintiff be engaged in a "common field of activity" with the defendant, which had previously been imposed by English courts.

More recently, two Australian cases involving the unlicensed use of images and themes connected with Paul Hogan's film "Crocodile Dundee" have had the result that effectively makes the tort of passing off in Australia a tort of misappropriation and misrepresentation in a commercial context.[117]

---

115. Number 2, 1984 156 CLR 414.

116. [1960] SR (NSW) 576.

117. *Paul Hogan* v *Koala Dundee Pty Ltd.* (1988) AIPC 90–527, *Hogan & Anor* v *Pacific Dunlop Ltd.* (1988) ATPR 90–902, (1989) ATPR 40–948 (Full Fed Crt).

Following the Hogan cases it seems that the only requirements that must be established in a character merchandising passing off action in Australia are:

(1) A misappropriation of the plaintiff's reputation; and
(2) A misrepresentation of the business connection between the parties which is likely to mislead people into believing that there is a business connection between the plaintiff and the goods and services of the defendant.

This contrasts to the English action of passing off which is still restricted **1.61** in its application in character merchandising cases by requiring the plaintiff to show they had acquired goodwill in their image and suffered actual or potential damage.

Case illustrations

In the case of *Paul Hogan* v *Koala Dundee Pty Ltd.*,[118] the actor, Paul Hogan, **1.62** brought proceedings against a shop which had made extensive use on its goods and signs of a koala bear character wearing the Mick Dundee hat and sleeveless vest. Mick Dundee was the lead character in the "Crocodile Dundee" series of films and was played by Paul Hogan.

In holding that an action of passing off had been made out in this case it was said:

> "In Australia the law now is that the inventor of a sufficiently famous fictional character . . . may prevent others using his character to sell their goods . . . even where he has never carried on business at all other than in the writing or making of the work in which the character appears."

In *Hogan & Anor* v *Pacific Dunlop Ltd.*,[119] Paul Hogan brought another **1.63** successful passing off action. This case concerned television and print advertisements for shoes. The advertisements contained an easily recognisable parody of the famous "knife scene" from the first "Crocodile Dundee" movie.

In that case it was held that the cause of action in passing off is complete when a relevant misrepresentation is made, "even though no actual deception and damage to the plaintiff can be shown to have resulted from it".

Australian cases have increasingly acknowledged the importance of the element of misappropriation in character merchandising passing off

---

118. (1988) AIPC 90–527.
119. (1988) ATPR 90–902.

actions. On appeal in the *Hogan & Anor* v *Pacific Dunlop* case, it was stated that the importance in character merchandising is, "The creation of an association of the product with a character, not the making of a precise representation."

In the *Hogan* v *Koala Dundee* case, it was said that the essence of the wrong done was not a misrepresentation as to the existence of a licensing arrangement but, "Wrongful misappropriation of a reputation or, more widely, wrongful association of goods with an image properly belonging to the applicant".

The relevant misrepresentation is to the sponsorship or endorsement of a product. However, it was clear in the public survey evidence provided in the *Hogan* v *Koala Dundee* case that this form of misrepresentation is something which the public neither notices nor cares about. The flexibility of the Australian courts has allowed for the misrepresentation to be established even in view of this degree of artificiality on the basis that, as stated in the *Hogan* v *Pacific Dunlop* case, the purchasing public would be aware in a general way of licensing practices.

Trade Practices Act

1.64   The Trade Practices Act 1974 (Cth) (TPA) is the main consumer protection legislation in Australia. It is a federal act which applies to all corporations engaged in trade and commerce in Australia. The TPA has been used in protection of personality cases in conjunction with, and as an alternative to, the Common Law action of passing off.

Section 52(1) of the TPA sets out a broad prohibition against corporations engaging, in trade and commerce, in conduct that is misleading or deceptive or is likely to mislead or deceive.

Section 53(c) and (d) of the TPA deal more specifically with reputation. These provisions prohibit a corporation falsely representing that goods or services have sponsorship, approval or affiliation that they do not in fact have. Section 52 of the TPA claims have been more successful than the narrower section 53 of the TPA claims in relation to character merchandising cases.

The similarity between a passing off and a section 52 of the TPA action is clearly apparent with the issues involved and the elements to be proved being essentially the same.

As mentioned previously, actions under section 53(c) and (d) of the TPA have not proved successful for character merchandising claimants. The reason for this is that the words "sponsorship", "approval" and "affiliation" in the sections have received specific judicial interpretation as something akin to formal or authoritative commendation.

Provisions of the TPA effecting media organisations are discussed further below under "Misleading or deceptive conduct". Consideration is given there to a publisher's defence provided for in the TPA. Section 85(3) of the TPA provides a defence to a publisher of an advertisement that contravenes Part V of the TPA if it can establish that it is in the business of publishing advertisements and did not know, nor had any reason to suspect, that the advertisement contravened Part V of the TPA.

Privacy

In Australia there is no general right of privacy. Recently, though, the   **1.65** New South Wales Reform Commission recommended an inquiry be held to consider whether a general tort of privacy should be introduced.[120]

Although individual privacy is not an absolute right embedded in either the Common Law or legislation, peripheral protection is afforded where a breach of personal privacy falls under another head of action. For example, interferences with privacy may constitute a breach of confidence, trespass, breach of copyright or an economic tort such as wrongful appropriation of professional reputation.

There are some Commonwealth and State acts which deal with particular areas of privacy protection in Australia. However, generally these have only limited application. For example, the Privacy Act 1988 (Commonwealth):

(1) Applies to Federal government agencies and departments and provides enforceable guidelines for the collection, use and storage of personal information;

(2) Sets guidelines for the collection, use and storage of tax file numbers and information connected with these which does extend to private sector collectors of tax file numbers; and

(3) Regulates the practices of credit reporting agencies and credit providers in relation to personal credit information.

At the time of writing, new privacy legislation is proposed to be intro-   **1.66** duced in NSW (later in 1996). The Privacy and Data Protection Bill 1996 (NSW)[121] offers some legal remedies for those who feel their privacy has been unjustifiably encroached on. It covers such situations as homosexuals

---

120. *Defamation*, New South Wales Law Reform Commission, Report number 75, Sydney 1995.

121. Before legislation is passed by both Houses of Parliament, it is in the form of a "Bill" rather than an "Act".

being "outed", or people who are HIV-positive having their HIV-status revealed. The current proposal is that such people could seek damages of up to A $40,000.

Examples of some of the more important mechanisms by which privacy of personal information and conduct is protected under Australian law, which are considered below, are:

(1)   Interception and listening devices legislation;
(2)   Common Law torts of trespass and nuisance; and
(3)   Broadcasting codes of practice.

Interception and listening devices legislation

1.67   In Australia, there is specific legislation prohibiting a person listening to or recording a communication passing over a telecommunications system without the knowledge of the person making the communication.[122]

A breach of this prohibition can give rise to a civil action against a party. The legislation provides that a court can grant civil remedial relief to a party to the relevant intercepted communication. The court is entitled to make such orders against the offender as the court considers appropriate, including punitive damages.[123]

The prohibitions in the Commonwealth interception legislation catch any listening or recording effected by a direct line into the telecommunications system, recording by means of a suction cup over a telephone receiver[124] and interception by a radio frequency scanner of a mobile phone communication.[125] There is conflicting authority as to whether the prohibition in the Commonwealth legislation extends to recording by a device placed next to a telephone receiver, or whether this situation instead falls within the state legislation regarding listening devices. This is on the basis that the conversation is no longer at this stage being intercepted in its passage over a telecommunications system, and could instead constitute a "private conversation" for the purposes of the state legislation.[126]

In Australia, there is specific legislation in all States prohibiting the use of a listening device to record or listen to a private conversation

---

122. Telecommunications (Interception) Act 1979 (Cth), s 7.

123. Telecommunications (Interception) Act 1979 (Cth), s 107A.

124. *R v Migliorni* (1982) 38 ALR 356.

125. *Edelsten v Investigating Committee of NSW* (1986) 80 ALR 85.

126. In *R v Curran* (1982) 50 ALR 745 at 767, it was held that the legislation did not apply to such a recording but the opposite view was taken in *R v Oliver* (1984) 57 ALR 543 at 548.

except in certain circumstances.[127] A private conversation is generally defined to mean words spoken by one person to another in circumstances that reasonably indicate that one or more of the parties to the conversation desire the words to be listened to only by the parties to the conversation.[128] In addition to this, in New South Wales, South Australia, the Australian Capital Territory and the Northern Territory, it is also prohibited for a party to the conversation to record the conversation without the other party's consent. Under the Victorian, Queensland, Tasmanian and Western Australian legislation, the recording of a private conversation by a participant to that conversation can be done without seeking the consent of the other participant or participants. In all States, a person who is not a party to the private conversation is prohibited from recording or listening to that conversation by means of a listening device unless all the parties to the conversation consent. Exceptions apply in all States if the use of a listening device to record or listen to a private conversation was done pursuant to a warrant.

Trespass and nuisance

Trespass

The Common Law tort of trespass can be used as a basis to prevent **1.68** breaches of privacy. A person in possession of premises is entitled to exclude others from those premises.[129] Trespass to land occurs where a person enters onto land without the express or implied consent of the occupier, enters on land with the occupier's consent but does not leave when asked to or places something on another's land without their consent.

It should be noted that filming or taking photographs while on a person's land where the person has given their consent to enter the land does not necessarily exempt a person from liability for trespass. The consent to enter land may be limited to an express purpose and filming or photography may be outside the scope of that purpose. There is no restriction imposed by laws of trespass in Australia for filming or photography by a party outside the occupier's land.[130]

---

127. Listening Devices Acts — 1992 (ACT), 1991 (TAS), 1990 (NT), 1984 (NSW), 1978 (WA), 1972 (SA), 1969 (VIC) and the Invasion of Privacy Act (1971) QLD.

128. Listening Devices Acts: 1992 (ACT), s 2; 1984 (NSW), s 3(1); 1972 (SA), s 3; 1991 (Tas), s 5(2); 1990 (NT), s 3(1); 1969 (Vic), s 3; 1978 (WA), s 3; and Invasion of Privacy Act 1971 (Qld), s 4.

129. *Colo v The Queen* (1994) 120 ALR 415.

130. *Bathurst City Council v Sabar* (1985) 2 NSWLR 104, at 106–107.

The remedy for trespass is damages, which can include aggravated or exemplary damages.[131] Furthermore, an injunction may be granted to restrain a threatened trespass. However, following the general principles regarding injunctions, where a film or photograph taken during the act of trespass can be remedied by an award of damages, an injunction will not be granted.[132]

Nuisance

1.69 The tort of nuisance may, in appropriate circumstances, afford some protection to individual privacy. Nuisance arises where a person "unreasonably" interferes with the use or enjoyment of land by the occupier.[133]

In Australia, an occupier has no particular right of freedom from view. Therefore, it is not nuisance to simply observe, film or photograph people or premises on land.[134] Although this is so, systematic surveillance or persistent telephone contact may amount to nuisance.[135]

Broadcasting codes of practice

1.70 In Australia, pursuant to codes of practice, broadcast news and current affairs programmes must not use material relating to a person's personal or private affairs except where it is in the public interest to broadcast such material. In addition to this, the broadcaster must display sensitivity when dealing with traumatic incidents.[136] Similar provisions apply in relation to radio broadcasts.[137]

Breach of confidence

1.71 The tortious action of breach of confidence serves to protect information that ought to be kept confidential because of the nature of the information or

---

131. *Lincoln Hunt Australia Pty Ltd.* v *Willisee* (1986) 4 NSWLR 457.

132. *Lincoln Hunt Australia Pty Ltd.* v *Willisee* (1986) 4 NSWLR 457, *Heritage Real Estate Pty Ltd.* v *Australian Broadcasting Commission* (unreported, NSW SC, Sharpe J, 21 July 1992).

133. *Victoria Park Racing and Recreation Grounds Co. Ltd.* v *Taylor* (1937) 58 CLR 479.

134. *Victoria Park Racing and Recreation Grounds Co. Ltd.* v *Taylor* (1937) 58 CLR 479.

135. *Alma* v *Nakir* [1966] 2 NSWR 396.

136. *FACTS Commercial Television Industry Code of Practice*, ss 4.3.4 and 5.

137. *FARB Commercial Radio Code of Practice*, s 2.2(e).

the circumstances in which it is imparted. Commonly, this action is used to protect trade secrets and confidential government information, although the categories of information and relationships of confidence are not closed.

Elements of the action

There are three basic elements that will create a legally enforceable **1.72** obligation of confidence. These are:

(1) The information has a "quality of confidence about it";
(2) The information was imparted to a person in circumstances or in a relationship giving rise to an obligation of confidence; and
(3) That person disclosed or used that information (or threatened to) without authorisation and to the detriment of the person entitled to prevent it.[138]

Even where these elements are made out, there are cases where the **1.73** public interest will still allow (or indeed compel) disclosure of the particular information. This public interest element is expressed in two ways. It operates as a defence to an action for breach of confidence, for example, the disclosure of information regarding criminal activities in the public interest. It also operates as a fourth element required to be made out in actions relating to confidential government information. A government plaintiff must show that the public interest in effective government compels the suppression of the confidential information.

Quality of confidence

To make out this element, the particular information must not have been **1.74** disclosed to the public already or to such a large section of the public such that it would be seen as having entered the public domain. This is a question of degree in each particular case.

In Australia, it was held that a passing mention of a police informer's name did not destroy the confidential quality of that person's name.[139] Even if the general nature of information has become common knowledge, the detail or specifics of a particular document may still retain a confidential character.[140] Likewise, it has been held (at least at an interlocutory stage) that the courts may prohibit the disclosure of

---

138. *Coco v A N Clark (Engineers) Ltd.* [1969] RPC 41, 47.

139. *G v Day* [1982] 1 NSWLR 24.

140. *Westpac Banking Corp v John Fairfax Group Pty Ltd.* (1991) 19 IPR 513.

information that is not confidential, if such disclosure would destroy the confidential nature of related information.[141]

Confidential information can take any form of expression. In Australia, the quality of confidence has been found in ideas that have not yet been documented.[142] The action for breach of confidence most commonly arises in respect of commercially valuable and sensitive material. However, it is not limited to this type of information. The protection extends to any personal information that is not public, or publicly available, and to government information that is protected in the public interest.

Obligation of confidence

1.75 The circumstances and relationships giving rise to an obligation of confidence are extremely broad. There is no set formula for determining if an obligation has been created. The obligation may be express or implied. It will arise in most employment contracts where the material sought to be protected is truly confidential information rather than general skill or knowledge that an employee develops as a result of his or her occupation.[143]

An obligation of confidence will be imposed on a person who wrongfully obtains confidential information. Where a person imparts information to a third party in breach of an obligation, the third party will generally also be subject to an obligation of confidence, if that third party knew (or ought to have known) that the information was imparted in breach of an obligation of confidence.

The protection of confidential information that is overheard or received by a person without being solicited is unclear. It may be that the question should be resolved with reference to the extent of the opportunity afforded to the recipient of the information to accept or reject the obligation of confidence.[144]

The lengths to which journalists or photographers may go to obtain confidential information has not been fixed in Australia. It appears that any information that is obtained by lawful means (*e.g.*, without the use of illegal listening devices) can be disclosed by a journalist without giving rise to liability for breach of confidence. There is commentary from the High Court that the courts will restrain the publication of information obtained improperly or surreptitiously; however, these terms remain undefined.[145]

---

141. *Falconer* v *ABC* [1992] AIPC 90–849.

142. *Talbot* v *General Television Corp Pty Ltd.* [1980] VR 224.

143. *Ansell Rubber Co. Pty Ltd.* v *Allied Rubber Industries Pty Ltd.* [1967] VR 37 and *Section Pty Ltd.* v *Delawood Pty Ltd.* (1991) 21 IPR 136.

144. McLachlan and Mallam, *Media Law and Practice* [12.1930].

145. *Commonwealth* v *John Fairfax* (1980) 147 CLR 39, 50.

Detrimental disclosure without authorisation

Once an obligation of confidence is found to exist, any unauthorised use **1.76** or disclosure of that information will amount to a breach of the obligation. This is so whether or not the information was used or disclosed intentionally, negligently or inadvertently. The need for, and extent of, detriment required on the part of the person owed the obligation of confidence has been debated in Australia. It has been suggested that although it is unnecessary to establish an action for breach of confidence, it will be relevant to determine whether any remedy will be granted.[146] Any requisite detriment need not be legal or even financial and can include such detriment as loss of privacy or hurt feelings.

Government information

Information relating to the government (or its operations) is subject to **1.77** an additional requirement before it is accorded protection under the tort of breach of confidence. The United Kingdom case of *Attorney General (United Kingdom)* v *Jonathan Cape*[147] established the balancing of public interests test. This test is that the public interest in protecting confidentiality for the effective operation of government must outweigh the public interest in disclosure for an action to arise.

Government information which, if disclosed, would be adverse to the public interest includes information relating to national security, relations with foreign governments or information which, if disclosed, would prejudice the ordinary business of government.[148]

The first difference from an ordinary breach of confidence action when dealing with government information is that the detriment suffered by a government plaintiff must be of a significantly different character to the detriment suffered by a private person or corporation. In *Commonwealth* v *John Fairfax & Sons Ltd.*, Mason J (as he then was) said that the relevant detriment is to the public interest in effective government rather than a particular government's detriment. He said:

"It can scarcely be a relevant detriment to the government that publication of material concerning its actions will merely expose it to public discussion and criticism. It is unacceptable in our democratic society that there should be a restraint on the publication of information relating to

---

146. *Corrs Pavey Whiting & Byrne* v *Collector of Customs* (Vic) (1987) 74 ALR 428.

147. [1976] QB 752.

148. *Commonwealth* v *John Fairfax & Son Ltd.* (1980) 147 CLR 39, 51–2 (Mason J).

45

government when the only vice of that information is that it enables the public to discuss, review and criticise government actions."[149]

1.78 This leads to the extra requirement imposed on a government plaintiff. It must show that disclosure is likely to injure the public interest. In essence, this is a reversal of the onus of proof, whereby the government must show that the public interest requires the suppression of information. In general, a court will not prevent the publication of information that merely throws light on the past workings of government as long as it does not prejudice the community in other respects.

In the recent case of *Commonwealth* v *John Fairfax Publications Pty Ltd.* & *Ors* (1995),[150] there was an indication that the implied constitutional freedom of political discussion (discussed above) will have an effect on the public interest balancing test. Bryson J found that the constitutional protection should be a relevant consideration and be accorded a high (but not paramount) importance in deciding whether the public interest required disclosure or suppression.

Defences

1.79 There are two types of defences to an action for breach of confidence, being justified disclosure and disclosure under compulsion of law.

Justified disclosure

1.80 The general rule is that there must be a "just cause or excuse" for disclosing the confidential information to a third party.[151] However, the application of this rule has led to developments in the United Kingdom that have not been adopted in Australia.

The narrowest expression of the rule is accepted in both jurisdictions, that is, that there is no confidentiality attaching to a crime or fraud.[152] In Australia, this has been expanded to include a contravention of the Trade Practices Act 1974 (Cth).[153] This approach has, however, been criticised as being too broad. In *A* v *Hayden* (No. 2),[154] Gibbs CJ stated that "iniquity" should be confined to serious crimes.[155]

---

149. *Commonwealth* v *John Fairfax* & *Son Ltd.* (1980) 147 CLR 39, 52.

150. Unreported, Supreme Court of New South Wales, 2033/95.

151. *Fraser* v *Evans* [1969] 1 QB 349, 362.

152. *Gartside* v *Outram* (1856) 26 LJ Ch 113, 114.

153. *Allied Mills Industries Pty Ltd.* v *Trade Practices Commission* (1981) 34 ALR 105, 126–41.

154. (1984) 156 CLR 532.

155. (1984) 156 CLR, 545–546.

Expansion of this rule in the United Kingdom was made in *Initial Services Ltd.* v *Putterill*,[156] where the court found "iniquity" to include any misconduct that ought to be disclosed in the public interest. This test has received limited acceptance in Australia; however, the requisite misconduct has been narrowly construed. In *A* v *Hayden* (No. 2),[157] it was held that disclosure of trivial wrongs or past misconduct that is unlikely to be repeated is not in the public interest. However, information concerning matters relating to the protection of the community from destruction, damage or harm or which is medically dangerous to the public, would fall within this approach to the defence.[158]

The second expansion of the general rule in the United Kingdom saw it being converted into the type of public interest balancing test outlined for government information. This test involves balancing the public interest in maintaining confidences against the public interest in knowing the truth.[159] This approach has not been generally accepted in Australia.[160] It may be that this approach will be seen as simply an application of the first expansion. This view was expressed by Powell J in *Attorney General* (*United Kingdom*) v *Heinemann Publishers Australia Pty Ltd.* (1987).[161]

One qualification to the defence of justified disclosure in a breach of confidence action is that any disclosure must be made to the appropriate body or group. The nature of the confidential information will often determine the breadth of disclosure which is justified. For this reason it is rare that a disclosure to the media generally will be protected by the defence. The general rule is that disclosure should be no more widespread than the public interest requires in the circumstances. In *Corrs Pavey Whiting & Byrne* v *Collector of Customs* (Vic) (1987),[162] Gummow J held that where information relates to a crime or serious misdeed of public importance, disclosure is only justified to a third party with a real and direct interest in redressing the crime or misdeed.

Disclosure required by law

A person will be protected from a breach of confidence action where the **1.81** information is required by law to be disclosed. The most common example

---

156. [1967] 1 QB 396.

157. (1984) 156 CLR 532.

158. *Commonwealth* v *John Fairfax & Sons Ltd.* (1980) 147 CLR 39.

159. *Lion Laboratories Ltd.* v *Evan* [1984] 2 All ER 417.

160. *Castrol Australia Pty Ltd.* v *Em Tech Associates Pty Ltd.* (1980) 51 FLR 184 and *Corrs Pavey Whiting & Byrne* v *Collector of Customs* (Vic) (1987) 74 ALR 428 at 445–450.

161. (1987) 8 NSWLR 341.

162. (1987) 74 ALR 428.

arises in respect of court orders for the purposes of litigation. In *Bacich* v
ABC (1992),[163] the court ordered that Australian Broadcasting Commission
journalists could be compelled to disclose the identity of their sources,
one of whom had himself committed a breach of confidence, for which
the plaintiffs wished to bring proceedings. The journalists would have a
good defence to an action for breach of confidence in disclosing the
identity of the source.

Disclosure of journalists' sources

1.82 As part of the Australian journalistic tradition and under rule three of the
Australian Journalists Association's Code of Ethics, a journalist owes a moral
obligation of confidence in respect of the identity of a source. The journalist
owes this obligation to the source him or herself. This professional
obligation arises most commonly when a journalist is called on to give
evidence as to the identity of their source in legal proceedings.

Australian courts have declined to recognise an evidentiary privilege
entitling a journalist to refuse to disclose evidence on the ground that it
would reveal information imparted in confidence or the identity of the
source of the information.[164] This obviously creates a tension between the
media attempting to gather and report information with the assistance of
informants (who provide such assistance confident of their anonymity)
and the courts' attempts to ensure that all evidence is available at trial.
There are few decided cases on the compulsory disclosure of journalists'
sources, as the issue only arises in the rare case where an informant does
not wish to be identified and the information has been published notwithstanding the fact that the source has not been so identified. The
question of compelled disclosure of the identity of a source will arise
either in a defamation proceeding or because an order for discovery has
been made.

In defamation actions, the so-called "newspaper rule" gives the
court a discretion to refuse to order a disclosure of sources in interlocutory proceedings, even if disclosure would be relevant to or assist
in the investigation of an issue at trial.[165] This rule applies to radio and
television and is not limited to news stories. However, this rule only
offers protection at the discovery stage and does not apply to the trial
itself.[166]

---

163. (1992) 29 NSWLR 1.

164. *McGuinness* v *Attorney General* (Vic) (1940) 63 CLR 73; *John Fairfax & Sons Ltd.* v *Conjuangco* (1988) 156 CLR 346.

165. *John Fairfax & Sons Ltd.* v *Conjuangco* (1988) 165 CLR 346; *Theiss* v *TCN Channel Nine Pty Ltd.* (1990) 5 BR 509.

166. *Wran* v *ABC* [1984] 3 NSWLR 241.

The newspaper rule relates only to the disclosure of material that would identify the source rather than the information supplied by the source, unless disclosure of the material itself would necessarily identify the source. The rationale for the rule has been expressed by the Australian High Court to be founded on the:

> ". . . special position of those publishing and conducting newspapers, who accept responsibility for and are liable in respect of the matter contained in their journals, and the desirability of protecting those who contribute to their columns from the consequences of unnecessary disclosure of their identity".[167]

1.83 The newspaper rule is further limited by the fact that it will not apply in an action for preliminary discovery to identify the source or author of a defamatory publication.[168] The High Court has said that an order for discovery will be granted where it is necessary to provide the applicant with an effective remedy.[169] Similarly, in the preliminary steps of a breach of confidence action, an order requiring disclosure of the identity of a source of leaked information may be compelled.[170]

There are no Australian cases supporting the United Kingdom position[171] that the courts have a discretion to permit a witness or party to refuse to disclose information on the ground that it was imparted in confidence. The New South Wales Supreme Court has interpreted those decisions as showing no more than the usual requirement that any question must be relevant.[172]

Various States are considering providing a legislative discretion to the judge to enable a journalist to protect his or her sources, as recommended by the Western Australian Law Reform Commission.

Remedies

1.84 Breach of confidence actions arise either where unauthorised disclosure or use has been threatened or where it has already occurred. Where the disclosure has only been threatened, a person will seek an interlocutory injunction to restrain the intended disclosure or use until a final hearing

167. *McGuiness* v *Attorney General* (Vic) (1940) 63 CLR 73, 104.

168. *John Fairfax & Sons Ltd.* v *Conjuangco* (1988) 165 CLR 346.

169. *John Fairfax & Sons Ltd.* v *Conjuangco* (1988) 165 CLR 346, 352–3.

170. *Bacich* v *ABC* (1992) 29 NSWLR 1.

171. As stated in *Attorney General* v *Clough* [1963] 1 QB 773 and *Attorney General* v *Mulholland* [1963] 2 QB 477.

172. *Re Buchanan* (1964) 65 SR (NSW) 9, 11.

can determine the matter. Where the disclosure or use has already occurred, an aggrieved person will usually seek damages or an account of profits.

The general approach in determining whether an interlocutory injunction should be granted is to determine if there is a serious question to be tried and if the "balance of convenience" favours the granting of an injunction.[173] There is some authority supporting the proposition that an applicant must make out a *prima facie* case in matters that involve public interest considerations.[174] The balance of convenience tests looks at the consequences to both parties if the injunction were granted. It usually involves a consideration of whether the applicant can be properly compensated with a monetary amount if the injunction is not granted and the consequences to the defendant if an injunction is granted. Because of the urgency of most applications for interlocutory injunctions, temporary injunctions can be granted on an *ex parte* basis.

Where an applicant makes out its case at a final hearing, a final injunction can be granted. Final injunctions may be refused where damages are an adequate remedy, where the plaintiff has engaged in improper conduct or used reprehensible means to protect the confidentiality of information or where the defendant has innocently obtained and used the information for an original venture of its own. The court may also impose ancillary orders including the return of materials and documents or the destruction of equipment and goods produced by the use of the confidential information.

An account of profits or damages may be awarded in addition to, or as an alternative to, injunctive relief. Damages are usually sought and granted when the information has already been disclosed or used and an injunction would serve little purpose. An account of profits is often awarded in commercial cases where a defendant has derived an advantage by means of an improper use of confidential information. The defendant is then obliged to account to the plaintiff for all profits derived from that use.

Because of the practical difficulties in determining the amounts actually derived from improper use or disclosure of confidential information, the courts are reluctant to award an account of profits unless it would be "practical or simple".[175] In *Attorney General (United Kingdom)* v *Heinemann Publishers Australia Pty Ltd.*,[176] an account of profits was awarded in relation

---

173. *Castlemaine Tooheys Ltd.* v *South Australia* (1986) 161 CLR 148; *Falconer* v *ABC* [1992] AIPC 90–849.

174. *Castlemaine Tooheys Ltd.* v *South Australia* (1986) 161 CLR 148.

175. *Aquaculture Corp* v *New Zealand Green Mussel Co. Ltd.* (number 2) (1986) 10 TPR 319, 322.

176. (1987) 61 ALJR 612.

to the *Spycatcher* book published in Australia, the contents of which were held to be based on confidential information.

Where a breach of confidence occurs in breach of a contractual obligation, damages have been recognised as an appropriate remedy. In equitable actions, damages are also available in lieu of an injunction.[177] In practice, in Australia damages are awarded where no other remedy is available.[178] The general approach is to attempt to restore the plaintiff to the same position as if the breach of confidence had not occurred.

Prohibited speech legislation

In Australia, tension has developed between free expression and individual privacy. As mentioned previously, the High Court of Australia has recently recognised a constitutionally guaranteed implied right of free speech.[179] In *Theophanous*, the judges expressed the view that the balance may have been tilted too far against free communication in favour of protection of individual reputation. **1.85**

To some extent the developments in the Australian High Court conflict with legislative initiatives. In recent years the Commonwealth and State legislatures have become increasingly responsive to public concern about individual privacy rights. Corresponding legislation prohibiting certain speech and conduct has been introduced including racial vilification and sexual harassment legislation.

For example, in Victoria the Equal Opportunity Act 1995 was recently introduced, replacing the former Equal Opportunity Act 1984. This Act prohibits discrimination in areas including employment, education, accommodation, club membership and sport.

There is also a specific offence created for publishing or authorising publication of an advertisement or notice that indicates that a party intends to engage in any conduct that is prohibited as discriminatory.

The attributes in relation to which conduct may be discriminatory are extensive and include age, lawful sexual activity, marital status, political belief, pregnancy, race, religious belief and sex.

The Federal Parliament recently amended the Racial Discrimination Act 1975 (Cth) to make it unlawful to do any act (other than in private)

---

177. See Supreme Court Act 1970 (NSW), s 68; Judicature Act 1876 (Qld), s 4; Supreme Court Act 1935 (SA), s 30; Supreme Court Civil Procedure Act 1932 (Tas), s 11(3); Supreme Court Act 1958 (Vic), s 62; Supreme Court Act 1935 (WA), s 25.

178. *Talbot* v *General Television Corp Pty Ltd.* [1980] VR 224.

179. *Theophanous* v *Herald* & *Weekly Times Ltd.* (1994) 182 CLR 104x.

if the act is reasonably likely to offend, insult, humiliate or intimidate another person and the act is done because of the race, colour or national or ethnic origin of the other person. Complaints about such unlawful acts can be taken to the Human Rights and Equal Opportunities Commission but the unlawful act is not an offence. Note also that the prohibition on offensive behaviour based on racial hatred does not render anything unlawful which is said or done in good faith in performing artistic works, in the course of genuine academic, artistic or scientific purpose or in publishing a fair and accurate report of any event or matter of public interest.

The Racial Discrimination Act also makes it unlawful to publish an advertisement or notice that indicates an intention to do something made unlawful pursuant to certain provisions of the legislation. The Act is very wide in this regard as it makes unlawful any act involving some distinction, exclusion, restriction or preference based on race, colour, descent or national or ethnic origin which has the purpose or effect of impairing the enjoyment of any fundamental freedom in all areas including the political, economic, social or cultural fields.

Misleading or deceptive conduct

1.86 Media organisations should be aware that the Trade Practices Act 1974 (Cth) (the "TPA") contains provisions which, if breached, may give rise to civil liability and the possibility of large fines imposed by the Australian Competition and Consumer Commission (ACCC), which replaces the former Trade Practices Commission.

Section 52 TPA prohibits a corporation engaging in misleading or deceptive conduct in trade or commerce. It also prohibits conduct that is likely to mislead or deceive. A breach of section 52 of the TPA may give rise to civil liability but not a fine. The ACCC, or any person, may seek an injunction to restrain a breach of section 52 of the TPA. Any person who suffers loss or damage as a result of the breach may seek damages and may also apply for appropriate rectification or relief.

There are other sections in the TPA in Part V (the Part within which section 52 of the TPA is found) which prohibit specific practices including:

(1) False representations in connection with the supply of services (section 53);
(2) Offering gifts or prizes without an intention to supply (section 54); and
(3) Bait advertising (section 66).

A breach of the specific prohibited practices in Part V of the TPA can   **1.87**
result in a fine of up to A \$400,000 (AUD) in the case of a corporation
and A \$40,000 (AUD) in the case of an individual. In addition to this an
injunction, disclosure, damages or other remedial order can be made.

Importantly, the TPA includes a "publisher's defence". Section 85(3)
of the TPA provides that it is a defence for a publisher of an advertisement
that contravenes Part V of the TPA if the publisher can establish:

(1)   He or she is a person whose business it is to publish or arrange for
      the publication of advertisements; and
(2)   He or she received the advertisement for publication in the ordi-
      nary course of business and did not know and had no reason to
      suspect that its publication would amount to a contravention of a
      provision of Part V.

This is an important defence for all media organisations who carry   **1.88**
advertisements. Although it provides no assistance in relation to the
organisation publishing its own material, it does provide a defence concerning the contents of advertisements accepted for publication.

A publisher should be aware of some general principles regarding
advertising in Australia as, although section 85(3) of the TPA provides a
publisher's defence, it may not be available if the advertisement gives
reason to suspect that it amounts to contravention of Part V of the
TPA. This is because the wording of the publisher's defence specifically excludes the operation of the defence where a publisher has reason
to suspect that publication would amount to contravention of Part V of
the TPA.

The court does allow a degree of latitude when considering whether
advertisements are in breach of the TPA but two situations require special
care. These are comparative advertising and character advertising.

Comparative advertising

If an advertisement is comparative (*i.e.*, listing features of a competitor's   **1.89**
product in comparison with the advertiser's product), the court looks
more critically at the advertisement because consumers are more likely to
view the advertisement as a fair and accurate comparison. Comparisons
should be accurate if used and be made between equivalent objects or
services.[180]

---

180. *State Government Insurance Commission* v *JM Insurance* (1984) ATPR 40–465.

Character advertising

1.90 As has been discussed above under personality protection, character advertising is an area in which care should be taken to being misleading or deceptive conduct. Advertisements using a competitor's character or the character of another company should be approached with utmost caution.

When a publisher is publishing its own material or is advertising its own organisation, it may be liable if it breaches provisions in Part V of the TPA.

Section 65A of the TPA provides a defence to "information providers" to breaches of specific provisions of Part V of the TPA where the publication is made in the course of carrying on a business of providing information. This defence is designed to protect publishers from actions relating to information published in news items. Advertisements are not protected by this defence.

It should be noted that a publisher is not exempt from the consumer protection provisions of the TPA in respect of the provision of information where the publisher has what is regarded as a commercial interest in the content of the information. This may occur, for example, where a newspaper has agreed to publish a "news" item about a product in exchange for the product supplier taking out advertising.[181]

---

181. *Advanced Hair Studio Ltd.* v *TUW Enterprises Ltd.* (1987) 19 FCR 1, *Horwitz Grahame Books Pty Ltd.* v *Performance Publications Pty Ltd.* (1987) 9 ATPR 48.27.

Canada

Chapter 2
Canada

Roger D. McConchie
Ladner Downs
Vancouver, Canada

Introduction

Legislative environment

Canada is a federation in which legislative power is exhaustively divided   **2.1**
between the national Parliament and the legislatures of the 10 provinces.[1]
Two northern territories, which do not have full provincial status, exercise legislative authority expressly delegated by Parliament. Except for
national laws concerning intellectual property, the civil liability of the
news media in Canada is largely governed by laws falling within the legislative jurisdiction of the provinces and the territories.

Civil defamation law, the source of most litigation against the news
media, is a matter of "property and civil rights". This subject was assigned
to the provinces by the Constitution Act, 1867[2] and has been delegated
to the Yukon and Northwest Territories by the national Parliament.[3]
On the same basis, provincial and territorial law defines the liability of the
news media for other civil wrongs including invasion of privacy, appropriation of personality, trespass to property, nuisance, breach of confidence,
injurious falsehood, and negligent publication causing emotional or
financial injury.

The provincial and territorial laws affecting the news media are not
uniform. Efforts to harmonise those laws have met with limited success.
The Uniform Law Conference of Canada, a non-governmental body whose
object is to promote the uniformity of legislation throughout Canada, has

---

1. Constitution Act, 1867 (United Kingdom), [formerly the British North America Act] reproduced in RSC
1985, app II, no. 5, ss 91 and 92.

2. Constitution Act, 1867, s 92(13).

3. Yukon Act, RSC 1985, c. Y–2, s 17(h); Northwest Territories Act, RSC 1985, c. N–27, s 16(h).

adopted a Uniform Defamation Act[4] and a Uniform Privacy Act.[5] No province or territory has fully enacted either of those model statutes. The Uniform Trade Secrets Act,[6] which codifies protection for sensitive business information, has not been implemented anywhere.

Another complication arises from the fact that the province of Quebec has a system of law which is fundamentally distinct from that of the nine Common Law provinces[7] and the two northern territories. Quebec's Civil Law has its roots in French custom and legislation whereas each of the Common Law provinces and the territories have inherited English law.

Quebec courts also approach legal issues differently. Judges give some weight to prior judicial decisions but they look first to statute law including the Civil Code of Quebec (1994), Quebec's Charter of Human Rights and Freedoms and Quebec's Press Act for answers to legal issues affecting the news media. In the rest of Canada, the courts primarily look to the principles of law and equity expressed in case precedents.

Intellectual property law is the constitutional responsibility of the national Parliament. It is largely codified and applies uniformly throughout Canada. The statutes of particular relevance to the news media include the Copyright Act and the Trade-marks Act.[8]

In general, the news media in Canada exercise ample rights of freedom of expression. Few prior restraints are imposed by the Civil Law. Certain prior restraints on the news media are mandated by the federal Criminal Code[9] and the federal Young Offenders Act.[10] These ban reports of certain aspects of criminal court proceedings, such as the identity of rape victims. Some provincial statutes ban publication of information involving juveniles. These criminal and quasi-criminal bans are outside the scope of this chapter.

Since the formal patriation of Canada's constitution from the United Kingdom in 1982, all Canadian legislation has been subject to constitutional challenge to the extent that it infringes anyone's "freedom of thought, belief, opinion and expression, including freedom of the press and other media of communication" which is guaranteed by section 2(b) of the Canadian Charter of Rights and Freedoms.[11] The Charter subjects

---

4. Uniform Defamation Act, Consolidation, CLIC, 1979, revised; see Proceedings of the 76 Annual Meeting, August 1994, Uniform Defamation Act, Rev., app D.

5. ULCC, Proceedings of the 76 Annual Meeting, August 1994, Uniform Privacy Act.

6. ULCC, Proceedings of the 69 Annual Meeting, August 1987, app I.

7. Alberta, British Columbia, Manitoba, Newfoundland, New Brunswick, Nova Scotia, Ontario, Prince Edward Island and Saskatchewan.

8. Copyright Act, RSC 1985, c. C–42; Trade-marks Act, RSC 1985, c. T–13.

9. RSC 1985, c. C–46.

10. RSC 1985, c. Y–1.

11. Part I of the Constitution Act, 1982, being schedule B to the Canada Act, 1982 (United Kingdom), 1982, c. 11.

this guarantee "to such reasonable rights prescribed by law as can be demonstrably justified in a free and democratic society." Nevertheless, the Charter allows all legislatures to over-ride freedom of expression for up to five years, by a simple declaration to that effect in the infringing statute.[12]

Canadian courts

Some lack of uniformity in the law governing media liability is due to the **2.2** fragmented structure of the Canadian judicial system. The Constitution Act, 1867 authorised each province to establish a provincial superior court of general jurisdiction, whose judges are appointed and paid by the federal government.[13] Pursuant to this authority, each province has created a two-level superior court system.[14] Most civil claims against the news media are filed and heard initially in the provincial or territorial superior trial court, from which there is a right of appeal to the respective provincial or territorial court of appeal. A further civil appeal to the Supreme Court of Canada requires leave from that court or from the provincial appellate court.

The Supreme Court of Canada consists of nine judges who are appointed and paid by the federal government. Three members of the court must come from the bench or bar of Quebec. Since 1949, when appeals to the Judicial Committee of the Privy Council (United Kingdom) were abolished, the Supreme Court of Canada has been the ultimate court of appeal for Canada. Its decisions are binding on all lower courts. The Supreme Court of Canada is entitled to over-rule its previous decisions but this power is used with restraint.

To the extent that there is no Supreme Court of Canada decision on point, the Common Law is free to develop differently in each province and territory. Courts observe the English law principle of *stare decisis* in the nine Common Law provinces and two northern territories. On this principle, legal rules expressed in the decisions of a provincial appellate court are binding on the trial court of the same province, but not on the

---

12. Constitution Act, 1982, ss 1 and 33.

13. Constitution Act, 1867, ss 96 and 100.

14. The trial-level court is called the "Court of Queen's Bench" in Alberta, Saskatchewan, Manitoba and New Brunswick; the "Supreme Court" in British Columbia and Newfoundland; the "Ontario Court — General Division" in Ontario; the "Supreme Court Trial Division" in Nova Scotia; and the "Superior Court" in Quebec. Prince Edward Island, the smallest province, has a Supreme Court divided into trial and appellate divisions. The appellate court in each other province is called the "Court of Appeal". The Yukon and Northwest Territories each have a "Supreme Court" and a "Court of Appeal".

trial courts of the other provinces. Some provincial courts of appeal consider themselves bound by their own prior decisions; others do not. Trial judges are not bound by prior decisions of judges of the same rank, but usually follow them unless persuaded there is good reason to differ.

The national Parliament has created a federal court system consisting of the Trial Division and the Federal Court of Appeal for the purpose of administering federal laws including the intellectual property statutes.[15] The Federal Court has concurrent original jurisdiction with the provincial superior courts in intellectual property matters, except in cases of conflicting applications for the registration of a copyright or trade-mark or cases in which it is sought to annul any registration of a copyright or trade-mark, in which event the federal court has exclusive jurisdiction.[16]

Basis of liability

2.3 This chapter will summarise the laws affecting the news media in the following subject areas: defamation, invasion of privacy, appropriation of personality, trespass to property, nuisance, breach of confidence, injurious falsehood, negligent publication causing, emotional or financial injury, copyright and trade-marks. It is impossible in this summary to record every nuance that distinguishes the procedural or substantive law of one province or territory from that of another. Accordingly, the chapter emphasises only the major points of difference. Copyright and trade-mark law, as mentioned previously, are uniform across Canada.

Defamation

2.4 The law of defamation constitutes the most significant civil restriction on freedom of expression in Canada and is the most frequent basis of civil litigation against the news media. Although Canadian damage awards for defamation have historically been modest, a 1995 ruling of the Supreme Court of Canada may signal a new trend.[17] In that ruling, the Supreme Court sustained the C $1.6-million verdict of an Ontario jury, placing a high premium on reputation and thereby renewing long-standing news media concerns about potential "libel chill".

---

15. Federal Court Act, RSC 1970, c. F–7.

16. Federal Court Act, s 20.

17. *Hill* v *Church of Scientology of Toronto*, [1995] 2 SCR 1130, (1995) 184 NR 1.

Defamation Law — Common Law Provinces and the Territories

Defamation law is firmly rooted in English jurisprudence and is largely unal- **2.5**
tered by statute. Despite the flood of print, radio and television media into
Canada from the United States of America, Canadian courts have to date
been reluctant to tailor Canadian libel law so that it fits neatly with American
libel principles. In the 1995 decision mentioned above, the Supreme Court
of Canada unequivocally rejected arguments that Canadian libel law
should be modernised to accord greater protection to libel defendants by
adopting United States First, Amendment principles that afford significant
protection to defendants for defamatory criticism of "public" persons.

Even before the Canadian Charter of Rights and Freedoms came into
force in 1982, legal and news media critics charged that Canada's defamation law was archaic and unnecessarily complex. Each of the provinces
and the two northern territories has defamation legislation but it modifies the Common Law in only a few aspects. Moreover, the defamation
statutes differ significantly, making it difficult for the national news media
to assess their potential civil liability accurately.

The news media in the Common Law provinces and territories face
special difficulties in the defence of defamation litigation. In those jurisdictions, liability for defamation is strict in the sense that it is no defence
for the news media to prove that it had no intention to defame, or that it
had no intention to refer to the plaintiff, or that it was unaware of the
plaintiff's existence, or that it did not know the extrinsic facts that would
make its words defamatory of the plaintiff. Moreover, the law presumes
that a defamatory statement is false and the onus therefore rests on the
defendant to prove truth.

Defamation Law — Quebec

The news media face different liability principles in Quebec. To obtain **2.6**
damages, a plaintiff in Quebec must prove that the author of the defamatory matter was guilty of an intentional wrong or negligence and that the
defamation caused "matériel" or "moral" prejudice. Malice is presumed,
however, if the defamatory statement is objectively injurious. Falsity is also
presumed and a news media defendant therefore has the onus to prove
the truth of the defamatory matter.[18] Liability may even arise from publishing true facts if there was no public interest involved, or if the sole
purpose was to injure the person defamed.[19]

---

18. *D (R)* c. *L (D)* (1992), 17 CCLT (2d) 35 [Que.SC]; *Van den Hoef* c. *Air Canada*, [1988] RRA 543 [Que.SC].

19. *Collins* c. *Hull (Ville)*, [1995] AQ no. 602 (12 October 1995); Baudouin, *La Responsibilité Civile*, 4ieme ed.
(Montreal, Que: Yvon Blais, 1994), at pp 235–237.

Quebec courts require news media defendants to meet a rigorous standard of care during the investigation and reporting of a defamatory story. The standard is that of a professional working in the information industry. A defendant will not be held liable if he or she satisfied this standard of care, even if the article was defamatory and false.[20]

The cause of action for defamation is not specifically codified in Quebec. It is based on a general duty described in article 1457 of the Civil Code of Quebec,[21] which provides:

> "Every person has a duty to abide by the rules of conduct which lie on him, according to the circumstances, usage or law, so as not to cause injury to another. Where he is endowed with reason and fails in this duty, he is responsible for any injury he causes to another person and is liable to reparation for the injury, whether it be bodily, moral or material in nature. He is also liable, in certain cases, to reparation for injury caused to another by the act or fault of another person or by the act of things in his custody".

2.7 Reputation is explicitly protected by article 35 of the Civil Code of Quebec, which states: "Every person has a right to the respect of his reputation and privacy."

Liability principles

2.8 In the Common Law provinces and territories, a publication that tends to lower a person's reputation in the estimation of right-thinking members of society generally, or to expose a person to hatred, contempt or ridicule, is defamatory.[22] What is defamatory may be determined from the ordinary meaning of the published words or matter, or from the surrounding circumstances, as they would be understood by the ordinary, reasonable and fair-minded reader.[23] The test is similar in Quebec.[24]

No Canadian legislature has defined what constitutes "defamatory" matter. The Report of the Saskatchewan Commissioners to the Uniform Law Conference of Canada in 1983 recommended a definition of

---

20. *Carpentier* c. *Radiomutuel Inc.*, [1995] AQ. no. 414 [Que.CA].

21. *Code civil du Québec* (1994); see also Quebec's Charter of Human Rights and Freedoms, LRQ 1977, c. C–12, art 4.

22. *Cherneskey* v *Armadale Publishers Ltd.*, [1979] 1 SCR 1067, at p 1079.

23. *Botiuk* v *Toronto Free Press Publications Ltd.*, [1995] 3 SCR 3, (1995), 126 DLR (4) 609.

24. *Collins* c. *Hill* (*Ville*), [1995] AQ. no. 602; *Dubois* c. *Société St-Jean Baptiste de Montréal*, [1983] CA 247 Baudouin, *La Responsibilité Civile*, 4ieme ed. (Montreal, Que: Yvon Blais, 1994), at pp 235–237; Vallières, *La Presse Et La Diffamation* (Montreal, Que: Wilson & LaFleur, 1985), at pp 5–8.

"defamation" to be included in the Uniform Defamation Act.[25] The Uniform Law Conference of Canada has since abandoned efforts at codification of a definition because of difficulties in arriving at a satisfactory wording.

Examples of allegations that courts have held to be defamatory include the following: accusations of corruption, dishonesty, criminal conduct, professional incompetence, personal bankruptcy, immorality and violation of legal standards.

Not all criticism is defamatory. It has long been held that people accepting or seeking public office can expect attack and criticism on the grounds that the public interest requires that their conduct shall be open to the most searching evaluation.[26] Further, insults and vulgar abuse, or statements merely in bad taste, are not defamatory.[27]

Defamation law protects not only the reputation and honour of individuals but the reputation and goodwill of a corporate business. Any legal entity that is capable of enjoying a reputation is entitled to sue for defamation, including non-profit bodies such as school boards, municipalities, and even charitable societies.[28]

Libel and slander

At Common Law, defamation consists of two torts, libel and slander. The **2.9** former is actionable without proof of damage; the latter requires proof of special damages except for three special situations.[29] Generally, libel is defamatory matter in writing or other permanent form. Slander is oral defamation, other than in a broadcast.[30] Many province defamation statutes provide that a defamatory radio or television broadcast is libel.

In Quebec, the Civil Law *distinguishes* between *diffamation* and *l'injure*. *Diffamation* consists of an imputation of facts that are *detrimental* to an

---

25. ULCC, Proceedings of 65 Annual Meeting, August 1983, app G, p 96.

26. *Martin* v *Manitoba Free Press Co.* (1892), 8 Man. R 50 at 72, aff'd (1892), 21 SCR 518.

27. *Vander Zalm* v *Times Publishers* (1980), 18 BCLR 210, 109 DLR (3d) 531 [BCCA].

28. *Hunger Project* v *Council on Mind Abuse (COMA) Inc.* (1995), 22 OR (3d) 29 [Ont.]; *Saar Foundation Canada Inc. c. Baruchel*, [1990] RJQ 2325 [Que.SC].

29. The three exceptions are (1) words imputing a loathsome, contagious disease; (2) words imputing a crime punishable by imprisonment; and (3) defamatory statements regarding fitness for, or conduct in, a profession, calling or business.

30. See *Burnett* v *CBC* (No. 2) (1981), 92 APR 181 [NSSC], (reporter sued for oral question alleged to be defamatory).

individual's honour. *L'injure* (abuse) occurs when *outrageous* statements are made, or when terms of contempt or invective are used, without the imputation of any fact.[31]

Innuendo: "popular" and "legal"

2.10 At Common Law, the plaintiff may complain about the literal meaning of the words published or broadcast and may allege that the words conveyed "popular" innuendo meanings to the average, ordinary, objective reader.[32] At trial, the court is entitled to consider the meaning of a news story or broadcast as a whole, taking into account the impression created by headlines, captions, graphics and photographs in the case of the print media, and images, facial expressions, tone of voice, symbols, and the dramatic juxtaposition of sound and text in the case of the broadcast media.[33] Omission of facts to enhance the dramatic impact of a story may create a defamatory effect.[34]

Quebec law similarly recognises that defamation may take the form of literal meanings or innuendo meanings.[35]

At Common Law, if extrinsic facts known to a special category of readers make an otherwise innocent statement defamatory, the plaintiff may plead a "legal" innuendo.[36] Quebec law also recognises claims based on legal innuendo (insinuation).[37]

Publication

2.11 Defamatory matter is not actionable unless it is published to someone other than the plaintiff. In the case of the news media, this element of the cause of action is easily established by a plaintiff.

Re-publication

2.12 Everyone who re-publishes or re-broadcasts a libel, whether or not they express agreement with it, may be held liable.[38] It is no defence, therefore,

---

31. *Gravel* c. *Arthur* (1991), 10 CCLT (2d) 174 [Que.CA], leave to appeal to SCC refused 20 February 1992.

32. *Botiuk* v *Toronto Free Press Publications Ltd.*, [1995] 3 SCR 3, (1995), 126 DLR (4) 609, at para 62.

33. *Lougheed* v *CBC* (1979), 98 DLR (3d) 264 [Alta.CA]; *Vogel* v *CBC*, [1982] 3 WWR 97; *Christie* v *Westcom Radio Group Ltd.* (1990), 51 BCLR (2d) 357 [BCCA].

34. *Colour Your World Corp.* v *CBC* (1994), 17 OR (3d) 308 [Ont.Gen.Div.].

35. 129675 *Canada Inc.* c. *Caron*, [1996] AQ 160 [Que.SC], Baudouin, *La Responsibilité Civile*, 4ieme ed. (Montreal, Que: Yvon Blais, 1994), at pp 235–237; *Brunelle* c. *Girard*, (1914), 23 BR 427.

36. *Botiuk* v *Toronto Free Press Publications Ltd.*, [1995] 3 SCR 3, (1995), 126 DLR (4) 609, at para 62.

37. *Compagnie de Publication de La Presse* c. *Giguère* (1908), CBR 268.

38. *Hill* v *Church of Scientology of Toronto*, [1995] 2 SCR 1130, (1995) 184 NR 1, at para 176.

for the news media to allege that it merely reprinted or re-broadcast what had previously been published by someone else or that the defamatory matter came from a wire service story.[39] Advertisements or other notices composed by third parties inspire many defamation claims.[40]

Joint liability

Everyone who has control over the printing or broadcasting or other **2.13** publication of material containing defamatory matter may be held liable in damages, even if they had no direct personal knowledge that the publication or broadcast contained the defamatory matter. Accordingly, publishers, editors, news directors, producers, printers, announcers and even distributors of print, broadcast or other media may be named as defendants in addition to the actual author of the defamatory matter.

Questions of law and fact

It is a question of law for the court whether a publication or broadcast is **2.14** *capable* of bearing an alleged defamatory innuendo.[41] Previous jurisprudence is sometimes helpful to courts in answering this question. It is a question for the jury (or the judge alone, in cases tried without a jury) whether a publication or broadcast is in fact defamatory.[42]

Identification of the plaintiff

Defamatory matter is not actionable unless it identifies the individual **2.15** plaintiff in some manner, or alternatively, bears an innuendo that identifies the individual plaintiff. It is a question of law whether the words are capable of interpretation as identifying the particular plaintiff. If so, it then becomes a question of fact whether reasonable people

---

39. *Macdonald v Mail Printing Co.* (1900), 32 OR 162, at 170 reversed in part (1901), 2 OLR 278 [Ont.CA]; *Thomson v CBC*, [1981] 4 WWR 289, at 298 [NWTSC]; *Allan v Bushnell Television Co.*, [1969] 1 OR 107 reversed in part, [1969] 2 OR 6 [Ont.CA]; *Chinese Cultural Centre of Vancouver v Holt* (1978), 7 BCLR 81 [BCSC]; regarding Quebec, see *Bergeron c. Rouleau* (1932), 38 RL 376; *Lemieux v Compagnie du Journal Le Monde* (1989), 2 RP 106.

40. *E.g., Allen v Bailey* (1995), 24 CCLT (2d) 212 [Ont.HC]: (an obituary).

41. *Ross v Lamport*, [1956] SCR 366; *Lefolii v Gouzenko*, [1969] SCR 3; *Vander Zalm v Times Publishers* (1980), 18 BCLR 210, 109 DLR (3d) 531 [BCCA].

42. *Booth v BCTelevision Broadcasting System* (1982), 139 DLR (3d) 88 [BCCA].

would conclude that the words refer to the plaintiff. The subjective intent of the author of the defamatory matter is not determinative of this issue.

Although corporations, incorporated societies, and municipalities[43] may be defamed because they possess a distinct legal identity, unincorporated groups have no cause of action.[44] Some courts have taken the view, however, that trade unions may be defamed even if they have no distinct legal personality.[45]

In 1994, the Ontario High Court dismissed a libel suit by one ex-pilot, filed on behalf of 25,000 surviving members of WWII Bomber Command, who alleged that a CBC television documentary portrayed their conduct as morally reprehensible. The trial court held that there cannot be a libel of a class or group because the defamatory matter must identify specific individuals. An appeal from this decision was dismissed on other grounds by the Ontario Court of Appeal.[46]

In 1994, the Ontario High Court also dismissed a libel action brought by the Mayor of Pembroke against an Ottawa sports columnist over an article complaining about Pembroke hockey fans. The article did not name the Mayor, nor did it suggest that each and every citizen of Pembroke committed the reprehensible acts attributed to the Pembroke hockey fans. Accordingly, the words of the article were not capable of referring to the plaintiff Mayor or to the residents of Pembroke.[47]

In Quebec, it has been held that when an identifiable group is so small that each member is personally harmed by defamatory statements (although not named), each member of the group may claim damages.[48]

In Quebec, a defamation claim is not necessarily extinguished by the death of the person defamed. Descendants may sue for defamation if it injures their reputation. In the Common Law provinces and the northern territories, the death of the person defamed extinguishes the cause of action.[49]

---

43. *Prince George (City)* v *BCT System Ltd.*, [1979] 2 WWR 404 [BCCA].

44. *McCann* v *The Ottawa Sun* (1994), 16 OR (3d) 672 [Ont.]; *Stark* v *Toronto Sun Publishing Corp.* (1983), 42 OR (2d) 791 [Ont.].

45. *Pulp & Paper Workers of Canada* v *International Brotherhood of Pulp, etc. Workers of Canada* (1973), 37 DLR (3d) 687 [BCSC].

46. *Elliot* v *CBC* (1994), 16 OR (3d) 677 [Ont.]; aff'd (1995), 125 DLR (4) 534 [Ont.CA].

47. *McCann* v *The Ottawa Sun* (1994), 16 OR (3d) 672 [Ont.].

48. *Trahan* c. *L'Imprimerie Gagné Ltée* (1987), 44 CCLT 33 [Que.SC].

49. *Davie* v *The Commissioner of the Yukon Territory and Antony Penikett* (26 April 1993), unreported, Whitehorse no. 602.90.

Civil statutes concerning group libel

Manitoba's Defamation Act prohibits libel of a race or religious creed **2.16** that is likely to expose its members to hatred, contempt or ridicule, or tends to create unrest or disorder. Any member of the race or creed is entitled to sue for an injunction to prevent the continuation and circulation of the libel.[50] This specific prohibition does not give a right to claim damages.

British Columbia's Civil Rights Protection Act[51] creates a civil cause of action for compensatory and exemplary damages and for an injunction with respect to any communication which is intended to interfere with the civil rights of a person or class of persons by promoting hatred or contempt, or the superiority or inferiority of a person or class, on the basis of colour, race, religion, ethnic origin or place of origin.

British Columbia's Human Rights Act empowers a tribunal to order payment of pecuniary and non-pecuniary damages for publications which indicate discrimination or an intention to discriminate against a person or a group or class of persons, or that are likely to expose a person or a group or class of persons to hatred or contempt because of their race, colour, ancestry, place of origin, religion, marital status, family status, physical or mental disability, sex, sexual orientation or age.[52] The tribunal may also grant a permanent injunction. Lack of intent to contravene the Act is no defence. No rulings have yet been made under this 1993 provision.

Defences to defamation claims

The basic defences to a defamation lawsuit in the Common Law jurisdic- **2.17** tions are truth, privilege and fair comment. The majority of defamation actions centre on these defences.

Justification

At Common Law, a defamatory allegation is presumed to be false. The **2.18** onus therefore rests on the defendant to prove the truth of the defamatory matter on a balance of probabilities based on the weight and preponderance of the evidence. If the defamatory matter alleges

---

50. RSM 1987, c. D–20, s 19.

51. SBC 1981, c. 12, s 1.

52. SBC 1984, c. 22, s 2(1), s 17, as amended by SBC 1993, c. 33.

criminal or corrupt conduct, the courts may require a higher degree of probability to be established by a defendant.[53]

The defence will succeed if the defendant proves the truth of the "sting" or "bite" or "gist" of the allegation. The defamation statutes of Ontario[54] and Nova Scotia[55] codify this aspect of the Common Law. They state that a defence of justification:

> ". . . shall not fail by reason only that the truth of every charge is not proved if the words not proved to be true do not materially injure the plaintiff's reputation having regard to the truth of the remaining charges".

2.19   In the Common Law provinces, malice does not void the defence of truth. In fact, the defence of truth may succeed even if the defendant did not know that the defamatory statement was true when it was printed or broadcast, or even if the defendant believed it to be false at that time.

Nevertheless, justification is a problematic defence for the news media in the Common Law provinces and territories. No publisher or broadcaster can be certain in advance that a judge or jury will believe its evidence. The court is free to accept or reject the whole or any part of the testimony of any witness. Evidence available at the time of the publication or broadcast may not be available at the trial of a defamation action many years later. In Canadian courts, hearsay testimony is generally inadmissible, unless it fits within one of the narrow exceptions to the exclusionary rule. Witnesses for the defence may be afraid to testify or may not be available at trial because of death or illness or for many other reasons. Whistleblowers about government misconduct might never be identified. Confidential sources, whose identity is known to the defendant journalist, might refuse to waive the defendant journalist's promise of anonymity.

In Quebec, the burden of proving truth also rests on a defendant.[56] However, truth is not a sufficient defence unless the defendant proves that publication of the defamatory facts was in the public interest.[57] Quebec courts have not developed a single test, however, for determining what constitutes the public interest.[58] Further, truth is not a defence if the sole purpose of the publication was to harm the person defamed.[59]

---

53. *York* v *Okanagan Broadcasters*, [1976] 6 WWR 40 [BCSC]; *Panglinan* v *Chaves* (1988), 52 Man.R (2d) 86 [QB].

54. Libel and Slander Act, RSO 1990, c. L–12, s 23.

55. Defamation Act, RSNS 1989, c. 122, s 9.

56. *Vitali* v *Morina* (1989), 1 CCLT (2d) 224 [Que.SC].

57. *Szabo* c. *Morisette* (1993), 18 CCLT (2d) 182 [Que.SC]; Vallières, *La Presse Et La Diffamation* (Montreal, Que: Wilson & LaFleur, 1985), at pp 90–103.

58. Vallières, *La Presse Et La Diffamation* (Montreal, Que: Wilson & LaFleur, 1985), at pp 90–103.

59. *Gravel* c. *Arthur* (1991), 10 CCLT (2d) 174 [Que.CA]; Vallières, *La Presse Et La Diffamation* (Montreal, Que: Wilson & LaFleur, 1985); *Baudouin, La Responsibilité Civile,* 4ieme ed. (Montreal, Que: Yvon Blais, 1994), at pp 235–237.

Privilege defences

At Common Law, there are occasions when the public interest in freedom of **2.20** speech over-rides the public and private interest in protecting individual or corporate reputation. In large measure, the occasions of Common Law privilege relate to the functioning of the institutions of government. The defence of privilege protects fair and accurate reports by the news media of the public proceedings of institutions such as Parliament, the legislative assemblies of the Provinces, the courts and quasi-judicial tribunals. Outside the context of reports of the functioning of public institutions, Canadian courts have generally been reluctant to accept media defences based on a Common Law privilege.

Statutory privileges

The federal Parliament, the provinces and the northern territories have **2.21** enacted certain statutory privileges applicable to the news media which recognise their special role in the functioning of Canadian democracy. Media critics charge that these statutory privileges are too narrow. Despite their limitations, these privileges have afforded valuable protection to the news media.

Reports of proceedings of government

The Federal Parliament of Canada Act requires that civil courts stay any **2.22** proceedings based on the publication of any copy of a report, paper, votes or proceedings originally published by or under the authority of the Senate or the House of Commons. In addition to that absolute privilege for publication of entire government documents, a defendant who publishes merely an extract or abstract enjoys a qualified privilege if he or she proves that it was published in good faith, and without malice.[60]

Federal legislation also creates a defence of qualified privilege for any fair and accurate report made in good faith, in a newspaper or any other periodical or publication in a broadcast, of an official report made by the federal Information Commissioner under the Access to Information Act,[61] by a Corrections Investigator made under the Corrections and Conditional Release Act,[62] by the Commissioner of

---

60. RSC 1985, c. P–1, ss 7, 8, 9.

61. RSC 1985, c. A–1, s 66(2).

62. RSC 1985, c. C–44.6, s 190(b).

Official Languages under the Official Languages Act,[63] and by the Privacy Commissioner under the Privacy Act.[64]

Each of the Common Law provinces and the Yukon and Northwest Territories have legislated, to varying degrees, qualified privilege defences for reports in newspapers and broadcasts of the proceedings of government bodies. (Saskatchewan's statute only applies to newspapers). Most such defences are embodied in defamation statutes:

Alberta:	Defamation Act, RSA 1980, c. D–6
British Columbia:	Libel and Slander Act, RSBC 1979, c. 234
Manitoba:	Defamation Act, RSM 1987, c. D–20
New Brunswick:	Defamation Act, RSNB 1973
Newfoundland:	Defamation Act, SN 1983, c. 63
Northwest Territories:	Defamation Act, RSNWT 1988, c. D–1
Nova Scotia:	Defamation Act, RSNS 1989, c. 122
Ontario:	Libel and Slander Act, RSO 1990, c. L–12
Prince Edward Island:	Defamation Act, RSPEI 1988, c. D–5
Saskatchewan:	Libel and Slander Act, RSS 1978, c. L–14
Yukon Territory:	Defamation Act, RSYT 1986, c. 41

2.23 Except for British Columbia, each defamation statute protects a fair and accurate report, published without malice in a newspaper or broadcast, of proceedings in the Senate or House of Commons of Canada, the Legislative Assembly of any province, or a committee of any of those bodies, except where neither the public nor any reporter was admitted. The Northwest Territories and the Yukon Territory statutes also apply to their respective legislative assemblies and to committees of those assemblies. Oddly, British Columbia's statute applies only to select committees of its own Legislative Assembly. It does not even apply to its own Legislative Assembly or to those of other jurisdictions.

The defamation statutes of Alberta, Manitoba, New Brunswick, Nova Scotia, Prince Edward Island, Newfoundland and Saskatchewan also recognise a privilege defence for fair and accurate, good faith reports of a public meeting, a meeting of a municipal council, school board, board of education, board of health, or of any other board or local authority formed or constituted under a federal or provincial statute, or of a committee appointed by any such board or local authority. The statutes

---

63. RSC 1985, c. 31 (4 Sup), s 75(2).

64. RSC 1985, c. P–21, s 67(2).

of Newfoundland and the Yukon Territory recognise an equivalent privilege but also extend it to boards constituted under statutes of the two territories. Ontario's legislation also extends a similar qualified privilege defence to the proceedings of "any administrative body that is constituted by any public authority in Canada" and to "any organisation whose members, in whole or in part, represent any public authority in Canada." British Columbia's statutory protection applies only to reports of a public meeting, or a meeting of a municipal council, school board, board or local authority formed or constituted under a British Columbia statute.

The defamation statutes of the two territories and the Common Law provinces (except Prince Edward Island, Saskatchewan and Ontario) also expressly recognise a qualified privilege defence for fair and accurate, good faith reports of meetings of commissioners authorised to act by letters patent, statute or other lawful warrant or authority. Nova Scotia and Ontario statutes protect fair and accurate reports of the proceedings of any commission of inquiry that is constituted by any public authority in the British Commonwealth. Nova Scotia's defamation statute also protects reports of "the proceedings of any administrative body that is constituted by any public authority in Canada".

The defamation statutes of each Common Law province and of the Yukon Territory provide that the privilege for reports of government bodies does not apply to the publication of any matter not of public concern or the publication of which is not for the public benefit.

Quebec's Press Act[65] does not apply to broadcasters. It provides only limited protection to newspaper publishers and writers.[66] The Press Act creates a qualified privilege for accurate reports of public proceedings of the federal Parliament and Quebec's legislative assembly (the "National Assembly") and committees of those bodies, and for reports of the Public Protector laid before the National Assembly.

Publication at the request of government

The defamation statutes of each of the Common Law provinces and the **2.24** territories provide that the publication in a newspaper or broadcast, at the request of a government department, bureau or office or public officer, of a report, bulletin, notice or other document issued for the information of the public, is privileged, unless it is proved that the publication was made maliciously. The Northwest Territories expressly extends the protection to include requests by the council of a municipality. Nova Scotia and Ontario expressly extend the protection to publication at the request

---

65. RSQ 1964, c. 48, art 10.

66. *McGregor* c. *The Montreal Gazette Ltd.,* [1982] CS 900 [Que.SC].

of any government entity if reports of that entity's proceedings are protected by the defamation statute. Saskatchewan expressly protects publications requested by the commissioner of police or chief constable.

The defamation statutes of each Common Law province and the Yukon Territory provide that the privilege for reports at the request of government does not apply to the publication of any matter not of public concern or the publication of which is not for the public benefit.

Quebec's Press Act enacts a qualified privilege for publication in any newspaper of any notice, bulletin or recommendation emanating from a Government or municipal health service, and for public notices given by the government respecting the solvency of certain companies or regarding the value of certain issues of bonds, shares or stocks.

None of the foregoing statutory provisions creates a general privilege defence for news media reports of police press conferences or police information.

Reports of court proceedings

2.25 The defamation statutes of each of the Common Law provinces and the two northern territories enact a qualified privilege defence for fair and accurate reports, published without malice, of proceedings publicly heard before a court exercising judicial authority, if published contemporaneously with the proceedings, and if they contain no comment. A report of in-camera proceedings is not protected. A report need not be verbatim, but any significant inaccuracies will defeat the privilege.[67]

Quebec's Press Act enacts a privilege for reports of public sittings of the courts if the reports are accurate.

Miscellaneous statutory privileges

2.26 Nova Scotia and Ontario have enacted a qualified privilege defence for fair and accurate newspaper or broadcast reports of the decisions of associations for the promotion of art, science, religion, or learning, or for the promotion of trade, business, industry or professional bodies, or for the promotion of sports, insofar as the decision relates to a member of the association.

Right of contradiction or explanation

2.27 In the Common Law provinces and the two northern territories, the above-noted statutory privileges are defeated if the defendant newspaper or broadcaster fails, on request, to publish or broadcast a reasonable statement by way of contradiction or explanation of the report or

---

67. *Wenman v Pacific Press Ltd.* (30 January 1991), unreported, Vancouver no. C891725 [BCSC].

other publication. In British Columbia, however, this stipulation does not apply to reports of court proceedings.

Common Law privileges

In large measure, the Common Law recognises a qualified privilege **2.28** defence for reports of government and court proceedings analogous to the above-noted statutory privileges. To the extent that the statutory privileges are narrower than those recognised by the Common Law, the news media may choose to rely on the latter. For example, British Columbia's Libel and Slander Act does not cover reports of proceedings of its Legislative Assembly. The news media must therefore rely on the Common Law.

At Common Law, an occasion of qualified privilege also arises where a publication is made in the performance of a legal, moral or social duty to a person who has a corresponding interest in receiving such a statement.[68] This privilege is defeated, however, if the dominant motive for publishing is actual or express malice.[69] Malice is not limited to spite, but includes any indirect motive or ulterior purpose that conflicts with the sense of duty or the mutual interest created by the occasion.[70] Malice may also be established by showing that the plaintiff spoke dishonestly, or in knowing or reckless disregard for the truth.[71] The privilege is also defeated, however, when the limits of the duty or interest have been exceeded.[72] In other words, if the information communicated was not reasonably appropriate to the legitimate purposes of the occasion, the defence fails.

Qualified privilege is not often a successful defence for defamatory news media publications or broadcasts. Only rarely have the courts found that a newspaper had a duty to publish the defamatory matter. In 1983, the British Columbia Supreme Court accepted a defence of qualified privilege by a consumer affairs reporter, because her defamatory article alleging that the plaintiff's product could cause death followed an earlier article by the same reporter recommending purchase of the plaintiff's product. Careless, impulsive or irrational conduct by the reporter did not negate her honest belief in the defamatory statement. Accordingly, the

---

68. *Hill* v *Church of Scientology of Toronto*, [1995] 2 SCR 1130, (1995) 184 NR 1, at para 144; *McLoughlin* v *Kutasy*, [1979] 2 SCR 311, at 321.

69. *Botiuk* v *Toronto Free Press Publications Ltd.*, [1995] 3 SCR 3, (1995), 126 DLR (4) 609, at p 3; *Hill* v *Church of Scientology of Toronto*, [1995] 2 SCR 1130, (1995) 184 NR 1, at para 144.

70. *Hill* v *Church of Scientology of Toronto*, [1995] 2 SCR 1130, (1995) 184 NR 1, at para 145.

71. *Netupsky* v *Craig*, [1973] 2 SCR 55, at 61–62.

72. *Hill* v *Church of Scientology of Toronto*, [1995] 2 SCR 1130, (1995) 184 NR 1, at para 146.

plaintiff failed to prove malice, which would have defeated the qualified privilege defence.[73] In 1994, the British Columbia Court of Appeal held that special circumstances will be required before a newspaper has a duty to publish defamatory matter and rejected the defendant newspaper's argument that its readers shared a common interest concerning Canadian immigration procedures and the admission of political refugees. The defendant newspaper had published articles alleging that the plaintiff had been a terrorist. The Court of Appeal also rejected the newspaper's request for recognition of a "fair report" privilege permitting news papers to publish defamatory reports on matters of public interest.[74]

In 1995, the Supreme Court of Canada expanded the Common Law defence of qualified privilege relating to reports of court proceedings.[75] Previously, the privilege applied to pleadings, affidavits and other filed documents only if they were read in open court or referred to in open court. The Court expanded the privilege to apply even to documents in court files that are never mentioned in open court. The privilege is defeated, however, if a published report is not reasonably appropriate in the circumstances existing at the time of publication.[76]

At Common Law, a fair and accurate report of statements in the federal Parliament or the provincial legislature is protected by qualified privilege, which is defeated by proof of malice on the part of the publisher or broadcaster.

In Quebec, it is dubious that a general defence of qualified privilege (*l'immunité relative*) exists for the news media. It may be that the only case where the news media can invoke good faith as a defence are those instances prescribed by the article 10 of the Press Act, which extends a form of privilege for accurate and good faith reports of proceedings of the government, notices, bulletins or recommendations emanating from a government or municipal health service, public notices given by the government or by a person authorised by it respecting the solvency of certain companies or regarding the value of certain issues of bonds, shares or stock, or reports of sitting of the courts provided they are not held in camera.[77]

Fair comment

2.29 Often called the cornerstone of free speech, fair comment may be the most important defence to defamation lawsuits arising from criticism

---

73. *Camporese* v *Parton* (1983), 47 BCLR 78 [BCSC].

74. *Moises* v *Canadian Newspaper Co.* (1996), 76 BCAC 263 [BCCA].

75. *Hill* v *Church of Scientology of Toronto*, [1995] 2 SCR 1130, (1995) 184 NR 1, at para 151–154.

76. *Hill* v *Church of Scientology of Toronto*, [1995] 2 SCR 1130, (1995) 184 NR 1, at para 155–156.

77. Vallières, *La Presse Et La Diffamation* (Montreal, Que: Wilson & LaFleur, 1985), at pp 104–110.

of politicians or other public figures. To succeed on this defence, the defendant must prove that the defamatory matter is comment on true facts, expressed or implied in the defamatory publication or broadcast, on a subject of public interest.[78] The defence fails if the ordinary reader or listener would regard the defamatory matter as fact rather than comment, or if the comment was actuated by malice. In a news story, every known background fact need not be published but enough facts must be published to demonstrate a basis for the comment.[79] The plaintiff has the burden of proving malice.

The comment need not be fair, in the sense of being reasonable by objective standards, as long as it was made honestly and without improper motives.[80] In the Common Law provinces, mere negligence in the research leading to the formulation of the defamatory comment does not constitute malice.[81]

In 1978, the Supreme Court of Canada ruled in *Cherneskey* v *Armadale Publishers Ltd.* that fair comment was not a defence available to a newspaper that published a letter to the editor, because the newspaper failed to prove that a defamatory comment in the letter also represented the newspaper's opinion.[82] The troubling implication of that decision for freedom of the press lead the northern territories and the Common Law provinces (except British Columbia, Saskatchewan, and Nova Scotia) to amend their defamation statutes. Alberta's amended statute provides that a defence of fair comment does not fail merely because the defendant did not share the defamatory opinion expressed by another person.[83] The defamation acts of Manitoba, Newfoundland, Prince Edward Island, Ontario, New Brunswick, the Yukon Territory, and the Northwest Territories are similar, but each also requires proof that a person could honestly hold the defamatory opinion;[84] moreover, the defence fails (except in Ontario) if the defendant knew the opinion was dishonestly expressed by its originator. New Brunswick's statute requires that the person expressing the defamatory opinion be identified.

The fair comment defence requires strict proof of all the facts published with the comment. Further, the defence does not apply to comments that impute corrupt or dishonourable motives to the plaintiff.[85] The

---

78. *Vander Zalm* v *Times Publishers* (1980) 109 DLR (3d) 531 [BCCA], at DLR pp 535–536.

79. *Holt* v *Sun Publishing Co.* (1978), 83 DLR (3d) 761 [BCSC].

80. *Sara's Pyrohy Hut* v *Brooker*, [1992] 1 WWR 556 [Alta.QB], aff'd [1993] 3 WWR 662 [Alta.CA].

81. *Camporese* v *Parton* (1983), 47 BCLR 78 [BCSC].

82. *Cherneskey* v *Armadale Publishers Ltd.*, [1979] 1 SCR 1067.

83. Defamation Act, RSA 1980, c. D–6, s 9(1).

84. RSM 1970, c. D–20, s 9(1); RSN 1990, c. D–3, s 11; RSPEI 1988, c. D–5, s 9(1); RSO 1970, 243, s 24; RSNB 1973, c. D–5, s 8.1(1), RSYT 1986, c. 41, s 8; RSNWT 1988, c. D–1, s 10(1).

85. Law Reform Commission of British Columbia, Report on Defamation (1985), at 25.

defamation statutes of Ontario[86] and Nova Scotia[87] have amended the Common Law to provide that the defence will not fail by reason only that truth of every allegation of fact is not proved, if the expression of opinion is fair comment having regard to such of the facts alleged or referred to in the words complained of, as are proved.

In Quebec, the law recognises a similar defence (*commentaire loyal*). Quebec law protects editorial comment but requires that it be clearly distinguishable from statements of fact. The editorial writer is required to exercise considerable caution to ensure the underlying facts are accurately recorded.[88] It appears, however, that the defendant must also establish that the opinion expressed is reasonably supported by the facts.[89] Comment based on a known untruth is not defensible.[90] It has been held that elected officials are proper targets of media comment, criticism and caricature, and may even be subjected to ridicule, as long as the media do not misrepresent the facts.[91]

Damages

2.30 In 1995, the Supreme Court of Canada in *Hill* v *Church of Scientology of Toronto*[92] rejected defence arguments there should be a "cap" for general damages in libel cases similar to the C $250,000 limit imposed by a 1978 decision of the court on damages for non-pecuniary loss for pain and suffering in personal injury cases. Instead, the Supreme Court of Canada unanimously endorsed the unprecedented C $1.6-million verdict of an Ontario civil jury, which included C $300,000 general damages, C $500,000 aggravated damages and C $800,000 punitive damages.

Hill v *Church of Scientology of Toronto* did not involve a media defendant (although news media were intervenors). It is worrying to the news media, however, because it does sanction harsh penalties for defamation. The huge sums awarded for general and aggravated damages, which dwarf past Canadian court awards, did not "shock the conscience" of the court, which is the test for appellate interference. Punitive damages are more susceptible to control by appellate courts but even this element of the jury's verdict was expressly held to be reasonable because of the

---

86. RSO 1990, c. L–12, s 23.

87. RSNS 1989, c. 122, s 9.

88. *Chaloult* v *Gagnon*, (1937), 43 RL 359.

89. *L* c. *Les Editions de la Cité*, (1960), CS 485.

90. *SRJ Consultants Inc.* v *Fortin* (1982), 20 CCLT 221 [QSC].

91. *Gravel* c. *Arthur* (1991), 10 CCLT (2d) 174 [Que.CA].

92. *Hill* v *Church of Scientology of Toronto*, [1995] 2 SCR 1130, (1995) 184 NR 1, at para 168.

defendant's "insidious, pernicious and persistent malice."[93] The defendant made its defamatory allegations knowing them to be false and it re-iterated the defamatory allegations throughout the trial and even after the jury award.

As a result of *Hill* v *Church of Scientology of Toronto*, massive jury libel awards for general and aggravated damages based on evidence of malice may be almost immune to appellate review. Large punitive damages awards are also more likely to survive appellate scrutiny. As a result, more time and money may be spent by libel litigants on malice issues in the discovery process, pre-trial investigation and at trial. It is premature to predict whether the frequency of defamation lawsuits will increase in Canada.

Compensatory damages

At Common Law, damages are presumed to flow from publication of a **2.31** libel. This principle is codified by the defamation statutes of all Common Law provinces except Nova Scotia, Saskatchewan and British Columbia. The defamation statutes of the Northwest Territories and the Yukon Territory merely provide that a defamation action may be commenced without alleging or proving special damage, *i.e.,* actual pecuniary loss.

Compensatory damages include general damages, special damages and aggravated damages. At Common Law, general damages for libel are at large, meaning that the court is entitled to make a subjective assessment without requiring proof of specific financial loss. In *Hill* v *Church of Scientology of Toronto*, the plaintiff did not prove financial loss. In fact, he received three promotions before the jury verdict, was elected to prestigious positions, and was appointed to the Ontario High Court before the Supreme Court of Canada's ruling. The Supreme Court of Canada said that its judgment in the *Hill* case will not lead to inflation in defamation awards but it remains to be seen whether the Court's prediction is valid. In 1996, an Ontario jury awarded a plaintiff lawyer C $600,000 general damages and C $100,000 aggravated damages over a newspaper sports column.[94]

Politicians, government officials, and professionals are frequent libel plaintiffs. Until *Hill* v *Church of Scientology of Toronto*, defamation damage awards to political figures that survived appellate scrutiny did not exceed C $135,000 and most were substantially below that sum.

In a 1992 judgment setting aside a trial judge's award of damages, the British Columbia Court of Appeal in *Derrickson* v *Tomat* discussed the subject of damage awards for defamatory statements made in the heat of political

---

93. *Hill* v *Church of Scientology of Toronto*, [1995] 2 SCR 1130, (1995) 184 NR 1, at para 203.

94. *Eagleson* v *The Globe Mail*, (7 August 1996) Ontario Court no. 92–CU63382.

controversy.[95] The majority ruled that the guarantee of freedom of expression entrenched in the Constitution by section 2(b) of the Canadian Charter of Rights and Freedoms requires that Courts exercise restraint in awarding damages for politically motivated defamation. Referring to prior jurisprudence suggesting that those who take on the burden of public life deserve more, rather than less, compensation when their reputations are sullied by their opponents, the majority held that courts now have a duty to develop the Common Law of libel damages in a manner consistent with the constitutional values reflected in the Charter. It remains to be seen if this view will be endorsed by the Supreme Court of Canada in a future case.

In 1995, the British Columbia Court of Appeal, in the course of dismissing an appeal from a trial award of compensatory libel damages to a senior government official, without deciding the point, expressed doubt that restraint in assessing libel damages for politically-motivated defamation should apply to defamation of civil servants, who are not allowed to explain their actions and who have not entered a public arena in such a way as to invite public discussion.[96]

In Quebec, the Charter of Human Rights and Freedoms recognises the distinction between pecuniary loss (*dommage matériel*) and non-pecuniary loss (*dommage moral*).[97]

Aggravated damages

2.32 At Common Law, aggravated damages may be awarded in circumstances where the defendant's conduct has been particularly high-handed or oppressive, thereby increasing the plaintiff's humiliation and anxiety arising from the defamatory statement.[98] Like general or special damages, aggravated damages are compensatory in nature. Their assessment requires consideration by the jury of the entire conduct of the defendant prior to the publication of the libel and continuing through to the conclusion of the trial. They represent the expression of natural indignation of right-thinking people arising from the malicious conduct of the defendant.[99]

In order for aggravated damages to be awarded, there must be a finding that the defendant was motivated by actual malice, which increased the injury to the plaintiff, either by spreading further afield the

---

95. 10 CCLT (2d) 1, leave to appeal to the SCC dismissed, [1992] 6 WWR viii.

96. *Newsome* v *Kexco Publishing Co. Ltd.*, (1995), 67 BCAC 297 [BCCA].

97. Vallières, *La Presse Et La Diffamation* (Montreal, Que: Wilson & LaFleur, 1985), at pp 76–82.

98. *Hill* v *Church of Scientology of Toronto*, [1995] 2 SCR 1130, (1995) 184 NR 1, at para 188.

99. *Hill* v *Church of Scientology of Toronto*, [1995] 2 SCR 1130, (1995) 184 NR 1, at para 189.

damage to the reputation of the plaintiff, or by increasing the mental distress and humiliation of the plaintiff. The malice may be established by extrinsic evidence derived from the libellous statement itself and the circumstances of its publication, or by extrinsic evidence pertaining to the surrounding circumstances that demonstrate that the defendant was motivated by an unjustifiable intention to injure the plaintiff.[100]

In assessing aggravated damages, the court may take into account whether there was a retraction and apology. If so, this may negate malice. Aggravated damages are more likely to be awarded if there was a repetition of the libel, or if the defendant's conduct was calculated to deter the plaintiff from proceeding with the libel action, or if the defendant engaged in a prolonged and hostile cross-examination of the plaintiff for a plea of justification which the defendant knew was bound to fail.[101]

Quebec law does not provide for an award of aggravated damages.

Punitive damages

At Common Law, punitive damages may be awarded in situations where **2.33** the defendant's conduct is so malicious, oppressive and high handed that it offends the court's sense of decency.[102] Punitive damages bear no relation to what the plaintiff should receive by way of compensation. Their aim is not to compensate the plaintiff, but rather to punish the defendant. It is the means by which the jury or judge expresses outrage at the egregious conduct of the defendant. They are in the nature of a fine that is meant to act as a deterrent to the defendant and to others.

Punitive damages are only to be awarded in those circumstances where the combined award of general and aggravated damages would be insufficient to achieve the goal of punishment and deterrence. Unlike compensatory damages, punitive damages are not at large. Consequently, courts have a much greater scope and discretion on appeal. The appellate review should be based on the court's estimation as to whether punitive damages serve the purpose of deterrence.[103]

In Quebec, the Charter of Human Rights and Freedoms permits the court to award exemplary damages in the case of an unlawful and intentional attack on reputation. The purpose of such damages is punishment and deterrence.[104] A defendant's testimony at trial, reiterating the alleged truth of defamatory matter, may constitute an intentional act that

---

100. *Hill* v *Church of Scientology of Toronto*, [1995] 2 SCR 1130, (1995) 184 NR 1, at para 190.

101. *Hill* v *Church of Scientology of Toronto*, [1995] 2 SCR 1130, (1995) 184 NR 1, at para 191.

102. *Hill* v *Church of Scientology of Toronto*, [1995] 2 SCR 1130, (1995) 184 NR 1, at para 196.

103. *Hill* v *Church of Scientology of Toronto*, [1995] 2 SCR 1130, (1995) 184 NR 1, at paras 196–199.

104. LRQ 1977, c. C–12, arts 4, 5 and 49; *Carpentier* c. *Radiomutuel Inc.*, [1995] AQ. no. 414 [Que.CA].

justifies an award of punitive damages.[105] A refusal to apologise may also be a factor in awarding punitive damages.[106]

Apology and retraction

2.34   At Common Law, a full retraction and apology may reduce the damages otherwise payable to the plaintiff. This defence is available even if the requirements of certain statutory defences cannot be satisfied.[107]

The defamation statutes of each of the Common Law provinces and the two northern territories provide that a defendant may give in evidence, in mitigation of damages that he or she offered to publish an apology, or did publish an apology, before the action, or shortly afterwards. (Saskatchewan's defamation statute only applies to newspapers).

The defamation statutes of the Common Law provinces and the two northern territories also provide that a plaintiff shall only recover actual damages (in some provinces referred to as "special damages") against a newspaper or broadcaster if the defamatory matter was published in good faith, there was reasonable ground to believe that it was for the public benefit, it did not involve a criminal charge, the publication took place in mistake or misapprehension of the facts, and a full and fair retraction was published, in as conspicuous a place and type as the defamatory matter. (Saskatchewan's statute limits this defence to newspapers). Alberta, Manitoba, New Brunswick, Nova Scotia, Prince Edward Island, and the Yukon and Northwest Territories also require that a full apology accompany the retraction. This defence does not apply to defamation of a candidate for public office published or broadcast within five days of the election (15 days in Saskatchewan).[108]

Quebec's Press Act stipulates that only actual and real damages may be claimed if a defendant newspaper establishes good faith and promptly publishes a full retraction in as conspicuous a place as the defamatory article.[109] The Press Act also requires the newspaper to publish a reply by the plaintiff, if it is of reasonable length and in appropriate terms. If such a retraction and reply are published without further comment by the newspaper, no lawsuit may be filed by the person defamed against

---

105. *Bouchard c. Bombardier* (1991), 10 CCLT (2d) 224 [Que.SC].

106. *Trahan c. L'Imprimerie Gagné Ltée* (1987), 44 CCLT 33 [Que.SC].

107. *Tait v New Westminster Radio Ltd.* (1984), 58 BCLR 194 [BCCA]; *Thomson v NL Broadcasting Ltd.* (1976), 1 CCLT 278 [BCSC].

108. RSA 1980, c. D–6, s 16; RSM 1970, c. D–20, s 17; RSNB 1973, c. D–5, s 17; RSN 1990, c. D–3, s 19; RSNWT 1988, c. D–1, s 19; RSNS 1989, c. 122, s 22; RSPEI 1988, c. D–5, s 18; RSS 1978, c. L–14, s 8; RSYT 1986, c. 41, s 18; RSO 1990, c. L–12, s 9; RSBC 1979, c. 234, s 7.

109. RSQ 1964, c. 48, art 5.

the newspaper.[110] These provisions do not apply if the article referred to a candidate at election time, or if it alleged a criminal offence.[111]

The defamation statutes of the Common Law provinces and the territories also provide that the defendant may prove in mitigation of damages that the defamatory matter was published or broadcast without actual malice and without gross negligence, and that before the lawsuit or at the earliest opportunity afterwards, the defendant published or broadcast a full apology. (Saskatchewan's statute only protects newspapers). Except in Ontario and British Columbia, a full and fair retraction must accompany the apology.[112] Ignoring pre-publication warnings issued by the target of the defamatory matter will make it difficult for the news media to rely on this defence.[113]

At Common Law, damages may also be mitigated by permitting the plaintiff to publish or broadcast a rebuttal.[114]

Notice requirements and limitation periods

Except for British Columbia, the defamation statutes of the Common **2.35**
Law provinces and the two territories require, as a precondition to a lawsuit, that a plaintiff serve on a newspaper or broadcaster written notice of an intention to bring a defamation action. (Saskatchewan's statute does not apply to broadcasters). Ontario's statute prescribes the shortest notice period: within six weeks of the defamatory matter coming to the plaintiff's attention.[115] Except for Saskatchewan, the other defamation statutes prescribe three months.[116] Saskatchewan only requires that the notice be given five days before a lawsuit against a daily newspaper, and 14 days before a lawsuit against a weekly. In British Columbia, the only requirement is that one clear day lapse between publication or broadcast of the libel and issuance of the writ; notice is not required.[117]

---

110. RSQ 1964, c. 48, arts 7 and 8.

111. RSQ 1964, c. 48, art 9.

112. RSA 1980, c. D–6, s 15; RSM 1970, c. D–20, s 16; RSNB 1973, c. D–5, s 16(1); RSN 1990, c. D–3, s 18; RSNWT 1988, c. D–1, s 18(1); RSNS 1989, c. 122, s 5; RSPEI 1988, c. D–5, s 17; RSS 1978, c. L–14, s 7; RSYT 1986, c. 41, s 17(1); RSO 1990, c. L–12, s 51; RSBC 1979, c. 234, s 6(1).

113. *Snider* v *Calgary Herald* (1985), 34 CCLT 27 [Alta.QB].

114. *Thomson* v *NL Broadcasting Ltd.* (1984), 58 BCLR 194 [BCCA].

115. RSO 1990, c. L–12, s 5(1).

116. RSA 1980, c. D–6, s 13(1); RSM 1970, c. D–20, s 14(1); RSNB 1973, c. D–5, s 13(1); RSN 1990, c. D–3, s 16(1); RSNWT 1988, c. D–1, s 15(1); RSNS 1989, c. 122, s 18(1); RSPEI 1988, c. D–5, s 14(1); RSYT 1986, c. 41, s 14(1).

117. RSBC 1979, c. 234, s 5.

Quebec's Press Act, which does not apply to radio or television, requires that notice of intention must be delivered three days before filing a lawsuit to allow the newspaper to rectify or retract the defamatory matter.[118]

Statutory limitation periods in each jurisdiction extinguish the cause of action for defamation. The limitation period is two years in Alberta,[119] Manitoba,[120] British Columbia,[121] New Brunswick,[122] Newfoundland,[123] and the Northwest Territories.[124] In Ontario,[125] an action against a newspaper or broadcaster must be commenced within three months after the defamatory matter came to the attention of the person defamed, but such an action properly brought may include a claim for any other libel by the same defendant within the year prior to the lawsuit. Nova Scotia,[126] Prince Edward Island,[127] the Yukon Territory[128] and Saskatchewan[129] prescribe a six-month limitation period.

The Quebec Press Act requires that a defamation action against a newspaper be brought within three months of the plaintiff learning of the publication, and in any event, within one year following publication.[130]

Injunctions: interlocutory and permanent

2.36   An interlocutory injunction before trial will not be issued for an allegedly defamatory publication or broadcast unless the words complained of are clearly defamatory, clearly untrue and clearly not fair comment. The court must conclude that any jury verdict favouring the defendant at trial would inevitably be considered perverse by a court of appeal. If the publisher of the defamatory matter says it will prove truth or some other defence, no interlocutory injunction will be issued.[131]

---

118. RSQ 1964, c. 48, art 3; *Lépine* c. *Proulx*, [1996] AQ 1197 [QSC].

119. Limitation of Actions Act, RSA 1980, c. L–15, s 51(a).

120. Limitations of Actions Act, RSM 1987, c. L–150, s 2(1)(c).

121. Limitation Act, RSBC 1979, c. 236, s 3(1)(c).

122. Limitations of Actions Act, RSNB 1973, c. L–8, s 4.

123. Limitation of Personal Actions Act, RSN 1990, c. L–15, s 4(b).

124. Limitation of Actions Act, RSNWT 1988, c. L–8, s 2(1)(c).

125. Limitations Act, RSO 1980, c. 237, s 6.

126. Defamation Act, RSNS 1989, c. 122, s 19.

127. Defamation Act, RSPEI 1988, c. D–05, s 15.

128. Defamation Act, RSYT 1986, c. 41, s 5(1).

129. Libel and Slander Act, RSS 1978, s L–14, s 14, newspapers only.

130. RSQ 1964, c. 48, s 2.

131. *Canada Metal Co. Ltd.* v *CBC* (1974), 44 DLR (3d) 329 [Ont.]; aff'd 55 DLR (3d) 42 [Ont.CA].

In one of the rare cases where an interlocutory injunction was ordered in a Common Law province, the British Columbia Court of Appeal in 1974 made the order because the defendant offered no evidence of the truth of its defamatory allegations and said it would broadcast them despite the lack of hard proof.[132]

In Quebec, the Court of Appeal sustained an interlocutory injunction against a defamatory advertisement that asked potential clients to boycott hotels owned by the plaintiffs.[133]

After trial, a successful plaintiff will be entitled to a permanent injunction against repetition of the libel. Violation of both the letter and spirit of an injunction can be punishable as either contempt of court or as the Criminal Code offence of disobeying an order made by a court.[134]

Scope of pre-trial discovery

Wide-ranging discovery of a reporter's work product and other unpub- **2.37** lished material may become increasingly common. It will often be relevant to malice, which is now an issue of critical importance as a result of the Supreme Court of Canada's decision in *Hill* v *Scientology*.

Canadian courts have not recognised a special media privilege for withholding relevant information. In 1995, the British Columbia Court of Appeal sustained a lower court order requiring a defendant broadcaster to permit the plaintiff to see unbroadcast videotapes of interviews, journalists' notes, and draft scripts of a national televised news programme about the financial status of the plaintiff bank. The Court rejected arguments by the television broadcaster that investigative reporting would be "chilled" if reporters realised their work product and notes would be the subject of scrutiny in the event of a libel action. The plaintiff bank was entitled to see non-broadcast material because it might have a bearing on the broadcaster's defence of truth.[135] Leave to appeal to the Supreme Court of Canada has been denied.

No legislation requires the production of tapes of broadcasts to persons who believe they have been defamed before they file suit. Any such legislation would probably have to be enacted by the federal Parliament, which has legislative jurisdiction over radio and television broadcasts.

---

132. *Church of Scientology of BC* v *Radio NW Ltd.*, [1974] 4 WWR 173 [BCCA].

133. *Malenfant* v *Larose*, [1988] AQ. no. 1878 [Que.CA]; *cf. Communications Voir Inc.* c. *Pelcom Marketing Inc.* (1994), 62 QAC 313.

134. Criminal Code, RSC 1985, c. C–46, s 127(1), s 718.

135. *Bank of British Columbia* v *CBC* (1995), 10 BCLR (3d) 201 [BCCA], leave denied (1996), 17 BCLR (3d) xxxi.

In 1994, the Ontario High Court ordered a defendant satirical magazine to disclose the names and addresses of the publisher, editor and writers involved in the magazine. The names were not published in the magazine, possibly to frustrate libel plaintiffs.[136]

Ontario recognises the so-called "newspaper rule", which allows the news media to maintain the confidentiality of news sources until trial. Canadian courts have recognised the existence of a discretion in the court not to compel journalists to testify so as to identify their sources.[137] No Canadian court, however, has yet recognised a constitutional right to refuse disclosure of confidential sources.

The Supreme Court of Canada has not yet definitively ruled whether the constitutional guarantee of freedom of expression and freedom of the press in section 2(b) of the Canadian Charter of Rights and Freedoms protects journalists generally from being compelled to reveal their sources. In the only case on confidential sources that has come before the Supreme Court since the Charter came into force, the Court held that the evidence did not prove the existence of a confidential relationship, and the Court declined to answer the constitutional question in the abstract.[138]

Failure to disclose a confidential source if ordered to do so by the Court could lead to a finding of contempt of court punishable by imprisonment and/or a fine, or to a charge under the federal Criminal Code of wilful disobedience of a court order.

Constitutional aspects of Defamation Law

2.38 Since enactment of the Canadian Charter of Rights and Freedoms in 1982, efforts have been made by libel defendants including the news media to persuade judges to modernise the Common Law to incorporate defences analogous to those available under the First Amendment to the United States Constitution as a result of the 1964 decision of the United States. Supreme Court in *New York Times* v *Sullivan*.[139] The First Amendment prevents politicians or public servants from suing for libellous statements made about their conduct or fitness for office unless they can prove that the defendant published the libel with malice, *i.e.*, "with knowledge that it was false or with reckless disregard of whether it was false or not".

---

136. *Hogan* v *Great Central Publishing Ltd.* (1994), 16 OR (3d) 808.

137. *McConachy* v *Times Publishers Ltd.* (1964), 50 WWR 389 [BCCA]; *Crown Trust* v *Rosenberg* (1983), 38 CPC 109; *Belzberg* v *BCTelevision*, [1980] 3 WWR 85.

138. *Moysa* v *Alberta Labour Relations Board* (1989), 34 CPC (2d) 97.

139. *New York Times* v *Sullivan*, 376 United States 254 (1964).

The Supreme Court of Canada's ruling in 1995 in *Hill* v *Church of Scientology of Toronto* dampens media hopes for significant change in the Common Law of defamation in the near future. The Supreme Court held that it is no defence to allege that the Common Law of defamation violates free speech rights guaranteed by the Charter unless the lawsuit is the result of government action. Unless government is the plaintiff, the Charter normally will not have direct application. If the Common Law is inconsistent with Charter values, however, the court can exercise its traditional jurisdiction to make incremental, cautious changes to the law. The onus is on a libel defendant, however, to prove that such changes are necessary in a free and democratic society.[140]

In *Hill* v *Church of Scientology of Toronto*, the Supreme Court of Canada left open the possibility that different principles might apply to assessing damages against media defendants. Even in *New York Times* v *Sullivan*, however, counsel for the defendant newspaper did not argue that journalists enjoyed preferred free speech rights over ordinary citizens. Freedom of expression in section 2(b) of the Charter applies to "everyone".

In *Hill* v *Church of Scientology of Toronto*, the Supreme Court of Canada unequivocally rejected defence arguments that the Common Law presumptions of falsity, malice and damages — which arise once a statement is found to be defamatory — must be reversed to reflect Charter free speech values.

In Ontario, it has been held that a Court Order requiring a libel defendant to publish a full apology and retraction is not an unjustifiable infringement of free speech rights guaranteed by the Charter.[141]

Invasion of privacy

In 1968, British Columbia became the first Common Law province to enact privacy legislation, thereby creating a new cause of action for invasion of privacy.[142] Manitoba followed in 1970,[143] Saskatchewan in 1974,[144] and Newfoundland in 1990.[145] The Civil Code of Quebec, 1994 also recognises a specific right of privacy and gives a cause of action for   **2.39**

---

140. *Hill* v *Church of Scientology of Toronto*, [1995] 2 SCR 1130, (1995) 184 NR 1, at paras 85, 92–98.

141. *Moore* v *Canadian Newspapers Co.* (1989), 60 DLR (4) 113.

142. Privacy Act, RSBC 1979, c. 336.

143. Privacy Act, CCSM 1970, c. P–125.

144. Privacy Act, RSS 1978, c. P–241.

145. Privacy Act, RSN 1990, c. P–22.

invasion of that right.[146] In the other seven provinces and the two territories, a measure of privacy protection is indirectly accomplished by the law governing trespass to real property, nuisance, breach of confidence and appropriation of personality.

Until recently, there have been only a few reported judgments in the Common Law provinces involving claims against the media for invasion of privacy either under the privacy statutes or at Common Law.

The cause of action for violation of privacy created by the statutes of British Columbia, Manitoba, Saskatchewan and Newfoundland do not require proof of damage.[147] In British Columbia, Saskatchewan and Newfoundland, the plaintiff must establish that the violation was intentional and without a claim of right.[148] In Manitoba, a negligent invasion of privacy is actionable but it must be substantial, unreasonable and without a claim of right.[149]

The privacy statutes contain certain safeguards for freedom of expression. Saskatchewan's statute provides that an act, conduct or publication is not a violation of privacy where it was that of a person engaged in news gathering for any newspaper or other paper containing public news, or for a broadcaster licenced by the Canadian Radio Television Commission, and was reasonable in the circumstances and necessary for, or incidental to, ordinary news gathering activities.[150] In Saskatchewan, a publication is also not a violation of privacy where there were reasonable grounds to believe the matter was of public interest or was fair comment on a matter of public interest, or it was privileged in accordance with defamation law.[151]

The British Columbia, Newfoundland and Manitoba statutes do not specifically exempt persons engaged in newsgathering. British Columbia and Newfoundland's legislation provide that publication is not a violation of privacy if the matter published was of public interest or was fair comment on a matter of public interest, or the publication was privileged in accordance with defamation law;[152] the defendant's belief is irrelevant. Manitoba's Privacy Act[153] protects publication of any matter if there were

---

146. Arts 35–41, 1457. Art 35 states: "Every person has the right to the respect of his reputation and privacy. No one may invade the privacy of a person without the consent of the person or his heir unless authorised by law".

147. RSBC 1979, c. 336, s 1(1), CCSM 1970, c. P–125, s 2; RSS 1978, c. P–241, s 2; RSN 1990, c. P–22, s 34.

148. RSBC 1979, c. 336, s 1(1), RSS 1978, c. P–241, s 2; RSN 1990, c. P–22, s 3(1).

149. CCSM 1970, c. P–125, s 2(1).

150. RSS 1978, c. P–24, s 4(1)(e).

151. RSS 1978, c. P–24, s 4(2).

152. RSBC 1979, c. 336, s 2(2).

153. CCSM 1970, c. P–125, s 5(f).

86

reasonable grounds to believe that publication was in (*not of*) the public interest, or it was privileged under defamation law, or fair comment on a matter of public interest.

In 1985, the British Columbia Supreme Court dismissed an action for breach of privacy where the defendant television station had videotaped events occurring in a furniture store's parking lot, which was visible to the general public passing by. The events were not private in the sense of being sheltered from public observation and related to a labour strike that was a matter of public interest.[154]

In 1993, the British Columbia Supreme Court dismissed arguments for an interlocutory injunction under the Privacy Act to restrain the broadcast of videotapes, holding that the plaintiff's interest in suppressing private facts did not outweigh the public's interest in ensuring the integrity of the news gathering process.[155] The Court stated it was unaware of any authority for the proposition that it is in the public interest to allow the Court to control the process by which news is gathered, analysed and edited. To the contrary, the law provides that the news gathering process is one that deserves the Court's protection.

In 1995, the British Columbia Supreme Court dismissed claims by a plaintiff who alleged her privacy had been violated by a newspaper that published her identity contrary to a publication ban made by a judge under the federal Criminal Code during criminal proceedings against the accused attacker. The jury had ruled that constituted a breach of privacy and awarded the plaintiff general damages of C $3,000 and punitive damages of C $15,000. The trial judge set aside the jury verdict because section 3(10) of British Columbia's Libel and Slander Act provides that a:

> "... fair and accurate report in a public newspaper of proceedings publicly heard before a court exercising judicial authority, if published contemporaneously with the proceedings, is privileged".

The publication of the plaintiff's name was part of a fair and accurate report **2.40** of court proceedings "publicly heard".[156]

In 1989, the Manitoba Court of Queen's Bench struck out an Affidavit by a third person listening to a telephone conversation between the plaintiff and the defendant on the ground the evidence was obtained by an invasion of privacy contrary to Manitoba's Privacy Act.[157]

---

154. *Silber* v *BC Broadcasting System* (1985), 25 DLR (4) 345 [BCSC].

155. *Doe* v *CBC* (1993), 86 BCLR (2d) 202 aff'd 216 [BCCA].

156. *F* v *Chappel and News Publishing Ltd.* (28 June 1995), unreported, Rossland no. 2362 [BCSC].

157. *Ferguson* v *McBee Technographics Inc.*, [1989] 2 WWR 499 [Man.QB].

None of the provincial statutes expressly define privacy. Saskatchewan, Newfoundland and British Columbia stipulate that the nature and degree of privacy to which a person is entitled are that which is reasonable in the circumstances, due regard being given to the lawful interests of others.[158] Commercial premises likely have only a low expectation of privacy.[159]

Saskatchewan and Newfoundland's privacy legislation provide that privacy is *prima facie* violated by auditory or visual surveillance, whether or not accomplished by trespass; listening to or recording telephone conversations; and use of letters, diaries or other personal documents.[160] Manitoba enumerates the same factors as examples of possible violations.[161] British Columbia enumerates only eavesdropping and surveillance as specific situations where privacy may be violated.[162]

Saskatchewan, Newfoundland and Manitoba confer broad remedial powers on the court including the power to award damages, grant an injunction, order an accounting of profits obtained by reason of the breach of privacy, and the power to order the defendant to deliver up all articles or documents that the defendant obtained as a result of the invasion of privacy.[163] British Columbia's statute is silent about remedies, but it has been held that punitive damages may be awarded for breach of the Privacy Act.[164] None of the statutes provide a mechanism for determining appropriate levels of damage awards and there are few reported damage awards to provide guidance to potential litigants. The statutes have engendered little litigation and damage awards have been relatively modest.

The Civil Code of Quebec (1994) provides that no one may invade the privacy of a person without the consent of the person or his heirs unless authorised by law. By way of illustration, it enumerates acts that may be considered invasions of privacy, including entering or taking anything in a dwelling; intentionally intercepting or using a person's private communications; appropriating or using a person's image or voice while that person is in private premises; keeping a person's private life under observation by any means; using a person's name, image, likeness or voice for a purpose other than the legitimate information of the public; and using a person's correspondence, manuscripts or other personal documents.[165]

---

158. RSBC 1979, c. 336, s 1(2); RSS 1978, P–22, s 6(1).

159. *Thomson Newspapers* v *Canada* (1990), 67 DLR (4) 163 [SCC].

160. RSS 1978, c. P–24, s 3.

161. CCSM 1970, c. P–125, s 3.

162. RSBC 1979, c. 336, s 1(4).

163. RSS 1978, c. P–24, s 7; CCSM 1970, c. P–125, s 4(1).

164. *ICBC* v *Somosh* (1983), 51 BCLR 344 [BCSC].

165. *Code civil du Québec* (1994), arts 35–41.

In provinces that do not have privacy statutes, recent jurisprudence appears to favour acknowledgement of a Common Law right to privacy.[166]

Before enactment of the 1994 version of the Civil Code of Quebec, that province's courts relied on the statutory protection against invasion of privacy implied in Quebec's Charter of Human Rights and Freedoms.[167] In a decision made before the Charter, a defendant broadcaster was found liable for a breach of privacy contrary to article 1053 of the former Civil Code, which provided that:

> ". . . every person capable of discerning right from wrong is responsible for the damage caused by his fault to another, whether by positive act, imprudence, neglect or want of skill".

A tabloid news announcer had suggested that viewers write and phone **2.41** the plaintiff, and ran his address and telephone number on screen.[168] In another case, however, a Quebec court refused to enjoin the commercial screening of a documentary film on the 1969 Woodstock festival, showing the plaintiff and a young woman cavorting naked.[169] In 1996, the Quebec Court of Appeal upheld a C $2,000 damages award against an artistic magazine and a photographer for publishing a photograph of a woman sitting alone on a street bench. The woman plaintiff was the focus of the photograph. The court suggested that had she been part of a larger group or of a newsworthy event, the public's right to information might have overridden her privacy rights. Generally, judgments of the Quebec courts suggest that newsworthy stories and articles about public issues and public figures are instances in which the public interest may override privacy rights.[170]

In Quebec, individual privacy has also been protected indirectly by the law of defamation. The defence of truth is not established by a defendant to a defamation lawsuit if there was no "public interest" in the subject matter.[171]

Manitoba has rejected the concept of a "false light" invasion of privacy[172] whereas one British Columbia court has held, in *obiter dicta* that it is a legitimate basis for complaint under British Columbia's Privacy Act. In that case, the plaintiff complained he was depicted in a false light

---

166. *Roth* v *Roth* (1991), 9 CCLT (2d) 141 [Ont.].

167. LRQ 1977, c. C–12, art 5; *Valiquette* v *Gazette*, (1991), 8 CCLT (2d) 302; *Aubry* v *Duclos and Les Edition Vice-Versa Inc.* (15 August 1996) unreported no. 500–09–00568–915 [QCA].

168. *Robbins* v *CBC* (1958), 12 DLR (2d) 35.

169. *Field* v *United Amusement Corp.*, [1971] CS 283.

170. *Deschamps* v *Renault Canada* (1977), C de D 937 [Que.SC].

171. Vallières, *La Presse Et La Diffamation* (Montreal, Que: Wilson & LaFleur, 1985), at pp 90–103.

172. *Parasiuk* v *Canadian Newspapers Co.*, [1988] 2 WWR 737.

attacking the television camera because the background to the altercation was not shown, but his action was dismissed on other grounds.[173]

Appropriation of personality

2.42　The Privacy Act of British Columbia creates a separate tort for misappropriation of a person's name or portrait for the purpose of advertising or promoting the sale or other trading in property or services.[174] The privacy statutes of Manitoba, Saskatchewan and Newfoundland treat commercial appropriation of personality as an aspect of the breach of privacy tort.[175]

In British Columbia, to render a newspaper, other publication or broadcaster liable for misappropriation of personality, the plaintiff must prove that his name or portrait was used specifically in connection with material relating to the readership, audience, circulation or other qualities of the newspaper, other publication or broadcaster. This safeguard is not found in the Manitoba, Newfoundland or Saskatchewan statutes.

In Quebec, the courts enjoined misappropriation of personality long before the Civil Code of Quebec, 1994, which clearly stipulates that use of a person's name, image, likeness and voice for a purpose other than the legitimate information of the public, is an example of an invasion of privacy.

In the Common Law provinces, even before enactment of the privacy statutes, the courts recognised a cause of action for misappropriation of personality. This cause of action remains important in Ontario and the other provinces that have no privacy statutes.[176]

In British Columbia, a civil lawsuit recently filed against the print and broadcast media under the Privacy Act raised novel and important privacy issues. The plaintiff was a witness to an unsolved murder. She was interviewed and photographed by television and by newspapers that ran stories identifying her by name, photograph or both. The plaintiff sued, *inter alia*, for damages for breach of privacy and negligence. The defendants asked the court to rule that the guarantee of freedom of expression in section 2(b) of the Canadian Charter of Rights and Freedoms constitutes a "claim of right" within the meaning of British Columbia's Privacy Act so as to justify an invasion of privacy. They also asked the court to rule

---

173. *Silber* v *BC Broadcasting System* (1985), 25 DLR (4) 345 [BCSC].

174. RSBC 1979, c. 336, s 3(1).

175. CCSM 1970, c. P–125, s 3(c); RSS 1978, c. P–24, s 3(c); RSN 1990, c. P–22, s 4(c).

176. *Krouse* v *Chrysler Canada* (1973), 1 OR (2d) 225 [Ont.CA]; *Racine* v *CJRC radio capital Ltée* (1977), 17 OR (2d) 370 [Ont.Co.Ct.].

that the identity of a witness, who consented to be interviewed on camera and photographed, is not a private fact, the revelation of which will support a cause of action for not breach of the Privacy Act. The case settled before trial leaving these questions unresolved.[177]

Trespass

There are few instances of trespass lawsuits against the news media in Canada.[178] Nevertheless, journalists must bear in mind the principles that emerge from Canadian trespass cases and from other British Commonwealth case law. **2.43**

Journalists have no general right of access to private property, even if a newsworthy event is happening on that property. Even public meetings occurring on private property are not accessible as of right by the news media. If asked to leave by the property owner, the reporter must do so.[179] Airports, hospitals, schools, shopping malls and government buildings are normally accessible to reporters but they may be a private property for the purpose of trespass law.[180] Like anyone else, reporters may be singled out and excluded from property even if other members of the general public are allowed on to the property.[181] The landowner's right to refuse access is absolute and need not be reasonably exercised.[182]

At Common Law, any unauthorised entry onto private property is a trespass entitling the person in possession to sue for an injunction and damages without proof of real loss or damage.[183] Nominal damages might be awarded in cases of a "technical" trespass involving no real injury.[184] If the trespass is done in a particularly high-handed manner, however, the court may award punitive damages.[185] A person who has an invitation or permission to enter land for a specific purpose commits trespass if he enters for another purpose.[186]

---

177. *Pierre* v *Pacific Press Ltd.* (1993), 83 BCLR (2d) 1 [BCCA]; [1994] 1 WWR 23, [BCCA], leave refused [1994] 2 WWR lxv [SCC].

178. *E.g., Silber* v *BC Broadcasting System* (1985), 25 DLR (4) 345 [BCSC].

179. *R* v *Peters* (1972), 16 DLR (3d) 143 [Ont.CA]; aff'd 17 DLR (3d) 128n [SCC].

180. *R* v *Page* (1965), 44 CR 350, [1965] 3 CCC 293 [Ont.].

181. *Russo* v *Ontario Jockey Club* (1987), 46 DLR (4) 359 [Ont.].

182. *Webb* v *Attewell* (1993), 18 CCLT (2d) 299 [BCCA].

183. *Boyle* v *Rogers*, [1922] 1 WWR 206 [Man.CA].

184. *Rusche* v *ICBC* (1992), 4 CPC (3d) 12 [BCSC]; *Little* v *Peers*, [1988] 3 WWR 107 [BCCA].

185. *Epstein* v *Cressey Dev. Corp.* (1990), 148 BCLR (2d) 311 [BCSC]; aff'd (1992), 65 BCLR (2d) 52 [BCCA]; *Webb* v *Attewell* (1993), 18 CCLT (2d) 299 [BCCA].

186. *R* v *Burko* (1968), 3 DLR (3d) 330 [Man.Ct.].

A licence to enter land will be implied in certain circumstances. If a walkway or driveway leading to a residence is not barred by a locked gate, and there is no sign or other indication that entry is forbidden, any member of the public may use the walkway or driveway to the entrance of the residence for the purpose of lawful communication with anybody in the residence.[187] If the occupant opens the door, the visitor is entitled to observe what is in plain view within the residence. If the occupant refuses permission to remain on the property, the visitor has a reasonable time to leave.[188]

Air space above a height necessary for the ordinary use and enjoyment of land and its structures is in the public domain.[189] Accordingly, an over-flight in the public domain is not a trespass.

A mistaken belief that one is not on private property is no defence,[190] but presence on the property must be voluntary.[191] For example, if a news reporter is pushed by a crowd onto private property, the reporter would not be liable for trespass.

The implied licence to approach the front door of a residence or to enter a building ordinarily accessible to the public does not necessarily extend to a journalist equipped with a video camera. Where practical, news media planning to enter private property for an extended period will obtain written consent. Museums, art galleries, theatres, and sports events may prohibit still photographs or videotaping. A journalist who ignores these prohibitions is a trespasser. Nevertheless, the occupant of the property is not entitled to seize a journalist's camera, film or videotape unless he has a warrant issued under the Criminal Code.[192] There appears to be no reported case where a Court in a Common Law province has granted an injunction against broadcasting a videotape created by a trespassing journalist.[193] Unless it involves a violation of privacy legislation, the news media do nothing unlawful by publishing still photographs, videotapes or film taken while trespassing.

Taking a photograph with a telephoto lens or in some manner without actually entering private property is not a trespass.

---

187. *R v Evans* (25 January 1996), unreported, no. 24359 [SCC]; *R v Johnson* (1994), 4 MVR (3d) 283 [BCCA].

188. *Nagel v Hunter* (1995), 6 WWR 246 [Alta.CA]; *R v Reed* (12 September 1995), Vancouver CA 19996 [BCCA].

189. *Didow v Alberta Power Ltd.* (1988), 5 WWR 606 [CA], leave to appeal to SCC refused, 99 NR 398 (note) SCC.

190. *Costello v Calgary (City)* (No. 2), 23 CCLT (2d) 125, 25 MPLR (2d) 24 [Alta.QB].

191. *Mann v Saulnier* (1959), 19 DLR (2d) 130 [NBCA].

192. *R v Vassallo* (1983), 131 DLR (3d) 145 [PEISC]; aff'd 4 DLR (4th) 685n [PEISC], leave to appeal to SCC refused 20 December 1983.

193. *Church of Scientology v Transmedia Productions Property Ltd.* (1987) ATR 80–100.

Nuisance

In the Common Law provinces, the civil cause of action for nuisance **2.44** provides a remedy for a breach of privacy that causes unreasonable interference with the enjoyment and use of land. Most reported cases arise in the context of matrimonial disputes.[194] Few claims involve the news media.

There appears to be no reported Canadian case where the news media has been successfully sued in nuisance, although claims have been made for "jump" or "ambush" interviews conducted by a reporter accompanied by a camera operator. A nuisance action over jump interviews or persistent surveillance of a plaintiff's residence or place of business is likely to fail unless the media's conduct is so severe that the plaintiff must abandon his or her entire programme of activities. It is not a nuisance for the news media to attempt a telephone interview, even if the phone call is to the plaintiff's residence during early morning hours, as long as the purpose is not harassment.

In a libel context, the British Columbia Supreme Court in 1982 expressed distaste for the defendant television station's "ambush" interviews, which took the plaintiff off guard and placed him in a bad light. The court held that the jump interviews in that case were part of a pattern of malicious manipulation of the facts, which increased the damage award against the broadcaster for libel.[195]

Continual shadowing of a person or their vehicle over an extended period has been held to constitute a nuisance, as has prolonged and intrusive surveillance of a private residence.[196]

Breach of confidence

No Common Law province or territory has enacted legislation that codifies **2.45** a regime of protection for business secrets, although the Uniform Law Conference of Canada adopted a Uniform Trade Secrets Act in 1987.[197]

At Common Law, a court may grant an injunction against the publication of confidential information or trade secrets that were obtained surreptitiously or improperly, or communicated in circumstances of confidence

---

194. *Motherwell* v *Motherwell* (1977), 73 DLR (3d) 62 [Alta.CA]; *Capan* v *Capan* (1980), 14 CCLT 191 [Ont.HC].

195. *Vogel* v *CBC* (1982), 21 CCLT 105; 35 BCLR 7 [BCSC].

196. *Poole* v *Ragen*, [1958] OWN 77 [Ont.] (police).

197. *MacDonald* v *Vapor Canada Ltd.*, [1977] 2 SCR 134.

that they will not be divulged.[198] However, damages are not awarded in the case of non-contractual breaches, unless the plaintiff can prove that it has suffered loss or profit or that the recipient has enjoyed a benefit as a result of the improper disclosure. An action for breach of confidence can be brought only by the person or organisation to whom the confidence is owed.

There are few reported Canadian cases involving claims against journalists for conspiring with sources to breach such a legal duty of confidentiality. There are instances where injunctions have been granted against the Canadian news media in respect of alleged promises of confidentiality made by a journalist to a source. To date, however, the breach of confidence action has rarely been employed against the news media in the Common Law provinces.[199]

Courts have recently enjoined the news media from publishing information that is subject to solicitor-client legal privilege. In 1994, for example, the Nova Scotia Supreme Court rejected a defendant broadcaster's argument that such an injunction would breach its freedom of expression guaranteed by the Charter, ruling that to refuse to protect the privacy of solicitor-client communications would substantially curtail their effectiveness.[200]

It seems that Canadian law recognises a public interest defence for publishing otherwise confidential information. In 1994, the Alberta Court of Appeal sustained a lower court order refusing an injunction against a broadcaster to restrain publication of allegedly confidential financial information relating to a shopping mall. The Court approved the proposition that suppressing private facts does not outweigh the public interest in ensuring the integrity of the news gathering process.[201]

The Civil Code of Quebec (1994) creates liability for the unfair use of secret or confidential information.[202] On the other hand, it also creates a public interest defence, where the purpose of disclosing trade secrets is to facilitate public health and safety. Before the Civil Code of Quebec (1994) came into force in January 1995, Quebec courts awarded damages for the unauthorised disclosure of personal information by professional advisors such as lawyers, priests or doctors. It appears that Quebec Civil Law borrowed principles expressed in the Common Law of other provinces concerning the protection of confidential information and business secrets.[203]

---

198. *Pharand Ski Corp* v *Alberta* (1992), 7 CCLT (2d) 225 [Alta.QB].

199. *Paddington Press Ltd.* v *Champ* (1979), 43 CPR (2d) 175 [Ont.HC]; *BW International Inc.* v *Thomson Canada Ltd.* (1996), 137 DLR (4th) 348 [Ont.].

200. *Amherst (Town)* v *CBC* (1994), 128 NSR (2d) 260, (1994), 22 CRR (2d) 129 [NSCA].

201. *Triple Five Corporation Ltd.* v *United Western Communications Ltd.*, no. 9403–0286–AC; leave to appeal to SCC denied, SCC. no. 21450; see also *Doe* v *CBC* (1993), 86 BCLR (2d) 202 aff'd 216 [BCCA].

202. *Civil civile du Québec* (1994), arts 1487, 1472.

203. Goudreau, "Protecting Ideas and Information in Common Law Canada and Quebec", (1993–94) 8 IPJ 189.

The Uniform Trade Secrets Act,[204] if enacted, would create a statutory cause of action against anyone who acquires a trade secret by unlawful means. It defines "trade secret" broadly to include any business information having economic value that has been the subject of reasonable efforts to prevent it from becoming generally known.[205] The Act would empower a court to grant interlocutory and permanent injunctive relief.[206] It exonerates a defendant who establishes that the public interest in disclosure of the trade secret outweighs the upholding of the trade secret.[207]

Injurious falsehood

At Common Law, injurious falsehood is the malicious publication of **2.46** falsehoods concerning the plaintiff that induces others to act in a manner that causes the plaintiff actual damage. Unlike defamation, the plaintiff need not prove injury to reputation.[208]

This claim includes interference with any potential advantage, even of a non-commercial nature. Depending on the content of the publication, the cause of action may be called slander of title,[209] slander of goods, trade libel, commercial disparagement, or malicious falsehood.[210]

The essence of injurious falsehood is that the disparagement of the plaintiff's property, products, business or services affects their marketability. At Common Law, the onus is on the plaintiff to prove that actual economic loss has occurred and will occur; falsity; and that the defendant acted maliciously with intent to cause injury without lawful excuse. Ordinarily, the plaintiff must be identified by name but identification by implication may be sufficient where the plaintiff enjoys almost exclusive dominance of the market.[211]

In Ontario, the Libel and Slander Act[212] modifies the Common Law by providing that in an action for slander of title, slander of goods or other malicious falsehood, it is not necessary to allege or prove special damage, if the falsehood is calculated to cause pecuniary damage to the plaintiff and is published in writing or other permanent form; or if the falsehood

---

204. ULCC, Consolidation of Uniform Acts, c. 47.

205. ULCC, Consolidation of Uniform Acts, ss 1(1), 6(1).

206. ULCC, Consolidation of Uniform Acts, s 8.

207. ULCC, Consolidation of Uniform Acts, s 10(1)(b).

208. *Manitoba Free Press* v *Nagy* (1907), 39 SCR 340.

209. *Geo Cluthe Manufacturing Co.* v *ZTW Properties Inc.* (1995), 23 OR (3d) 370 [Ont.Div.Ct.].

210. *Frank Flaman Wholesale Ltd.* v *Firman* (1982), 20 CCLT 246 [Sask.QB].

211. *Church & Dwight Ltd.* v *Sifto Canada Inc.* (1994), 22 CCLT (2d) 304 [Ont.Gen.Div.].

212. Libel and Slander Act, RSO 1990, c. L–12, s 19.

is calculated to cause pecuniary damage to the plaintiff in respect of any office, profession, calling, trade or business. Further, the statute provides that the plaintiff may recover damages without proving actual loss.

Malicious falsehood claims frequently arise from advertisements in newspapers or broadcasts. In most cases, however, the news media are not named as defendants unless the publication or broadcast occurred despite a warning from the plaintiff. The plaintiff will rarely be able to prove malice on the part of the news media, which is an essential element of the claim.

The courts permit businesses to make general, unfavourable comparisons of competitive merchandise with their own goods.[213] This right does not extend, however, to specific, false comparison between the plaintiff's and the defendant's goods or to false, disparaging statements regarding particular aspects of the plaintiffs' goods.[214]

A newspaper has been held liable for falsely and maliciously publishing that the plaintiff had discontinued its business, thereby causing special damage to the plaintiff.[215] On the other hand, where a defendant newspaper mistakenly reported that the plaintiff's husband and three children were killed in a car accident, the action was dismissed because the plaintiff proved negligence but not malice.[216]

Negligent publication causing emotional or financial injury

2.47　In the Common Law provinces and territories, the news media do not have a general duty of care to investigate the accuracy of their news stories, nor do they have a duty to warn readers or listeners that their news stories may be inaccurate. Further, there is no Common Law or express statutory duty of care not to expose a person to humiliation or emotional distress by publication of true statements.[217] Recent jurisprudence, however, is beginning to erode these principles in some provinces.

In 1993, the British Columbia Supreme Court awarded damages to a plaintiff who was inadvertently identified by the defendant newspaper

---

213. *Future Shop Ltd.* v *A & B Sound Ltd.* (1994), 93 BCLR (2d) 40 [BCSC].

214. *United Communications Inc.* v *Bell Canada* (1995), 29 CPC (3d) 159 [Ont.Gen.Div.]; *Church & Dwight Ltd.* v *Sifto Canada Inc.*, (1994), 22 CCLT (2d) 304 [Ont.Gen.Div.].

215. *Sheppard Publishing Co.* v *Press Publishing Co.* (1905), 10 OLR 243 [Ont.CA].

216. *Guay* v *Sun Publishing Co. Ltd.*, [1953] 2 SCR 216.

217. *Roed* v *BC Association of Professional Engineers* (1988), 29 BCLR 59 [BCCA].

contrary to a court order under the national Criminal Code banning publication of her identity.[218] In 1995, the Ontario High Court made a damage award against a newspaper for negligently breaching a similar publication ban.[219] In 1995, a British Columbia jury made a modest award of damages against a newspaper for negligently breaching a similar publication ban.[220] These three recent trial level decisions are cases of first impression that raise difficult issues concerning the relationship between statutory publication bans and private law duties of care. At some future date, appellate courts will have to decide whether Criminal Code publication bans do create or evidence a private law duty of care on the part of the news media to make reasonable inquiries to determine whether a publication ban has been pronounced in a criminal case; and if so, to refrain from publishing banned information.

A recent case in British Columbia courts raised the question whether a person who witnesses a crime in a public place, and consents to be interviewed, has a right of action in negligence against a newspaper for publishing her identity. The news media defendants alleged that the Canadian Charter's guarantee of freedom of expression entitled the media to publish the identity of a witness to a public crime, who voluntarily comes forward, without being answerable in negligence for any foreseeable personal injury caused to the witness by the fugitive criminal, or as a result of psychological stress caused by fear of the criminal. This case settled before these issues were decided by the court.[221]

Copyright

The national Copyright Act[222] enacted by Parliament is the sole source of copyright in Canada.[223] It incorporates as domestic law the 1928 Rome revision of the Berne Convention, the 1952 Universal Copyright Convention, and the copyright provisions of the North American Free Trade Agreement between Canada, the United States of America and Mexico. The Act was recently amended to comply with the Trade-Related Intellectual Property Rights provisions of the World Trade Organisation Agreement. **2.48**

---

218. *C (PR)* v *Canadian Newspaper Co.* (1993), 16 CCLT (2d) 275.

219. *(R)* v *Gary Nyp and Southam Inc.* (3 May 1995), unreported, Kitchener no. 3215/92 [Ont.HC].

220. *F* v *Nelson Daily News* (2 June 1993), unreported, Rossland no. 2362 [BCSC].

221. *Pierre* v *Pacific Press Ltd.* (1993), 83 BCLR (2d) 1 [BCCA]; [1994] 1 WWR 23, [BCCA].

222. Copyright Act, RSC 1985, c. C–42.

223. *Hutton* v *CBC* (1989), 29 CPR (3d) 398 [Alta.QB], aff'd (1992), 41 CPR (3d) 45 [Alta.CA].

The Copyright Act does not create a copyright in facts, knowledge, information or ideas[224] but it does protect the *expression* of such matters[225] if four statutory criteria are met, namely originality, fixation,[226] nationality of creator, and place of first publication. This protection extends to expression in print, broadcast or electronic form.

There is little reported copyright litigation involving the news media. Nevertheless, both on the news/editorial and on the advertising side of the business, newspapers and broadcasters must be acutely aware on a daily basis of the requirements of copyright law.

Copyright protects every original literary, dramatic, musical and artistic work, which includes ". . . every original production in the literary, scientific or artistic domain, whatever may be the mode or form of its expression . . .".[227] In determining whether a work is original, Canadian courts generally apply the "sweat of the brow" test rather than artistic novelty or quality.[228] Most news stories, editorials, letters to the editor, advertising and other published or broadcast news media content are capable of satisfying this requirement.

The Rome Revision of the Berne Convention does not apply to news of the day or to miscellaneous information that is simply in the nature of items of news. The Convention provides that serial stories, tales and all other works, whether literary, scientific or artistic, whatever the object, published in the newspapers or periodicals of one of the subscribing countries, may not be reproduced in the other countries without the consent of the authors.[229] As an exception, the Convention stipulates that articles on current economic, political, or religious topics may be reproduced by the press unless such copying has been specifically prohibited. Where articles are copied, the source must always be clearly indicated.[230]

Canadian print and broadcast media routinely appropriate the substance of news stories reported by other news media. There are few reported judgments, however, involving claims by news media against other news media defendants for infringement of copyright in news articles or broadcasts.

It is unclear whether the Copyright Act provides protection to the results of public opinion polls that are frequently commissioned by the Canadian

---

224. *Gribble* v *Manitoba Free Press Ltd.*, [1931] 3 WWR 570 [Man.CA].

225. *Goldner* v *CBC* (1972), 7 CPR (2d) 158, at 161 [FCTD].

226. Except for a musical work.

227. RSC 1985, c. C–42, s 2, "every original literary, dramatic, musical and artistic work".

228. *University of London Press Limited* v *University Tutorial Press Limited*, [1916] 2 Ch. 601 [United Kingdom]; *Canadian Admiral Corporation* v *Rediffusion Inc.*, [1954] Ex.CR 382; *U&R Tax Services* v *H&R Block Canada Inc.*, (20 June 1994), unreported, Federal Court no. T–891–89.

229. Copyright Act, RSC 1985, c. C–42, at schedule III, art 9(1).

230. Copyright Act, RSC 1985, c. C–42, art 9(2).

news media. The point has not been litigated, however, and the Canadian news media routinely print or broadcast the substance of polling results obtained by their competitors.

Copyright protection does not apply to the names of people, goods, services, businesses, or companies although they might enjoy trade-mark protection.

The requirement of "fixation" means that the expression to be "in some material form, capable of identification and having a more or less permanent endurance".[231] This requirement is automatically satisfied in the case of print media. For the broadcast media, it is satisfied by recording the work on tape, video or film prior to or simultaneously with its broadcast. Recording will extend copyright protection to scripted news programmes, unscripted talk shows, and broadcasts of live events such as sports or news events.[232]

The creator of the work must be a Canadian citizen or resident, a British subject, or a citizen, subject of, or ordinarily resident in a Berne Convention country, or any member of the World Trade Organisation, or any country adhering to the Universal Copyright Convention.[233] Even if the creator does not meet these citizenship or residence requirements, copyright protection will apply to any work first published in Canada or elsewhere in the British Commonwealth, or a WTO or Berne Convention country.

Copyright may subsist in a collective work, which the Copyright Act defines to include:

> ". . . a newspaper, review, magazine, or similar periodical . . . and any work written in distinct parts by different authors, or in which works or parts of different works of different authors are incorporated."[234]

This relatively recent addition to the Copyright Act might create copy-   **2.49**
right in a "broadcast day" but the point has not been adjudicated.

Copyright exists immediately on creation of the work and survives for 50 years after the year of the creator's death. No registration is necessary but a certificate of registration is evidence that copyright subsists in the work and that the person registered is aware of the copyright. In most countries, including Canada, copyright also protects the moral rights of the creator.[235] Infringement of moral rights occurs if the work is, to the

---

231. *Canadian Admiral Corporation* v *Rediffusion Inc.*, [1954] Ex.CR 382.

232. *Tyson Sports Inc.* v *Mansion House (Toronto) Ltd.*, [1990] 1 FR 448 [FCTD]; *FWS Joint Sports Claimants* v *Canada (Copyright Board)* (1991), 36 CPR (3d) 483 [FCA].

233. Copyright Act, RSC 1985, c. C–42, s 5(a).

234. Copyright Act, RSC 1985, c. C–42, s 2, "collective work".

235. Copyright Act, RSC 1985, c. C–42, ss 14.1, 14.2.

prejudice of the honour or reputation of the author, distorted or mutilated or otherwise modified or used for promotion in association with a product, service, cause or institution.[236] The person whose moral rights are infringed has an independent right to sue for injury to his or her reputation, even if copyright is not infringed,[237] and for injunctive relief.

Freelance news reporters enjoy copyright that staff reporters do not. Unless there is an agreement to the contrary, unlike freelancers, staff reporters have no copyright in their contributions to newspapers, magazines, periodicals, or to television or radio broadcasts. The employer owns the copyright. When the work is an article or other contribution to a newspaper, magazine or similar periodical, however, in the absence of agreement to the contrary, the author retains the right to restrain the publication of the work otherwise than as part of a newspaper, magazine or similar periodical.[238]

Infringement of copyright entitles the copyright holder to sue for damages including general, special, aggravated and punitive damages, for an accounting of profits, and for an injunction to restrain further infringement.[239] Generally, an infringer must pay to the plaintiff all profits earned from the infringement.

Where it would be customary to grant a licence, damages may be measured as the amount of royalty normally payable.[240] Punitive damages may be awarded where the defendant's conduct has been high-handed, or tainted by fraud or malice.

The Copyright Act contains special defences reflecting the public interest in freedom of expression. The Act provides that it is not an infringement of copyright in an address of a political nature delivered at a public meeting to publish a report thereof in a newspaper.[241] Further, it is not an infringement of copyright to publish in a newspaper a report of a lecture delivered in public, unless the report is prohibited by conspicuous written or printed notice posted at the main entrance of the building where the lecture is given, and in a position near the lecturer.[242]

Infringement is not committed by any fair dealing with any work for the purposes of criticism, review or newspaper summary, if the source and the author's name, if given in the source, are mentioned.[243] It is a question

---

236. Copyright Act, RSC 1985, c. C–42, s 28.2(1)(a) and (b).

237. Copyright Act, RSC 1985, c. C–42, s 34(1.1); *Pollock* v *CFCN Productions Ltd.* (1983), 73 CPR (2d) 204 [Alta.QB].

238. Copyright Act, RSC 1985, c. C–42, s 13(3).

239. Copyright Act, RSC 1985, c. C–42, s 34(1).

240. *Allen* v *Toronto Star Newspapers Ltd.* (1996), 129 DLR (4) 171 [Ont.Gen.Div.]; *Bemben & Kuzych Architects* v *Greenhaven-Carnagy Developments Ltd.* (1992), 45 CPR (3d) 488 [BCSC].

241. Copyright Act, RSC 1985, c. C–42, s 28.

242. Copyright Act, RSC 1985, c. C–42, s 27(2)(e).

243. Copyright Act, RSC 1985, c. C–42, s 27(2).

of fact in each case whether there has been fair dealing. The provision is interpreted narrowly. Ordinarily, reproducing the entire work will not constitute fair dealing unless the work is short or, in the case of the visual arts, the criticism or review would be meaningless otherwise. In the latter case, the news media would ordinarily be advised to obtain written copyright permission. It is unclear whether a parody of a copyrighted work is defensible under the "fair dealing" defence.

On the other hand, a news reporter who takes written notes of a public speech may be entitled to copyright protection for his or her notes, and has a cause of action against other reporters who rely on a verbatim copy, or undertake substantial borrowing.[244] This principle is less significant today than in the past, given the ubiquitous use of tape recorders and videocameras. Even in the past, however, this principle did not prevent competitors from publishing independent, identical records of the same speech, as long as they arrived at their version independently.

The Copyright Act also stipulates that anyone may take and publish a photograph of any architecture, sculpture or work of artistic craftsmanship if it is permanently situated in a public place or building.[245] This exemption does not apply to objects that travel from one location to another, nor does it protect videotaping.

The news media routinely confront copyright issues relating to photographs which the Copyright Act defines to include "photo-lithograph and any work expressed by any process analogous to photography".[246] Whether made from negatives or by polaroid or modern electronic processes, photographs enjoy copyright protection. A person who commissions a photograph is deemed to be the first owner of copyright if they paid money or other valuable consideration for the photograph, and the photograph was created after and because of the commission.[247] This deemed ownership does not apply if there is an agreement that the photographer will retain copyright. Freelance photographers who take photographs on speculation retain copyright unless they sell the negatives, in which case the courts normally rule that copyright has been assigned to the purchaser unless there is an express agreement to the contrary. Copyright will exist in a photograph of a commonplace article or scenery, even if anyone else could take a similar photograph.[248]

Photographs of crime or accident victims commissioned by the victim's family enjoy copyright protection. Although written consent to publication

---

244. *Walter* v *Lane* (1900) AC 539.

245. Copyright Act, RSC 1985, c. C–42, s 27(2)(c).

246. Copyright Act, RSC 1985, c. C–42, s 2 "photograph".

247. Copyright Act, RSC 1985, c. C–42, s 13(2).

248. *Ravary* v *Teledirect*, (19 April 1995), unreported, Actions 500–05–01, 2826–911.

is required under the Copyright Act, in practice this is not always obtained by the news media. If photographs are stolen from the copyright owner, publication may be enjoined by the court. Canada has not yet seen the development of "chequebook journalism" where newsworthy private photographs are auctioned to news competitors.

Copyright in a video, film, television broadcast or cable programme is infringed by taking a photograph of any image forming part of such a work.

The news media often avoid copyright infringement claims by appropriate contracts with contributors, wire-services, and other sources of material. Copyright protection applies to personal or business letters, whether in final or in draft, and whether intended for internal or external publication. A letter to the editor of a newspaper conveys an implied licence to its publication, and implied agreement to abridgement for reasons of space. Furthermore, submission of an article to a newspaper implies a licence for publication, subject to payment of appropriate compensation.[249]

Clipping services which do not copy articles or broadcasts, but merely buy or otherwise lawfully obtain newspapers, magazines, or periodicals and distribute them, do not infringe copyright.[250]

Publication of purloined private correspondence has recently resulted in copyright infringement claims against the news media, but there are few reported judgments.

Press Releases involve an implied licence to copy or publish after any indicated embargo time.

The Copyright Act prescribes a regime of compulsory licensing. Where publication of a book is begun in a serial form outside the British Commonwealth or other countries to which the Copyright Act applies, the Copyright Board may grant a licence where the owner has refused to grant a licence to publish the book in serial form in Canada.[251] Compulsory licences may also be granted where the copyright holder cannot be located. Recently, where a textbook publisher wanted to re-publish a letter to the editor published in a Canadian newspaper, the Copyright Board issued a non-exclusive licence to the publisher on payment into trust of the normal fee, to be paid to the writer if he or she came forward.

It is possible that a defence of public interest can be raised in defence to an action for infringement of Crown copyright[252] in circumstances where there is a need for full and free disclosure of information on the

---

249. *Springfield* v *Thame* (1903), 89 LT 242; *Hall-Browne* v *Iliffe and Sons Ltd.* (1928–35) MCC 88.

250. *Fetherling* v *Boughner* (1978), 40 CPR (2d) 253 [Ont.HC].

251. Copyright Act, s 22.

252. *R* v *James Lorimer* & *Co.* (1984), 77 CPR (2d) 262 [Fed.CA].

grounds of public health or safety. There are no judicial statements whether a defence of public interest may be raised to infringement of private copyright in Canada, but Canadian courts would probably follow British jurisprudence, which recognises such a defence in limited circumstances.[253]

Trial courts have held that Copyright law is a reasonable limit on freedom of expression that is demonstrably justifiable in a free and democratic society. No case has reached the Supreme Court of Canada that involves a Charter free speech challenge to any restrictions imposed by the Copyright Act or by regulations made under that statute.

Trade-marks

The national Trade-Marks Act, which largely codifies trade-mark law, **2.50** contains no provisions that are specially applicable to the news media. Problems occasionally arise, however, in connection with comparative advertising or advertising by small businesses seeking to exploit the goodwill attached to well-known trade-marks.

At Common Law, a business could obtain perpetual trade-marks protection for a mark by using it in connection with a service or product. The Act gives the owner of a trade-mark the right to the exclusive use of that mark to be identified with goods or services.[254]

A trade-mark is a word, symbol, logo, design or shape of goods, or a combination of these elements, used to distinguish the goods or services of one person or organisation from those of another in the market place. The advertising departments of the Canadian news media attempt to identify unauthorised use of the trade-marks but it is an impossible task. Normally, where unauthorised use occurs, the trade-mark owner draws this fact to the attention of the news media and warns against re-publication or re-broadcast. Damages claims against the news media, absent wilful re-publication in the face of such warnings, are very rare.

One provision in the Trade-Marks Act of potential concern to the print and broadcast media stipulates that no one shall use a trade-mark registered by another person in a manner that is likely to have the effect of depreciating the value of the goodwill attaching thereto.[255] The few reported cases on this provision support the proposition that although the defendant's use of the trade-mark must be in relation to goods or

---

253. *E.g., Beloff v Pressdam Ltd.*, [1973] 1 All ER 241 [Ch.D].

254. Trade-marks Act, s 19.

255. Trade-marks Act, s 22(1).

services before the prohibition can apply, it is not necessary for the infringing defendant to be in direct commercial competition with the trade-mark owner. It is enough if the defendant uses the trade-mark to earn a commercial profit in relation to goods and services.[256]

No reported case has tested this provision prohibiting depreciation of a trade-mark in the context of a newspaper, a magazine, or a television or radio broadcast. In one reported case involving a business defendant which marketed a parody product and was defended on the basis of the Charter's guarantee of freedom of expression, a trial court ruled that the most liberal interpretation of "freedom of expression" guaranteed by section 2(b) of the Charter does not embrace the freedom to depreciate the goodwill of registered trade-marks, nor does it afford a licence to impair the business integrity of the owner of the marks merely to accommodate the creation of a spoof.[257]

It appears, however, that use of a parody of a trade-mark to give added impact to a news story, editorial or commentary is not prohibited by the Act.

Conclusion

2.51 On the whole, the Canadian news media enjoy significant freedom of expression that is only minimally restrained. Since the entrenchment of free speech rights in Canada's constitution in 1982, the media have less reason to fear that future laws, whether made by legislatures or by judges, will erode that freedom. Before the Charter, the Supreme Court of Canada stated on numerous occasions that free speech is crucial to the functioning of Canada's parliamentary democracy.[258] Recent decisions of Canada's highest court suggest that free speech will be given even more respect as a result of the Charter.[259]

---

256. *Rôtisseries St-Hubert Ltée* c. *Le Syndicat des travailleurs (euses) de la Rôtisseries St-Hubert de Drummondville* (CSN) (1986), 17 CPR (3d) 461 [Que.SC].

257. *Source Perrier SA* v *Fira-Less Marketing Co.* (1983), 70 CPR (2d) 61 [FCTD].

258. Reference *Re Alberta Statutes*, [1938] SCR 100; *Switzman* v *Elbling*, [1957] SCR 285.

259. *Edmonton Journal* v *Alberta (Attorney-General)* (1989), 64 DLR (4) 577; *CBC* v *Dagenais* (1995), 120 DLR (4) 12; *RJR-MacDonald Inc.* v *Canada* (1995), 127 DLR (4) 1.

England and Wales

Chapter 3
England and Wales

Alan Williams
Denton Hall
London, England

Introduction

There are a number of areas where liability issues may arise in the context $\quad$ **3.1**
of the exploitation of material in the media, whether such exploitation is
analogue or digital; these issues may arise irrespective of the medium of
publication; they apply equally to print-on-paper publishing as to electronic publishing.

English law is not alone in finding some of the questions about liability
in the context of new technologies to be a difficult one. It is particularly
in the area of the new technologies that law is grappling with credibility.
How does one control information which can travel round the world in
seconds (though it often is infuriatingly slow); how can laws of, for
instance, obscenity not be thought flat-footed when they were designed
to cope with "publication" in one territory, where the publisher and
distributor and bookseller were identifiable and they now have to cope in
an era when all may be overseas and not subject to English jurisdiction?
What is publication?

The law must strike a fine balance between censorship and freedom
of expression. This chapter cannot hope to provide the answers, but it
does at least offer a brief perspective on the state of English law which
at least in copyright terms, is one of the most up to date laws in the
world. The same cannot, unfortunately, be said of the English law of
defamation.

Publishing has never been so easy, but nor has it been potentially
so fraught with unknown and unexpected dangers. In this Chapter we
take a brief look at defamation and malicious falsehood; blasphemy
and obscenity; official secrets; reporting restrictions; confidentiality;
data protection; copyright and performance rights and moral rights;
passing off; trade-mark patents and registered design infringement;
forgery and counterfeiting; consumer protection; legislation and
product liability; encouragement to indulge in illegal conduct and

race relations. That is quite a *tour d'horizon* so it cannot be comprehensive. Fuller text books on the relevant subjects provide more information and guidance.

Defamation

3.2   The English[1] law of defamation is held by many to be far too restrictive of the right of free expression: England has no provision comparable to the First Amendment in United States law and although English legal theory is that you can publish anything you like as long as it is neither unlawful nor illegal, there is so much that is both unlawful and illegal that any kind of investigative journalism is fraught with difficulties.

Any attempt at major reform seems to fall foul of England's lack of an established law of privacy and every call for liberalisation of defamation law seemingly must be balanced by proposals for the introduction of a law of privacy. The Press is not alone in denouncing any privacy proposals. The result is deadlock.

Definition of defamation

3.3   Under English law, a statement is defamatory if, in the circumstances of publication, it lowers the subject in the opinion of right thinking people generally[2] or it exposes that person to hatred, contempt or ridicule;[3] makes one shun or avoid that person;[4] disparages their reputation in relation to their work;[5] or damages the business reputation or goodwill of a company.[6]

To be actionable, the statement must have been "published". This means made available to one or more people[7] (by whatever medium). The plaintiff must also establish that the words are capable of a defamatory

---

1. References to "English" and "England" relate equally to England, Wales and Northern Ireland, but do not relate to Scotland, where here are some substantive differences in the Law. References to the "United Kingdom" relate to England, Wales and Scotland.

2. *Sim* v *Stretch* [1936] 2 All ER 1237 at 1240.

3. *Parmiter* v *Coupland* (1840) 6 M&W 105 at 108; *Sim* v *Stretch, ibid.*

4. *Youssoupoff* v *MGM Pictures Ltd.* (1934) 50 TLR 581 at 587.

5. *Drummond-Jackson* v *BNA* [1970] 1 All ER 1094 at 1104, [1970] 1 WLR 688 at 699.

6. *Jones* v *Jones* [1916] 2 AC 481 at 507.

7. *Pullman* v *Walter Hill* & *Co Ltd.* [1891] 1 QB 524 at 529, CA.

meaning[8] (a question for the judge);[9] and that he has been identified — the test is whether reasonable people knowing the plaintiff would take the words as referring to him.[10] The plaintiff need not prove he has suffered damage[11] nor need he prove that the libellous statement is untrue.

There is a distinction between libel, which is (broadly) the written or recorded (or televised) word, and slander, which is the spoken word. This distinction is important largely because with libel damage is assumed whereas with slander it must be proved. Most on-line communications have a sufficient degree of permanence to be classified as libel rather than slander.

Publication

A statement will clearly have been published when included in the screen display of a CD-ROM or other multimedia product sold to the public. In the case of an on-line service such as the Internet, where a defamatory message has been sent to a bulletin board news group (BBS), open either to all users or just to subscribers of a particular on-line service provider, that message will have been published where the BBS operates like a conventional notice-board and allows any user who has access to it to read all the messages on the board. Similarly, the sender of a defamatory e-mail will be liable where third parties read that message in the same way as more traditional mail, as will the sender of a defamatory statement appearing on the pages of the World Wide Web which is read by a third party. **3.4**

Title to sue

Individuals who are identifiable (even though they are not necessarily named) as well as companies and corporations may bring an action for libel. It is unlikely that non-trading organisations, such as a county council or the Government, may do so, unless an official is identifiable (when he or she could sue). If sufficiently small, groups of individuals may have an action. **3.5**

---

8. *Capital and Counties Bank Ltd.* v *George Henty & Sons* (1882) 7 App Cas 741 at 745.

9. *Rubber Improvement Ltd.* v *Daily Telegraph Ltd.*; *Rubber Improvement Ltd.* v *Associated Newspapers Ltd.* [1964] AC 234.

10. *Knupffer* v *London Express Newspaper Ltd.* [1944] AC 116 at 119.

11. *Hobbs* v *CT Tinling & Co. Ltd.*, *Hobbs* v *Nottingham Journal Ltd.* [1929] 2 KB 1 at 17, CA per Scnetton LJ.

On-line defamation

3.6   Until recently, the use of on-line services had not resulted in wide-scale defamation litigation. While the Internet makes it easy to publish defamatory messages, it is also easy to type in a reply and set the record straight. Further, users can ask the service provider running a service to act if a specific message goes too far. On many BBS, users will see both the original message and the response it generates displayed together. However, as the law in England stands at the moment, this does not make any difference to whether or not a plaintiff may bring an action for defamation, although it could bear on any damages awarded. It would be a significant step for the courts or legislators to allow a different standard to develop for on-line communications from that applicable to other areas of life.

Persons liable for defamation

3.7   When a defamatory message is published, it is not just the author who may be held liable. Everyone who takes part in the publication of a defamatory statement can be jointly and severally liable alongside the author:[12] this includes the editor, the publisher, the printer, the warehouser, the wholesaler, the retailer and even the newspaper boy.

Over the years the parameters of this joint and several liability in traditional media distribution have become established through case law. So, for example, where the material complained of is contained in a CD-ROM a plaintiff could elect whether to sue all the parties responsible for its publication, from the creator to the retailer, or to sue any one or more of them separately. However, the position on-line is not so clear; by the very nature of a service such as the Internet, the author of a libellous message may:

(1)   Be unidentifiable or untraceable. Various technical devices can be used to disguise or hide the true identity of an Internet user and it is far easier to reach a large number of people anonymously with the Internet than with other publishing media;

(2)   Be outside the jurisdiction of the victim's courts. The ease with which messages on the Internet may cross international borders in comparison with traditional distribution channels for books and magazines or CD-ROMs is of great importance. The victim of a

---

12. *R v Paine* [1606] 5 Mod Rep 163 at 167.

libellous statement may find its author far from the jurisdiction of the English courts and practically impossible to sue; and

(3) Have insufficient funds to meet the claim. Plaintiffs will pick out whom they perceive to have a "deep pocket"; the author may simply not be worth suing.

Defamation — service providers

The most likely candidates for the plaintiff to sue are the service providers   **3.8** that allow a user access to the Internet or the particular destinations such as a BBS. For this purpose, "service provider" could include anyone who provides a service or product that allows third parties to post material on-line, including access to advertising space or other interactive services, and could extend to many multimedia producers.

Applying the laws of defamation to a service provider is not straight-forward. If the service provider successfully argues that it operates a "telematic" service, *i.e.*, a communication system for the exchange of information in the same way as a telephone company or the Post Office, but simply using a different medium, it should be no more liable for delivering a libellous message than the Post Office is for delivering a libellous letter or British Telecom for defamatory comments made over the phone or sent by fax. Such an analogy seems valid for e-mail between individuals. If, however, facilitation or participation in sending a message to a BBS is more akin to publishing a book or broadcasting a television or radio programme (in that the messages are necessarily disclosed to a section of the public), should the service provider be liable?

The difficulty is that the level of involvement of different service providers in the control and editing of messages and content on their network varies considerably. A service provider may merely set up a system and not take an active part in controlling messages that appear, just as a company providing transmitters or satellites may play no part in the selection or production of programmes appearing on the television channels it broadcasts. From a practical perspective, it is certainly difficult for the larger service providers to vet the number of messages appearing daily on a BBS. While smaller service providers may be able to censor subject-matter — indeed, they may advertise this service to users who do not wish to receive certain types of material — identifying whether or not a message is defamatory, as a book or CD-ROM publisher usually must do, will usually be far harder than spotting pornographic or other controversial content. On the other hand, some material may obviously fall into the "dangerous" category and thus require vetting by a careful "publisher".

Thus, service providers' liability will depend on whether they fit into the traditional categories of publisher, printer, distributor or vendor.

If the courts decide that service providers should be treated as publishers, they will only have the same defences as the author. These are principally:

(1) Proving the truth of the message;
(2) Establishing that it was fair comment; and
(3) Establishing that absolute or qualified privileged attached to the publication.

3.9 This general liability has been used by libel plaintiffs through the years, but few to better effect than the late Robert Maxwell, to stifle unwelcome comment.

It raises a tricky problem for live broadcasters who are liable for whatever goes out over the air; and it raises problems for, for example, access providers and bulletin board operators who "handle" tens of thousands of messages a day without much real chance of checking every item.

Defamation Act 1996

3.10 The Defamation Act 1996 was introduced with the objective of resolving this conundrum. It is too early to be definitive, but the balance of opinion (and certainly the opinion of this author) is that it has not succeeded in its objective. The Defamation Act 1996 seeks, among other things, to remove from liability a class of publisher now called "secondary publishers" unless they knew or should have known of the defamatory material. It provides that the primary publishers (the commercial publishers, the author and the editor) will bear the same liability as publishers have always done. It defines:

(1) An editor of a defamatory statement as "a person having editorial or equivalent responsibility for the content of the statement or the decision to publish it"; and
(2) An author of a defamatory statement as "the originator of the statement, but does not include a person who did not intend that his statement be published at all".

3.11 The main defences available to authors, editors or publishers will basically be proving the truth of the statement or establishing that it was fair comment or subject to privilege.

However, the Defamation Act 1996 does not consider a person to be an author, editor or publisher of a defamatory statement if they are only involved:

"... in processing, making copies of, distributing or selling any electronic medium in or on which the statement is recorded, or in operating or providing any equipment, system or service by means of which the statement is retrieved, copied, distributed or made available in electronic form . . ."

Or: **3.12**

". . . as the operator of or provider of access to a communications system by means of which the statement is transmitted, or made available, by a person over whom [he] has no effective control".

This provision was intended to provide protection for Internet service **3.13** providers who have no editorial control over the material carried on their service, but from the wording it is unclear how a court would interpret the definition. No English court has yet addressed the issue of how Internet or on-line services should be treated in defamation law. Cases that have so far arisen have settled out of court.

Even if a secondary publisher were held to fall within the above exception, it could still be liable for a defamatory statement if it did not take "reasonable care in relation to its publication". It would not be liable, however, if it did "not know, and had no reason to believe, that what [it] did caused or contributed to the publication of a defamatory statement". In assessing whether a publisher exercised reasonable care the court should look at "the extent of [its] responsibility for the content of the statement or the decision to publish it", "the nature or circumstances of the publication" and "the previous conduct or character of the author, editor or publisher [of the statement in question]".

Clearly, then, if the publisher were transmitting an on-line version of a satirical magazine like *Private Eye*, it would need to take more care than if it were publishing an on-line train timetable. With no additional guidance, it is unclear what actions of the publisher would need demonstrate that it had taken reasonable care without bringing itself within the role of editor or publisher.

The safest analysis of the law as it stands is to acknowledge that if someone comes within the definition of publisher, editor or author, there has been no change in liability. It remains important that where possible, the primary publisher receives warranties and indemnities from content suppliers that material is not defamatory and that any material it creates itself is cleared for defamatory content.

Defences

To succeed in defending a libel action a defendant must establish any of the **3.14** following:

(1) That the words are not capable of a defamatory meaning;
(2) That they were not published (*e.g.*, a "Private & Confidential" letter sent to the person defamed);

(3)   That there was no identification; or

(4)   That he has one of the following defences.

3.15   The defences include:

(1)   Justification;
(2)   Fair comment;
(3)   Privilege;
(4)   Death; and
(5)   Statute of limitation.

3.16   Justification will be a complete defence if the publisher can prove that on the balance of probabilities the statement is true.[13] It is vital to note that the statement will be presumed to be false unless the publisher can prove it.

The fair comment defence applies if the statement is a "fair comment made in good faith and without malice on a matter of public interest".[14]

Privilege covers an accurate and contemporaneous report of proceedings in Parliament or public judicial proceedings notwithstanding that such report may include defamatory material since such report will be "absolutely privileged"; in other words, it cannot be sued upon.[15] A defence of "qualified privilege" is also available in certain situations where the publisher has a "legal, social or moral duty" to publish,[16] for example, non-contemporaneous reports of court proceedings or information set out in shareholders' circulars. Qualified privilege, however, does not protect investigative journalism generally. Where qualified privilege attaches to defamatory material it is protected unless the defendant can be proved to have been acting maliciously. (Malice, for this purpose, means publishing something known to be false, not necessarily with any feelings of spite or ill-will).

It is not possible to libel someone who is dead.[17] Libel actions can only be brought by the individual who has been libelled and not that person's family or estate. Thus, a libel action will die with the plaintiff or the defendant.

---

13. The law will not permit a man to recover damages in respect of all injury to a character which he either does not, or ought not, to possess: *McPherson v Daniels* (1829) 10 B&C 263 at 272.

14. *Campbell v Spottiswoode* (1863) 3 B&S 769; *Slim v Daily Telegraph Ltd.* [1968] 2 QB 157 at 170 and 179 [1968] 1 All ER 497 at 503 and 508.

15. *Munster v Lamb* (1883) 11 QBD 588 at 600, CA.

16. *Davies v Snead* (1870) LR 5 AB 608 at 611.

17. *Hatchard v Mège* (1887) 18 QBD 771, DC; *Broom v Ritchie & Co.* 1905 6F (Crof Sess) 942.

The Limitation Act 1980, as amended by the Defamation Act 1996, section 5, provides that no proceedings may be instituted after the expiry of one year from a fresh publication.

Previous publication is not a defence, but it may impact on the question of damages if the plaintiff might have been expected to have seen the publication, and did nothing about it.

Potentially defamatory material can be published if one of the available defences applies, but this only serves to reduce the likelihood of a libel action or give the publisher a means successfully to defend it. To avoid a libel action completely one must not publish defamatory material.

On a practical basis, defamation clearance for publishers is usually framed in terms of a balance of risk in view of those likely to take action. It will be much harder for lawyers to advise clients where the traditional territorial controls of print publishing no longer exist, allowing on-line content to reach anywhere in the world and defamation actions to be brought in any jurisdiction. Defamation law in England is less favourable to defendants than the law of most other countries. Further, small service providers are unlikely to be willing to take the financial risk of losing a defamation action and would probably decide to settle any such suit out of court. Such decisions will depend on the availability of defamation insurance cover and, while insurance companies are currently quoting cover for service providers, they clearly will not want to be exposed to open-ended liability.

Libel actions in England are very technical, long-winded and expensive. Either party can ask for a jury trial and the rules are such that evidence of a plaintiff's character can only be introduced in respect of the allegation complained of, and not generally.

While truth is a defence, it is truth that is provable in court. A defamatory statement is no less defamatory because it is true. It is proof of the truth that provides a defence. It does not matter how much care an author or publisher has taken to check material, if the truth cannot be proved, there is no defence. Nor is it a question of what the author meant to say — what counts is what the ordinary reader understands the passage to mean.

Legal costs and juries' awards have been very high and the decisions of juries are unpredictable. It is now possible for the judge to give limited advice to the jury on how to approach calculating the award and for the judges on appeal to reduce the award without having to order a retrial.

The Defamation Act 1996 has introduced two reforms intended to speed up libel actions. The first is an offer of amends procedure and the second a summary jurisdiction route allowing a judge without a jury to award up to £10,000 by way of damages. There are difficulties with both.

115

Remedies

3.17 Various remedies are available to a plaintiff, including injunctions and actions for damages.

Damages

3.18 Damage will be presumed and need not be proved, but the basic rule is that damages are compensatory and not punitive. If a defendant pleads a defence of justification that subsequently fails, the jury may award "aggravated" damages, which are intended to be punitive. "Special" damages can be awarded where a defendant has suffered actual pecuniary loss, or if a defendant is proved to have calculated the prospect of material advantage, "exemplary" damages may be awarded.

The Court of Appeal now has the power to re-assess damages.

Injunction

3.19 A permanent injunction will normally be awarded at the end of an action that has been won by a plaintiff. This aims to prevent the defendant from repeating the defamatory statement.

Other issues

Legal aid

3.20 No legal aid is available for libel actions. Since usually all the plaintiff must establish is that the words are defamatory, the onus of proof (usually of a defence) lying with the defendant means that the plaintiff has the advantage in libel actions.

On-line defamation jurisdiction

3.21 The cross-border nature of electronic communications adds a new dimension to the problem of libel. Internet users can type in a message in the United Kingdom that can travel across many nations around the world and be read in a dozen or more countries at once. Each State may claim jurisdiction if one of its citizens has been defamed. The author may be untraceable. The Internet Service Providers (ISPs) or bulletin boards in each country therefore present obvious and ready targets. This is not a very satisfactory position for anyone.

116

Malicious falsehood

A malicious falsehood involves spitefully, dishonestly or recklessly making **3.22**
an untrue (or false) statement about a person, and which is calculated
to cause that person to suffer special pecuniary damage. An author
may, however, rely on the defence of good faith if he honestly believed
in the truth of the statement. The advantage to a plaintiff of an action
in malicious falsehood is that legal aid is available. The disadvantages
are that the onus of proof lies with the plaintiff and that damage must
be proved. The action is now used quite frequently alongside both
defamation and passing off claims.[18]

Blasphemy and obscenity

The English obscenity and blasphemy law applies not only to traditional **3.23**
newspaper publishing but also to on-line products. Screening software
can help monitor obscene or blasphemous material where a high volume
of material must be screened, but it should be noted that a United
States court has held the use of screening software as a sign that a service
provider acted as a publisher and not a mere distributor.[19] Warranties from
third parties will be advisable.

"Indecent" material is material that embarrasses the sexual modesty
of ordinary people and will usually not affect freedom of expression or
art. It is generally confined to maintaining decorum in public places.
Sending indecent material through the post may affect the distribution
of magazines and is a criminal offence (although prosecution is usually
confined to unsolicited mailings).

Penalties for offences in this area involve unlimited fines or imprisonment (maximum term is three years). There are difficulties in securing
prosecutions so prosecuting authorities often seek a seizure order.

Distribution of pornographic or sexually explicit material is control-
led by a range of legislation.[20] There are also the Common Law offences
of conspiracy to corrupt public morals[21] and outraging public decency.[22]

---

18. *Vodafone Group Plc and Anor* v *Orange Personal Communications Services Ltd.*, *The Times*, 31 August 1996.

19. The United States Telecommunication Act 1996 effectively reversed this decision.

20. Obscene Publications Acts 1959 and 1964, Criminal Justice and Public Order Act 1994, Protection of
Children Act 1978 and Criminal Justice Act 1988, Post Office Act 1953, Unsolicited Goods and Services Act 1971,
Telecommunications Act 1984, Indecent Displays Control Act 1981, Local Government (Miscellaneous Provisions)
Act 1982, Customs Consolidation Act 1876, Video Recording Acts 1984, Broadcasting Act 1990.

21. *Shaw* v *DPP* [1962] AC 220, 45.

22. *Knuller Ltd.* v *DPP* [1973] AC 435.

Obscene Publications Acts 1959 and 1964

3.24 It is an offence under section 2 of the 1959 Act to publish an obscene article whether or not for gain. The 1964 Act extends the offence to include having an obscene article for publication for gain, but mere possession of an obscene article alone is not an offence.

Section 1(2) defines an article as anything containing or embodying matter to be read or looked at or both, any sound record, and any film or other record of a picture or pictures. Section 1(3) of the 1959 Act defines publish to cover any distribution, circulation, sale, hiring, giving, lending, showing, playing or projecting. This was extended by section 168(1) of the Criminal Justice and Public Order Act 1994 to include "where the matter is data stored electronically (a person publishes where he) transmits that data". As a result, it is submitted that a content provider uploading obscene material on a server in the United Kingdom for transmission on the Internet will fall within the offence. It is, however, not altogether clear whether a service provider would also be caught. Where a service provider holds obscene material that has been uploaded onto a server under its possession and control it may be considered to be publishing that material and/or having obscene material for publication for gain. Where, however, a service provider acts merely as a conduit through which obscene material passes, being sent to or from third parties, it may be considered not to be publishing that material and that instead it acts only as a "common carrier" in a similar way to a telephone company or the Royal Mail.

Section 1(1) of the 1959 Act defines an article as obscene if its effect is, if taken as a whole, such as to tend to deprave and corrupt persons who are likely, having regard to all relevant circumstances, to read, see or hear the matter contained or embodied in it. The requirement to deprave and corrupt has been interpreted by the courts to be much narrower than sexual explicitness.[23] It goes beyond immoral suggestion or persuasion and must constitute a serious menace.[24]

Reference to persons who are likely to read, see or hear involves a relative test of the effect of the article on the minds of the primary readership or audience.[25] The standard for material available only to adult consumers in a licensed sex shop will differ from that applicable to material available to the general public in a high street newsagent and, in turn, between "top shelf" material and other material available in a newsagent. Similarly, where the Act applies, the obscenity test for material

---

23. *Darbo* v *DPP* [1992] Crim LR 56; [1992] COD 65.

24. *Knuller* v *DPP* [1973] AC 435.

25. *DPP* v *Whyte* [1972] 3 All ER 12.

on the Internet, which is freely accessible for anyone to download, could be wider than for material that can only be accessed by adult consumers who are specifically requesting the material to be made available to them.

There is no requirement for a guilty intention to deprave and corrupt. The obscenity test will be satisfied where the prosecution establishes the fact of the publication and the effect of the article published. However, the degree of knowledge possessed by those publishing the obscene material is relevant to the defence under section 2(5) of the 1959 Act, which provides that a person will not be convicted if he can prove that he had not examined the obscene article and had no reasonable cause to suspect that his publication of it would render him liable to conviction. If a person has not inspected the material, he may remain liable if there were suspicious circumstances or if he benefited from an increased profit margin to cover a risk factor; but a truly "innocent" person will have a defence.

The approach of the courts in analogous defamation cases demonstrates the need for the publisher to act in a responsible manner and clarifies the circumstances in which a publisher or distributor ought to suspect the contents of a publication (*e.g.*, satirical magazines and known soft-porn titles). In the context of the Internet, it can be seen that, while a content provider uploading obscene material onto a server for transmission on the Internet will not have a defence, a service provider that did not inspect the material and had no reason to suspect its contents will arguably have a defence. Potentially obscene material will often be easy to spot but it may not always be clear whether a service provider should have cause to suspect and inspect material on its server.

There is a further defence under section 4 of the 1959 Act where the publisher can establish that his publication of the obscene material is justified as being for the public good, is in the interests of science, literature, art or learning, or of other objects of general concern. Thus, obscene material made available or transmitted on the Internet for the public good will not be illegal.

Under section 43 of the Criminal Courts Act 1973 and section 69 of the Criminal Justice Act 1988, where a person is convicted of an obscenity offence in relation to computers, it is the practice of the police to ask the court to order forfeiture of equipment, which may have a deterrent effect.

Protection of Children Act 1978 and Criminal Justice Act 1988

Under section 1 of the 1978 Act, it is an offence to distribute or show, or to possess with a view to distributing or showing, or to publish or cause to be published any advertisement likely to be understood as conveying   **3.25** that the advertiser distributes or shows (or intends to distribute or show) any indecent photograph of a child under 16.

Under section 160 of the 1988 Act, it is an offence to possess an indecent photograph of a child under 16.

Section 84 of the Criminal Justice and Public Order Act 1994 extends both of the above offences to apply to indecent "pseudo-photographs" of a child, that is an image made by computer graphics or otherwise which appears to be a photograph. There is no need for the image to have been based on a child — it could originally have been an adult but modified to look like a child. There is no definition of photograph in either the 1978 or 1988 Acts. Both provide that photograph will include films and video recordings and it is submitted that a photograph in digital form transmitted on the Internet could be caught as a pseudo-photograph whether or not it is also considered to be a photograph.

Neither the 1978 Act nor the 1988 Act provide a definition of indecent. The courts have defined it as something that offends the ordinary modesty of an average man, offending against recognised standards of decency at the lower end of the scale — thus, an image may be indecent but not obscene.[26] The indecent article must infringe current community standards within the context of its publication — as adjudged by jury deliberation.[27]

Section 1(4) of the 1978 Act provides a defence to anyone charged with distributing, showing, possessing or intending to show or distribute indecent photos if that person:

(1) Has a legitimate reason to do so; or
(2) Has not seen the photos and does not know nor has any cause to suspect them to be indecent.

3.26 Section 160 of the 1988 Act provides the same defences, and also provides a defence if the photograph was sent to the accused without any prior request by him or on his behalf and he did not keep it for an unreasonable time. Thus, a content provider uploading such material on to a server for transmission on the Internet and a user who had knowingly downloaded and viewed that material would not have a defence unless, for example, they were doing so for *bona fide* medical purposes or, in the latter case, the material had been unsolicited and the user did not keep it for an unreasonable time. The position of an Internet access provider is not clear. Where an access provider holds indecent photographs of children on its server, it will clearly be possessing the material, but the extent to which it may rely on the defence of not having seen the photographs and having no cause to suspect them will depend on the circumstances of each case.

---

26. *R v Stanley* [1965] 1 All ER 1035.
27. *A-G v IBA* [1973] 1 QB 629.

Post Office Act 1953

Under section 11 of the 1953 Act, it is an offence to enclose in a postal **3.27**
packet any indecent or obscene print, painting, photograph, lithograph,
engraving, cinematograph film, book and written communication or any
indecent or obscene article whether similar to the above or not. Postal
packet is defined as every packet or article transmissible by post and so is
unlikely to apply to the Internet.
     The offence is committed by the person who posts and not by the Post
Office.

Unsolicited Goods & Services Act 1971

Under section 4 of the 1971 Act, it is an offence to send or cause to send **3.28**
to another person any book, magazine or leaflet or advertising material
for any such publication that he knows or ought reasonably to know is
unsolicited and which describes or illustrates human sexual techniques.
Unlike the 1953 Act, sending or causing to send is not limited to posting.
This offence could be applied to content providers transmitting advertising for this type of material on the Internet, but not necessarily the
material itself, as a court may not consider digitised material on the Internet
as a book, magazine or leaflet.

Telecommunications Act 1984

Under section 43 of the 1984 Act it is an offence to send by means of a **3.29**
public telecommunication system a message or other matter that is
grossly offensive or of an indecent, obscene, or menacing character or send
by those means, for the purpose of causing annoyance, inconvenience or
needless anxiety to another, a message that is known to be false or persistently
make use for that purpose of a public telecommunications system.
     This offence can extend to such material transmitted over the Internet
only in so far as it is sent over a public telecommunications network. Both
content providers and Internet access providers could be caught by this
provision. No defence of the kind available under the 1978 Act is provided
for. It should be noted that if this offence were applied successfully it
would widen the definition of illegal material on the Internet from
obscene to merely indecent.

Indecent Displays Act 1981

Under section 1 of the 1981 Act, it is an offence to display indecent matter **3.30**
in, or so as to be visible from, any public place. Public place is defined as

any place to which members of the public have or are permitted access (whether on payment or otherwise) except a place where the public are permitted access only on payment for that display or a shop or any part of a shop to which the public can only gain access after passing an adequate warning notice[28] if in both cases persons under 18 years of age are not permitted to enter. Matter is defined as anything capable of being displayed except an actual human body or part thereof. It expressly does not apply to television or licensed cable services, exhibitions in art galleries or museums, Crown or local authority exhibitions, performance of a play or films screened in licensed cinemas.

It is perhaps arguable that a site on the Internet to which access is unrestricted falls within the definition of public place, but the outcome of a prosecution is highly uncertain. However, the concept under this Act of warning notices may be a sensible one to apply to indecent material on the Internet — indeed, one that is already used by many content providers on screen displays appearing before access to the indecent material itself.

Local Government (Miscellaneous Provisions) Act 1982

3.31   Section 2 of the 1982 Act enables local authorities to licence sex shops and sex cinemas. Schedule III defines sex shops and cinemas as any premises, vehicle, vessel or stall used for a business which consists to a significant degree of selling, hiring, exhibiting, lending, displaying or demonstrating sex articles or other things intended for use in connection with or for the purpose of stimulating or encouraging sexual activity or acts of force or restraint which are associated with sexual activity or use to a significant degree the exhibition of moving pictures, by whatever means produced, which are concerned primarily with the portrayal of, or primarily deal with or are intended to stimulate or encourage sexual activity or acts of force or restraint that are associated with sexual activity or genital organs or urinary or excretory functions.

The extent to which these provisions could allow local authorities to licence premises on which servers linked to the Internet are connected is not clear. Data transmitted over the Internet may not be considered to be articles, but may in some circumstances be moving pictures.

---

28. *E.g.,* "WARNING: Persons passing beyond this notice will find material on display which they may consider indecent. No admittance to persons under 18 years of age."

Customs Consolidation Act 1876

Under section 42 of the 1876 Act, it is an offence to import indecent or **3.32**
obscene prints, paintings, photographs, books, cards, lithographic or other
engravings, or any other indecent or obscene articles. The word articles
has been interpreted to extend to statues, chessmen, dildos, inflatable
rubber women, and penis-shaped plastic mouth organs but it does not
appear to catch digitalised material transmitted on the Internet which on
resolution into user readable form becomes an obscene article.

The European Community Court of Justice[29] has effectively applied
the provisions of Article 30 of the Treaty of Rome to prevent the above
applying in the case of importation of merely indecent material into the
United Kingdom from other Member States where dealing in such material is not per se illegal in the United Kingdom.

It is the view of the customs authorities that the 1876 Act cannot be
extended to non-tangible material imported into this country and that
the law would need to be amended to catch Internet transmissions of
indecent or obscene material.

Video Recording Act 1984

Under the Video Recording Act 1984, it is an offence to supply video **3.33**
works in this country that have not been classified by the British Board of
Film Classification unless they fall into one of the exempt categories provided for in the Act. Video work is defined as any series of visual images (with
or without sound) produced electronically by the use of information
contained on any disc or magnetic tape and shown as a moving picture.
Reference to the use of a disc or magnetic tape means that visual images
on the Internet are unlikely to fall within this classification system.

Broadcasting Act 1990

The 1990 Act for the first time applied the Obscene Publications Act 1959 **3.34**
to radio and television by enacting that, for the purposes of the 1959 Act,
a person also publishes an article to the extent that any matter recorded
on it is included by him in a programme included in a programme
service. The 1990 Act also sets out the framework for the regulation of
broadcast media generally.

---

29. *Conegate* v *Customs & Excise* [1986] 2 All ER 688.

Note: the Independent Television Commission decided not to take any action against an "adult" website on the grounds that what was being shown did not come within the definition of a television programme service as defined by the 1990 Act. There will undoubtedly be further development in this area.

Conspiracy to corrupt public morals

3.35 This Common Law offence has been excluded in relation to films by the Criminal Law Act 1977 and broadcast media by the 1990 Act. The Obscene Publications Act has also excluded it for publications falling under that Act, but it may still be applied to other indecent publications and has been used in the last 20 years against distributors of child pornography. The Court of Appeal has described the offence as one that may be revived "to guard the moral welfare of the state against attacks which may be more insidious because they are novel and unprepared for."[30] As such, it could be used to prosecute unsuitable material on the Internet.

The Government will wish to examine whether this Common Law offence should be disapplied to the Internet as it has been in relation to broadcast material.

Outraging public decency

3.36 Outraging public decency[31] is another vague Common Law offence similar to conspiracy to corrupt public morals and was used to successfully prosecute an art gallery exhibiting human foetuses in 1989. It could apply to the Internet.

Blasphemy

3.37 Indecent descriptions applied to sacred subjects may amount to the crime of blasphemy.

The publication of contemptuous, reviling, scurrilous or ludicrous matter relating to God, Jesus Christ, the Bible or the formularies of the Church of England is a criminal offence. There has only been one prosecution in the last 75 years. The publisher must intend to publish,

---

30. *Conegate* v *Customs & Excise* [1986] 2 All ER 688.
31. *Shaw* v *DPP* [1961] 2 All ER 446.

but he need not intend that the words amount to blasphemy. The offence is punishable by fine and imprisonment at the discretion of the court.

Adapting to modern technology

R v *Fellows*[32] illustrates how the English courts are willing to bring the law into line with modern technology. In his Court of Appeal judgment, Lord Justice Evans stated, "There is enormous public disquiet at the potential which the Internet offers for the international transmission of pornography".   **3.38**

The case involved two men sentenced to imprisonment for exchanging obscene material over the Internet. The first defendant had compiled an archive of pornographic material stored on a server linked to the Internet. Access to the server was only provided to those given a password, either because they were vouched for by existing password holders or because they provided additional material of a similar kind. One such recipient and provider of additional data was the second defendant. Both men were charged with various offences under the Protection of Children Act 1978 and the Obscene Publications Act 1959 (as amended in 1964).

The Criminal Justice and Public Order Act 1994 amended both Acts — as a Parliamentary select committee stated at the time to ensure that the legislation applied to "the new horror of computer pornography" — so that the definition of "photograph" in the Protection of Children Act included "data stored on a computer disc or by other electronic means which is capable of conversion into a photograph" and so that the Obscene Publications Act's definition of "publish" included transmitting electronically stored data.

The defendants had committed the acts in question prior to these amendments. They argued that since Parliament had deemed it necessary to make such amendments, the law had not extended to those acts. The Court of Appeal had to examine how legislation, created before Parliament could have envisaged the capabilities of modern on-line technology, should be applied to persons using the Internet. It held that legislation could be construed to extend not just to what was known at the time of its creation, but also to future developments by virtue of the particular wording used. The fact that Parliament may have subsequently amended the legislation does not alter the original wording's meaning or influence a court's own interpretation of it. The Court of Appeal then held that "photograph" and "article" in the unamended Acts were wide enough to include data on a hard disc.

---

32. *The Times*, 3 October 1996, CA.

The Criminal Justice and Public Order Act 1994 amendments to the Protection of Children Act 1978 and the Obscene Publications Act 1959 now mean that in many cases the law on illegal pornography will certainly apply to the Internet. Uncertainties remain as to the meaning of "distributing" or "showing" under the Protection of Children Act in the context of the Internet and to what extent the amended Obscene Publications Act restriction on transmitting electronic data requires active steps. *R* v *Fellows* also did not look at the wider issue of the liability of ISPs or other hosts through which persons like the appellant can act. It does provide a useful example of how courts might interpret other legislation drafted before the rise of the Internet.

Contempt of court

3.39 Strict liability contempt is committed if a publication "creates a substantial risk that the course of justice in the proceedings in question will be seriously impeded or prejudiced".[33] Strict liability means that the prosecution does not need to prove that the publisher intended to prejudice the proceedings. The publication must be of the nature which could tip the final verdict or produce a situation in which the jury would have to be discharged.

Proceedings must be "active": the active period is generally from the arrest of the defendant or the issue of a warrant for his arrest until the proceedings are concluded on acquittal, sentence, verdict or any decision putting an end to the proceedings. Civil proceedings become active when the case is set down for trial until the proceedings are concluded by whatever method.

The penalties for contempt are fine or imprisonment.

Danger areas

3.40 Danger areas in this context include: criticising the decision to prosecute which can be particularly dangerous if prosecution witnesses are likely to be influenced; anticipating the course of the trial; reporting on the defendant's character and previous convictions; publishing the defendant's

---

33. Contempt of Court Act 1981 s 2(2).

photograph in criminal cases where the identification of the defendant is in issue can also lead to liability; and undermining or intimidating witnesses.

Informed speculation as to the issues which are likely to be raised is not contempt provided no opinion is expressed as to the way those issues should be resolved, and would not amount to unlawfully anticipating the course of the trial. The Attorney General has now said that "wanted" photographs will not be subject to prosecution. Suggesting that a witness is untruthful or otherwise unreliable or making payments to witnesses prior to giving evidence is dangerous because of the risk of bias as a result of the payment.

Third parties who have knowledge of the court order and deliberately flout the order render themselves liable for contempt.[34]

Defences

The publisher may claim as a defence that he did not know and had no **3.41** reason to suspect that the proceedings were active. The public interest defence is available where a publication is made in good faith as part of a discussion on matters of general public interest, and the risk of prejudice to particular proceedings is merely incidental to the discussion.

Official secrets

It is a criminal offence to publish official secrets covered by the Official **3.42** Secrets Acts. The Acts protect certain limited classes of official information and the topics that they earmark for this protection include security and intelligence, defence, international relations, and information which if disclosed would result in or be likely to result in the commission of offences. There are, therefore, inherent dangers in publishing material relating to these topics, but since the Official Secrets Act 1989 this danger has largely been removed for material relating to public health, housing and environmental matters.

The penalty on conviction is imprisonment.

---

34. *Attorney General* v *Guardian Newspapers* [1988] 2 WLR 805.

Reporting restrictions on juvenile offenders and proceedings generally

3.43 The Children and Young Persons Acts of 1933 and 1969 lay down strict provisions regarding the reporting of proceedings in a juvenile court. Reports must not reveal details of either the person against whom proceedings are taken or the witness in the proceedings, including name, address, school, picture, or any other information that may help identify them. Any breach of these provisions will result in a fine. Where an action is brought in any other court, the court may direct which details may be reported.

Reports of proceedings in Magistrates Courts and of committal proceedings are restricted to certain specified information such as the name of the Court and the names of the Judges, the names, addresses and ages of the offender and witness, and the offence, etc.

Privacy — confidentiality

3.44 At present, there is no action for an invasion of privacy in the United Kingdom. Existing areas of law do to a certain extent protect these concepts, but it is widely argued that these are inadequate.

Primarily actions for breach of confidence approach such protection of privacy. Infringement of copyright, defamation or harassment and physical intrusion actions may also be applied in certain circumstances and with limited effect, toward this end.

Breach of confidence

3.45 An action for breach of confidence requires that:

(1) The information must have the necessary quality of confidence;
(2) It must have been imparted in circumstances importing an obligation of confidence; and
(3) There must be an unauthorised use to the detriment of the party communicating it.[35]

3.46 The confidential information must be particularised — it cannot be general.

---

35. *Coco v AN Clark (Engineers) Ltd.* [1969] RPC 41 at 47–48 per Megany J; *Dunford & Elliot Ltd.* v *Johnson & Firth Brown Ltd.* [1978] FSR 143 at 148, CA; *Jancan & Platt Ltd.* v *I. Barget Ltd.* [1977] FSR 260 at 276–277, CA.

Examples

Members of the intelligence services are under a lifelong obligation to **3.47** maintain the confidentiality of the information imparted to them in the course of their service. For other employees, the obligation must be limited in scope and time to avoid restraint of trade. For the memoirs of cabinet ministers, protection remains until such time as the disclosure of information would no longer undermine the doctrine of joint cabinet responsibility. In the context of revealing sources, the Judge can make an order if he thinks it is necessary in the interests of justice, national security or for the prevention of disorder or crime to disclose these. However, the recent willingness of the courts to order disclosure is now to be taken to the European Court of Human Rights as being contrary to Article 10 of the European Convention on Human Rights relating to freedom of expression.

Defences

It is a defence where information is in the public knowledge or public **3.48** domain;[36] where iniquity is involved (the plaintiff has behaved disgracefully or criminally); public interest is furthered (*e.g.*, information relating to a crime, not necessarily committed by the plaintiff).

Inadequacy

Arguably, breach of confidence relates only to information and would there-**3.49** fore not apply to directly apprehended events such as photographs taken surreptitiously. It relates only to confidential information, which may exclude some private or personal information. It protects relationships importing an obligation of confidence rather than simply the information itself.

Data protection infringements

The Data Protection Act 1984 is intended to give protection against **3.50** the use of personal information that is inaccurate, incomplete or irrelevant, the possibility of access to personal information by unauthorised

---

36. See the "Spycatcher" affair.

persons and the use of personal information for a purpose other than that for which it was collected.

For information to be covered by the Act it must be:

(1)   In a form that can be processed by equipment operating automatically in response to instructions given for that purpose; and

(2)   Personal data.

3.51   Personal data consists of information that relates to a data subject who can be identified from the information or from that and other information in the possession of the data user. To state that the individual is a doctor, lives in a certain village and drives a certain car may be enough to identify him.

The most important procedure for data users in respect of such information is the requirement to register. Failure to register constitutes a criminal offence.

Copyright and related rights

3.52   The issue of copying third party material is a very relevant one. The ethos of the Internet is very much a copyright-free one at the moment. That will change as commercial exploitation on and of the Internet increases. The safe advice must be that content intended to be used must have been cleared for exploitation in the relevant medium. If it is third party material, consent will need to be negotiated, unless an agreement exists granting the necessary rights for the relevant medium.

Copy Clearance

Employee-generated works

3.53   If the author of the copyright work in question is an employee and the work was created "in the course of employment", the employer is the first owner of the copyright in that work, subject to any agreement to the contrary.[37] Thus, content produced in the course of his (or her) employment for a publisher by an employed journalist will be owned by the publisher and may be exploited by the publisher in any media, or by anyone to whom the publisher licenses or assigns that right. Indeed,

---

37. Copyright Designs and Patents Act 1988, s 11(2).

extended employment contracts may go further and ensure that rights are assigned expressly in any work produced by any employee at any time while he is still an employee of the publisher.

Freelancer and consultants

Where the publisher was not the employer of the author of the relevant **3.54** copyright work, the publisher will have to ensure that it holds the correct rights. Freelance material will often have been acquired at short notice with merely an implied licence to publish. It would be open to question as to whether this licence extended from print publishing to cover on-line services, certainly until such use becomes standard custom and practice. If the publisher intends to use archive material, it may need to go back and ensure that it has the appropriate rights. Journalists' unions in both the United States and United Kingdom have threatened action against publishers for using material in on-line services claiming it had been cleared only for print-on-paper rights.

Other content

Print material may include photographs and artwork that must also be **3.55** cleared for on-line use. In addition, on-line services are also likely to involve sounds, music, other images and video. These will have their own clearance problems, particularly music.

Use of material that has not been properly cleared or licensed would be a primary infringement of copyright by the act of copying that material. Section 17 of the Copyright Designs and Patents Act 1988 defines copying as including storing "in any medium by electronic means" and making copies of any kind of copyright work "which are transient or incidental to some other use".

Rental and lending rights

Since 1 January 1997, the restricted acts include rental and lending in **3.56** respect of almost all copyright works. This has been introduced into United Kingdom law, broadly with effect from 1 April 1997, along with the concept of an inalienable right to equitable remuneration. The person who owns the rental right is responsible for the payment of the equitable remuneration. In the absence of agreement on what is equitable, and in fact at any time thereafter, the question can be referred to the Copyright Tribunal for a ruling.

There are "fair dealing" and other exceptions but these are usually more limited in their application than many people are willing to believe.

Remedies

3.57 The remedies that a court could grant to the copyright owner as a result of infringement of copyright include:

(1) An injunction to prevent continued use;
(2) Damages for any loss that the owner has suffered as a result of the infringement, or an account of profits gained from the infringing use;
(3) If relevant, seizure of, for instance, the equipment responsible for the infringement; and
(4) Delivery up of infringing copies, and of articles used to create the infringing material.

3.58 As a result, it is vitally important that users:

(1) Ensure that they obtain appropriate rights in material created whether by freelance staff or third party authors; and
(2) Where possible obtain appropriate warranties and indemnities from third parties supplying material.

Moral rights and performers' rights

3.59 In addition to copyright, many works have moral rights attached to them that are exercisable by the author. This concept causes anxiety, especially for those of the Common Law tradition. Many producers of multimedia products have identified moral rights as a serious legal barrier, given the commercial and technical need to re-edit and change the source material at the time it is produced in digital form.

The Copyright Designs and Patents Act 1988 introduced moral rights formally into United Kingdom law. These are the right to be identified as author (right of paternity), the right to prevent derogatory treatment of the work (the right of integrity), the right not to have a work falsely attributed and a very strange right of privacy (owned by the person who commissions the work not by the person(s) who appear in it) in photographs and films taken for private and domestic purposes.

Infringement of a moral right is actionable as a breach of statutory duty owed to the person entitled to the right. Accordingly, damages and an injunction are available.

The 1988 Act specifically excludes the paternity right in the case of employees who produce works in the course of their employment and the right to object to derogatory treatment is restricted to where the employee has actually been identified as the author of the work. For others, a publisher may be able to rely on the exemption of both rights:

"... in relation to publication in a newspaper ... or similar periodical ... of a literary, dramatic, musical or artistic work made for the purposes of such publication".[38]

It has yet to be established whether an on-line service could be a "similar periodical". **3.60**

Under United Kingdom law, moral rights can be waived, or authors can consent to use. Accordingly, it will be important to ensure that the appropriate waivers of third parties' moral rights are obtained or adequate warranties from third party suppliers to that effect. Typical wording for such a waiver may be:

"... [the Author] hereby unconditionally and irrevocably waives in favour of [the Publisher] any moral rights or droite moral or similar or analogous right to which [the Author] may be entitled in any jurisdiction in relation to [the Work] ...".

Since different jurisdictions approach moral rights in different ways, it is important to be aware of potential difficulties in the international context. **3.61**

The case brought in France, where moral rights are highly appreciated, by the Estate of John Huston against the French broadcaster La Cinq illustrates this. In 1986 Turner Entertainment acquired the rights to the 1950 film "Asphalt Jungle", which had been made in black and white by John Huston and produced by MGM in America. In 1988, still in America, Turner colourised the film and then licensed La Cinq to broadcast the colourised version on French television.

At first instance, the French Court held that colourisation was capable of modifying the perception of the film by a viewer and that accordingly the Estate could object to it. In 1989, the Court of Appeal in Paris overturned that decision, considering that American law should apply and that any rights that John Huston had had, had been assigned to Turner. In 1994, the Court of Appeal in Versailles quashed the judgment of the Court of Appeal in Paris and seems to have adopted the reasoning of the Court of First Instance in 1988. The Court of Appeal said that the

---

38. Copyright Designs and Patents Act 1988, s 79(6).

applicable law was that of the country where protection was being claimed. Under French law the right of integrity could not be assigned and accordingly remained vested in the estate of John Huston. It went on to decide that colourising a black and white film amounted to an infringement of that right.

While rights should be cleared across all jurisdictions of exploitation, cognisance must still be taken of inalienable rights in other territories. New technology exacerbates this: a film can be withdrawn from a particular territory, but electronic rights know no boundaries. What will happen when the "Asphalt Jungle" is distributed digitally in its colourised version? The European Commission has in mind that it will prepare a Directive aimed at harmonising moral rights laws in the European Union, but its prospects are unclear.

The English courts have not had many opportunities to consider moral rights. One decided case is *Noah* v *Shuba*,[39] concerning, *inter alia*, false attribution of authorship. English courts are likely to approach remedies much more in financial terms than the nominal award of one franc and the restoration of honour, which seem to characterise French awards.

Part II of the Copyright Designs & Patents Act 1988 now confers performers' copyright.[40] Where such performances are to be used in the form of music, video or voice recordings, the appropriate consents should be obtained or the publisher given warranties to that effect. Typical wording for such a consent may be:

> ". . . [the Performer] hereby irrevocably grants all consents including (without limitation) all consents required pursuant to Part II of the Copyright Designs & Patents Act 1988 and/or any statutory modification, amendment or re-enactment thereof for the fullest possible exploitation of the [Performance] [in all media throughout the world] [in accordance with the terms of this Agreement]."

Passing off

3.62 An action for passing off is designed to protect goodwill. There are five minimum characteristics necessary to create a valid passing off cause of action:

(1) A misrepresentation calculated to lead to confusion in the minds of the general public as between the plaintiff's and defendant's respective goods;

---

39. *Noah* v *Shuba* [1991] FSR 14.

40. As amended by the Copyright and Related Rights Regulations 1996 (which came into force on 1 December 1996).

(2) Made by a trader in the course of trade;

(3) To prospective customers of his or ultimate consumers of goods or services provided by him;

(4) Which is calculated to injure the business or goodwill of another trader (in the sense that this is a reasonably foreseeable consequence); and

(5) Which causes actual damage to a business or goodwill of a trader by whom the action is brought or will probably do so.

It is necessary to distinguish between name protection and product **3.63** protection.

Infringement of trade-mark, patent or registered design

Patents

Infringement of patents can occur, for example, by knowingly supplying **3.64** the means for working an invention unless what is supplied is a "staple commercial product", *e.g.*, publishing the method of assembly of a patented product.

Trade-marks

Infringement of trade-marks is by trader B using trader A's mark (or a **3.65** mark so nearly resembling it as to be likely to be misleading) for trader B's goods and services.

Infringement of a registered design

A proprietor of a registered design has the exclusive right: **3.66**

(1) To make or import for sale or hire or for use for the purposes of trade or business; or

(2) To sell, hire or offer or expose for sale or hire, an article in respect of which the design is registered and to which that design or a design not substantially different from it has been applied for.

It is an infringement to do any of these things without the licence of the **3.67** registered proprietor. It is also an infringement to make anything or enable any article to be made in respect of which the design is registered and to which the design (or a design not substantially different from it) has been applied without the licence of a registered proprietor.

Infringement of an unregistered design

3.68   There is design right protection for qualifying designs. This applies to both functional and aesthetic designs that are "original" (and correspondingly not "commonplace"). Unregistered design right lasts for a maximum period of 15 years dating from the year in which a design was first recorded in a design document or an article was first made to that design. Unregistered design right is infringed by any person who copies a design (or a substantial part of it) in an article, and by those who intentionally or negligently deal with such articles.

Forgery and Counterfeiting Act 1981

3.69   Under the Forgery and Counterfeiting Act 1981, it is a criminal offence to make or use or, alternatively, copy and use the copy of any document, stamp, Inland Revenue stamp or mechanical, electronic or other means of recording or storing information (*e.g.*, a cassette) with the intention of inducing somebody to accept it as genuine and by reason of so accepting it to do or not to do some act to his or any other person's prejudice.

Infringing the consumer protection legislation including price indications

3.70   The public and consumer bodies have for many years been concerned at the difficulty in distinguishing between genuine reductions and false comparative price claims. One of the purposes of the Consumer Protection Act 1987 is to combat this. Section 20 of the Act makes it an offence if in the course of business a person gives (by any means whatsoever) to any consumers an indication that is misleading as to the price at which any goods, services, accommodation or facilities are available. Pursuant to the provisions of the Act, a Code of Practice relating to price indications has been published: a failure to comply with this Code will be evidence that an offence under the Act has been committed. The Code includes "dos and don'ts" in relation to price comparisons, actual price to the consumer and price indications that become misleading after they have been given. References to "value" or "worth" should be avoided.

Product liability

Product liability is liability for unfit, defective or dangerous products. **3.71** "Product" normally denotes movable goods such as chairs or cars, together with certain intangibles like gas and electricity. The liability of those associated with their manufacture or sale takes two main forms. First, there is liability to pay damages, enforceable through civil court action either for negligence or under the Consumer Protection Act 1987 or under the Sale of Goods Act 1979 for breach of the implied promise by the seller that goods are of merchantable quality and fit for their purpose. The second is liability to criminal prosecutions for breaches of statutes and safety regulations.

Section 3 of the Consumer Protection Act defines "defect" so that a product is defective if its safety is not such as persons are generally entitled to expect. In determining this, there is to be taken into account the marketing and advertising of the product, its presentation, and instructions and warnings supplied with it. The temptation in marketing and advertising is to stress the product safety. It is important to avoid exaggeration however, because unjustifiable claims may lead to a defect being deemed to exist. Appropriate instructions and warnings are important. They must be clear, comprehensible and appropriate to all kinds of purchasers. It is desirable to distinguish between what is harmful to the product and harmful to the user; in the latter case headings such as "danger" or "warning" are needed.

Software of merchantable quality

It is not clear whether software counts as "goods" and is therefore **3.72** covered by the Sale of Goods Act 1979, but in cases where arguably software is goods, questions of "merchantable" quality become relevant. Software can be characterised as tailor-made or off-the-shelf. Perhaps off-the-shelf software comes more easily within the "goods" definition.

What can reasonably be expected of off-the-shelf software is perhaps what a reasonably well-informed purchaser would expect when buying it: comprehensive and comprehensible user manuals and magnetic discs which can be read without trouble on the computer for which they were

137

designed; a programme which corresponds with the description of what it will and will not do. It was thought that it would be naive of a customer to expect software to be wholly free of defects, except trivial items; but see below!

As to tailor-made software, a contract for services is governed by the Supply of Goods and Services Act 1982.

In the *St. Albans* case,[41] the mere fact that a contract was negotiated between two substantial companies was held not to take the exemption clauses incorporated into it outside the provisions of the Unfair Contract Terms Act 1977. The software in question was purchased by St. Albans District Council. It was found to be defective. The defendant, ICL, claimed that the software was still at the development stage so no contractual term could be implied to require it to supply a programme that would perform the expected function. The award of damages was made notwithstanding a standard term in ICL's conditions, which purported to restrict ICL's liability to £100,000.

The Court of Appeal held that a limitation clause in a standard form of contract would be deemed unreasonable if it failed to satisfy the Unfair Contract Terms Act. The judge believed that there would be a term implied at Common Law that the programme was "reasonably capable of achieving the purpose specified in the statement of user requirements in St. Albans' invitation to tender".

Encouraging readers to indulge in illegal conduct

3.73 It is an indictable offence at Common Law for a person to incite or solicit another to commit an offence,[42] even though no such offence is either committed or attempted. The penalty for incitement is imprisonment or a fine or both, at the discretion of the court.

For an incitement to be complete, there must be some form of actual communication with a person whom it is intended to incite. Where, however, a communication is sent with a view to incite, but does not reach the intended recipient, the sender may be guilty of an attempt to incite. Incitement is complete though the mind of the person incited is unaffected.

To prove incitement, it is necessary to show that the accused sought to persuade or encourage another to commit an act that would constitute a crime if done by that other, but it is no defence that, at the time of the incitement, the offence incited would not have been committed, or that it could not thereafter be committed owing to physical impossibility or police action.

---

41. *St. Albans City and District Council* v *ICL, The Times*, 14 August 1996, CA.

42. *R* v *Higgins* (1801) 2 East 5; *R* v *Gregory* (1867) LR ICCR 77.

If the person who incites believes that the crime can be accomplished by the means suggested, he commits an offence although the crime incited cannot be accomplished by those means, but there is no offence of incitement where he does not believe that the crime can be thus accomplished, even if the person incited believes that it can.

One example of encouraging readers to indulge in illegal conduct would be seditious libel. This Common Law offence can be committed by "promoting ill-will and hostility between different classes of Her Majesty's subjects".[43] There must be proof of incitement to violence against the State. There must be an incitement to disorder and violence. A person may be said to have a seditious intention if the words incite persons to commit any crime or disturbance of the peace, such as a racist attack. Another example may be a car advertisement where viewers and readers are encouraged to break the speed limit.

Race relations

While discriminatory behaviour has been legislated against by the Race **3.74** Relations Act 1976, there is little control of such attitudes in publishing. The underlying philosophy is that people should have freedom of expression which will give them the right to entertain ideas of any kind and to express them publicly.

There is, however, a public order offence in relation to discriminatory material, which was first introduced in Britain in 1965 after several years of serious racial violence. The theory was that while freedom of expression must be maintained, the mode or manner of the expression of certain views should be regulated in the interests of the freedom of an individual to go about his business in public without being subjected to insults or assaults.

The Public Order Act 1986 makes it an offence to publish threatening or abusive or insulting material either with an intention to provoke racial hatred or in circumstances where such hatred is likely to be stirred up by publication. "Racial hatred" is defined to mean hatred against a group defined by colour, race or national origin, and therefore includes Jews and Sikhs[44] but excludes, for example, Muslims. The term "racial group" is not defined by reference to religion and so offered no assistance to Muslims who claimed that the book, *The Satanic Verses*, was directed against them as a group.

---

43. *Cf.* "Race Relations", below.

44. *Mandla* v *Dowell Lee* [1983] 1 All ER 1062.

It is also an offence to possess racially inflammatory material with a view to publication in circumstances where racial hatred is likely to be stirred up. An author or publisher will not be at risk if they can show that they collated the material to condemn it. There is also protection for books of genuine historic interest, subject to the Attorney General's consent to publication.

It is a defence for an accused who is not shown to have intended to stir up racial hatred to prove that he was not aware of the content of the material and did not suspect, and had no reason to suspect that it was threatening, abusive or insulting.

Note: Some of this material has been extracted with consent from *Multimedia: Contracts, Rights and Licensing* written by the author, Alan Williams, and published by FT Law & Tax.

France

Chapter 4
France

Kathie D. Claret and Laurent Rouzeau
Archibald Andersen
Neuilly-sur-Seine, France

Introduction

A variety of legal foundations form the basis of liability of the media in   **4.1**
France; the single most important remains the cause of action based on
defamation. The discussion which follows will concentrate on defamation
and, on certain other grounds, including violation of privacy, untrue
news and general tort principles.

Defamation

History

In 1881, when the Law on the Freedom of the Press was passed (LFP),[1]   **4.2**
defamation became a specifically defined legal offence. This Law, largely
influenced by the Third Republic's liberalism, was mainly intended to
establish a status for the press and to protect freedom of expression and
opinion of journalists.

Prior to 1881, notwithstanding the prohibition of duels, insults to
honour and reputation often led to bloodshed. When confronted with
the attitude of such "honourable men", the courts displayed leniency. In
1880, seven deaths attributed to duels were officially recorded. Three
years after the adoption of the Law on the Freedom of the Press, eight
more victims had fallen "on the field of honour". In time, however, the
LFP had an effect on attitudes; victims of defamation came to prefer legal
to physical battles.

---

1. *Loi sur la Liberté de la Presse*, 29 July 1881 (LFP).

The legislative road to this point was long and difficult. Under the laws of the *Ancien Regime*, defamation was punished via various edicts, which took into account the rank and social origins of the defamer and of the victim to determine the sanction. When the victim was the King, the defamer risked losing his life. At that time, there were no legal distinctions between insults and defamation, which included both malicious gossip and untrue allegations. Dareau, in his *Traité des injures dans l'ordre judiciaire* (1775), wrote that:

". . . gossip as well as libel may be at the root of defamation, because a person may injure another by the publication of evil, be it actual deeds or only imagination".

4.3 However, the law's uncertainty and the arbitrariness of judicial decisions did not allow a balance to be struck between freedom of expression and respect for the rights of individuals.

In 1810, the Criminal Code first distinguished between "injurious insult" and "defamation", on the basis that only untrue statements could give rise to actionable defamation. The Law of 17 May 1819 introduced the general misdemeanour of defamation, calumny and scandal-mongering. Defamatory statements were punishable in every case, regardless of whether they were true or false. The law would admit evidence of the truth of the facts only when the defamation targeted the authorities, various State entities or civil servants. When individuals were involved, evidence of the truth of the statements was not allowed, and the defamer was automatically punished unless he could prove his good faith. The Law of 29 July 1881 strengthened this system, without allowing evidence of the truth of statements when individuals were involved. It was only via the *Ordonnance* (Executive Order) of 6 May 1944 that this "truth defence" (*exceptio veritatis*) was included in the 1881 Law. The objective of this *Ordonnance* was to offer a quasi-impunity to those denouncing collaborators and sympathisers with the Nazi regime, in the troubled context of the post-war period.

Even though it has been slightly modified to take social and political changes into account, the Law of 29 July 1881 is still the cornerstone of French defamation law.

The Law distinguishes between defamation of individuals and various categories of defamation considered "special" and including defamation towards public entities, the dead, civil servants and others.

In addition to the repressive measures of the Law of 29 July 1881, general tort principles set forth in articles 1382 and 1383[2] of the French

---

2. Civil Code, article 1382: "Any human action which causes harm to another person creates the obligation on the person due to whom it happened, to repair it." Article 1383: "A person is responsible for the harm he causes, not only through his acts, but also through his negligence or imprudence." [All translations are unofficial].

Civil Code also provide assistance to the victims of defamation, who may benefit from broad compensatory measures.

Overview

The legal definition of defamation was established by articles 29 *et seq.* of **4.4** the Law of 29 July 1881 on the Freedom of the Press (LFP). Although the LFP and its implementing texts targeted defamation principally within the context of the press, it applies equally to persons and media unrelated to the world of journalism.

Pursuant to the LFP, defamation may form the basis of either a criminal or a civil action.

Definitions

Article 29 of the Law of 29 July 1881 defines defamation as: **4.5**

> ". . . any allegation or imputation of a fact which taints the honour or the reputation of the person or entity about whom or which the fact is imputed".[3]

The same article defines the notion of injurious insult, often associated **4.6** with the misdemeanour of defamation, as "any outrageous expression or term of contempt or abuse which does not include an allegation of fact".

Article 32 of the LFP provides that defamation of individuals is a misdemeanour "punishable by imprisonment of five days to six months and/or a fine of FRF 150 to FRF 80,000".

Distinction between injurious insult and defamation

Reason for the distinction

The distinction between the legal concepts of injurious insult and defama- **4.7** tion is important as it is impossible under article 53 of the LFP to bring suit for both injurious insult and defamation based on a single occurrence. It is possible, however, to bring an action for both defamation and injurious insult where, for instance, a written document contains certain terms which are defamatory and others which constitute injurious insult.[4]

---

3. French law draws no distinction between written and oral defamation.

4. Cass. crim., 22 February 1966.

Means of distinction

4.8   In practice, to distinguish between injurious insult and defamation, the question is asked as to whether the allegations in question can be refuted by contrary evidence. Should such be the case, an action for defamation would normally be appropriate; if not, an otherwise defamatory statement which expresses an opinion or a value judgment would normally constitute the basis for an action for injurious insult.

Defamation, properly speaking, must be based on a specific act which can without difficulty, be the subject of proof or an adversarial debate.[5] For example, it is possible for someone who is described as a "criminal" to furnish evidence to the contrary and thus to demonstrate that the allegation is defamatory. Alternatively, it would be much more difficult to prove that one is not a "nasty character"; the courts would normally hold this to be an injurious insult.

Recourse to extrinsic elements

4.9   For the many cases which border on injurious insult or defamation, case law gives the courts the possibility to rely on elements which are "extrinsic" to the writing or utterance in question. The *Cour de Cassation* (Supreme Court) has decided that:

> ". . . terms which in themselves are non-defamatory may constitute defamation due to circumstances extrinsic to the writing. Such circumstances must be invoked before the trial judges, who alone have the jurisdiction to establish the existence and the nature thereof".[6]

Distinction impossible

4.10   There are nonetheless cases where it is nearly impossible to distinguish injurious insult from defamation. In such cases, the courts normally hold that there has been defamation.[7]

Publicity element

4.11   To establish the misdemeanours of defamation and injurious insult, the statements must be publicised. In the absence of publicity, these offences

---

5. Cass. crim., 2 December 1980.

6. Cass. crim., 23 November 1965.

7. Cass. crim., 9 July 1982.

are re-characterised as non-public injurious insult and are punished as minor offences under Criminal Code, articles R 621–1 or R 624–3,[8] falling within the jurisdiction of the *Tribunal de Police* (Police Court).

Elements of Defamation

While leaving journalists and the media a broad power to criticise, the **4.12** legislature, conscious of the need to avoid an over-burdening of the courts by oversensitive plaintiffs, has nonetheless established certain rules to be followed.

Article 29 of the LFP, as amended by the Executive Order of 6 May 1944, defines defamation and establishes the terms of its application.[9] It imposes five essential conditions for establishing the misdemeanour of defamation:

(1) The allegation or imputation of a specific fact;
(2) Liable to taint honour or reputation;
(3) Targeting a specific person;
(4) Made in bad faith; and
(5) Which has been published.

Imputation or allegation of a specific fact

A specific fact

To constitute defamation, the utterances or writings in question must be **4.13** based on specific facts which if true would exempt the accused from liability upon furnishing evidence of the truth of the facts in question. In

---

8. CA Aix, 7 February 1994; Criminal Code, article R 621–1: Non-public defamation of a person is punished by the fine provided for minor offences of the first class. Criminal Code, article R 624–3: Non-public defamation committed about a person or a group of persons due to origin or membership, real or otherwise, in an ethnic group, race or established religion is punished by the fines provided for minor offences of the fourth class. Criminal Code, article R 610–1: Offences, as well as the classes to which they belong, are determined by the *Conseil d'Etat.*

9. LFP, article 29: "Defamation is constituted by any allegation or imputation of a fact which taints the honour or reputation of a person or entity about whom or which the fact is imputed. Direct publication or reproduction of such an allegation or imputation is punishable, even if made so as to cast doubt or if targeting a person or entity who is not explicitly named, but whose identification is made possible due to the terms of speeches, shouts, threats, writings or printed matter, posters or signs."

contrast, injurious insult allows for no exonerating evidence, as it is based on no specific fact. A recent decision stated:

> ". . . the term 'Nazi' could be an injurious insult but its use alone, without imputation of a particular fact, would not constitute defamation. Neither the drawing of nor allusion to a 'little Polish Nazi' alone could constitute defamation, where no particular act has been specifically attributed to either of the persons depicted."[10]

4.14 The *Cour de Cassation* has the authority to decide whether or not allegations or imputations are sufficiently specific to constitute the offence of defamation. A fact must be ascertainable, but it is not necessary that it be described in detail. An allusion, where sufficiently clear and precise to identify the intended person, may be sufficient to constitute the misdemeanour or defamation.

The Court of Appeal of Paris thus stated that publication by the satirical newspaper *Le Canard Enchaîné* of a caricature entitled "Le Pen's Dream", which showed a parachutist in uniform plunging a "chained duck" into a bathtub full of water, alluded to the imputations of torture allegedly conducted by Mr. Le Pen during the war in Algeria. Such a caricature, although humorous and understandable only to those aware of Mr. Le Pen's past, was nonetheless held to be defamatory.[11]

Form

4.15 Authors may greatly vary their styles in an attempt to avoid punishment, although it is of little importance. Thus, interrogatory or utterances casting doubt, simple hypotheses, suspicions or insinuations may constitute defamation.[12] Utterances issued in a conditional style or vague forms such as "they say that" or "they told us that" might equally contain defamatory utterances.

Facts liable to taint honor or reputation

Definition

4.16 According to Professor Chavanne:[13]

> ". . . honour is a quality which, for a citizen, consists of having nothing for which to reproach himself which is contrary to good morals, and reputation, is the idea that others have of a person".

---

10. Paris Court of Appeal, 1 June 1995.

11. Court of Appeal, 15 January 1986.

12. Cass. crim., 12 October 1993.

13. Chavanne, Drago and Boinet, *Droit de la Presse*, August 1994, Editions Litec, Paris, p 140, paragraph 41.

The courts do not always distinguish between "facts liable to taint honour" **4.17** and those "liable to taint reputation" and use the two expressions alternatively and cumulatively without attaching any particular importance thereto.

Existence of harm

The law speaks of "facts liable to taint", which would seem to imply **4.18** that actual harm is not an indispensable element to establishing the misdemeanour. Actual harm sustained will normally play a role only in determining damages and not in the characterisation *per se* of the misdemeanour of defamation.

Common knowledge

Even if the facts in question are common knowledge, the misdemeanour **4.19** of defamation may exist. Only the amount of the fine might be adjusted.

Due to the rule of *volenti non fit injuria*, reporting facts about which a person himself has boasted and made public is not defamation.

Victim's status and opinion

In evaluating any taint to honour and reputation, the courts are not **4.20** limited by their evaluation of the status of the person who has been defamed, nor by his own opinion of honour or morals. The victim's opinion as to the utterances or writings in question does not play a major role in establishing the misdemeanour of defamation. The Criminal Division of the *Cour de Cassation* has affirmed:

> ". . . the offence had not been established based on the victim's subjective evaluation, which had made a choice between the imputations made about him and the presumed opinion of his readers, while the laws which prohibit and punish defamation protect all persons, without providing any exception based on such elements . . .".[14]

The victim's notion of honour and reputation is also unimportant. The **4.21** *Cour de Cassation* has declared on this subject that "judges do not need to inquire into [the victims'] personal and subjective ideas regarding the concepts of honour and reputation".[15]

---

14. Cass. crim., 28 January 1986.
15. Cass. crim., 2 July 1975.

To evaluate the misdemeanour of defamation, judges conduct an abstract analysis.

Examples

4.22 The following examples may help to better understand what might taint a person's honour and reputation. Imputations or allegations of criminal convictions are slurs on honour. Thus, one may not with impunity treat someone as "a murderer", particularly if the offence was pardoned.[16] Private life is a sensitive domain; judges consistently hold that defamation has been committed when the right to privacy is threatened. One may not, therefore, call someone a "homosexual"[17] or accuse him of being "the son or daughter of a criminal".[18] In the event of violation of the right to privacy, article 9 of the Civil Code[19] is often invoked instead of defamation, most notably due to the short statute of limitations applicable to defamation proceedings and the greater flexibility of the Common Law procedures. Professional ability also merits defending. One is, therefore, free to like or dislike an attorney's pleadings or a doctor's opinion, but one may not question his professional competence, knowledge or intelligence.

A specific person

4.23 So that the misdemeanour of defamation be found to have been committed, it is imperative that a natural person, a legal entity or one of the institutions named in articles 30 and 31 of the LFP[20] be the subject thereof.

Identifying the victim

4.24 Article 29 of the LFP specifically states that the misdemeanour of defamation may be committed even against a person who is "not specifically

---

16. Cass. crim., 23 June 1980.

17. CA Paris, 20 February 1986.

18. Cass. crim., 10 March 1955.

19. Civil Code, article 9: Everyone has the right to respect of his private life. Judges may, without prejudice to reparation for the damage suffered, provide for other measures, such as sequester, seizure, etc., which are intended to impede or curtailing harm to the intimacy of private life; such measures, where necessary, may be issued as an interim order.

20. LFP, article 30: of the Courts, Tribunals, Public Entities, the Army, Naval and Air Forces, Official Entities, and the Public Administration.

named [but] whose identification is possible". The person need not be named; it is sufficient that the judges can identify the person from intrinsic and extrinsic elements at their disposal. The Criminal Division of the *Cour de Cassation* has emphasised that "the fact that only the initiated could recognise the person being targeted does not impede a finding of defamation".[21]

Although it suffices that the person or persons who is or are the subject the writings or utterances be identifiable or recognisable thereby, the remarks must not be purely technical and must actually focus on one natural person or legal entity. For the Court of Appeal of Paris, "a purely technical comment which contains no professional judgment" does not constitute defamation.[22]

Plurality of victims

Case law allows a defamation action in the event of a plurality of victims **4.25** if they are all identifiable. All persons targeted by allegations or imputations may act together or separately against the author. The *Cour de Cassation* has declared:

> ". . . when the defamatory imputations were made with a vague description liable to throw suspicion on a plurality of persons, each of those persons has a basis for requesting reparation for the damage which has thereby been caused to him".[23]

Using the same principle, the *Cour de Cassation* convicted a newspaper **4.26** which had published an article personally charging four mayors who had been removed from office for administrative irregularities. Although the mayors in question were not named, they were sufficiently identifiable and as "the imputations were aimed at a limited group of persons, each person who was tainted by suspicion had the right to demand reparation".[24]

More recently, the Paris *Tribunal de Grande Instance* affirmed this in a case of defamation targeting a *Conseil Municipal* (town council). That court held that:

> ". . . when an official entity is composed of a limited number of persons, each of its members may consider himself personally targeted by the injurious insults or defamatory imputations about said entity, and in

---

21. 24 July 1934.

22. 21 January 1985.

23. Cass. crim., 21 April 1923.

24. Cass. crim., 2 October 1953.

consequence is allowed individually to file an action for the suppression of an insult which taints his honour or reputation".[25]

Incidental victims

4.27 It is an issue whether, given that the victim has the right to file suit, members of the immediate family, spouses, ascendants and offspring also have standing to sue. Case law is clear on this issue: either the direct victim is still living and he alone has the right to sue for defamation, or he is deceased and his family might have the possibility to act on the basis of article 34 of the LFP, which permits such cases, where it is possible to taint the honour of those living via the memory of the deceased.

As long as the victim is still living, family members may file only a civil liability suit.

Victims with or without legal personality

4.28 Legal entities are protected by article 29 of the LFP.[26] The difficulty resides in determining whether they, or their members, were being targeted. A legal entity's personality is sometimes so tied to that of its members that it is difficult to distinguish between them. For example, the *Comité National de Défense contre l'Alcoolisme* was authorised to file a suit in defamation against an article which spoke of "militant alcoholics". One would be justified in thinking that only the members of the committee had a basis for filing a defamation suit in this case. The court decided otherwise, holding that:

> ". . . the Comité National de Défense contre l'Alcoolisme is sufficiently described by the terms 'anti-alcoholism' or 'anti-alcoholics', because in belonging to the anti-alcoholics, it is even one of the main incarnations of anti-alcoholism in France".[27]

4.29 According to case law, groups without legal status have no standing to sue on behalf of victims of defamation, to whom that right is reserved. The Court of Appeal of Colmar has held:

> ". . . where defamation is generally aimed at certain groups of citizens lacking a legal status, a social class or a profession, it may not be suppressed, unless some or all of the members of these groups can deem themselves to have been personally targeted; the Law of 29 July 1881

---

25. Paris, 28 April 1987.
26. Cass. crim., 22 March 1966.
27. *Tribunal de Grande Instance* Paris, 8 July 1970.

specifically lists, in its articles 30 and 32, a certain number of groups of people or entities which it protects against defamation; the legislature makes no provision other than in these cases, and there may be no defamation when the allegations are directed against a group of people not included in those lists; such is the case of homosexuals, who, insofar as the law suppressing sexism has not been promulgated, do not constitute a legally-protected entity. A defamation suit may nonetheless be individually instituted by the members of that group who may have the right to consider themselves personally targeted by the imputations; without proof that homosexuals had been sufficiently designated to have suffered personal harm, a civil suit is inadmissible".[28]

Associations and unions

4.30 Associations may only institute legal proceedings based on article 29 of the LFP when they are personally targeted. As they do not represent the interests of a profession, they may not act in the name and on the behalf of the persons being defamed. The Law of 1 July 1972 on the Fight against Racism has made an exception for associations which fight racism. They are authorised to act even where they are not themselves targeted by the imputations and allegations.

The same rules apply to suits by unions, which may only institute proceedings where they have been personally targeted. For example, the veterinarians' union may not file a suit in defamation against the author of utterances made against the profession in general.[29] The *Cour de Cassation* has added that:

". . . even though untrue, utterances which taint only a profession as a whole and do not cast aspersions on any particular person will not constitute the misdemeanour of defamation and injurious insult in the meaning of articles 29, 32 and 33 of the Law of 29 July 1881".[30]

4.31 However, under article L 411–11 of the *Code du Travail* (Labour Code),[31] a union may file suit in any jurisdictions so that the collective interests of the profession it represents be respected "without it being necessary for all of its members to have been victims of accusations".[32] Thus, the

---

28. 27 June 1983.

29. Cass. crim., 2 May 1956.

30. Cass. crim., 5 May 1964.

31. Article 411–11 of the Labour Code provides: "[Unions] have the right to be a party to legal proceedings. They may exercise all rights reserved to the civil complainant in criminal proceedings regarding the facts bearing either directly or indirectly on the collective interest of the profession they represent."

32. *Tribunal de Grande Instance* Paris, 16 February 1977.

Chambre Syndicale des Experts Professionnels en objets d'arts et de collection was allowed to proceed with its action for damages pursuant to tort law, based on utterances made in an article which sought to severely discredit the profession.[33]

Product or service defamation

Criticism exclusively of a service or product

4.32 Case law has clearly stated that only attacks on identifiable persons are susceptible of being penalised as defamation. The *Cour de Cassation* has emphasised that:

> ". . . where they do not involve the individual or legal entity, assessments of a business or industrial undertaking's products, services or performance, even where excessive, do not fall under the provisions of article 29 of the Law of 29 July 1881".[34]

4.33 If the critique is of products, a defamation action cannot be instituted because:

> ". . . defamation presumes an imputation directed against a person and does not exist in the event of disparagement of a product; the same is true where the writings concerned target essentially a product".[35]

4.34 This makes it very difficult for professionals whose profession, services or products are attacked to have their detractors convicted on the basis of defamation.

The *Cour de Cassation* has recently reiterated that the fact that an article and television programme invite the public to renounce wearing fur, to protect certain animal species, does not constitute a defamatory attack on the furrier profession.[36]

Similarly, when called on to rule on the lot of an article criticising the use of homeopathic products, the *Tribunal de Grande Instance* of Paris held that:

> ". . . neither the laboratory nor the homeopathic pharmaceuticals union can consider themselves to have been the victims of systematic denigration of pharmaceutical medications where the speaker of the published

---

33. *Tribunal de Grande Instance* Paris, 16 February 1977.

34. Cass. crim., 8 February 1994.

35. *Tribunal de Grande Instance* Paris, 18 April 1984.

36. Cass. civ. 2e, 17 February 1993.

utterances, even if they are accompanied by drawings of a satirical nature, does not exceed his right freely to criticise and manifests no desire to do harm".[37]

Criticism implicating a trades- or businessperson

A defamation action will be admitted if, in attacking the product or the service offered, the critique also implicates the trades- or businessperson's honesty, good faith or professionalism. **4.35**

The *Tribunal Correctionnel* of Paris (Criminal Court) has held that a consumer magazine's disclosure of the failings of the French medical system, which closely linked the quality of medical services to those of the professional concerned, did not justify "that a doctor be personally targeted and criticised in terms and by means which bear on his reputation and competence".[38] The Paris Court of Appeal has also stated:

> "An evaluation of the quality of food served in an establishment is subjective and may be freely expressed; the terms used may be quite severe when the critiques are well-founded and pertinent, but should not bear on a restaurateur's professional reputation. If they exceed the limits of free expression of a specialised journalist, they constitute a fault for which he owes reparation. Thus, is the case should a critic proceed, with no basis for complaint, to a denigration of a restaurateur's professional capabilities which was rendered even more shocking because, in expressing himself with irony and in a humorous tone, he ridiculed the restaurant owner".[39]

Tainting business reputation

While criticism of products and services may not be the basis of a defamation suit, it may nonetheless taint a brand's image and/or a business's reputation and so forming the basis of a civil action for damages under general tort principles. For example, publishing an article entitled "Warning, health fraud; beware of modern charlatanism", which reproduced an ad regarding a slimming treatment, tainted the business reputation of the enterprise concerned.[40] **4.36**

In such a situation, a business or tradesperson may file suit for unfair competition or denigrating behaviour if the critique comes from a

---

37. 20 November 1985.

38. 2 December 1978.

39. 22 April 1980.

40. *Tribunal de Grande Instance* Paris, 6 March 1969.

competitor, or a civil liability suit for misleading information if the critique emanates from a non-competitor third-party.

Judges' strict supervision

4.37 The *Cour de Cassation* reserves the right to verify whether the defamation actually targets a particular person and, to this end, examines the contents of the writings or utterances in issue. It has emphasised that it has the prerogative:

> ". . . to exercise its authority as to knowing whether the utterances which are the subject of the indictment contain legal elements of public defamation as defined in articles 29 and 32 of the Law of 29 July 1881".[41]

4.38 That court nonetheless exercises no authority over the extrinsic elements, whose examination it leaves to the trial judge. One decision illustrates this traditional doctrine in recalling that:

> ". . . the trial judges' evaluation as to the description of the person being defamed is sovereign when it is based on elements which are extrinsic to the text in question".[42]

Wrongful intent

Presumption of bad faith

4.39 Article 35 *bis* of the LFP puts forth the principle that "any reproduction of an imputation which has been held to be defamatory will be considered to have been made in bad faith". The principle of presumption of bad faith runs counter to the rules which govern not only customary law, but also nearly all other press-related misdemeanours which themselves rely on a presumption of good faith. This presumption of bad faith is justified by the theory that a person who issued or published defamatory utterances could not reasonably have been ignorant of tainting the honour and reputation of one or more other persons.

This principle relies on the "theory of intent"; in matters involving defamation in general, the courts consider that, failing proof to the

---

41. 26 May 1987.

42. Cass. crim., 16 January 1969.

contrary, wrongful intent exists. President Tanon, of the *Cour de Cassation*, explains that wrongful intent is:

> ". . . consciousness of the act such as it is defined by law; the conscience is, with free will, and independent of any particular harmful intent or any other purpose on the part of the actor, the necessary and sufficient condition for criminal conviction".

Thus, where clearly the act was voluntary and its author was fully aware **4.40** that the utterances or writings being made would taint someone's honour and reputation, the defamer's guilt speaks for itself without any need to consider motives for the act. The *Cour de Cassation* has noted on numerous occasions:

> ". . . imputations whose defamatory nature trial judges must evaluate are rightly deemed to have been made with harmful intent. It is not necessary for the court . . . expressly to establish their author's bad faith".[43]

The lone fact that a person issues or has published defamatory utterances **4.41** is sufficient to characterise a presumption of wrongful intent. The onus is thus on him to furnish proof of his good faith. The *Cour de Cassation* has not ceased to emphasise:

> ". . . defamatory imputations imply the intent to harm the person whose honour or reputation they taint. That intention may only be disproved if the author of the defamatory writing, who alone has this burden of proof, succeeds in establishing evidence of facts to prove his good faith. Consequently, the judges need not put themselves in his place to determine whether the person targeted was harmed in error . . .".[44]

Instances of bad faith and special circumstances

Bad faith is presumed to exist; the courts will not consider any motive **4.42** which might have led one to make defamatory utterances or the fact that the defamer believed in the accuracy of his assertions.

The *Cour de Cassation* has clearly stated that "faith in the accuracy [of one's assertions] does not suffice to destroy the presumption of bad faith"[45] and that:

> ". . . a defamatory writing is, by law, said to be published with wrongful intent. This presumption fails only in the presence of evidence which is

---

43. Cass. crim., 12 June 1987.

44. Cass. crim., 8 July 1986.

45. Cass. crim., 18 May 1954.

sufficient to gain admission of good faith. Neither faith in the accuracy of the evidence, nor the absence of personal animosity constitutes such evidence".[46]

4.43 The intention to inform the public is not justification in and of itself:

"According to a consistent doctrine, neither the credibility of the facts which have been imputed, the absence of personal animosity on the part of the author of the imputation towards the person targeted, the opinion he might have of his act's legality, the belief in the reality of the facts alleged, the affirmation of the absence of any defamatory intent, nor, finally, particularly because it is a journalist in question, the desire to inform the public, excludes harmful intent".[47]

4.44 This doctrine is constantly recalled by the *Cour de Cassation* in similar terms, as it affirms that:

". . . neither the faith in the accuracy of allegations, even if such faith were proven, nor the intention to inform the public, constitutes exculpatory evidence".[48]

4.45 That a fact is public knowledge does not affect the presumption of bad faith. This knowledge might no doubt have an influence on the amount of damages paid to the victim, but not on the existence of the misdemeanour.

The same is true for remorse and retraction. They do not eliminate defamation, but might attenuate its financial consequences.

Provocation, likewise, has no impact on the existence of the misdemeanour; case law emphasises that "defamatory utterances do not become less so due to being a response to another utterance, even if the latter was defamatory".[49] But if the defamatory utterances were not public, they would be likened to a non-public injurious insult and their author could benefit from the excuse of provocation provided by article 33 of the LFP.

Finally, the existence of an election period provides no justification *per se.* Even if during such a period debate is livelier and the wish to provide better information to the voters is obvious, journalists and various other parties involved in the campaigns must be on their guards, despite a relative leniency on the part of the courts not to surpass the limits allowed by case law, which has consistently reiterated that there "is no exception to this rule during election periods".[50]

---

46. Cass. crim., 3 June 1975.

47. *Tribunal de Grande Instance* Auxerre, 22 June 1965.

48. Cass. civ., 14 November 1973.

49. Cass. crim., 3 May 1972.

50. Cass. crim., 3 May 1972.

Even then, the persons targeted by the defamation must be party to the political campaigns because:

". . . while the intention to inform voters might, during a political campaign and under certain conditions, constitute justification of the good faith of the authors of the imputations, it is otherwise when the latter target a person who is not a candidate".[51]

Justification, good faith and legitimate motives

The case law defining and specifying the conditions for applying defama-   **4.46**
tion begs the issues of the fundamental principle of freedom of speech and how the obligation to respect the honour and reputation of persons can be reconciled with it.

Freedom of expression, the right to know and inform the public

Given the incessant flow of news and the need to report with the least   **4.47**
possible delay, journalists do not always take the time to verify the accuracy of what they are disseminating, hence the numerous opportunities for defamation.[52]

Case law establishes relatively simple principles to determine journalists' margin for manoeuvre; in each case, they are applied depending on the judges' sovereign examination of the facts, and flexibility must be used in adapting them to other cases. The following examples illustrate how the case law has achieved a balance between the misdemeanour of defamation and the principle of freedom of speech and expression, especially with regard to journalists.

The courts constantly recall the fundamental principle of freedom of expression. The *Tribunal de Grande Instance* (TGI — High Court) of Paris emphasised that:

". . . the author of a work . . . who had made a presentation in the form of a debate and which held itself out as objective because it disclosed the pros and cons of the current of modern Christian thought in moderate terms devoid of excessive aggression, may not be held to have committed a fault

---

51. Cass. crim., 28 February 1989.

52. The Law of 27 July 1849 established the misdemeanour of false news and penalises "the publication or reproduction made in bad faith of false news, manufactured or falsified items, as well as those falsely attributed to a third party where such news or items are likely to disturb the public peace" or "would shake the armed forces' discipline or morale or impede the nation's war effort" (article 27).

as a result of having, even in an erroneous or improper manner, placed the plaintiff to the defamation action at one of the extremes of the debate, without casting a serious and inadmissible taint to the free expression of his thought or personal opinions".[53]

4.48   The courts stress the fact that:

". . . although any utterance of a defamatory nature is deemed to have been formulated in bad faith and with harmful intent, such a presumption disappears when the judge takes note of proof which works to the accused's benefit".[54]

4.49   In relying on these general principles, judges have held that:

". . . journalists' responsibility to inform their readers cannot go so far as to authorise the publication of articles which might harm someone's reputation . . ."[55]

4.50   that a journalist who reproduces:

". . . obvious and well-known facts with the sole intention of informing his readers may be sued in defamation when he gives this information a polemic and aggressive form . . .",[56]

4.51   but that "when the purpose of the information sought seems serious and legitimate enough to justify the means used", the rules might be relaxed.[57]
These decisions, even though old, establish valid precedents. Significantly, it has been held that a journalist may not avoid being sued for defamation "by pleading only the need to inform",[58] but that:

". . . where the circumstances show that the authors of the articles were careful to conduct the preliminary investigations and verification which are normally necessary to accomplishing their task of providing information . . ."[59]

4.52   the rules might be eased:

"It is only in the domain of political polemic bearing on opinions and doctrine related to the role and functioning of the State's basic institutions that the good faith exception, particular to defamation, is not necessarily subordinated to prudence in the expression of thought."[60]

---

53. 23 March 1983.
54. Cass. crim., 23 June 1964.
55. CA Aix, 11 March 1909.
56. CA Douai, 1 February 1904.
57. CA Paris, 5 May 1948.
58. Cass. crim., 12 June 1987.
59. CA Paris, 10 December 1986.
60. Cass. crim., 11 June 1981.

A journalist may freely reproduce various facts, without fear of being sued **4.53** in defamation, to the extent that he adds no personal, disagreeable, erroneous or subjective remarks or commentary to them. He should thereby avoid falling into what the *Cour de Cassation* calls the digression of "tendentious exaggeration, systematisation and presentation".[61]

A simple bit of gossip or slight exaggeration will not suffice to establish defamation; a journalist may often successfully invoke the *exceptio veritatis* while always taking care not to violate the right to privacy.

Literary, artistic and scientific criticism

Although the freedom to criticise is often expressly invoked by the courts, **4.54** it remains conditioned by the fact that such freedom may not exceed a certain level of tolerance which the Court of Cassation recalls using a classic formula:

> ". . . although it is true that critics must enjoy great freedom to express their opinions as to the value of artistic, literary or scientific works which they are asked to judge, they will not be allowed impunity to combine those opinions with defamatory digressions".

While it is usual to recite this principle, judges are left with a wide margin **4.55** of subjective evaluation and interpretation. For example, it has been held that to accuse a writer of not having written the work which made him famous, when he was in fact the work's author, was defamatory.[62] Alternatively, according to the High Court of Paris:

> ". . . the act, by a literary critic, of saying that a book is of a pathetic intellectual level which uses the most vulgar prejudices and means to achieve its goal, would not constitute defamation of the book's author, as long as neither his honour nor reputation, nor his professional nor private character is denigrated or questioned, and one could not incidentally deem the allegations or imputations issued by the critic to apply literally to the author himself, but only to his work".[63]

Nor does saying that an actress is "too old to play 35-year old women and **4.56** too young to play grannies" constitute defamation.[64]

Moreover, artistic, literary and scientific criticism will be justified to the extent that it does not question the author's personal and professional

---

61. Cass. crim., 12 June 1978.

62. Cass. crim., 10 October 1973.

63. 5 April 1968.

64. CA Paris, 31 May 1988.

capabilities: all criticism which goes beyond the work *per se* risks being penalised under article 29 of the LFP.

It is useful to recall the unequivocal court decision which stated that:

> ". . . the critic's rights in the fields of art, science and literature do not permit defamation. The critic is certainly freely allowed to attack the work, but the person of the author, his honour, reputation and character, and his artistic, scientific or literary integrity must be respected. Criticism of the work must not be confused with unjust denigration of the author's person and actions".[65]

4.57 A critique itself, even if made in a controversial and lively tone, must remain objective and focused on the work which is the subject thereof.

Consideration of "greater interests"

4.58 When the greater interests of the State or the services which are essential to its proper running, such as the State education system, justice or defence, are at stake, case law freely admits that certain actions in defamation will not be considered admissible, even when the journalist or defamer had not taken all of the necessary precautions. The *Cour de Cassation* thus decided:

> ". . . good faith regarding the utterances, which constitutes exculpatory evidence particular to defamation, is not necessarily subordinate to prudence in the expression of the thought when the discussion bears on a State's fundamental interests, even where that State is foreign".[66]

4.59 The Paris High Court has stated that, as the education system is a sensitive domain, which is of primary importance for children and the country itself, parents might legitimately, when faced with a teacher's intransigence, "call for collective action to protect their children's morals" and consider "it their duty to act when faced with harm to this greater interest". The Court added that "their attitude demonstrated a respectable preoccupation that the court could not reproach" and that "as a consequence, they are well founded in pleading their good faith".[67]

---

65. *Tribunal de Grande Instance* Auxerre, 22 June 1965.

66. Cass. civ., 28 November 1984.

67. *Tribunal de Grande Instance* Paris, 18 December 1974.

Express criticism as part of professional duties

There are cases where defamation is justified by the fact that the party **4.60**
who commits the defamation is obliged to do so, due to circumstances or
to his position.

Thus, a prefect who, in a letter addressed to a mayor, reiterated the
conclusions of an inquiry by the administration into the award of a
contract, and called the mayor's attention to the fact that his deputy had
committed serious irregularities "bordering on the criminal", was held
to have committed no transgression of a defamatory nature.[68]

Similarly, the Court of Appeal of Montpellier has held that reports
made by government officials to their superiors noting the dishonourable behaviour of agents under their authority:

> ". . . cannot constitute a personal offence which may be separated from
> their duties when, even though such reports were unfavourable, they were
> not motivated by enmity or a personal interest".[69]

To shelter himself from a defamation action, a higher official must avoid **4.61**
all particularly disagreeable or outrageous utterances in his reports and
internal memoranda which might lead one to think that he is settling a
personal matter which has no relation to his duties.

Similarly, the president of a professional union may not spread information according to which his administrative secretary-general "abandons
himself to malicious lies in the hope of hiding his incompetence". These
utterances, in the absence of proof sufficient to establish the union president's good faith, were held to constitute defamation,[70] as they were directed
against the person of the secretary-general, tainted the latter's reputation
and honour and thus exceeded the acceptable legal limits of criticism.

Accordingly, it has been said that the only critiques which are punishable are those which "surpass the acceptable limits of debate among the
members of a group".[71]

Complaint and reporting

Good faith will also be presumed to exist and the charge of defamation **4.62**
will be set aside where it results from the instigation of a complaint or
reporting of a criminal or tortious act to the Public Prosecutor.[72]

---

68. *Conseil d'Etat*, 28 March 1969.

69. 20 March 1980.

70. Cass. crim., 17 March 1980.

71. Cass. crim., 1 December 1971.

72. Cass. req., 7 February 1887.

Publicity

4.63 Even though article 29 of the LFP does not expressly specify this, the element of publicity is indispensable in establishing the misdemeanour of defamation. Without this element, otherwise defamatory utterances are classified as injurious insults punishable by article R 621–1 of the Criminal Code.[73]

Means of publicity

4.64 Article 23 sets out the various means of publicity within the meaning of the LFP, and includes speeches, shouts or threats made in public places or meetings; writings or printed matter which are sold, distributed, offered for sale or exhibited in public places or at meetings; posters or signs exposed to public view; and audio-visual matter. Despite being amended by the Legal Decree of 29 July 1939, article 28 is still applicable to press offences and adds to the means of publicity provided by article 23, the offering for sale, distribution or exhibition of drawings, engravings, paintings, emblems or images.

It has been held that the LFP's list of media used for injurious insult or defamation is not exhaustive; although such list should doubtless be revised so as to refer expressly to new means of communication and informational technologies, the Paris Court of Appeal, for example, has held that an on-line data-processing terminal reproducing a commentary on an article could serve as a medium for defamation.[74]

Difficulties of application

4.65 While, in theory, the condition of publicity may seem relatively straight-forward, the courts are, in practice, often confronted with fairly sensitive situations, as illustrated by the following examples.

For the *Cour de Cassation*, comments sent by letter to a third party with an announcement that the letter would be published in the near future were held nevertheless to retain their confidential nature in the absence of such actual publication, and were not therefore held to be defamatory.[75]

---

73. Cass. crim., 16 March 1971.

74. 27 September 1993.

75. Cass. crim., 3 June 1976.

Similarly, in a case where a company director had, during a meeting of the workers' committee, called an employee a "thief" for having stolen a work tool and then had the meeting minutes posted in the factory, the *Cour de Cassation* held that the director should be sued not for defamation but only for non-public injurious insult.[76] The utterances made before the workers' committee were deemed not to have been adequately published as to constitute defamation, particularly since they could be justified by the need for freedom of speech during such a meeting. Thus, although the minutes were posted on the company's bulletin board, the court held that the imputations were not defamatory because they did not go beyond a relatively limited circle of persons, the company's employees, who were united by the same community of interests.

Hence, it is not particularly easy to apply the publicity criterion where the notion of a "group of persons united by a community of interests" is also present. The problem of the public or private nature of meetings and shareholders' meetings, and that posed by distributions of pamphlets bearing defamatory charges, serve as a good illustration of this difficulty.

In a case where a letter had been addressed to 32 families, the trial court held that it had:

"... not been established or even alleged that this correspondence circulated openly or had been addressed to addressees other than the 32 families involved; the condition of publicity is therefore lacking and it is a case of non-public defamation comparable to the offence of non-public injurious insult".[77]

On the other hand, the *Cour de Cassation* affirmed that: **4.66**

"... a letter attached to a professional report had been sufficiently published so as to constitute defamation where — the appeals court — found that this report not only could have been read by persons other than the addressees, but was also addressed to persons outside the corporate group, even to non-subscribers".[78]

Shareholders' meetings

Case law has not generally characterised shareholders' meetings as   **4.67** public, no matter how numerous the participants were. Defamation

---

76. 9 July 1982.

77. Trib. Corr., Paris, 18 December 1974.

78. Cass. crim, 22 February 1966.

may be found, however, if debates were public and the utterances made unrelated to the subject of the meeting.[79]

The distribution of a circular letter to shareholders to convene them to the general shareholders' meeting did not amount to publication within the meaning of the 1881 Law.[80] However, within the meaning of article 23 of the Law of 29 July 1881, "the element of publicity exists if the [circular letter] is distributed to one or more third parties unrelated to the group"[81] of people united by a community of interests.

It has been held that when journalists of the financial press were present at shareholders' meetings, the debates acquired a public nature,[82] on condition that the authors of the defamatory statements knew of the presence of persons unrelated to the shareholders' group.[83]

Pamphlets as a defamation medium

4.68 With regard to pamphlets, the *Cour de Cassation* has followed nearly verbatim the case law regarding shareholders' meetings and has deemed the element of publicity to be missing when the distribution of pamphlets was to "a group of persons united by a community of interests",[84] as in the case of a distribution of pamphlets conducted at the workplace or on corporate premises.

In a recent decision, however, the Paris Court of Appeal found that the distribution of pamphlets in a school amounted to publicity since such distribution was conducted during a school open-day when persons from outside the school were present.[85]

Exceptio veritatis

4.69 At the outset, the *exceptio veritatis* was designed to allow citizens to denounce the Administration and its agents for abusive conduct without fear of prosecution.[86]

---

79. Montpellier Court of Appeal, 31 March 1966.

80. Cass. crim., 1 December 1971.

81. Cass. crim., 15 July 1981.

82. Cass. crim., 27 November 1920.

83. Cass. crim., 29 December 1921.

84. Cass. crim., 13 May 1986.

85. CA Paris, 13 May 1995.

86. Article 35(1) and (2).

In cases involving defamation of individuals, the defamers were not authorised to provide evidence of the truth of their allegations. However, they were not completely without defence since they could disclaim responsibility by invoking their good faith. The courts therefore treated bad-faith defamers, who had acted with the intention to do harm, more severely than journalists who had only reported well-known facts, even if the publication of the latter was likely to be prejudicial to the honour and reputation of the individual in question.

Similarly, certain courts have acquitted defamers, despite finding the terms in question defamatory, on the grounds that they had acted in good faith.[87] The *Cour de Cassation* even acquitted a journalist on the ground that he was acting in good faith, notwithstanding the fact that the manager of the newspaper for which he worked was convicted of defamation.[88]

The 6 May 1944 *Ordonnance* greatly broadened the extent to which the *exceptio veritatis* may be invoked. The "truth exception" may now be implemented in all cases, except those involving the right to privacy, facts dating back more than 10 years, and offences which have been pardoned, lapsed or have given rise to sentences which were pardoned or revised.[89] It is now possible for a defamer to justify his acts by invoking good faith and the *exceptio veritatis*, either together or separately, depending on the case.

When the facts in question are more than 10 years old, the flexible "good faith" principle may be invoked to discharge the defamer. The *Cour de Cassation* has clearly stressed that even if the accused cannot prove the truth of a defamatory utterance, he may establish his good faith by other means.[90] Furthermore, as the conditions for admitting the *exceptio veritatis* are particularly strict, especially with regard to the statute of limitations and rules of evidence, the good faith defence is often raised secondarily.

Note that when the *exceptio veritatis* is allowed, even when it results in the acquittal of the defamer, his civil liability may still be raised in relation to other torts, particularly if the incriminating behaviour amounts to an abuse of the freedom to criticise.

Conditions of application

The criteria for applying the *exceptio veritatis* are relatively strict. They are **4.70** enumerated in both article 35, which deals with the substantive rules, and in article 55, which provides procedural rules.

---

87. Seine Trib. Civ., 26 March 1926.

88. Cass. crim., 30 December 1904.

89. LFP, article 35.

90. Cass. crim., 15 February 1962.

167

As these criteria are a matter of public policy, their non-fulfilment may be raised for the first time at the appellate level or before the *Cour de Cassation.* Judges are also entitled to record any non-fulfilment of these criteria on their own initiative.

Substantive rules

Exceptio veritatis and defamation of individuals

4.71 Following the adoption of the *Ordonnance* (Executive Order) of 6 May 1944, certain scholars and judges considered that the LFP only accepted the *exceptio veritatis* as a defence with regard to the first two paragraphs of article 35, *i.e.*, defamation related to "legal entities, the Army, the Navy and the Air Force, official entities and persons listed in article 31" such as civil servants, public officials, etc. Case law over the years has taken a more liberal approach based on article 35(3), which states that, except in certain specific cases, "the truth of defamatory statements may always be proved", so as to admit that the *exceptio veritatis* is available in all defamation cases, including cases involving individuals.

Evidence of the truth of the facts is admissible even if the facts involve an individual and the defamation was committed in the press or by any other means. Applying this broader approach, the *Cour de Cassation* must vacate:

> ". . . decisions which, far from seeking to know whether the imputations fell under one of the exceptions whereby evidence of the truth is not admitted as a defence, held that the effect of the Ordonnance of 6 May 1944 was not to legitimise evidence of the truth of the facts, other than in the cases dealt with in the first two paragraphs of article 35".[91]

4.72 Significantly, proof of the truth of otherwise defamatory statements or facts is now admitted in both criminal and civil proceedings.[92]

Complete, absolute and irreproachable evidence

4.73 Evidence as to the truth of a defamatory imputation must be "complete and absolute and correspond to the full scope of the imputations".[93]

---

91. Cass. crim., 12 October 1954.

92. Cass. civ. 2e, 4 November 1988.

93. Cass. crim., 16 March 1948.

Objectivity and need for the information

A critic, even when he can prove the truth of the facts alleged, must not   **4.74**
surpass their actual scope. For instance, the Paris *Tribunal Correctionnel* has
penalised a consumers' association for having called a producer a "thief",
when he could only be blamed for having infringed the applicable
economic and sanitary regulations.[94] On the other hand, judges may
exhibit leniency when there is an imperious need to inform the public.
The Paris *Cour d'Appel*, for example, decided to dismiss a case against a
journalist "when the purpose of the information seemed serious and
legitimate enough to justify the means".[95]

Faithful to its precedents, the Paris *Cour d'Appel* has also held that the:

> "National Consumer Institute (INC) did not overstep the task to inform
> the public entrusted to it by the legislature when, in one of its magazine
> articles and in radio and television programmes, the defects of cameras
> were carefully presented, without excess and without the intent to dispar-
> age, since the INC is not bound to provide the public with merely neutral
> data consisting exclusively of figures, but may enlighten its readers by
> pointing out in simple, direct and unambiguous evaluations, the products'
> characteristics".[96]

Non-public defamation

It seems that the LFP did not envisage the application of *exceptio veritatis*   **4.75**
to cases of non-public defamation. Non-public defamation is likened to
non-public injurious insult and has been classified as a minor offence
under article R 621–1 of the Criminal Code. This unfortunate oversight
is nevertheless mitigated in certain cases by the possibility of avoiding a
criminal sanction by invoking the exculpatory excuse of provocation.

However, in a 24 April 1973 decision, the Paris *Tribunal de Grande
Instance* raised the *exceptio veritatis* in a non-public defamation case. This
apparently unique judgment stated:

> ". . . the admission of such evidence cannot be refused solely on the basis
> that the statements were not public, since this defamation is intrinsically
> susceptible of evidence to the contrary and article 35 contains no provi-
> sions forbidding evidence of the truth of non-public defamatory facts".

---

94. 18 November 1981.

95. Paris *Cour d'Appel*, 5 May 1948.

96. 4 December 1985.

Judges' role

4.76 Judges should not search for proof of the truth of the facts alleged.[97] They have no power to supplement or perfect the method of evidence which the law leaves solely to the accused to provide, while regulating its conditions of admission.[98]

It has been held that in inquiring as to whether the allegedly defamatory facts are true or false, an instructing judge (*Juge d'instruction*) exceeds his authority.[99] Thus, such a judge's scope of activities is narrower than usual since the *Code de Procédure Pénale* (Criminal Procedure Code) generally authorises him to carry on "all proceedings deemed useful to reveal the truth".[100]

The trial judges have the sovereign duty to infer from documents and testimony the justifying circumstances asserted by the accused and:

"... the Cour de Cassation must corroborate whether the said judges drew all the deductions that were implied from their findings, and whether their motives are free of deficiency and contradiction".[101]

Formalities

4.77 Certain provisions impose formalities that must be strictly complied with for a defamer to avail himself of the *exceptio veritatis*.
Article 55 stipulates that:

"... when the accused wishes proof of the truth of the defamatory facts to be admitted, in accordance with article 35 of the LFP, he must within 10 days of service of the summons, serve his answer on the public prosecutor or the plaintiff, at their chosen domicile, depending on who initiated the summons, which includes:

"(1) The facts, the truth of which he intends to prove, as stated and characterised in the summons;
"(2) Copies of his documentary evidence; and
"(3) The names, occupations and addresses of the witnesses he intends to call."

---

97. Cass. crim., 5 November 1963.
98. Cass. crim., 21 November 1989.
99. Cass. crim., 4 November 1986.
100. Article 81, paragraph 1.
101. Cass. crim., 20 December 1966.

This answer must elect domicile to be the *Tribunal Correctionnel*, "under **4.78** penalty of losing the right to prove the truth".

Article 55 is inseverable from article 56, which states:

". . . within the following five days, and at least three full days before the hearing, the plaintiff or the public prosecutor, depending on the case, must serve the defendant, at his chosen domicile, with copies of his documentary evidence and the names, occupations and addresses of the witnesses he intends to call to offer contradictory proof, under penalty of losing this right".

These two articles lay down specific and complex regulations which are a **4.79** matter of public policy. Non-compliance with these rules must automatically be recorded by the judges; violation thereof may be raised for the first time before the *Cour de Cassation*.

Evidence

On the grounds of *exceptio veritatis*, the accused is entitled to use and **4.80** produce only evidence in the form of written documents and oral testimony. These documents and testimony must normally date back to before the defamation; proof of acts which occurred between the date of defamation and service of the summons as provided in article 55 of the LFP has, however, been admitted in exceptional cases.[102] The accused may not use as proof facts or elements which have occurred after the act giving rise to the suit.[103]

In no case may the accused adduce means of proof other than those listed in articles 55 and 56. Even the plaintiff's admission of the allegation's truth is insufficient to allow the accused to establish his good faith and "these circumstances cannot dispense the accused from complying with the applicable legal procedure provided to establish it".[104]

Time limit

Failure to comply with the 10-day period described above, which is a **4.81** matter of public policy, will deprive the accused of the possibility to

---

102. Cass. crim., 17 December 1979.

103. Cass. crim., 24 October 1989.

104. Cass. crim., 5 November 1970.

prove the truth of the facts, except in the event of *force majeure*. The *Cour de Cassation* has clearly stated that:

> "... having neglected to serve his answer as provided by article 55 of the LFP, in the legally allotted time, the accused loses his right to furnish the Court with proof of the truth of the defamatory fact; as a result, defamation must be punished, without regard to whether the statements were true or false".[105]

4.82 The 10-day period which is granted to the accused for serving the plaintiff or the public prosecutor with the means of proof he intends to use cannot be extended; distance of the defendant from the place of suit, for example, is not a valid reason for extension.[106] Courts have considered that the period should not, moreover, be measured in full 24-hour days;[107] for example, service cannot take place on the 11th day, even when the 10th day is a holiday.

The date of the first summons to appear in court is used as the period's starting date. As a consequence, if one party is absent and is not represented by counsel or omits to disclose his answer,[108] or decides to oppose a judgment handed down in his absence,[109] the time period will not be renewed, nor will it be in the case of a transfer of the proceedings.

Because this time limit is a matter of public policy, the judge may invoke it himself; and failure to comply with this time limit requirement may be raised for the first time even at the level of the *Cour de Cassation*.

Due hearing of the parties

4.83 Unlike usual procedure, proof of the truth in defamation cases can result only from due hearing of the parties and not from elements provided by the pre-trial investigation of the case. The hearing may consider only properly served documents, and oral testimony only of the witnesses whose names and addresses were communicated during the 10-day period starting on the day of the summons.[110]

Article 55 of the LFP strictly limits the debate to the elements properly served. In no case may judges consider evidence which has not been properly served, even when it arises from well-known facts.[111]

---

105. 6 March 1952.

106. Cass. crim., 24 June 1986.

107. Cass. crim., 2 August 1884.

108. *Procédure par défaut — in absentia.*

109. *Procédure d'opposition.* Opposition to a default judgment involves challenging the judgment in front of the same judge who issued it, to insure that the new ruling encompasses factual as well as legal issues.

110. Paris Court of Appeal, 27 January 1988.

111. Cass. crim., 20 May 1954.

Obligation to put forward precise facts and to characterise the defamation

Facts stated by the accused and of which he intends to prove the truth **4.84** must be precisely defined. The *Cour de Cassation* has stated:

> "Article 55 of the Law of 29 July 1881 requires that the accused precisely state the facts set forth and characterised in the summons, the truth of which he intends to prove. This specification is necessary even though the accused intends to prove all the facts indicated in the quotation under scrutiny. This is an essential formality which must be complied with, under penalty of losing the right to prove the truth".[112]

Contradictory evidence by the victim

The offer of proof produced by the accused in the 10-day time limit may **4.85** be followed by contradictory evidence, at the discretion of the private party claiming damages or by the public prosecutor himself.[113] This counter evidence allows the victim to demonstrate bad faith and malicious intent on the part of the accused. It must be produced within five days following notification of the accused's offer of proof.

This time period may not be extended under any circumstances. Items of evidence produced by the plaintiff may not be used against him as proof of the truth of the allegation deemed defamatory and thus may not discharge the defamer.[114]

The good faith defense

An accused who fails to comply with the strict conditions of article 55 but **4.86** who may avail himself of one of the three cases provided by article 35 of the LFP (violation of the right to privacy, facts dating back more than 10 years, pardoned or lapsed offences) may still attempt to establish his good faith in accordance with the customary processes of law.

The possibility of invoking the good faith defence somewhat alleviates the rigidity of articles 55 and 56 of the LFP. For example, the *Cour de Cassation* has expressly recognised the possibility of an accused using documents more than 10 years old to establish his good faith.[115]

---

112. Cass. crim., 29 November 1994.

113. LEP, article 35.

114. Cass. crim., 20 May 1954.

115. Cass. civ., 29 June 1988.

Control by the Cour de Cassation

4.87   While trial judges are sovereign with regard to the evaluation of documents and testimony submitted to them, the *Cour de Cassation* still verifies that:

> ". . . they clearly stated to what extent the circumstances were established, whether they accurately assessed their correlation to the defamatory imputations and whether they properly conducted the evidentiary procedure".[116]

4.88   The supervision of the *Cour de Cassation* is limited to an essentially extrinsic control. It evaluates the nature and significance of the writings which are submitted to it, and determines whether the writings or utterances constitute injurious insult or defamation.[117]

Exclusion of the exceptio veritatis

4.89   Since promulgation of the *Ordonnance* of 6 May 1944, the *exceptio veritatis* may always be invoked except, as stipulated in article 35:

> ". . . where the imputation refers to the person's private life, dates back more than 10 years, or establishes a lapsed offence or a conviction which was eradicated by rehabilitation or on retrial".

4.90   The cases where the *exceptio veritatis* may not be invoked are not limited to criminal trials, but also include cases for civil liability.

Imputations concerning private life

4.91   Case law in general tends to hold that information which may have political, economic or social consequences falls into the public domain and may be revealed without fear. Where it is considered that information concerns both public and private life, judges have admitted the possibility to invoke the *exceptio veritatis*.

This approach remains vague, however, and the courts are frequently called on to decide whether the facts presented to them are matters of private or public life. The possibility to invoke the *exceptio veritatis* depends on this distinction.

To make this distinction, courts often take into account the type of person who has allegedly been defamed. Courts tend to be more

---

116. Cass. crim., 5 December 1952.
117. Cass. crim., 15 June 1984.

lenient when a well-known person, such as a movie star or a famous singer, has been the target of defamation.

Nevertheless, allegations of cohabitation,[118] homosexuality[119] or prostitution in a private apartment[120] have consistently been considered invasions of privacy.

Facts dating back more than 10 years

Facts dating back more than 10 years or relating to an offence which has **4.92** been pardoned or has lapsed, or which has given rise to a conviction which was discharged or was retried, are allotted a special status which normally precludes the possibility to invoke the *exceptio veritatis*; this results from the legislative intent to maintain law and order while allowing for pardon and forgetting.

Legal immunities

The Law provides for immunity with regard to defamation, in the following **4.93** cases:

(1) Immunity for parliamentary speeches and reports;
(2) Immunity for minutes of public political meetings;
(3) Immunity for reports on court hearings and the publication of legal decisions; and
(4) Immunity for speeches and writings submitted to the courts.

Parliamentary speeches and reports

Article 41 of the LFP states that: **4.94**

> ". . . no cause of action shall arise from speeches made in the National Assembly or the Senate, or from reports or any other matter printed on behalf of either parliamentary body".

---

118. Bourges Court of Appeal, 30 October 1945.
119. Paris Court of Appeal, 20 February 1986.
120. Paris, 30 May 1988.

4.95　This immunity has a perpetual and absolute character. It benefits not only members of Parliament but also any other person called to intervene in the course of the debates or before parliamentary commissions. Within this context, the author of defamatory allegations will not be held legally accountable therefor.

　　This immunity only extends exclusively to function-related acts. Moreover, it does not extend to speeches given before other types of assemblies, such as deliberations of the Economic and Social Council or municipal or regional Councils.

Minutes of public political meetings

4.96　Article 41 of the LFP leaves total freedom to the press to report on parliamentary debates, on the condition that the reported discussions not be deformed or interpreted and that the various opinions expressed be related objectively.

　　Aside from the above restriction, journalists have total freedom as to the form and style used in their reports.

Reports on court hearings and the publication of legal decisions

4.97　Article 41(3) specifies that:

> "... no cause of action in defamation or injurious insult shall arise from accurate summaries [of court hearings] recorded in good faith, speeches made or written documents produced before the Courts".

4.98　This immunity is conditioned on the objectivity and good faith of the journalists' summaries which must present the views expressed by the opposing parties in an unbiased manner. It does not extend to cases on which it is forbidden to report, such as defamation, paternity, child support, alimony and divorce cases, nor does it extend to *in camera* proceedings.

Speeches and writings submitted to the courts

4.99　The immunity for speeches and writings submitted to the courts[121] extends to the parties, their representatives or counsel. Judges are excluded, but benefit from a specific form of immunity due to their office.

　　For parties and their counsel to benefit from this immunity, the otherwise defamatory statements or writings must be made or submitted before

---

121. LFP, article 41(3).

the judges in charge of the case and while the case is still pending. This immunity does not extend to defamatory facts alien to the case in question.

When statements in court or writings submitted to the court overstep the acceptable bounds of freedom of expression and due process, article 41 authorises the court to order the party making injurious speeches to pay damages.

The Law of 15 June 1982 removed from judges their option to suspend temporarily a defaming attorney for a maximum of two months, or six months in the event of a subsequent offence.

At present, attorneys risk disciplinary proceedings before the *Conseil de l'Ordre* (bar association disciplinary committee), where the public prosecutor or the injured party's attorney files a claim for in-court defamatory or injurious utterances.

Specific cases of defamation

Specific rules and penalties apply to defamation with regard to the **4.100** particular persons, groups or institutions referred to below. All other cases of defamation towards individuals or groups having legal status must comply with the rules previously discussed.

Defamation of the courts, the military, official entities and public administrations

According to article 30 of the LFP: **4.101**

> ". . . an act of defamation committed against the courts, tribunals, public entities, the Army, naval and air forces, official entities, and the public administration, will be punished by imprisonment ranging from eight days to one and a half years and/or a fine ranging from FRF 300 to FRF 30,000".

This applies to all courts of law, including civil, administrative and **4.102** exceptional jurisdictions. Proceedings may be initiated by an executive committee meeting of the entity which has been the subject of the defamation.

As regards defamation related to the military, only the Minister of Defence is empowered to file a claim.

As the LFP does not define "public entities", a definition has been given by case law. These are "permanent national bodies exercising part of the national authority and which may, at any time, hold general meetings".[122] The National Assembly, the Senate, the Ministers' Council and Town Councils are included in this category.

As regards the "public administration", only entities enjoying "public prerogatives' power" can be considered to be a part thereof. For this reason, a savings and loan association, the *caisse d'epargne*, is not considered to be part of the public administration.[123] The distinction between the public administration and public entities is that entities belonging to the public administration cannot hold general meetings.

In all the cases provided for by article 30, for a statement to be held defamatory, it must necessarily designate the victim with precision and be linked to the institution concerned.

When the target is a private individual, article 30 proceedings are not applicable.

Injurious insults are dealt with by article 33(1):

> ". . . insulting remarks made by the same means to bodies or persons designated in article 30 and 31 of this Law will be punished by imprisonment ranging from six days to three months and/or a fine ranging from FRF 150 to FRF 80,000".

Defamation of a member of a ministry or of one of the Houses of Parliament or a civil servant

4.103 Article 31 of the LFP states:

> ". . . defamation committed by the same means, based on their offices or capacity, of one or more members of a Ministry; one or more members of either House; a civil servant; a public servant or official; a minister of a State-subsidised religion; a citizen charged with a public service or authority, whether temporary or permanent; or a juror or a witness, based on his testimony, will be subject to the same penalty as provided in article 30".

4.104 While these defamation victims have in common that they are all part of the public authority, they still need to be carefully distinguished from each other.

---

122. Cass. crim., 8 March 1955.
123. Cass. crim., 10 February 1883.

The qualification as "public person" is not sufficient to define the capacity and functions of the person concerned. The *Cour de Cassation* has clearly stated that in applying article 31:

> ". . . it is necessary to recall the precise terms of the quoted text, which must be narrowly interpreted since it relates to a criminal matter, and in addition, to a limited list of persons having a public character and protected as such. By using in his writings the general and imprecise character of 'public person', the private plaintiff failed to specify which of the varied and different characters referred to by the law he intended to mention, thereby failing to establish the misdemeanour".[124]

4.105 The cases generally hold that article 31 deals with defamation involving acts accomplished by the victim in the course of his employment, and the abuses of position he might have committed. These actions are evaluated, not from the point of view of any underlying motive or the author's intention, but with respect to their subject matters.[125]

According to Henri Guillot, *Avocat Général* for the Paris Court of Appeal, "public servant" or "official" means:

> ". . . either the officials belonging to a government office and who exercise official duties, or individuals holding the title of public official and who could be classed in the category of citizens responsible for a public service if their legal status does not give them a narrower role in the public administration".

4.106 Police officers, members of the military and constables fall into this category.

Case law has progressively applied the term "citizen responsible for a public service" to any person who is vested with some public authority, however insubstantial.

For example, case law has decided that mayors, town council members, sworn officials of the SNCF (French national railroad) and sworn highway and road authorities fall into this category. On the other hand, the president of a departmental hunting federation, attorneys and town clerks have been excluded from this status.

The jurors referred to in article 31 are exclusively those who are under oath and testify at a *Cour d'Assises* proceeding (criminal courts of original and appellate jurisdiction).

As for the "witnesses" covered by article 31, these include only witnesses who have been sworn in to testify in an actual proceeding; the

---

124. 20 November 1985.

125. Cass. crim., 16 December 1986.

witnesses heard by investigators in a police matter are not protected by article 31, because they have not been sworn in.[126]

In the event utterances or writings contain charges of both a public and private nature, doctrine holds that article 31 nonetheless applies where those charges cannot be separated without deforming them. It is thus the public nature of the defamation which would prevail.

Defamation based on ethnic origin, nationality, race or religion

4.107 Article 32(2) of the LFP provides:

> "[Defamation] of a person or group of persons based on origin or non-membership in an ethnic group, nation, race or recognised religion will be punished by imprisonment of one month to a year and/or a fine of FRF 300 to FRF 300,000".

4.108 This offence was added to the LFP in 1972, in the hope of providing an effective response to new causes of public disturbance and threats to both individual and State security. Until that time, only the concepts of race and religion had been covered by article 32.

In application of article 32 as modified, the High Court of Meaux has held on 5 July 1990 that the act of writing an article denying the existence of gas chambers and genocide perpetrated by Nazis during World War II constituted defamation of a group of persons based on their ethnic origin and religion.

On the other hand, the Paris Court of Appeal has specifically stated that:

> ". . . the act of denouncing the arrogance of young French people of North African origin and of asserting that they seem to benefit from impunity and privileges did not harm their honour. This is also true of the references to their violent behaviour during a demonstration, as this did not target all young French people of North African origin".[127]

4.109 An action may be instituted by the *Ministère Public* (Department of the Public Prosecutor) without any preliminary action on the part of the person or group of persons which was the subject of the defamation.

Moreover, an association which has been in existence for at least five years as of the date of the alleged defamation, and whose stated purpose is to fight racism, may be a civil party to the action, on the condition that it obtains the consent of the person who has been specifically targeted.

---

126. CA Paris, 23 February 1883.

127. CA Paris, 30 January 1991.

Article 32 also provides that in the event of conviction in any of the cases mentioned in its paragraph 2, the court may order the posting or the publication of its decision or the insertion of a *communiqué* in the newspaper or periodical at fault.

Finally, article 33(3) provides that the maximum penalties for injurious insult based on ethnic origin, nationality, race or religion are imprisonment of up to six months and a fine of up to FRF 150,000.

Defamation of the memory of the deceased

According to article 34 of the LFP: **4.110**

"Articles 31, 32 and 33 are only applicable to defamation or injurious insult of the memory of the deceased intended to taint the honour or reputation of the living legal heirs, spouses or sole legatees".

To establish the misdemeanour described by article 34, three conditions **4.111** must be fulfilled:

(1) The elements necessary to constitute the misdemeanour of defamation must be fulfilled, thus rendering articles 31, 32 and 33 applicable;
(2) The attacks on the memory of the deceased must taint the honour and reputation of those living; and
(3) The defamer must have intended to harm the heirs, spouses or sole legatees via the defamation of the memory of the deceased. This element is indispensable. According to case law, "the misdemeanour of article 34 can only be constituted if there is at least a direct or indirect allusion made to a living heir; this is achieved only if the author of the article intended to and did taint the honour and the reputation of the living heirs".[128]

The deceased's character

The characterisation of the offence must be determined in consideration **4.112** of the personal situation, character and position of the deceased during his lifetime, and not those of his survivors.

In the event of defamation prior to the victim's death, the heirs may only pursue a defamation action if the deceased had instituted such action during his lifetime.

---

128. Cass. crim., 22 March 1960.

Nature of action

4.113 The survivors have no grounds for a defamation action as mere representatives or heirs of the deceased. The action is personal to them based on a wrong which has been done to them due to "a solidarity of honour uniting the members of a family beyond the grave".[129]

The offence is not established where the defamatory writing or utterance not only failed to mention the heir, but made no allusion, even indirectly, to him.[130]

If the survivors themselves are targeted by the charges, either openly or by insinuation, and not the deceased, who only serves as a pretext, article 34 will no longer apply; depending on the case, either article 31, article 32 or article 33 will be applicable.

The heirs may bring a civil action for defamation of the deceased either in addition to or in conjunction with the public prosecution. However, where the defamatory charges are related to the deceased's character and position prior to his death, a civil action may only be accessory to the public prosecutor's case.[131] The civil court's lack of jurisdiction in this regard is a matter of public policy.[132]

Right to respond

4.114 In addition to the classic penalties, article 34(2) offers heirs, spouses and sole legatees the right to respond to defamatory charges in "newspapers" and "written periodicals".[133]

Procedural considerations

4.115 The rules of procedure which govern defamation are stringent and restrictive, and often deviate from customary law.

---

129. Trib. Civ. Seine, 12 June 1902.

130. Cass. crim., 22 March 1960.

131. LFP, article 46.

132. Cass. civ., 26 June 1922.

133. This right to respond is not particular to defamation of the memory of the deceased or defamation in general; LFP, article 13 notes that the right to respond is accorded to "any person named or described in a newspaper or periodical". It is independent of the public prosecutor's suit or a civil action based on an injurious insult or defamation (CA Paris, 21 April 1976). It must be exercised within one year of the day of publication; it is the person who was the subject of the attack who must establish its form and content. Article 13(4) sets out the extent of the right of response, which should theoretically be "limited to the length of the article which induced it". Victims of defamation, independently of the repressive measures offered by the LFP, and the general principles of civil liability set forth in the Civil Code, may thus always assert their right to respond.

Criminal jurisdictions

Public prosecution

Subject matter jurisdiction

The *Cour d'Assises* formerly had jurisdiction over matters of defamation. **4.116** Given, however, an increasing tendency toward the "correctionalisation" of defamation,[134] the Executive Order of 6 May 1944 granted jurisdiction over all press matters to the *Tribunal Correctionnel* (lower criminal court) except, according to article 45, with regard to inducements to commit the felonies and misdemeanours listed in article 23 of the LFP.

Territorial jurisdiction

The court with territorial jurisdiction over matters relating to defamation **4.117** is the relevant court for the place where the offence was committed. When defamation is committed by means of the press or audio-visual aids, the offence is said to have been established wherever the writing or broadcast was received. If the defamation was committed by letter or telephone, the place of the offence is where the letter or the telephone call was received.

With regard to defamation committed by means of the international press or television programmes or radio broadcasts received in several countries, French case law on private international law holds that the legal jurisdiction of the place of damage must take precedence over that of the act generating the offence. The Paris Court of Appeal has declared that:

"... the most appropriate means of determining the legal relationship, in the event where the place of the guilty deed and that of the damage are different, is the law of the place where the damage happened".

In the event where the defamation has effect in several countries, the laws **4.118** of those two countries must be applied.[135]

---

134. "Correctionalisation" consists of deeming an act which is actually a felony to be a misdemeanour, thereby removing it from the jurisdiction of the *Cour d'Assises* to that of the *Tribunal Correctionnel*. This deviation by custom from legally established jurisdictional rules may only take place with the consent of the victim, the accused and the relevant *Tribunal Correctionnel*. Although not legally proper, this practice is accepted and even in some cases ratified by the law.

135. CA Paris, 7 March 1988.

Institution of a case by the public prosecutor

Statute of limitations

4.119 Based on article 65 of the LFP, the statute of limitations for a defamation action is three months beginning on the date the offence is committed or the date of the last act of pursuance of legal proceedings.[136]

This statute of limitations applies to all press offences covered by the LFP. The brevity of the period is a matter of public policy,[137] and therefore non-compliance with the statute of limitations may be raised at any level of the proceedings; the victim is not presumed to have waived his rights to do so on the grounds that he did not invoke the statute of limitations at the level of the first instance trial.[138]

Calculation of the period

4.120 The statute of limitations period is calculated from the date the defamation is committed to exactly three months later, not on a basis of three times 30 days.[139] If a daily paper is published on 13 February, the statute of limitations will have run as of 13 May. No extension is made if the latter date falls on a holiday.

The starting date for the statute in respect of writings is the date of their publication, that is, the date they are in fact offered to the public. In the case of a book, for example, defamation is committed on the date of initial publication, not the last date on which the book is offered for sale.[140] When a book issued in several successive editions is said to contain defamatory comments, the statute of limitations begins to run as of the first date of issue of each edition.[141] Each edition or reprinting thus has a separate three-month statute of limitations.

When defamation is committed by means of a periodical, the statute begins to run as of the actual date of publication, defined as the date on which the periodical is made available to the public, not the fictitious date on the cover which may have a purely commercial purpose.[142] The Paris High Court has held, however, that when a newspaper bears a publication date, this date should be considered to be the actual date of publication with regard to third parties as well as the public prosecutor.[143]

---

136. Cass. civ. 2e, 27 February 1991; Cass. civ. 2e, 17 March 1993.
137. Cass. civ., 25 May 1971.
138. Paris, 25 April 1969.
139. Cass. crim., 1 June 1953.
140. Cass. crim., 5 January 1974.
141. Cass. crim., 8 January 1991.
142. CA Paris, 28 January 1977.
143. *Tribunal de Grande Instance* Paris, 7 July 1987.

The High Courts hold that it is the first act of publication which must be taken into account. If a publication bears two dates, the statute of limitations begins to run as from the first of such dates.[144]

Where a magazine bears the dates of the beginning and end of the week, the judges will use that of the beginning of the week. For a monthly magazine, the statute begins running as of the first day of the month.

When pamphlets are used as the means of defamation, the statute of limitations must generally be determined as from the date of the first publication of the pamphlet concerned.[145]

The statute begins to run even if the victim does not or cannot yet know of the offence.[146]

The statute of limitations may be interrupted or suspended in certain circumstances.

Interruption must result from the unequivocal desire of the public prosecutor or the plaintiff to achieve the acts necessary to preserve his rights. Interruptive acts include the public prosecutor's indictment,[147] investigatory acts (hearings, interrogatories, letters rogatory), complaints by parties joining the action and claiming damages, direct summonses, even made before a judge lacking jurisdiction,[148] and properly made notifications of a decision of the criminal division of the *Cour de Cassation* transferring the case to a new jurisdiction.[149]

On the other hand, non-interruptive acts include mere complaints, the deposit of a sum of money with the clerk of the court or[150] minutes of declarations whose purpose is to gather information or made in the context of a preliminary investigation ordered based on a complaint.[151]

The statute of limitations in a public prosecutor's action will be suspended when there is a legal obstacle or an insurmountable impossibility which prevent the plaintiff from acting.

This would be the case, for example, of a request for a new trial to the court of appeals[152] or in the case of parliamentary immunity when the trial judge failed to accomplish the interruptory acts in the time allotted and when it has been established that it was impossible for the victim-plaintiff to take action.[153]

---

144. *Tribunal de Grande Instance* Paris, 27 June 1985.

145. Cass. crim., 2 October 1990.

146. Cass. crim., 23 October 1978; Cass. crim., 1 December 1981.

147. Cass. crim., 11 October 1961.

148. Cass. crim., 29 November 1955.

149. Cass. crim., 6 May 1986.

150. Cass. crim., 4 March 1971.

151. Cass. crim., 30 October 1989.

152. Cass. crim., 19 April 1983.

153. Cass. crim., 27 October 1987.

The statute will not be suspended due to the facts that the accused was a minor,[154] his ignorance of the offence[155] or the lack of action by the public prosecutor, because the victim could have interrupted the running of the statute by directly summoning the accused.[156]

Limits on public prosecution

4.121 The prosecution of defamation committed by means of the press or any other means will automatically be pursued on the request of the public prosecutor.[157]

Article 48 creates six exceptions, which require the prior filing of a complaint for the commencement of a defamation action:

(1) In the event of injurious insult or defamation of the courts, tribunals and other entities, prosecution will take place only on request after deliberation in an executive committee meeting. Where the entity in question has no executive committee, the head or minister of the entity must file the complaint;

(2) For injurious insult or defamation of one or more members of a House of Parliament, the prosecution must be initiated by one of the persons involved;

(3) For injurious insult or defamation of civil servants, a public servant or official or citizens responsible for a public service or authority, prosecution must be initiated by the interested parties or ministers who have been the subject thereof;

(4) In the event of defamation of a juror or witness, the person involved must file suit;

(5) For offences involving foreign heads of state or their diplomats, these persons must file a complaint with the Ministry of Foreign Affairs, who will forward it to the Ministry of Justice; and

(6) Finally, prosecution of defamation of individuals must be instigated by the person involved.

4.122 Once a properly filed complaint has been brought before him, the French public prosecutor has the choice of instituting a trial, proceeding by direct summons or dismissing the complaint. The plaintiff always has the possibility of joining the case or directly summoning the accused.

---

154. *Tribunal de Grande Instance* Seine, 22 May 1964.

155. Cass. crim., 22 March 1890.

156. Cass. crim., 2 December 1986.

157. LFP, article 47.

Private prosecution

Individual victims of defamation also have the option of instituting a civil **4.123**
suit in accordance with the principles of customary law (article 32(1)).
The same is true for cases of injurious insults.

Other specific victims of defamation have no choice:

> "A civil suit arising from defamation as provided for and punishable by
> articles 30 and 31 may not, except in the event of the death or pardon of
> the author of the charges, be prosecuted separately from the public
> prosecution . . ."

(article 46 of the LFP).   **4.124**

Articulation of the offense

If the public prosecutor instigates an action, he is required to set forth **4.125**
and characterise the defamation by citing the applicable texts in his
indictment instituting the case (article 50 of the LFP).[158] The statement
of the case consists of a detailed written presentation of the passages likely
to constitute defamation. It is not necessary that the writing be reproduced in its entirety in the indictment, but only that the key passages be
supplied.[159] Failure of the prosecutor properly to characterise the alleged
defamation will result in the action being definitively dismissed.

Characterization

To further the prosecution, the complaint joining the party claiming **4.126**
damages must also fulfil requirements exorbitant of customary law
imposed by article 50. The victim must state and characterise the charges
in his complaint in the most detailed and complete possible manner. He
is considered bound by this characterisation and may not subsequently
amend it. The instructing judge is also bound thereby.

---

158. Article 50 states: "If the public prosecutor instigates an action, he must, in his indictment, set out and
characterise the provocations, outrageous comments, defamation and injurious insults whose prosecution is
being undertaken, indicating the texts whose application is requested, under penalty of having the prosecution
dismissed".

159. Cass. crim., 17 March 1981.

It is not unusual for defamation to be mixed with injurious utterances. Where injurious insult and defamation are indistinguishable, the courts must give priority to defamation over injurious insult.[160]

Deeds may not, therefore, be characterised as "defamatory or injurious"[161] or as "defamatory or at least injurious",[162] under penalty of rejection by the court.

Defamatory utterances may also constitute the misdemeanour of false accusation (*dénonciation calomnieuse*). In such a case, it is the offence of false accusation which would be accepted[163] because false accusation carries heavier penalties.[164]

Similarly, an alleged defamation will be subsumed in a prosecution for violation of a professional secret to the extent that the two concepts overlap, since the latter is punishable by heavier penalties, *i.e.*, one year of imprisonment and/or a penalty of FRF 100,000.[165]

Liability for defamation

4.127 According to article 23 of the LFP, directors of publications are held liable for offences committed through the press. They may be held liable not only for writings but also for drawings, images or emblems which are publicly diffused.

This liability does not exclude accomplice liability on the part of other participants in the offence. Articles 42, 43 and 44 of the LFP establish a chain of liability, starting with the director of the publication and ending with sellers, distributors and those who post notices.

Directors or editors of publications are first in order of liability, followed by authors, then printers, sellers, distributors and those who post notices. As a result of this chain of liability, when directors are held liable, authors may only be prosecuted as accomplices. In the

---

160. Trib. Corr. Melun, 14 June 1982.

161. Cass. crim., 3 June 1982.

162. Cass. crim., 26 June 1984.

163. Bourges, 1 August 1883.

164. New Criminal Code, article 226–10: "Accusation, effected by any means and directed against a particular person, of an act which is such as could lead to judicial, administrative or disciplinary sanctions and which is known to be either wholly or partially inaccurate, when it is made against either an officer of the court, a police or security officer, or an authority having the power to pursue it or to present the case to the authority having jurisdiction, either the hierarchical superiors or the accused's employer, is punishable by five years' imprisonment and a FRF 300,000 fine".

165. New Criminal Code, article 226–13.

meaning of the Law of 1881, journalists are liable for their writings, words, drawings, etc., only as accomplices.[166]

In the case of defamation through the press by an individual who is not a journalist, the individual's liability will be that of principal author of the offence, rather than an accomplice thereto.

Civil procedure

Inseparable civil action and public prosecution

In principle, a civil action for damages is autonomous of the prosecution **4.128** in a criminal case. A civil defamation action may, therefore, be initiated separately, except when it is based on the defamatory misdemeanours as described in articles 30 and 31 of the Law; in those rare cases, civil courts completely lack jurisdiction.

Civil court jurisdiction

Where a complaint for defamation is properly filed in civil court, the **4.129** provisions established in the Code of Civil Procedure apply, with the exception of the statute of limitations. The specific statute of limitations provided by the LFP remains applicable.

However, proceedings may, alternatively, be instituted in civil courts based on article 9 (violation of privacy) or articles 1382 and 1383 (general tort principles) of the Civil Code; in such cases, it would be unnecessary to comply with the criteria applicable to the misdemeanour of defamation, including the brief statute of limitations.

Faced with the brief statute of limitations and the complexity of the procedure provided by the LFP, victims of defamation thus often prefer to rely on the above provisions of the Civil Code.

Other grounds for potential liability

In addition to the general principles of tort liability set forth in articles **4.130** 1382 and 1383 of the Civil Code, liability of the media may frequently be based on false news misdemeanours and violation of right to privacy.

---

166. In French law, accomplice liability is not distinguishable in terms of liability *per se* since the liability of the principal will be the same as that of the accomplice. The distinction, however, is interesting, because in certain cases the sentence may differ even when offences are similar.

False news misdemeanors

4.131 The Law of 1881 also deals with publication of false news or distortion of information. Moreover, the criminal law has dealt with these issues through various means. For instance, article 433 of the Law of 24 July 1966 on commercial companies[167] punishes the publication of false news aimed at obtaining subscriptions to securities or deposits of funds; article L97 of the Electoral Code[168] punishes publications likely to mislead voters, or cause abstention during election time.

The Paris Court of Appeal has sentenced to one-year imprisonment, on the basis of article 322–14 of the Criminal Code,[169] an individual who during the 1995 terrorist bombings gave false alarm by making several anonymous phone calls to the police.[170]

As for the Law of 1881 itself, article 27 punishes:

> ". . . publication or reproduction by any means whatsoever, of false news, of fabricated, forged or falsely attributed items, when, if carried out in bad faith, it has disturbed the peace, or would have been likely to disturb the peace . . ."

4.132 as well as false information "of a nature to weaken discipline or morale of the armed forces". This article strictly defines the conditions for the application of the misdemeanour of false news, which is constituted only if the following four elements are present:

(1) False news;
(2) Liable to disturb the peace or hinder war efforts or undermine the discipline or morale of the armed forces;

---

167. Article 433. "Will be punished by one to five years imprisonment and a fine from FRF 2,000 up to FRF 60,000 or only one of these sentences: Those who, knowingly, while establishing a depositor's certificate which acknowledges subscriptions and deposits, have declared sincere and truthful subscriptions which they knew were fictitious or declared that the funds which were not permanently at the disposal of the company had been effectively deposited, or given to the depositor a list of shareholders mentioning fictitious subscriptions or deposits of funds which were not permanently at the disposal of the company."

168. Article L97. "Those who, with the help of false news, slanderous rumours or other fraudulent manoeuvres, will have surprised or mislead voters, or caused one or more voters to abstain from voting, will be punished by a sentence of one month up to one year imprisonment and by a fine from FRF 360 up to FRF 7,200."

169. Article 322–14. "To communicate or disclose false information with a view to make people believe that a destruction, damage, or a deterioration dangerous for the people will be, or has been committed, is punished by two years imprisonment and a fine of FRF 200,000. The same sentence is given in case of communication or disclosure of false information making people believe in the occurrence of a disaster and likely to prompt a useless intervention of assistance."

170. *Cour d'Appel de Paris*, 10 October 1995.

(3) Bad faith; and

(4) Publication.

The legislator has strictly limited article 27's scope of application and **4.133**
defined the conditions of its implementation, taking into account that
since journalists may not always have the time or the means to verify the
information they receive and on which they report or comment, it would
not be meaningful to punish them each time they publish erroneous
information. Courts have decided that "mere negligence to verify the
news being published does not amount to the bad faith element required
in a criminal cause of action".[171]

Publication or circulation of false news

Article 27 is only applicable to the case of diffusion of false news. In this **4.134**
regard, the definition of "news" is strictly construed: opinions or fore-
casts are not affected. On the other hand, "news" does not necessarily
mean current news; it may also include old facts newly discovered.

Article 27 applies only to positive actions (publication, reproduction,
distortion, etc.). Accordingly, those who simply refrain from publishing
information essential for maintaining peace or for the morale of the
armed forces could not be punished on the basis of this article. Silence is
not a ground for punishment even if the consequences of silence may at
times be more dire than those resulting from the publication of false news.

To verify the conformity of information to the truth, judges seek only
objective truth, on the basis of an overall analysis. Mere mistake is not
enough; there must be an actual lie.

Scope of application

The scope of application of article 27 is strictly limited since the informa- **4.135**
tion concerned must be likely to disturb the peace and/or weaken the
discipline or morale of the armed forces. Two distinct misdemeanours
are included in article 27.

Mens rea

There is a bad faith element in the misdemeanour. In respect of press-related **4.136**
crimes, bad faith is never presumed, except in defamation cases. As a
result, the public prosecutor has the burden to prove the untrue character

---

171. Cass. crim., 19 March 1953.

of the information and the malicious intent of the author. Mere thought-lessness and imprudence of a journalist who did not take the care to verify his information is not normally punishable.

Publication

4.137　The Law punishes publication, circulation or reproduction of false news by any means. It is sufficient that the news had been published or was meant to be published.

Proceedings and punishments

4.138　The criminal division of the *Cour de Cassation*, in a decision dated 25 February 1986, decided that article 27 protects the national commu-nity as a whole and not individual citizens taken separately. Consequently, proceedings may not be initiated by private parties; rather, only the public prosecutor may initiate such an action.

Article 27 punishes by imprisonment of between six months and three years and/or a fine of FRF 3,000 to FRF 300,000, those responsible for the dissemination of false news likely to disturb the peace. In cases of dissemi-nation of false news likely to weaken the discipline or morale of the armed forces, or to hinder the war efforts of the nation, those responsible may be imprisoned for between one year and/or five years and fined between FRF 3,000 and FRF 900,000.

Violation of right to privacy

4.139　Long protected by articles 1382 *et seq.* of the Civil Code, the right to privacy has been specifically codified pursuant to the Law of 17 July 1970. Article 9 of the Civil Code specifies, ". . . everyone is entitled to have his private life held in respect". Protecting private life means safeguarding privacy of the person whether at home or in any public place, and allowing the individual the peaceful enjoyment, free from harm, of his private life, which are essential to freedom and personal development.

The right to privacy ranks first among such individual rights as the right to one's image, or to the respect of one's name or voice. Although these rights are separate and distinct, they may often be subsumed in the right to privacy.

Article 9 of the Civil Code stands out, due to its autonomous character. Any violation of privacy is punishable without any need to provide evidence of the existence of any offence or damage.

Limits on right to privacy

A clear delimitation of what constitutes privacy is difficult to determine. **4.140**
It is a constant, however, that all persons, even public figures, "an
entertainment artist, whatever his reputation"[172] and "the statesman . . . like
any citizen",[173] have the right to privacy.

Private life and press freedom

The absence of a clear definition of private life raises a problem, particu- **4.141**
larly with respect to the freedom of the press as "the rights to privacy may
be in conflict with those on freedom of information".[174]

Generally, protection of private life terminates when the public has a
rightful interest to know the condition and situation of the person
concerned and when such person plays a role in the economic, political, social and artistic life. It is thus clear that private life will enjoy
greater protection when the person concerned is not a public figure.
However, a clearly private individual does not benefit from absolute
protection:

> ". . . the limits of the right to information of the public are not overstepped
> and there is no case of harm to private life when a newspaper printed the
> address and published a picture of the home of victims of an attack, as
> such publication was directly associated with a news event of general
> interest which took place in a precise place".[175]

Persons who hold certain offices or who enjoy a certain public reputation **4.142**
are entitled to lesser protection:

> ". . . with respect to people who hold positions attracting attention from
> the public due to the impact they have on economic life, transparency is
> required in connection with their assets which then become an item of
> information within the limits set by the specifically personal and private
> character of certain information linked to the person, her/his way of life
> and that of her/his family".[176]

The limits between private life and the freedom of the press are all the **4.143**
more ambiguous as nothing specifically defines their respective scopes of

---

172. Paris Court of Appeal, 26 March 1987.

173. *Tribunal de Grande Instance* of the Seine, 26 February 1968.

174. High Court of Paris, 4 July 1984.

175. Paris Court of Appeal, 5 March 1986.

176. Paris Court of Appeal, 20 October 1987.

application. The considerable amount of litigation in this regard is a good illustration of the high degree of uncertainty which prevails in this field.

The recent controversy on the private or public character of the health of the former President of the French Republic provides an example of the difficulty to give clear answers. The judges who ruled in connection with the publication by François Mitterrand's personal physician of a book on his health condition considered that the disclosures made in the book "represent a particularly serious intrusion in the privacy of François Mitterrand's family life and in that of his spouse and children".[177]

Harm to private life and defamation

4.144 Harm to private life may sometimes be coupled with defamation.[178] However, the notions are legally dissimilar and the courts must often review and recharacterise the qualification of the offence set forth by the parties. In leading cases, it was considered that "the charge of unsettled manners and sexual obsession does not represent defamation but rather harm to private life"[179] or even:

> ". . . the publication of someone's picture during a social gathering is considered a defamation as the article which accompanies alleges that the person has traded the stolen jewels".[180]

4.145 Nevertheless, it is not infrequent for victims to invoke both notions alternatively and even cumulatively.

By a judgment of 26 November 1975, the *Cour de Cassation* confirmed a decision which had admitted "not only the existence of defamation, but also of harm to private life". In this case, the *Cour de Cassation* decided that the:

> ". . . the claim for redress based on harm to private life and harm to the right of effigy falls outside the reach of the three month statute of limitations instituted by article 65 of the Law of 29 July 1981 on the press, whether or not the judges deciding on the merits of the case had recognised the existence of a defamation".[181]

---

177. Summary proceedings, Paris, 18 January 1996.
178. Cass. civ., 26 November 1975.
179. Paris High Court, 2 March 1988.
180. Paris Court of Appeal, 4 October 1984.
181. Cass. civ., 26 November 1975.

Interest of an action based on article 9 of the Civil Code

Compared with article 1382, article 9 of the Civil Code provides a variety **4.146** of efficient measures for redress:

> "The judges may, without prejudice to compensation for the damages suffered, prescribe any measures, such as impounding, attachment and others, to prevent or terminate a harm to the intimacy of private life; these measures may, in case of urgency, be ordered in summary proceedings".[182]

On the other hand, article 1382 of the Civil Code may apply if the victim **4.147** of otherwise defamatory remarks, which do not represent a harm to private life, does not wish, or is not in a position, to proceed in criminal court or to meet the brief statute of limitations applicable to defamations and nevertheless wishes to obtain compensation for the damages suffered.

Finally, it should be noted that in certain situations involving, for example, the publication of a book or an article containing both defamatory remarks and a harm to private life, the victims may be well advised to opt for the application of article 9 of the Civil Code. In a defamation action, the instructing judge may only distrain four copies (article 51[183] of the Law of 29 July 1881) so as to ascertain the reality of the offence. However, if the victim pursues summary proceedings before the civil jurisdiction, the judge may order an immediate provisional or conservatory attachment or impounding of all copies.

---

182. Article 9, paragraph 2 of the Civil Code.

183. Article 51. "... Immediately after the public prosecutor's charge, the investigating judge (*juge d'instruction*) may, but only if the deposit of documents prescribed under article 3 and 10 above is not made, order the seizure of four copies of the writing, newspaper or drawing incriminated".

Germany

Chapter 5
Germany

Matthias Prinz
Prinz Neidhardt Engelschall
Hamburg, Germany

Introduction

Germany's legal system is — in principle — based on codified law. Media   **5.1**
law's rapid change through a number of judicial precedents has resulted
in inadequately unified codification of the law. Thus, the basis of German
media law is a law of precedents. Case law supplements the only partial
codification. Since a landmark decision[1] of the German Federal Court of
Justice (*Bundesgerichtshof*) — the highest court for civil matters — in 1954,
it is established that a human individual is not only protected in its human
dignity[2] and the free development of his or her personality[3] but that also
a general personal right exists. This is a most important, far-reaching
inclusive right (*Rahmenrecht*). It protects the individual not only against
the state but also against other individuals and private companies including media companies.

In 1983, the Federal Constitutional Court (*Bundesverfassungsgericht*) — the
highest German Court and a guardian of the basic law — established a
right to informational self-determination (*Recht auf informationelle Selbst-
bestimmung*) in view of the modern means of data processing. Especially
with the constant development of technology in the areas of the
new "information highway" and multimedia, this right is of great
importance.

German media law is characterised by individual cases, but an overview
of the most important violations of the general personal right can be
useful.

---

1. BGHZ 13, 334.

2. Basic Law (*Grundgesetz* — GG), art 1(1).

3. Basic Law, art 2(1).

Publication of false facts

5.2 The protection against the dissemination of false factual statements is of great importance. Intentional lies or false reports resulting from insufficient research work are prohibited in the media. In any such case, personal rights are infringed. No public interest justifies such infringements. They are always inadmissible.

Publication of true facts

5.3 In special circumstances, even the publication of true facts and opinions can violate a person's privacy rights. An example is the publication of statements given with the intention to damage a person's dignity and reputation without any public interest justifying the violation.

The general personal right includes a protection against indiscretions, *i.e.*, against the disclosure of private facts. In this respect, the general personal right is similar to the American "right to privacy".[4] German courts have defined several special areas of protection (the sphere of secrecy, the intimate sphere, the sphere of privacy and the social sphere). Proceedings in the area of the intimate sphere deserve the most protection. In the area of the public sphere, there is no protection.

Commercial exploitation of a person in the media

5.4 The general personal right protects against commercial appropriation of a person's identity or characteristics, *e.g.*, through unauthorised advertising.[5] In German case law, there are several examples for this kind of violation: the publication of a fictitious exclusive interview,[6] the publication of a letter to the editor without the permission of the author[7] or the unauthorised processing of personal data in electronic systems.[8]

Further protection is offered through the right to free expression of one's own life. In principle, everybody has the right to decide if and to what extent others are allowed to disclose parts of his or her life.[9] Infringements have, however, to be accepted if there is a legitimate public

---

4. Warren and Brandeis, *Harvard Law Review*, Vol 4, 1890, p 220.

5. BGHZ 36, 346; 30, 7; compare the "appropriation cases" in American law.

6. BVerfGE 34, 269.

7. BGHZ 13, 334.

8. BGH NJW 84, 1886.

9. BVerfGE 35, 202 Lebach; 51, 148.

interest in information. Such a right does not exist, for example, when the affected person is involved in current matters that are of a high public interest.

Protection of one's own picture

Publication of pictures through photography or film without the permission of the person that is shown on the picture can be a violation of the personal rights (*Recht am eigenen Bild*). Celebrities (so-called "absolute persons of contemporary history", such as the President of the Federal Republic of Germany or the Queen of England) must, however, mostly allow their pictures to be published. In the same way, depicting people in connection with current events can — in particular cases — be allowed.   **5.5**

Causes of action

An individual has a cause of action before a civil court if his or her personal rights are violated. Possible remedies are an injunction, a reply or retraction as well as pecuniary damages and damages for pain and suffering (monetary compensation); in addition, a criminal cause of action based on defamation, slander or calumny[10] or on the violation to a person's right to his or her own picture.[11]   **5.6**

False statement of facts

An assertion of fact is given when the content of the allegation can be proven to be true or false. It differs from a mere opinion. An opinion is based on beliefs and does not allege to be true. For example, if somebody asserts: "This singer has sung very badly" this is a case of individual judgment, an expression of a belief. In contrast, the declaration: "The singer has performed a playback and has not sung live" is an assertion of fact. The verification of such an assertion is possible.   **5.7**

    To distinguish is often difficult. If it is said that a businessperson has "gone broke" this is considered to be an assertion of fact. The content of the assertion is: "The person has become bankrupt" or "is insolvent".

---

10. *Strafgesetzbuch*, s 186.

11. Law on Copyright in Works of Art (*Kunsturhebergesetz* — KUG), s 33.

If, however, it is said that the businessperson "knows how to make a good bankruptcy", it is not an assertion of fact but a mere expression of opinion. Here, subjective elements prevail.[12]

The distinction between assertions of facts and mere opinions is central in German media law. In case of false factual statements, the infringed individual can allege an injunction, a retraction or monetary compensation. In case of mere opinions, the individual has substantially fewer causes of action. Usually, these subjective statements are protected by the constitutional right of freedom of opinion.[13]

The right to reply

General

5.8   The right to reply provides a special right to the individual who is affected by a media publication. He has the right to supplement the published text through his reply in the same section as the text complained of appeared in and in the same type and manner as to attract the same measure of attention among the readers.[14] In Germany, 45 statutory rules regulating the right to reply exist. Each state has its own rules regarding the right to reply. Separate rules for the press, public broadcasting corporations and private broadcasting corporations exist (a unified law exists only in the states of Berlin and Brandenburg). There are many differences in details.[15] The essentials, however, are mostly common.

Individual concern

5.9   Only a person directly affected by the factual statement has a right to demand a reply.[16] A person is affected if there is an invasion in his or her own sphere of interest (*Interessensphäre*). For example, parents are affected by reports about their minor children.

Even legal entities such as private or public companies can be affected as well as organisations having a partial legal personality which can assert a legal cause of action or can be sued in court.

---

12. *Bundesgerichtshof*, AfP 1994, 218.

13. Basic Law, art 5 I — BVerfGE 42, 163.

14. *Bundesgerichtshof*, NJW 1976, 1198, 1201.

15. See Prinz, NJW 1993, 3039.

16. This is called *Betroffenheit*.

Dissemination of a factual statement

A media enterprise disseminates an assertion of facts not only when it **5.10** claims authorship but also when it makes use of another's assertion of facts. If the press uses expressions such as "it is reported that . . .", or "as it is heard . . .", a right to reply is usually available since the press organ is hereby disseminating the statement.

The same holds true for letters to the editor.[17] Therefore, an individual affected by a letter to the editor has the right to reply.

Content of the right to reply

The general rule is: "Fact for fact". The words of the reply must refer to **5.11** the previous incorrect information. The content of this original report must be given in a correct way. This is most important to the courts. In complicated cases, it can even be helpful to repeat the exact wording of the original report. In such a way it can be avoided to change its meaning. Examples for the link to the original report are:

> "In the paper Number 2/97 of 3 January 1997, page 11, it is asserted under the headline 'This even knocks down the strongest man' that I dismissed three managers last week without notice."

The then following reply must refer to the original report against which **5.12** it is directed. A mere negation, such as "This is untrue", is sufficient.[18]

The injured individual also has the right to present a counter-version. He must, however, confine himself to factual comment, for example, "The truth is that I dismissed none of my employees".

The court generally does not review the truthfulness of the asserted facts in the reply. The affected individual, however, has no right to lie. That means: If the content of the reply is evidently or known by a court of law to be incorrect, the plaintiff has no right to demand its publication. There is no justified interest in its being printed.

Extent of the right to reply

The reply must be of appropriate size. Most of the state laws assume that **5.13** this is the case if the length of the reply does not exceed the volume of the text complained of. The affected individual may, however, exceed it if this is necessary to give an understandable and concentrated answer

---

17. OLG Hamburg, AfP 1983, 345.

18. *Oberlandesgericht* Hamburg, AfP 1980, 106.

to the assertion of fact given in the original text. The courts should apply a generous standard in evaluating this.[19]

Formal conditions

5.14　A number of special conditions must be met to have a reply printed:

> (1)　The reply must be given in writing and must bear the signature of the injured party or legally recognised representative;
> (2)　If there is no personal signature, the reply is not valid; and
> (3)　Stamps, facsimile signatures and the like are not sufficient.

5.15　The courts disagree on the question whether it is sufficient to send the reply by fax. For some courts,[20] a fax is sufficient; for others it is not.[21]

　　The demand for a reply must be communicated immediately to the publisher or the responsible editor. This means it must be done without an unreasonable delay.[22] The statute of limitations commences when the affected individual gets first notice of the original report. A rule of thumb is that a reply is never too late when it reaches the publisher or the responsible editor within 10 days after publication of the original report.

All-or-Nothing-Principle

5.16　The All-or-Nothing-Principle is of great importance. It signifies that the reply must meet the formal conditions in every respect. The absence of any such condition — even if there is only one word too much or too little — relieves the publisher from the duty to publish the reply. The publisher has no obligation to inform the affected person about the reasons for not publishing the reply.

　　If the publisher refuses to print the reply, the affected person may seek relief through an interim injunction. This must be filed at the court situated at the publisher's place of business. If the court considers the reply inappropriate, the affected person must change his text and first demand — out of court — that the publisher publish the new version. If the publisher does not comply, the affected person must begin a new cause of action before a court. It can be necessary to repeat this practice until an acceptable version is found.

---

19. *Oberlandesgericht* Hamburg, AfP 1985, 53.

20. For example, the courts of appeal of Saarbrücken (*Oberlandesgericht* Saarbrücken, AfP 1992, 287); the district court of Cologne (*Landgericht* Köln, AfP 1995, 684).

21. Court of Appeal of Hamburg (*Oberlandesgericht* Hamburg, AfP 1989, 746).

22. Compare Civil Code (*Bürgerliches Gesetzbuch* — BGB), s 121(1): *ohne schuldhaftes Zögern.*

Most laws have a statute of limitations of three months for the reply. If no court action is taken within this limit, the individual is barred from demanding the publication of the reply.

Injunctive relief

The affected person can seek injunctive relief against the person making **5.17** a false factual statement concerning that person. He has the same right against the person who disseminates such a statement. For the assertion of an injunction, it is sufficient to set forth the objective unlawfulness. It is not necessary to prove intent or negligence on the part of the person making or disseminating the statement.

Another condition for the successful assertion of an injunction is that the alleged violation of rights is imminent or that there is danger of a repeated violation. The courts usually assume that there is danger of repetition if there was a prior violation of rights through prior publication. An injunction can also be granted if the affected person has proven that he has reliable information of a forthcoming violation of rights. In reality, this is seldom the case. It cannot be assumed that a media company that has started to inquire about a certain case is in danger of publishing an article that violates individual rights.[23] Mere research work does not necessarily result in later publication. Thus, a danger of committing a violation can only be assumed if the affected person has knowledge about the content of an already completed article.

Right to correction or revocation

A person whose rights are violated by the publication of untrue facts can **5.18** demand a correction, revocation or retraction of the untrue statement.[24] The plaintiff claiming this right must prove that the disputed factual statements were in fact false.[25] This means that the plaintiff bears the risk of doubts.

In formulating the declaration to retract, it is important that the content is not disproportionate compared to the content necessary for the elimination of the infringement. The declaration is not allowed to be a humiliation of the person who must correct his or her prior statement.[26]

---

23. *Oberlandesgericht* Hamburg, AfP 1992, 279.

24. *Bundesgerichtshof,* GRUR 1970, 254.

25. *Bundesgerichtshof,* NJW 1976, 1198.

26. *Bundesverfassungsgericht,* NJW 1970, 156.

A simple revocation is usually phrased like "I hereby revoke the assertion . . .". It is possible to add ". . . as false". If doubts about the real facts remain, it can be demanded that the statement include information about the real occurrences. This is called a qualified revocation or correction. Such a procedure is helpful to prevent speculation. For example, a declaration such as: ". . . our asserted statement that Anton Müller was convicted of perjury is hereby revoked as untrue". It remains, however, unclear whether Müller was convicted of other offences or if the proceedings did not yet come to an end. Here, an addition should be considered: "Anton Müller has nothing to do with the matter. There has been a confusion of names".

Monetary compensation

Pecuniary loss

5.19 A pecuniary loss resulting from a wrongful false factual statement must be compensated. The injured person must prove causality. He must prove that the damage occurred as a consequence of the publication of the false factual statement. This is usually difficult. For example, if the profits of a company decline after publication of a false factual statement in a newspaper, this decline is not necessarily the result of a certain press report. Another possible reason could be tougher competition, a changed market situation, etc. The award of damages in German media law is therefore rare.

Immaterial losses

5.20 Courts award pecuniary damages in case of a violation of personal rights only if the violation is substantial and if no other compensation is available.[27] In the past, damage awards were very low — almost negligible. An example is the case in which a magazine reported under the headline "H (name of the singer): No to a paternity test . . .", that a well-known singer had an illegitimate child. The singer was awarded damages in an amount of DM 10,000.[28]

The Federal Court of Justice (*Bundesgerichtshof*) has stated that the amount of pecuniary damages should result in a real incentive to desist.[29] Thus, higher monetary damages can be expected for the future. This

---

27. *Bundesgerichtshof*, NJW 1995, 861, 864.

28. *Oberlandesgericht* München, AfP 1990, 45.

29. NJW 1995, 861; see Prinz, NJW 1995, 817.

decision, however, is restricted to intentional or grossly negligent violations motivated by the desire to increase circulation. In most cases of violations of personal rights, this is not the case. Therefore, it still holds true for negligent violations that: as long as the affected person cannot prove any pecuniary losses and as long as there is no "severe infringement", the publisher is at no financial risk. The affected person can regain his or her reputation through a revocation, an injunction or a reply, but he cannot profit from the violation.

Statements of opinion

The situation is completely different with regard to statements of opinions.[30] **5.21** Article 5(1), first sentence of the German constitution guarantees the "right to free expression of opinions": "Each person has the right to freely express and distribute his opinion in words, writing and pictures . . .".

This fundamental right protects the freedom of opinion in the interest of the free development of personality as well as in the public interest in a democratic process. According to the Federal Constitutional Court, this right is constitutive for such a process.[31] In case of an expression of opinion, there is no right to injunction, reply, retraction or monetary compensation.

There is an exception for the so-called defamatory criticism (*Schmähkritik*). Such criticism is found if the criticism is not only relentless and insulting but leads to an intentional dishonour of one's dignity.[32] Defamatory criticism was, for example, assumed when the author Heinrich Böll was called the spiritual co-author of terrorism[33] or when an officer in the army was called a military slave-owner (*Wehrsklavenhalter*).[34]

In case of such defamatory criticism, the affected person can seek injunctive relief and, if the above-mentioned criteria are met, also monetary damages. He has nevertheless no right to a reply or a revocation.

The right to one's own picture

Portraits can only be distributed or publicly shown with the permission of **5.22** the portrayed person.[35] Exceptions where no permission is necessary are

---

30. Compare the distinction at "False statement of facts".

31. *Bundesverfassungsgericht*, AfP 1992, 59 with further reference.

32. *Bundesgerichtshof*, NJW 1974, 1762.

33. *Bundesverfassungsgericht*, NJW 1980, 2072.

34. LG Kaiserslautern NJW 1989, 1369.

35. *Kunsturhebergesetz*, s 22.

laid down in section 23 of the *Kunsturhebergesetz*. The permission required in section 22 is not needed for distribution and exhibition of:

(1) Portraits of contemporary history;
(2) Pictures where the persons are only accessories to the landscape or another locality;
(3) Pictures of meetings, demonstrations and similar events in which the depicted persons participated; and
(4) Portraits which have not been ordered as long as the distribution or exhibition serves a high interest of art.

5.23 The right does not extend to the distribution and exhibition that violates a legitimate interest of the portrayed person or, if he is dead, an interest of his relatives.

The most important cases in the area of the right to one's own picture are the "portraits of figures of contemporary history". The courts make a distinction between absolute and relative persons of contemporary history.

"Absolute persons of contemporary history" are persons that have a special place in society because of their position in society or because of their extraordinary achievement.[36] Among these persons are important politicians, athletes, musicians or leading figures of the economic life. They may be portrayed if no legitimate interest is violated. A legitimate interest is violated, among others, if the picture is used for advertising or if the picture portrays their intimate or private life.

The intimate sphere protects the most intimate part of the personality of a human being. Sexual habits, health problems, pregnancies, sexual relations to other people and the like are protected from the public eye and the publication of details.

The private sphere protects the general private life with family and friends from public scrutiny. It is not confined to the area inside one's own house. According to a recent decision of the Federal Court of Justice,[37] privacy is protected even in public places under certain circumstances. This can, for example, be the case if an absolute person of contemporary history sits down in a garden restaurant and expects not to be recognised. Pictures of such situations can only be published with the permission of the absolute person of contemporary history.

"Relative persons of contemporary history" have become prominent because of their connection to an event of contemporary history. An example is a criminal who attracted attention because of his crimes.

---

36. *Oberlandesgericht* Hamburg, AfP 1995, 665.

37. NJW 1996, 984; see Prinz NJW 1996, 953.

Relative persons of contemporary history can only be portrayed in context with the contemporary event, for example, a former head of a correctional institution of the former German Democratic Republic in a book about prisons in the GDR.[38] The publication in another context ("Women behind bars") is inadmissible.

If the right to one's own picture is violated, the affected persons can seek injunctive relief. With regard to pecuniary damages, they can choose among three different ways to calculate the damages:

(1) Compensation for the real damage;
(2) Collect the profit which the injurer gets through the publication; and
(3) Claim an appropriate "licence fee".[39]

The third variant, the "licence analogy", can be awarded only if the permission to print the picture is usually paid for. This is, for example, the case when an athlete allows his picture to be used for commercial advertising but not in the case of a person who is photographed while walking in the street and who is then shown in the newspaper. **5.24**

Finally, the affected person has a right to compensation for immaterial damages under certain conditions.[40]

Private life and intimate sphere

Factual statements

Even if a statement is true, the dissemination can be a violation of private life or intimate sphere. For example, texts that are not meant for the public can only be cited with the prior permission of the author. Examples are diaries, personal notes, internal remarks, and letters that are not meant to be published. The same is true for descriptions of domestic life,[41] pecuniary circumstances[42] or medical problems of a person. In a particular case, however, a right to publish can be granted after comparing the personal rights of the individual with the fundamental rights of freedom of opinion and freedom of the press.[43] For example, it is possible that the public interest in information outweighs the personal rights if **5.25**

---

38. *Landgericht* Hamburg, AfP 1994, 321.
39. *Oberlandesgericht* München; NJW–RR 1996, 95.
40. See "Formal conditions" above.
41. *Bundesgerichtshof,* NJW 1981, 1366, 1367.
42. *Oberlandesgericht* Hamburg, AfP 1992, 376.
43. *Bundesverfassungsgericht,* NJW 1991, 2339.

the press acts with a "legitimate interest" (*in Wahrnehmung berechtigter Interessen*), for example, to disclose abuses.

Pictures

5.26   Even absolute persons of contemporary history generally need not allow publication of their private sphere without permission. Their right to an undisturbed private life secured from publicity has priority over the public interest in information. Therefore, permission is necessary for all pictures that show obviously private situations. This, for example, is true for pictures showing a celebrity in her garden.[44] According to a decision of the Federal Court of Justice,[45] there can even be — as described above — a protected private sphere outside the private home. This protected sphere is invaded if somebody publishes a picture taken secretly in such a situation or taken by surprise.

    In case of such an unlawful infringement of the private life or intimate sphere, the affected person can seek injunctive relief and/or monetary damages.

Questions of procedure

Immediate activity

5.27   Before the plaintiff brings an action before the court, a number of formalities must be met in press law. Since the statutes of limitation for the whole procedure are very short,[46] a close and efficient co-operation between client and lawyer is necessary. The affected person should send a copy of the newspaper, magazine or of the television or broadcasting transmission to his lawyer as soon as he learns about an infringement. In addition to this, he should prepare a list of all false factual statements together with a thorough explanation.

Territorial jurisdiction

5.28   In German law, the plaintiff often must file several actions in different fora.

---

44. *Landgericht* Hamburg, Decision of 5 July 1995 — 324 O 192/95.

45. *Bundesgerichtshof*, Judgment of 19 December 1995 — VI ZR 15/95, compare above "Monetary compensation".

46. Ten days in the case of the right to reply.

An injunction, a revocation, pecuniary damages and damages for pain and suffering can, however, be sought at one court in one unified procedure. Because of the so-called "flying jurisdiction", according to section 32 of the German Civil Code of Procedure (*Zivilprozeßordnung*— ZPO), each German court has jurisdiction in whose district the affected paper is regularly distributed, respectively where the television or radio programme can be received. Accordingly, the plaintiff has the free choice of jurisdiction.

Media law demands a specific knowledge and a special understanding for wording and interrelations. Therefore, it is always recommended to choose a court with a special jurisdiction for media law or one with a special chamber for media law. A media law chamber that decides only media law cases presently exists only in Hamburg (*Zivilkammer* 24). This chamber had to decide 762 media-related cases in 1994 alone. In some other district courts, there is a special jurisdiction for media law. There, however, the number of cases decided each year lies significantly below the usual number of the Hamburg court.

In case of the right to reply, there is no free choice of court. Here, the plaintiff always must go to the court situated where the publisher or the broadcaster has its domicile. In most of the cases, this will be the district court (*Landgericht*) of Hamburg since most German publishers have their domicile in Hamburg.

Principal proceedings

After the preliminary rulings that are only necessary for replies and injunctive reliefs and which last only a few weeks or even a few days, there are regular principal proceedings. **5.29**

The right to revocation, pecuniary damages and damages for pain and suffering (monetary compensation) can only be claimed in such a regular court proceeding. Injunctive relief can also be awarded in such a procedure. This is, however, only recommendable if the statute of limitation of the preliminary procedure has already run out or if there is an extremely difficult case to solve.

Mandatory representation by a lawyer

District courts have jurisdiction if the value of the claim is over DM 10,000. In media law cases, this is regularly the case. In district courts, there is an obligation to be represented by a lawyer. Therefore, the plaintiff must seek representation by a lawyer who is admitted to the bar at the local court. **5.30**

211

Alternative actions

5.31 There are also other ways to fight against untrue and defamatory press and broadcasting statements. In reality, however, these are less important.

Complaint at the Press Council

5.32 If a defamatory statement was published in a press organ, the affected person has the right to lodge a complaint with the German Press Council.

Members

5.33 The German Press Council consists of 20 honorary members. They represent publishers and journalists in equal parts. Of these 20 members, 10 are part of the so-called Complaints Committee, which is responsible for processing the incoming complaints.

Procedure

5.34 Any person believing that a German press organ has reported a specific case in an untrue or defamatory way has the right to lodge a complaint with the German Press Council. The individual does not even need to be directly affected.

At the Press Council, there is no obligation to be represented by a lawyer. Since most of the publishers have specialised legal departments, it is, however, recommended to entrust an attorney with the complaint.

After a complaint has been communicated to the Press Council, it will be sent to the attacked press organ, mostly to the responsible editor. Thereby, the paper or magazine has the opportunity to describe the situation from its point of view.

The Complaints Committee then deliberates on the complaint in a non-public meeting. A standard developed by the Press Council in 1973 is the Press Code, which regulates the ethical and moral standards of professional journalism. In addition, the Complaints Committee can make use of a number of recommendations for press practice of the German Press Council. The Press Council developed these during its long-term activity and published them in its yearbooks.

The Complaints Committee decides about the complaint with the majority of the members present at the meeting. If one member lodges an objection, the case will be presented to the plenary meeting of the Press Council in which all 20 members will participate. If the accusation is found to be valid, the Press Council has the choice among several sanctions. Depending on the severity of the violation, a mere notice to the responsible editors, a written disapproval or a non-public censure will be given. The most severe sanction of the Press Council is the so-called public censure. According to article 16 of the Press Code, each censured press organ has the obligation to print the public censure in full. There are no remedies against decisions of the Press Council.

Enforcement

The Press Council has no executive power. To enforce its sanctions, it can **5.35** only rely on its moral authority. Unlike in Sweden, for example, the Press Council cannot even impose a monetary fine to add significance to its censures. As a result, the censures of the Press Council are not taken seriously by the German press. Its significance is low. In 1994, there were 250 complaints, which led to 11 public censures of which the publishers only printed seven notwithstanding their obligation to publish.

Complaint about a television or radio broadcast

Against statements in programmes of the public and private broadcasting **5.36** stations, the affected person usually has the informal right to a complaint. Since German broadcasting is divided into private and public broadcasting and also because the German states have the legislative power with regard to broadcasting, there are many different procedures in case of such a complaint.

Public broadcasting

Most of the broadcasting laws for the public broadcasting stations have **5.37** no explicit regulation concerning complaints on programmes.

Where there is a statute regulating such a procedure, the affected person has the right to due process and to a decision. This, however, does not imply that the complaint must be solved in favour of the complainant.

If there is no statutory regulation of a complaint, nevertheless everybody has the right to address the manager of a broadcasting station as the responsible person with a complaint. Then, however, there is no right to a specific procedure nor a right to a decision.

Private broadcasting

In most state media laws that regulate private broadcasting in Germany, **5.38** there is no regulation of a procedure for a programme complaint, with a few exceptions. Accordingly, the affected person can only lodge an informal complaint with the State Media Institution (*Landesmedienanstalt*) from which the broadcasting corporation has received its licence. This institution works as a reviewing organ for these licenced broadcasting corporations. In the few exceptional cases of a special statute regulating programme complaints, the requisite procedure must be followed.

Penal report

5.39 Besides the protection granted by the Civil Law, the person offended by a defamatory media report can make use of the criminal law through a penal complaint (*Strafanzeige*).

   The freedom of opinion granted in article 5(I) of the basic law is explicitly restricted in paragraph II by the right to human dignity. Here, some rules of criminal law apply.

Insult

5.40 The central misdemeanour relating to the honour of a person is the insult (*Beleidigung*). It is given if there is an intentional declaration of disregard or disrespect of another person's dignity. Such an insult can be committed by defamatory factual statements or expressions of opinion to the defamed person. The dissemination, which means the declaration towards third persons or to the public, is only included in section 185 if it was an expression of opinion. Dishonouring factual statements, no matter if they were true or false, are regulated in sections 186 and 187 of the Criminal Code (*Strafgesetzbuch* — StGB). Thus, according to section 185, media organs are only punishable if they intentionally disseminate defamatory expressions of opinions.

Slander

5.41 A person will be punished for slander if he makes or distributes factual statements concerning a third person that can humiliate this person or are appropriate to lower his esteem in public opinion unless the statement is true and this can be proven.

   The burden of proof lies with the person who makes the statement or disseminates it. To violate section 186 of the StGB, it is therefore sufficient if the truth of the statement cannot be proven even if it should objectively be true.

Formal insult

A statement of facts that is proven to be true can still be punishable if the **5.42** form and the circumstances of the assertion and the dissemination contain a defamation.[47] The limits of such a defamation must be narrow because of the specific importance of free reporting. They have, however, to include the so-called defamatory criticism (*Schmähkritik*) if the intention to hurt is predominant and substitutes the intention to inform. Even very caustic criticism must be admitted if it is true and if the will to inform is the main force behind the criticism.

Calumny

Regarding media reports the offence of calumny (*Verleumdung*)[48] has less **5.43** importance. There is a case of calumny if somebody asserts or disseminates a false statement of facts although he knows that his statement is untrue. In media reports this will rarely be the case.

Disparagement of a deceased person

The honour of dead persons is protected by section 189 StGB. Disparage- **5.44** ment of the memory of a deceased person (*Verunglimpfung des Andenkens Verstorbener*) is regulated by sections 185–186 StGB. However, the facts of the case are to be interpreted restrictively. Only acts included in section 185 StGB of some intensity are included in section 189 StGB. Basically, in German law the protection of personal rights ends with the death of a person.

Violation of the right to one's own picture

A person publishing a picture of a third person without authorisation **5.45** faces a prison sentence for up to one year if an affected person files a penal report. This is, however, a quite unusual proceeding. This violation of this right is known as *Verletzung des Rechts am eigenen Bild*.[49]

General remarks

Above, the different possible proceedings against dishonouring state- **5.46** ments in the press and broadcasting programmes in Germany have been

---

47. *Strafgesetzbuch*, s 192.

48. *Strafgesetzbuch*, s 187.

49. *Kunsturhebergesetz*, s 33.

briefly presented. Specialised legal knowledge is necessary to discover what procedures may be available and what success is likely. Media law has rapidly changed in recent years, in the same way as the media itself. Each year there are new precedents that change everything. It can be stated that nowadays several possibilities exist to defend individuals and companies against damaging reports. The protection of personal rights is becoming stronger and stronger. Whoever's rights are violated by the media in Germany does not need to resign. The injured party should seek information as soon as possible about the present state of law and the specific possibilities in the particular case within the very short time limit that begins to run as soon as that person has knowledge of the media publication that violates his or her rights.

Japan

Chapter 6
Japan

Masao Horibe and John Middleton
Hitotsubashi University, Faculty of Law
Tokyo, Japan

Introduction

In the developing information society of Japan today, the volume of **6.1** information produced and disseminated by the print and especially the electronic media continues to increase rapidly. As the level of consumption remains limited, suppliers are obliged to convey material which will appeal to consumers, and this excessive competition and commercialism have led to some serious violations of individuals' rights to reputation and privacy. In recent years, the expression *hodo higai* (damage caused by media reporting) has been used frequently to refer to a multitude of sins committed by the media — most notably, the wholesale invasion of privacy and defamation of individuals in the course of reporting crime — and the experiences of several *hodo higaisha* (victims of media reports) have been well documented.[1] With the continuing development of the nation's information society, the likelihood of further infringements can only be expected to increase.

Amid this environment, many commentators, including academics and lawyers, have criticised the current state of Japanese journalistic ethics and discussed how the media could be made more accountable for such violations. For their part, media organisations have also considered what could be done to prevent such abuses and what forms of relief should be made available to the victims of them.

Nevertheless, issues of Japanese media liability, unlike other social problems such as pollution and consumer affairs, are complicated by the fact that they cannot be solved simply by regulating the media's activities. One must always bear in mind the threat to the constitutional guarantee

---

1. See, for example, Tsukuru Shuppan (ed.), *Hodo higai: 11 nin no kokuhatsu* [Damage Caused by Media Reporting: Eleven Personal Complaints], Tsukuru Shuppan (Tokyo, 1991).

of freedom of expression[2] which inevitably ensues from demands for the protection of reputation and privacy through media regulation. Certainly, in a capitalist society, the media often possess private characteristics as profit-making enterprises. However, the same media also perform the public function of acting as a vehicle for the freedom of expression essential to the facilitation of citizens' rights to know and to have access to information. Hence, the problem here is always how best to balance the conflicting public interests of the protection of reputation and privacy on the one hand and freedom of expression on the other for the greater good of society as a whole.

In this chapter, we discuss the law relating to freedom of expression and the protection of the rights to reputation and privacy in Japan and introduce some recent examples of abuses of freedom of expression by the Japanese media.

Freedom of expression in Japan

The jurisprudence of free speech

6.2　That freedom of expression is valued so highly in Japanese society today can be attributed in part to the suppression of free speech concomitant to the rise of militarism in the 1930s. The ascent of militarism, a movement which triggered Japan's involvement in the Second World War, was characterised by the stifling of free expression in general and dissident expression in particular. Compelled to serve as government propaganda organs throughout the War and subject to legal restrictions and government pressures until its conclusion, the Japanese media came to appreciate the value of free speech and remain determined not to repeat the errors of the past.

The other prevailing justifications for free expression reflect the strong Western influence on Japanese political and legal thought in the nineteenth century. Freedom of expression is considered:

(1)　To be essential to the development of human personality;
(2)　To serve as the best method for discovering the truth by establishing a free market of ideas;
(3)　To guarantee self-government; and
(4)　To co-ordinate the social needs for stability and change.

---

2. Constitution of Japan of 1946, article 21.

The postwar conception of free expression has also shaped government   **6.3**
policies toward the media. As a result of this, contemporary Japan is
considered to be one of the few industrialised nations which guarantees
freedom of expression effectively.[3]

The constitutional guarantee of freedom of expression

The Japanese Constitution, which was promulgated on 3 November 1946   **6.4**
and entered into force on 3 May 1947, explicitly guarantees freedom of
expression, including that of the press. Article 21 provides:

> "(1) Freedom of assembly and association as well as speech, press and all
> other forms of expression are guaranteed.
> "(2) No censorship shall be maintained, nor shall the secrecy of any
> means of communication be violated."

This Constitution, enacted under the aegis of the Occupation, replaced   **6.5**
the Meiji Constitution of 1889, which provided, "Japanese subjects shall,
within the limits of law, enjoy the liberty of speech, writing, publication,
public meetings and association."[4] In contrast to the Meiji Constitution,
which recognised free expression only "within the limits of law",[5] today's
Constitution appears to guarantee unlimited press freedom. However,
the Supreme Court has held that reasonable and necessary restrictions,
designed to protect the public welfare, may constitute valid limitations on
the press.

The Court views the public welfare justification as permitting limited
restrictions on the exercise of freedoms. Article 12 of the Constitution
states:

> "The freedoms and rights guaranteed to the people by this Constitution
> shall be maintained by the constant endeavour of the people, who shall
> refrain from any abuse of these freedoms and rights and shall always be
> responsible for utilising them for the public welfare."

---

3. For further discussions of the law in this area, see Beer, "Defamation, Privacy, and Freedom of Expression
in Japan", 5 *Law in Japan* 192 (1972); Kim, *Japanese Journalists and Their World*, University Press of Virginia
(Charlottesville, 1981); Beer, *Freedom of Expression in Japan: A Study in Comparative Law, Politics and Society*,
Kodansha International (Tokyo, New York and San Francisco, 1984); Horibe, "Press Law in Japan" in Lahav
(ed.), *Press Law in Modern Democracies: A Comparative Study*, Longman (New York and London, 1985), pp
315–338; Beer, "Freedom of Expression: The Continuing Revolution" in Luney and Takahashi (eds), *Japanese
Constitutional Law*, University of Tokyo Press (Tokyo, 1993), pp 221–254.

4. Constitution of the Empire of Japan of 1889, article 29.

5. Under the Meiji Constitution, the judiciary possessed no power to review the constitutionality of any law
enacted by the Diet (National Parliament): 16 *Keishu* 193 (Great Court of Judicature, 3 March 1937).

6.6   Article 13 provides:

> "All of the people shall be respected as individuals. Their right to life, liberty, and the pursuit of happiness shall, to the extent that it does not interfere with the public welfare, be the supreme consideration in legislation and in other governmental affairs."

6.7   Similar limitations on the exercise of certain economic freedoms are contained in articles 22 and 29. A number of decisions by the Supreme Court have suggested that the Constitution permits or requires greater restriction of economic freedoms than civil liberties such as freedom of expression.

The role of the courts in protecting free speech

6.8   Article 81 of the Constitution vests the Supreme Court, as guardian of the Constitution, with broad powers of judicial review: "The Supreme Court is the court of last resort with power to determine the constitutionality of any law, order, regulation or official act."

The ambiguous wording of article 81 has proven fertile ground for questions regarding the nature of the power of judicial review. It was unclear, for instance, whether inferior courts could also exercise this power until the Supreme Court ruled in 1950 that such courts could indeed consider a statute's validity.[6] Another question was whether the Court was empowered to comment on abstract problems of constitutionality in the same manner as the German Constitutional Court. The Supreme Court held:

> "Courts do not possess the power, in the absence of a concrete legal dispute, to hand down abstract decisions covering the future and relating to doubtful disputes concerning the interpretation of the Constitution and other laws, orders, and the like."[7]

6.9   While the Supreme Court has never declared a statute restricting press freedom to be unconstitutional, the courts have played a significant role in developing the jurisprudence of free speech.

Regulation of the media

6.10   As Japan has no general press laws, the laws of defamation and invasion of privacy play a vital role in regulating the print media. The freedom of

---

6. 4 *Keishu* 88 (Supreme Court, 1 February 1950).

7. 6 *Minshu* 783 (Supreme Court, 8 October 1952).

expression and the press guaranteed by article 21 of the Constitution are balanced against the rights to reputation and privacy under the Civil and Penal Codes.[8] Apart from instituting legal proceedings for defamation and invasion of privacy, aggrieved persons may lodge complaints with the Civil Liberties Bureau of the Ministry of Justice and the various bar associations, which can make non-binding recommendations that may or may not have the desired effect.

The electronic media is further regulated by the provisions of the Broadcasting Act of 1950.

Defamation

Japanese law defines defamation as reducing the respect of another in **6.11** the community or lowering such person in the estimation of his/her peers. Group libel, in the strictest sense of the term, is not recognised.

From the perspective of Anglo-American law, the Japanese law of defamation is relatively straightforward, perhaps partly as a result of the limited number of actions brought to date. Japanese litigants are spared many of the quirks of the English Common Law, such as the distinction between libel and slander and the various categories of defamatory meaning (*i.e.*, literal meaning and popular and legal innuendoes). As the experiences of Japan's keenest litigant, Kazuyoshi Miura (to be introduced below) demonstrate, it is possible for lay people to mount successful actions against the media without legal representation.

Criminal defamation

No discussion of the Japanese media's civil liability would be complete **6.12** without some mention of the criminal law. Section 230 of the Penal Code provides that a person who injures the reputation of another by publicly alleging facts, whether true or otherwise, may be sentenced to imprisonment, with or without hard labour, for a term not exceeding three years or be fined up to JPY 500,000.[9] Defamation of a deceased person is not actionable unless the defamatory statement is false.[10] Prosecutors indict defendants at the request of defamed parties, but retain a discretion as to whether to take action or not.

---

8. See discussion of sections 709, 710 and 723 of the Civil Code and sections 230 and 230–2 of the Penal Code below.

9. Penal Code, section 230(1).

10. Penal Code, section 230(2).

The Penal Code distinguishes between ordinary defamation and defamation involving the public interest. If indicted, the press attempts to prove truth under section 230–2, which provides:

"(1) When the statement as defined in [section 230(1)] relates to matters of public concern and has been solely for the purpose of promoting the public interest, the person making such statement shall not be punished if the truth thereof is established on inquiry into its truth or falsity.

"(2) In applying the provision of the preceding subsection, facts concerning the criminal act of a person against whom prosecution has not yet been instituted shall be deemed to be facts relating to matters of public concern.

"(3) When the statement as defined in [section 230(1)] relates to facts concerning a public employee or a candidate for elective public office, the person making such statement shall not be punished if the truth thereof is established on inquiry into its truth or falsity."

6.13　The defence of truth (justification) is thus permitted only in cases in which the allegedly defamatory statements relate to "matters of public concern" and have been "solely for the purpose of promoting the public interest". Generally speaking, matters are of public concern if, by their nature, they are of public or national importance or have attracted public attention or criticism. The press maintains that the very fact of publication creates a presumption that the matter is of public concern, but the courts have disagreed. The Tokyo High Court held in 1953 that a magazine article reporting a rumour that executives of several publishing companies had been bribed to keep certain criminal scandals secret did not constitute a matter of public concern.[11]

The Supreme Court formulated a new test for "matters of public concern" in 1981 in a case involving criticism of the private life of a well-known public figure by the monthly magazine *Gekkan Pen*.[12] The magazine published articles in March and April 1976 accusing Daisaku Ikeda, honorary chairman of the *Soka Gakkai Buddhist lay* organisation, of having had intimate relations with two female adherents. The Tokyo District Court's conviction of the magazine's editor for criminal defamation in June 1978[13] was first upheld by the Tokyo High Court,[14] but later overturned by the First Petty Bench of the Supreme Court. The Supreme Court held that even the private behaviour of a private person could be of public concern, depending on the nature of a person's social activities and the

---

11. 6 *Kosai Keishu* 367 (Tokyo High Court, 21 February 1953).

12. 1000 *Hanrei Jiho* 25 (Supreme Court, 16 April 1981).

13. 978 *Hanrei Jiho* 132 (Tokyo District Court, 29 June 1978).

14. 978 *Hanrei Jiho* 130 (Tokyo High Court, 12 December 1979).

extent of his/her influence on society through such activities. In view of the organisation's public importance and Ikeda's social influence as a public figure, Ikeda's affairs were matters of public concern subject to section 230–2, and the case was referred back to the lower courts for re-examination. The accused was subsequently convicted on the basis that the truth of the magazine's allegations had not been proved and the editor lacked a reasonable ground to believe that they were true.[15]

The requirement of proving truth as a defence, traditionally the main issue for the press in both civil and criminal defamation cases, was relaxed in relation to criminal defamation by the decision of the Grand Bench of the Supreme Court in the *Yukan Wakayama Jiji* (Wakayama Evening Times) case in 1969.[16] In that case, the editor of a regional newspaper was prosecuted for publishing, as part of a series headlined "The Sins of the Vampire, Tokuichiro Sakaguchi", an article in February 1963 criticising the publisher of a sensationalist tabloid for attempting to corrupt public officials by offering to suppress stories of their misdeeds in return for payment. The defendant's conviction was upheld by the Osaka High Court, but ultimately reversed by a unanimous judgment of the Grand Bench of the Supreme Court, which set forth a new rule to be applied in criminal defamation actions against the press. Under this rule, a media defendant, rather than having to prove the truth of an allegedly defamatory statement as part of its defence, need only show that the statement was made under the mistaken but reasonable belief, based on reliable materials and a reliable source, that it was true. Statements made in good faith are not actionable since the court will not impute a criminal intent to the publisher.

Civil defamation

Section 723 of the Civil Code provides that defamation is a tort for which **6.14** the payment of compensatory damages and/or other "suitable measures" (such as the publication of an apology or retraction) may be required:

> "If a person has injured the reputation of another, the Court may, on the application of the latter, make an order requiring the former to take suitable measures for the restoration of the latter's reputation either in lieu of or together with compensation for damages."

The publication of an apology does not necessarily imply any personal **6.15** recognition of wrongdoing on the part of the defendant, and is used frequently both in and out of court to settle disputes.

---

15. 1128 *Hanji* 32 (Tokyo High Court, 18 July 1984).

16. 23 *Keishu* 975 (Supreme Court, 25 June 1969).

Under sections 709 and 710, the defendant is required to compensate the plaintiff in respect of both pecuniary and non-pecuniary damage, regardless of whether such injury was to the person, liberty or reputation of another or to his property rights, for intentional or negligent violation of the plaintiff's rights:

> "Section 709. A person who violates intentionally or negligently the right of another is bound to make compensation for damage arising therefrom.

> "Section 710. A person who is liable in compensation for damages in accordance with the provisions of the preceding section shall make compensation therefor even in respect of non-pecuniary damage, irrespective of whether such injury was to the person, liberty or reputation of another or to his property rights."

6.16 The Civil Code makes no specific provision for the granting of injunctions, but the Grand Bench of the Supreme Court held in the *Hoppo Janaru* (Northern Journal) case[17] that injunctions may be used to eliminate existing or prevent future violations. In doing so, the Court held that injunctions do not constitute a form of censorship prohibited by article 21(2) of the Constitution since they are a judicial act and not the result of an administrative process. However, since injunctions do constitute prior restraints, they should only be granted on the basis of clear and strict conditions and generally not in cases where the allegedly defamatory statements relate to public employees or candidates for elective public office. Nevertheless, where such statements are false or not made solely for the public benefit, and the plaintiff will suffer severe and irreparable damage if publication is allowed, then injunctions may be granted as an exception to this rule.

In contrast to section 230–2 of the Penal Code, the Civil Code does not specifically render non-actionable statements which are true, relate to matters of public concern, and are made solely in the public interest. However, the Supreme Court held in 1966 that the above principle in the Penal Code applies equally to civil cases and that the publisher need only have a reasonable belief that the statements were true.[18]

Since the repeal of the Newspapers Act in 1949, there has been no statutory provision recognising the right of reply. For a while it was thought that section 723 of the Civil Code might provide a basis for asserting this right, but the Second Petty Bench of the Supreme Court rejected this proposition in 1987.[19] In that case, the Japan Communist Party (JCP) asserted such a right in a defamation suit brought against the

---

17. 40 *Minshu* 872 (Supreme Court, 11 June 1986).

18. 20 *Minshu* 1118 (Supreme Court, 23 June 1966).

19. 41 *Minshu* 490 (Supreme Court, 24 April 1987).

Sankei Shimbun, Japan's fifth largest daily newspaper. The newspaper had published an advertisement by the Liberal Democratic Party which ridiculed the JCP and charged it with making a proposal contrary to its party platform. Although the Tokyo District Court stated in general terms that the constitutional right to freedom of speech included a right of reply, it refused to grant the plaintiff's demand unless the original advertisement was found to be defamatory.[20] The Tokyo High Court, however, deleted the section of the District Court's opinion which discussed the right of reply[21] and the claim was rejected again on appeal to the Supreme Court.

Invasion of privacy

The term *puraibashii* (privacy) seems to have first appeared in Japanese **6.17** literature in the 1920s, but was not recognised to any great extent in the academic world until the late 1950s. The best efforts of Japanese scholars since then have failed to produce any translation which has gained public acceptance, but almost all Japanese citizens today are familiar with the expression borrowed from English and use it in their everyday conversations.

The concept of privacy was brought to the attention of the public in 1961 when a prominent politician named Hachiro Arita brought an action for invasion of privacy, using that term in his statement of claim, against popular novelist Yukio Mishima and his publisher for an unauthorised *roman-à-clef* entitled *Utage no ato* (After the Banquet) based on his marital affairs.[22]

As a result of this lawsuit, the benefits of such notions as "private lives", "personal affairs", and "personal secrets", of which public awareness had only been vague, were crystallised into a new household word, "privacy". Much research was conducted into the approaches of the American and other foreign legal systems to this concept, and not surprisingly, it was the works of Warren and Brandeis[23] and Prosser[24] that attracted most scholarly attention. The first major work to appear in Japanese was *Puraibashii no kenri* (The Right of Privacy), published by Masami Ito in 1963.

The Tokyo District Court recognised the right in September 1964 on the basis of sections 709 and 710 of the Civil Code and awarded the

---

20. 857 *Hanrei Jiho* 30 (Tokyo District Court, 13 July 1977).

21. 981 *Hanrei Jiho* 43 (Tokyo High Court, 30 September 1980).

22. 15 *Kakyu Minshu* 2317 (Tokyo District Court, 28 September 1964).

23. Warren and Brandeis, "The Right to Privacy", 4 *Harvard Law Review* 193 (1890).

24. Prosser, "Privacy", 48 *California Law Review* 383 (1960).

plaintiff JPY 800,000 in damages, which was at that time the largest award of damages made for either defamation or privacy. The Court, however, denied the plaintiff's request that an apology be published on the ground that, unlike defamation cases, it is impossible to restore the *status quo ante* once there has been an invasion of privacy.

In creating the right of privacy, the Court declared that respect and protection of an individual's dignity in a society of mass communications was no longer a matter of mere ethics, but rather a personal interest elevated to a legal right, to be protected against unlawful infringement. The Court defined the right of privacy as "the legal right and assurance that one's private life will not be unreasonably disclosed to the public", and found that it was recognised in statutory provisions concerning certain aspects of privacy and guaranteed under the constitutional requirement that all people be respected as individuals.[25]

This judgment was welcomed by lawyers, but criticised by the literary community for curtailing freedom of expression. The media has since attempted to respect the right of privacy as a matter of public morality, while continuing to emphasise the importance of press freedom. The general prevailing opinion is that since both privacy and media freedom are important democratic interests, the facts of a particular case will determine which interest will be paramount.

A right to one's own likeness (and thus not be photographed without one's consent) was recognised in a decision of the Grand Bench in 1969[26] as an aspect of the right to privacy guaranteed by article 13 of the Constitution,[27] but appears to have little effect on the intrusive newsgathering activities of the more sensationalist programmes and publications. A motorist's claim that the use of a speed camera was an infringement of this right has since been rejected by the Second Petty Bench of the Supreme Court.[28]

Recent trends in litigation

6.18   Actions for defamation and invasion of privacy in Japan have been comparatively rare until recently and awards of damages small by international standards, enabling the media to publish and broadcast with little fear of litigation. During the 1990s, there has been a significant increase in both the number of successful civil actions brought against

---

25. Constitution, article 13.

26. 23 *Keishu* 1625 (Supreme Court, 24 December 1969).

27. *Supra.* section 5.5.

28. 40 *Keishu* 48 (Supreme Court, 14 February 1986).

the media and the scale of damages awarded. It is still unclear at this stage whether this growing propensity of complainants to seek legal remedies rather than pursue the traditional course of *nakineiri* (crying oneself to sleep) will continue long-term, but the media have expressed concern at the prospect of being sued and the increasing amounts of damages will no doubt provide potential litigants with an additional incentive to proceed.

Much of the discussion of this phenomenon focuses on the lawsuits brought by Kazuyoshi Miura, a former entrepreneur who attracted unprecedented media attention for his involvement in the fatal shooting of his wife, Kazumi, in Los Angeles in 1981. Playing the role of the poor husband who had also been shot in the ambush, he gained some sympathy for the first two years, before a reputable weekly magazine opened the floodgates to a stream of highly sensational and inaccurate reports by the mainstream media by suggesting in a series of investigative articles that all might not have been as it appeared. Despite being sentenced to life imprisonment in March 1994 for conspiring to murder Kazumi to collect JPY 155-million in insurance on her life, Miura has continued to protest his innocence and brought more than 200 defamation and privacy actions,[29] a large proportion of which have been successful, sending shock waves through the media.

It is significant, and a credit to the Japanese legal system, that Miura has been able to do this from behind bars (since his arrest in 1985) and without legal representation, although he is believed to have had some access to general legal advice through his contact with criminal counsel and knowledge of the offending reports through the efforts of his supporters. Miura maintains that he has acted alone through financial necessity rather than choice and been reassured by the fact that defendants in defamation cases bear the burden of proving the truth of all allegations made.[30]

The growing number of civil lawsuits

Between 1990 and 1993, there was a three-fold increase in the number of **6.19** judgments handed down in civil actions in which damages for defamation and invasion of privacy were sought.[31] In both 1990 and 1991, a total of

---

29. Furukawa, "'Rosu giwaku' jiken hodo no kyokun" [Lessons from the Reporting of the "LA. Suspicions" case], *Jurisuto* (no. 1038, 1 February 1994), pp 43–47.

30. Miura, "Masu media to taito ni tatakaeru saiban no susume" [Fighting the Mass Media on Equal Terms in Court] in Tsukuru Shuppan (ed.), *Hodo higai: 11 nin no kokuhatsu* [Damage Caused by Media Reporting: Eleven Personal Complaints], Tsukuru Shuppan (Tokyo, 1991), pp 195–220.

31. Akiyoshi, "Meiyo-puraibashii kanren hanrei no genjo" [The Current State of Judgments Relating to Reputation and Privacy], *Jurisuto* (no. 1038, 1 February 1994), pp 48–54.

19 judgments were handed down. This figure increased to 44 and 62 in 1992 and 1993 respectively. Of these, the ratios of those brought by Kazuyoshi Miura to those brought by others were 8:11, 9:10, 28:16, and 37:25. Miura thus brought 82 (57 per cent) of the 144 actions determined in this four-year period.

The success rates calculated as the proportion of total cases in which damages were awarded for 1991–1994 were 12 out of 19 (63.2 per cent) in 1990 and 1991, 28 out of 44 (63.6 per cent) in 1992, and 32 out of 62 (51.6 per cent) in 1993. Miura's individual success rates for the same years were slightly higher: five out of eight (62.5 per cent), seven out of nine (77.8 per cent), 19 out of 28 (67.9 per cent), and 23 out of 37 (62.2 per cent) respectively.

The increasing awards of damages

6.20   By international standards, awards of damages for defamation and invasion of privacy by Japanese courts have been low traditionally. The fact that the same judges have continuously awarded scales of damages in personal injury cases that are among the highest in the world[32] suggests that they place a higher value on human life and physical well-being than on reputation and privacy. They are also sensitive to the precedents laid down by their peers and loath to award higher damages than have been allowed in other cases of a similar nature.

Another important reason for the small awards of damages is that juries[33] are not used to assess damages or award the high punitive damages which constitute a large proportion of the figures which become headlines in other countries.

The average damages awarded in all defamation and privacy cases over the period 1990–1993 was JPY 939,000, including legal costs. Interestingly, the average awarded Kazuyoshi Miura was a third of that awarded other plaintiffs: JPY 570,000 as opposed to JPY 1.59-million. These figures seem especially low when one considers the high cost of living in Japan and the huge circulations of Japanese newspapers and magazines and large television network audiences.[34] However, there has been a noticeable

---

32. Japan ranked third highest alongside the United Kingdom and behind the United States and Australia in a worldwide survey conducted by the Tokio Marine and Fire Insurance Company of damages payouts in personal injuries cases in 1990. See Tokyo Kaijo Kasai Hoken Kabushiki Kaisha Kigyo Songaibu (ed.), *EC no songai baisho suijun to sosho-bengoshi jijo: Amerika to EC 12 kakoku no hikaku chosa kara* [Personal Injury Awards, Civil Procedures and Lawyers in EC Countries], *Jitsugyononihonsha* (Tokyo, 1994), p 22.

33. Juries were used in Japan from 1 October 1928 until the suspension of the Juries Act on 1 April 1943. While there are no plans to reintroduce the jury system in the near future, there is rigorous debate within the bar associations and academic circles as to the potential advantages and disadvantages of doing so.

34. For example, the average circulations of the morning editions of the three major national daily newspapers, the *Yomiuri Shimbun*, *Asahi Shimbun*, and *Mainichi Shimbun* for the period July–December 1995 were 10.06-million, 8.26-million, and 3.98-million respectively.

increase in the amounts of damages awarded since then, with the Tokyo District Court awarding the highest damages against a media defendant for libel — JPY 5-million — in March 1995.[35] Such awards of damages attract media attention and should they become more common, they will no doubt have a positive effect in reducing the extent of unethical practices such as the manufacturing of news.

Self-regulation

Japan has no independent, self-regulatory body, such as a press council **6.21** or ombudsman, to deal with complaints against the media. Most complaints are dealt with in-house by employees of the offending publisher or broadcaster, who may or may not act impartially. As Japanese journalists are perceived first and foremost as employees of their companies and not as independent professionals working in the public interest,[36] it is doubtful that aggrieved persons will trust them entirely to act impartially as arbitrators and conciliators for them.

The Japan Newspaper Publishers and Editors' Association, established in 1946 by the nation's daily newspapers, has formulated Canons of Journalism as its moral charter. The code's preamble recognises the important role of the press in rebuilding a democratic and peace-loving nation by adherence to high ethical standards. The Canons provide for:

(1) Freedom of the press;
(2) A sphere of news reporting and editorial writing;
(3) The principle of editorial comment;
(4) Impartiality;
(5) Tolerance;
(6) Huidance, responsibility and pride; and
(7) Decency.

Although anyone may notify a breach of the rules of ethics to the **6.22** Association, the Canons of Journalism provide no enforcement mechanism for such violations. The Association does have power under its Articles of association to expel a newspaper from membership for violating its code, but has never exercised this option.

---

35. 872 *Hanrei Taimuzu* 298 (Tokyo District Court, 14 March 1995).

36. Maezawa, *Watchdog: A Japanese Newspaper Ombudsman at Work*, Cosmohills Publishing (Tokyo, 1994), p 223.

Among Japanese commentators,[37] there is some support for the creation of an independent British-style Press Complaints Commission or Swedish-style Ombudsman, but such proposals remain controversial. There are some domestic precedents of self-regulation in the fields of film censorship and advertising standards which might provide some guidance as to how such bodies should be set up, but it appears unlikely that either the print or electronic media will take such initiative in the foreseeable future.

The Broadcasting Act

6.23 The Broadcasting Act, enacted in 1950 for the regulation of broadcasting for the public welfare, assures freedom of expression in the electronic media by guaranteeing the impartiality, integrity and autonomy of broadcasting as one of the purposes of the Act.[38] Under section 52–16(2), the Minister of Posts and Telecommunications may refuse to renew the broadcasting licence of a broadcaster which has failed to conform to the standards of freedom of expression specified by ministerial ordinance.

Section 3–2(1) provides that in producing programmes for the domestic market, broadcasters shall:

(1)   Not harm public security and good morals;
(2)   Be politically impartial;
(3)   Broadcast news without distorting facts; and
(4)   With regard to controversial issues, clarify the points at issue from as many angles as possible.

6.24 As broadcasts of inaccurate material can cause immense damage to reputations, section 4(1) of the Broadcasting Act requires broadcasters to broadcast corrections in cases where an aggrieved person has lodged a valid complaint within a specified period of the broadcast. This system of correction broadcasts is intended to provide those whose rights to reputation, trust and such have been infringed by inaccurate broadcasts with a quick and simple means of restitution. Such victims can demand within three months of the broadcast that the broadcaster air a correction, and the broadcaster must conduct an investigation forthwith and

---

37. *See*, for example, Tajima, "'Hodo higai' kyusai seido no shiminteki kaikaku no tankyu: kujo moshitate seido to hanronken no shisutemu o megutte" [A Study of the Civil Revolution for Relief Mechanisms for Damage Caused by Media Reporting: Systems for Complaints and the Right of Reply] in *Jiyu to seigi* [Freedom and Justice], August 1994, pp 21–29.

38. Broadcasting Act, section 1.

broadcast a correction within two days by appropriate means if, upon such inquiry, the falsity of the statements made is confirmed. Section 4(2) provides that the same shall apply in cases where the broadcaster has discovered false matter in its broadcasts by any other means. Neither of these provisions precludes an aggrieved person from bringing an action for damages against the broadcaster in accordance with the provisions of the Civil Code.[39]

Broadcasters are also required under section 5 to maintain records of programmes broadcast for a period of three months to enable aggrieved persons to confirm their contents.

The systems for the broadcasting of corrections in section 4 and the maintenance of records in section 5 date back to 1950 and 1959 respectively, but were modified by amendments to the Broadcasting Act and some related ordinances in 1995. Prior to these amendments, aggrieved persons were able to seek corrections and broadcasters were required to maintain programme records for only two weeks after broadcasts. Broadcasters were also only required to maintain records with respect to programmes featuring news or news commentary and could keep such records in whatever form they desired, whether it be in printed (script) form or as audio-visual recordings.

It was clear to the Ministry of Posts and Telecommunications (MPT) that the broadcasting environment in Japan had changed dramatically since the introduction of the systems in the 1950s and that some amendment to existing laws was desirable. Not only had the media's social influence grown markedly with the ever-increasing types of media and number of media participants, but the rights consciousness of citizens, as reflected in the greater number of lawsuits brought against the media for defamation and invasion of privacy, had also matured. Many had commented that the two-week period for seeking corrections was too short for the adequate relief of aggrieved persons, and the Ministry responded by recommending that the periods specified in sections 4 and 5 be extended to three months. These amendments entered into force in May 1995.

New ordinances relating to the method of maintenance of programme records and the types of programmes for which records must be kept were also introduced in November 1995 to improve the existing relief mechanisms for aggrieved persons in the light of the technological advances made in recent years. As a result of these amendments, programme records must now be maintained exclusively in audio-visual form[40] and in respect of all programmes, save those relating to economic market conditions, natural phenomena and sport[41] or motion pictures,

---

39. Broadcasting Act, section 4(3).

40. Cabinet Ordinance for the Broadcasting Act (1995), Rule 1.

41. *Id.*

cartoons, dramas, theatrical performances, music, information about transport, traffic or public sporting events, and advertisements relating to broadcasters' own or others' commercial activities.[42] These exceptions were deemed desirable for the protection of economic rights which might be violated should records of such programmes be required.

These amendments have been well received as improving aggrieved persons' prospects of obtaining appropriate relief for infringements of their rights by the electronic media. The challenge now is to educate the public of its hitherto seldom-used right to seek corrections and to see that broadcasters fulfil their legal obligations to broadcast such corrections in an appropriate manner.

Some recent abuses of freedom of expression

6.25 While Japanese journalists are quick to defend the constitutional guarantee of freedom of expression, many are also apt to forget the media's duty and responsibility not to abuse that right pursuant to article 12 of the Constitution:

> "The freedoms and rights guaranteed to the people by this Constitution shall be maintained by the constant endeavour of the people, who shall refrain from any abuse of these freedoms and rights and shall always be responsible for utilising them for the public welfare."

6.26 In this section, we introduce three recent abuses of freedom of expression — namely, the false reporting of news, the denial of historical fact, and the inclusion of subliminal images in broadcasts — and another potential one, political bias, as illustrations of the general deficiency of journalistic responsibility in the Japanese media as a whole in the 1990s.

False reporting of news

6.27 The problem of false reporting is pervasive in Japan[43] despite the emphasis placed on accuracy in the codes of conduct of the various

---

42. Ministerial Ordinance for the Broadcasting Act (1995), Rule 1(5).

43. See Middleton, "Reporting Fiction as Fact: The Problem of Misrepresentation and Invention by the Japanese Media" in Taylor (ed.), *Asian Laws Through Australian Eyes*, Law Book Company (Sydney, 1997), ch. 13.

associations of newspaper, magazine and book publishers and the standards laid down for commercial and public broadcasters.

Apart from the obvious dangers of libel and invasion of privacy, such reporting tends to diminish the credibility of the media as a whole. Credibility has been described as the central pillar of the media's strength, but fragile in nature, and when consumers dismiss a bizarre tabloid headline as fiction, they tend also, whether consciously or unconsciously, to tar other media operators with the same brush.[44] Consumers of news, having invested their time and trust in the media, have a legitimate expectation that the media will be fair and honest in providing the truth.[45]

False reporting may take a number of forms, including reports of fictitious characters and events, manufactured quotes and interviews, faked and doctored photographs, false letters to editors and advice columns, wrong attribution of quotes, misuse of quotation marks, abridgement or modification of quotes without the speaker's consent, misleading headlines and captions, suppression or distortion of facts, embellishment of facts to such an extent that a false impression is created, and colouring of news. One has only to open a newspaper or switch on a television on any given day in Japan to see numerous examples of these.

Three common forms of false reporting in Japan are *netsuzo*, *kakidoku*, and *yarase*. *Netsuzo* can be translated as "the manufacturing of news" in English and, in its broadest sense, encompasses *kakidoku* and *yarase*.

In one documented case, a group of sportswriters, wishing to quote a professional baseball player named Hideo Nomo, who was unavailable for comment at the time, agreed on a common quote on the basis of what they thought the pitcher would say in the circumstances and attributed it to him.[46] The player's approval was not sought until after publication of the statement the following day. The National Press Club of Japan published an account of the incident, written by one of the sportswriters involved, in its bulletin without any comment that it had been a breach of journalistic ethics, which suggests that the level of consciousness of journalists regarding the unethical nature of *netsuzo* is low.

Kakidoku means "to write and benefit" and can be explained as the reporting of conjecture as fact in the mere hope that it will prove correct. A magazine might claim, for instance that the reason why an actress married suddenly was because she was pregnant at the time. If the report turns out to be correct, all well and good, but if not, then the risk of being sued is minimal and the readers will soon forget. The

---

44. Russell, *Morals and The Media: Ethics in Canadian Journalism*, UBC Press (Vancouver, 1994), p 16.

45. *Id.*, pp 4–5.

46. Maezawa, *Watchdog: A Japanese Newspaper Ombudsman at Work*, Cosmohills Publishing (Tokyo, 1994), pp 105–108.

benefit of selling additional copies with a "scoop" outweighs the risk of publishing a possibly inaccurate statement.

Yarase means "to make someone do something" and may be defined as a staged simulation portrayed as a real event. Some common forms of *yarase* are the surreptitious use of models to illustrate news stories and actors to re-enact events in the news bulletins and current affairs programmes of commercial broadcasters.

Several cases of systematic distortion and invention have been exposed in Japan[47] and popular magazines occasionally feature articles listing recent cases involving the major dailies. In recent years, it has been deliberate falsifications by staff of the national public broadcaster, NHK, and the *Asahi Shimbun* that have attracted most attention.

In the autumn of 1992, NHK broadcast a two-part documentary series about the Mustang region in Nepal which included several misrepresentations, including staged scenes of altitude sickness, landslides and quicksand, and a policeman and dead horse portrayed falsely as a border guard and the pet of a young child. NHK responded to public and governmental criticism of the programmes by conducting a thorough inquiry, airing an apology, suspending the chief director and punishing six of his superiors five months after the initial broadcasts. Similarly, the acts of a photographer of the *Asahi Shimbun* in defacing coral in coastal waters off Okinawa in April 1989 to illustrate an article about environmental protection led to the resignation of the head of the company the following month. These two cases are well-known, but are by no means isolated. Revelations of false reporting by these and other media operators appear in the popular press on a regular basis and can be considered the mere tip of the iceberg.

Denial of historical fact

6.28   The willingness of Japanese magazine publishers to sacrifice journalistic responsibility and publish almost anything to boost circulations was highlighted in the *Marco Polo* case. The February 1995 issue of *Marco Polo*, a monthly magazine published by Bungei Shunju with a circulation of some 250,000 copies, carried a 10-page feature article authored by a 38-year-old Japanese physician, denying the existence of Nazi gas chambers during the Holocaust. The publication of the article provoked a heated response from diplomats, journalists and Jewish leaders, some of whom co-ordinated an unsuccessful effort to press the magazine to

---

47. See, for example, Magami, "'Kyoho' no kozo: Shimbun wa naze misuriido suru no ka?" [The Construction of False Reporting: Why Do Newspapers Mislead?], Bungei Shunju (Tokyo, 1989).

publish a retraction. Only after several companies withdrew their advertisements from the magazine at the request of the Simon Wiesenthal Center in Los Angeles did Bungei Shunju announce that it would discontinue publication of the magazine and recall all copies of the February issue. The company's president published an apology, dismissed the magazine's chief editor, and later resigned himself to restore public trust in the company.

Inclusion of subliminal images in broadcasts

The use of subliminal images by the Japanese media first attracted public **6.29** attention in June 1994 when the Administrative Commission of the Motion Picture Code of Ethics expressed concerns at the insertion of one or two frames of unrelated pictures in thirty-eight sections of the Japanese cinema version of the Shochiku production, *Rampo* to stimulate viewers' subconscious. The film company had advertised the inclusion of the images and insisted that the frames did not contain any material which would violate the Commission's Code of Ethics, but hinted that it would remove such images from the video version of the film.

A year later, Tokyo Broadcasting System (TBS) was condemned by the National Association of Commercial Broadcasters for having surreptitiously included subliminal shots of Shoko Asahara and Fumihiro Joyu, leader and spokesman respectively of the Aum Supreme Truth religious cult, and Daisaku Ikeda, honorary chairman of the *Soka Gakkai Buddhist lay* organisation, in two news specials on 7 and 14 May 1995. Several different kinds of visuals were inserted at various points in the programmes, and reportedly could hardly be recognised by the naked eye since they remained on screen for a mere one-thirtieth to twenty-two thirtieths of a second each. The first programme included several close-ups of Asahara in scenes of sightseers at the cult's Kamikuishikimura compound and youths riding a roller-coaster at an amusement park, while the second included ones of Joyu and Judas Iscariot in footage of the fatal stabbing of Aum member, Hideo Murai, in an attempt to attract viewers' attention and raise their sense of tension.

The use of subliminal images by TBS was criticised by the National Association of Commercial Broadcasters as a breach of its Code of Ethics and by the MPT as a violation of the Broadcasting Act which had eroded public confidence in broadcasting in general. The Ministry requested that TBS investigate the case and submit a report of its findings, and the head of the Broadcasting Bureau issued a written warning demanding that the network adopt strict measures to prevent any recurrence TBS apologised to viewers and punished five executives, including the news bureau chief and producer and director of the programme, by lowering their salaries for two to three months.

Ironically, a TBS news programme had criticised another commercial network, Nippon Television (NTV), at the beginning of May for broadcasting the rerun of a 1989 cartoon programme with new subliminal close-ups of Shoko Asahara, leading the National Association of Commercial Broadcasters to issue a warning to the production company.

NTV became the focus of attention again in January 1996 when it was suspected of having inserted subliminal images 0.07 seconds long in footage shown on a daytime sensationalist chat show the previous month. The network responded that the images were unintentional and mere editing errors, highlighting the difficulties that an aggrieved person might face in establishing liability in such a case.

Public broadcaster NHK amended its Domestic Programme Standards to prohibit the use of subliminal devices in September 1995.

Danger of political bias

6.30 The significance of section 3–2(1) of the Broadcasting Act, which requires political impartiality in broadcasting and was modelled on the fairness doctrine once upheld in the United States, was brought home to citizens in 1993 as a result of the Tsubaki incident.

In September 1993, Asahi National Broadcasting Company (Television Asahi) news bureau chief, Sadayoshi Tsubaki, made controversial remarks at a meeting of the National Association of Commercial Broadcasters suggesting that he had urged his staff to slant their coverage of the July lower house election campaign in such a way as to help oust the then ruling Liberal Democratic Party from power and assist other parties form a coalition government. The following month, he was summoned as a sworn witness to the House of Representatives' Political Reform *Ad Hoc* Committee to explain his remarks. In his testimony, Tsubaki apologised and endorsed the results of an in-house study which had concluded that the company's election reporting had not been biased. Television Asahi also apologised for his remarks, saying they went against the spirit of neutrality and political fairness, and cut the salary of its chief executive officer.

The MPT renewed the broadcasting licence of Television Asahi in November 1993 on condition that it take "necessary measures" whenever allegations of bias are made. After Television Asahi submitted a report to the MPT in August 1994 stating that records of the broadcasts in question had indicated that they were fair and impartial, the head of the Broadcasting Bureau issued a warning to the network, noting that the Television Asahi had not violated the Broadcasting Act but requesting that the company improve its in-house training to prevent any future recurrence of such incidents.

Japanese debates on the fairness of broadcasting and freedom of speech seem shallow compared to those in the United States, and discussions of the Tsubaki case have remained for the most part undeveloped and superficial. It is a shame that Japanese society has missed a golden opportunity to have more substantial discussions, not only in the media but in other circles as well, about the meaning and value of freedom of expression, including the validity of the House of Representatives' controversial summoning of Tsubaki only on the basis of the Broadcasting Act's fairness clause.

Conclusion

In Japan's developing information society, freedom of expression is guar- **6.31** anteed effectively by the Constitution, but open to abuse by a media more concerned with circulation and ratings figures than the protection of reputation and privacy through responsible, ethical journalism. The excessive competition and commercialism among the media have led to some serious violations of individuals' rights, and with the continuing development of the nation's information society, the likelihood of further infringements can only be expected to increase.

Complainants of defamation and invasion of privacy by the media traditionally avoided litigation, but have begun recently to assert their legal rights with encouraging results, as judged from the success rates of their claims and the increasing sums of damages awarded them. The lawsuits brought by Kazuyoshi Miura have been exceptional, but demonstrate the fact that lay people with limited legal knowledge can bring successful actions against the media on their own, at least in cases where the assertions made in the defamatory reports are patently false or the infringement of privacy is blatant.

Japanese courts have shown they can be trusted to balance fairly the opposing constitutional rights to reputation and privacy on the one hand and freedom of expression on the other, but until recently have undervalued individuals' intangible rights in calculating damages in defamation and privacy cases.

Media organisations clearly need to make greater efforts to fulfil their duty to the public to defend freedom of expression and respect other constitutional rights by operating responsibly in accordance with their existing codes of ethics. The media should take this opportunity to create self-regulatory industry bodies to provide aggrieved persons with satisfactory non-legal, ethics-based forms of relief, which would demonstrate the media's resolve to uphold high standards of journalistic ethics and avoid the prospect of costly, time-consuming legal action. Given the opportunity to seek vindication quickly and inexpensively from a truly independent body, many complainants of defamation and invasion of privacy would surely choose this over the protracted and potentially costly alternative offered by the courts.

The Netherlands

Chapter 7
The Netherlands

W.J.H.T. Dupont,
C.J.M. van Berkel, and E.J.M. Jeunink
Molengraaff Instituut Privaatrecht, Universiteit Utrecht
(Center for Intellectual Property Law)
Utrecht, The Netherlands

Introduction

In the Netherlands, until the beginning of the 1980s, the media did not   **7.1**
take the invasion of name, reputation and of privacy seriously from a legal
point of view. This development, as appears from case law and commentaries, is still going on today. An important aspect of this development is
how the Dutch courts have been required to examine the unlawfulness
of statements and the role of the fundamental rights in this respect, in
particular the right to freedom of expression. The way in which this right
has been phrased under the Dutch Constitution has caused problems. A
second problem has been caused by the question how this fundamental
right under domestic law relates to the international human rights treaties that the Netherlands has ratified, in particular the European Convention
of Human Rights (ECHR). Thus, this chapter will deal first with the
Dutch Constitutional system treatment of freedom of expression and its
relationship to article 10 ECHR before discussing civil remedies to defamation and protection against invasion of privacy and data protection.
This chapter does not deal with other liabilities faced especially by the
media, such as copyright infringement, obscenity or incitement.

Protection of name and reputation

Three levels of protection exist in the Netherlands in relation to defama-   **7.2**
tory statements in the media.[1] Since only one of these, *i.e.*, protection by

---

1. See also on this subject F.W. Grosheide, freedom of the press and freedom of the person — civil aspects
of defamation in The Netherlands and in Europe, forthcoming in European Review of Private Law.

way of an action in tort, is strictly of a Civil Law nature, the two other possibilities will be dealt with only briefly. These are criminal law and the *Raad voor Journalistiek* (Press Council). The discussion of the Civil Law protections offered to the person will also deal with the remedies available to the individual.

Media's legal position — freedom of expression

7.3   Information given in respect of persons or companies may be harmful to those involved. It is of importance to these persons or companies that damage is repaired. However, it is in the media's interest to be able to continue to fulfil its function to inform and hold opinions. This means that there may be a conflict of interests in respect of which the law must lay down norms. Often the media when sued for defamatory publications, pleads as a defence that it exercised a social function: to inform the public and to reveal public disorder. This social function must be taken into account by the court in deciding on the claim. The social function defence plea is based on article 10 ECHR and article 19 of the International Covenant of Political and Civil Rights (Covenant) and the case law in this respect.

Besides the constitutional protection mentioned above, protection of freedom of expression under the international treaties is important in its own right. The international treaty provisions, article 10 ECHR and article 19 of the Covenant, are treaty obligations that according to article 93 of the Dutch Constitution, "are binding on anyone", often referred to as "directly applicable" provisions.[2] It follows from article 94 Constitution that treaty obligations take precedence over national statutory provisions, *i.e.*, precedence not only over primary and subordinate legislation, but also precedence over the Constitution itself.

This is important in two respects. Firstly, the treaty obligations can be invoked in the Dutch courts insofar as they offer more protection than is provided for under article 7 of the Dutch constitution. Article 7 protects all manifestations of the freedom of expression; the treaty provisions, however, explicitly protect acts of communication, such as the freedom to receive and impart information.

There are also drafting differences between the treaty provisions and the Constitution in respect of the restrictions. Thus, article 7 of the Constitution primarily prohibits preventive restrictions to the freedom of expression in general, whereas articles 10(2) ECHR and 19 of the Covenant exhaustively list the exceptions to these freedoms and for the protection of which

---

2. *Hoge Raad*, 18 April 1961, *Nederlandse Jurisprudentie* (NJ) 1961, 273 (article 10 ECHR) and *Hoge Raad*, 11 February 1986, NJ 1986, 673 (article 19 of the Covenant).

interests they may be invoked. Therefore, the treaty provisions, in particular article 10(1), offer more possibilities for a balancing of interests than article 7 of the Constitution does. Article 10(2) requires an examination to assess whether in view of the restrictive listed values, a domestic measure or an order which limits the freedom of expression may be considered "necessary in a democratic society". Secondly, the protective scope of the treaty provisions is wider than under article 7 of the Constitution. Article 7(4) explicitly excludes commercial advertising from protection, whereas the treaty provisions do offer this protection, because advertising falls within the definition of the freedoms of opinion and information under articles 10 ECHR and 19 of the Covenant.[3]

In view of the precedence of article 10 ECHR over article 7 of the Dutch Constitution, it is important to ask whether and if so, to what extent the freedom of the press can be subjected to restrictions. Put briefly, the case law indicates that the ECHR strongly emphasises protection of political and social criticism and discussion, as a result of which restrictions and penalties seldom stand the test of the European Court of Human Rights.[4]

In spite of the recognised precedence of article 10 ECHR over article 7 of the Constitution, it has long been unclear whether the Dutch courts and in particular the *Hoge Raad* directly applied article 10 ECHR in claims for damages concerning defamatory publications.[5] There are two reasons for this lack of clarity. Firstly, for the courts to directly apply article 10(2), the courts must acknowledge *drittwirkung* or horizontal effect (between private parties). Authors, however, have differed on whether the Dutch courts and in particular the *Hoge Raad* have acknowledged this effect.[6] Secondly, assuming the *Hoge Raad* has indeed acknowledged the horizontal effect of article 10, it has long been uncertain whether the *Hoge Raad* in

---

3. JM de Meij, *Uitingsvrijheid*, Amsterdam 1996, pp 45–47 and *Hoge Raad*, 13 February 1987, NJ 1987, 899.

4. *Sunday Times/United Kingdom*, ECHR 26 April 1979, Volume 30; Barthold, ECHR 25 March 1985, Volume 90; *Lingens/Austria*, ECHR 9 July 1986, Volume 103; *Oberschlick/Austria* 23 May 1991, Volume 204; *Swabe/Austria*, ECHR 28 August 1992, Volume 242–B; *Observer and Guardian/United Kingdom*, ECHR 26 November 1991, Volume 216; *Sunday Times, Number 2/United Kingdom*, ECHR, 26 November 1991, Volume 217; *Thorgeirson/Iceland*, ECHR 25 June 1992, Volume 239; *Castells/Spain*, ECHR 23 April 1992, Volume 236; *Jersild/Denmark* ECHR 23 September 1994, Volume 298; *Bluf/Netherlands*, ECHR 9 February 1995, Volume 306–A; *Prager and Oberschlick/Austria*, ECHR 26 April 1995, Volume 313; *Tolstoy Miloslavsky/United Kingdom* ECHR 13 July 1995, Volume 323.

5. The *Hoge Raad* is the highest court only deciding on the merits of the case.

6. For instance, AG Franx in *de Telegraaf, Hoge Raad*, 27 January 1984, NJ 1984, 202, finds that the *Hoge Raad* acknowledged this in *Hoge Raad,*, 25 June 1965, NJ 1966, 115, whereas this is denied by van Dijk and van Hoof, *European Convention in theorie en praktijk*, 2nd ed., Nijmegen 1982, p 360 footnote 784 and by Schuijt, "Is de Hoge Raad bang voor uitingsvrijheid?", AMI 1990, pp 83–89. See also Burkens, who finds that acknowledgement neither follows from this case nor from any other, Burkens, *Algemene Leerstukken van Grondrechten naar Nederlands Constitutioneel Recht*, Zwolle 1989, pp 185 *et seq.*

laying down criteria, actually took account of the way in which exceptions to the freedom of expression are phrased under article 10(2).

Probably until 1995, based on the *Hoge Raad's* reasoning, often the only conclusion which could be arrived at was that the *Hoge Raad* did not directly apply article 10(2).[7] In the past, some authors have criticised the *Hoge Raad's* examination.[8]

Three levels of protection

Protection of individuals by way of the Criminal Code

7.4   The Criminal Code (*Wetboek van Strafrecht*) also offers protection against defamatory press publications, etc. Given the purpose of this chapter this topic will not be dealt with extensively. Some special remarks concerning protection of privacy are made further below.

Protection through the Press Council

7.5   Complaints in respect of a "journalistic behaviour" can be lodged with the Press Council. The Press Council has operated, albeit in a different composition and under a different name, since 1948. In 1982, the Council became a foundation and widened its basis. Today, the Dutch Society for Journalists, the broadcasting organisations, organisations for publishers and the *Genootschap van hoofdredacteuren* (Bond for Senior Editors) participate in the Press Council. Since the Press Council is not a disciplinary organisation, but a "council of opinion", it can best be qualified as a complaints commission. According to article 3 of its articles of association, only those persons who are directly affected can lodge a complaint concerning "journalistic behaviour". Those "directly affected" include societies representing a certain interest, if in light of their purpose, they are directly affected. Under article 3 of the articles of association, the test is phrased as follows:

> "[W]hether the bounds are exceeded, of that what in view of the requirements of journalistic responsibility is considered socially acceptable."

7.6   Rulings of the Council are not binding. They do not result in any enforceable penalty. There is no appeal from rulings of the Council. Prior

---

7. See also JM Meij, *Uitingvrijheid*, 2nd ed. Amsterdam 1996, pp 154 *et seq.*

8. See Schuijt, *Is de Hoge Raad bang voor uitingsvrijheid?* AMI 1990, at pp 83–89 and — more moderate — Dupont, in: Grosheide (ed.) *Hoofdstukken Mediarecht*, Alphen a/d Rijn 1991, at p 112.

to or together with a procedure before a civil court, a complainant sometimes lodges a complaint with the Press Council. According to some authors, this leads to the unwanted effect of the civil court literally adopting the ruling of the Council or attaching too much importance to it.[9]

Protection through the civil courts

Examination of defamatory statements

Article 6:162 *Burgerlijk Wetboek* (Civil Code — BW) regulates infringe-   **7.7**
ments against name and reputation.

It has been unclear for a long time whether the Dutch courts and in particular the *Hoge Raad* acknowledged the precedence and the direct applicability of article 10 ECHR. Rather the *Hoge Raad* took a purely Civil Law approach, balancing two high-quality social interests, on the one hand, the individual's interest not to be exposed in press publications to rash suspicions and, on the other hand, the public interest that disorder be revealed.[10] An example of this approach was demonstrated in *Gemeenteraadslid/X*, which was the leading case until 1995.[11] In this case that concerned revelations of disorder by the press, the *Hoge Raad* laid down a number of guidelines for the courts to assess the lawfulness of statements. The facts were as follows: a member of the town council submitted a letter written by her to the Council Committee on Social Welfare and at the same time sent a copy to a journalist with the daily newspaper *De Gelderlander* and to the newsletter of a political party, *de Tribune*. *De Gelderlander* published the letter before the Town Council meeting took place; *de Tribune* published the letter a few weeks later. Both publications contained sections from the letter which suggested that Mr. Y, a member of the board of government-subsidised children protection's agencies, had entered into shady real estate deals that had nothing to do with child protection, to enrich himself at the expense of public funds.

In the proceedings that followed, the *Hoge Raad* held that the *Gerechtshof* (Court of Appeal) not having considered several circumstances, had

---

9. See Korthals Altes, "Is de Raad voor Journalistiek overbodig?", *Massacommunicatie* 1988/3, at p 263 and Oppenoorth, "De Raad voor Journalistiek en de strijd om de informatievrijheid", *Mediaforum* 1994/2, at p 15.

10. See Schuijt, "Is de Hoge Raad niet meer bang voor uitingsvrijheid?", *Informatierecht* AMI 1996, number 3.

11. *Hoge Raad*, 24 June 1983, NJ 1984, 801 (ann. MS).

based its decision on a too narrow interpretation of the term unlawfulness. The *Hoge Raad* held in respect of the lawfulness:

> "In examining this question there are basically two high-quality opposing interests at stake: on the one hand the interest of individuals not to be exposed to defamation by the press; on the other hand the interest that public disorder, which may affect society should not be allowed to continue because of lack of knowledge with the general public, resulting from the inability of the responsible public bodies in today's complicated society to pay equal attention to all matters that deserve attention, leaving aside the possibility of other factors which may hinder the ending of certain disorder."

7.8 The Court postulated that which of these interests ought to be decisive depends on the circumstances, and in a case like this particularly on:

(1) The nature of the published suspicions and the seriousness of the expected consequences for the person who is the subject of the suspicions;

(2) The seriousness — from the public interest perspective — of the disorder that the publication aims to reveal;

(3) The extent to which, at the time of publication, the suspicions were based on the available facts;

(4) The wording of the suspicions, in relation to the factors listed under (1) to (3);

(5) The degree of probability that even without the contested press publication, the goals in the public interest could have been reached in another way that is less harmful to the other party and has a reasonable chance of success; and

(6) A possible limitation of the harm caused by the publication to the injured party, in view of the chance that the statement in question would have attracted publicity, also without the contested submission to the press.

7.9 This *Hoge Raad* judgment has long been regarded as a landmark case.[12] The judgment not only lays down criteria for press publications but has a more general scope as well, since it is held to mean that the answer to the question about the lawfulness of a statement in other cases also depends

---

12. See also annotation by Brunner, *Vara Bom/LSP, Hoge Raad*, 27 January 1984, NJ 1984, 803; and Asser-Hartkamp III, number 283, Zwolle 1994.

on a balancing of interests, the result of which depends on all circumstances of the case,[13] or in a more recent explanation of the case by the *Hoge Raad*:[14]

> "A judge's judgment should be based on a balance of both — in the more often cited case — opposing interests, but the question which one of the interests in the matter put before him ought to be decisive, depends on all circumstances of the case, which must be considered interrelated. Basically it is left to the judge who decides over the facts to determine what the specific characteristics of the case are and what weight they should have. In the 1983, case under [(1)–(6)] only a few relevant factors were mentioned, the case did not require a judge to examine at least all of these factors and account for these in his judgment".

Early in 1995, the *Hoge Raad's* case law showed a change.[15] The *Hoge Raad* now explicitly applies article 10 ECHR. In *Parool BV/ Van Gasteren*, it stated that since the action was against a journalist and a press body and therefore the awarding of damages would interfere with the right to freedom of expression, the court should examine whether the infringements meet the conditions of article 10 ECHR before the damages sought could be awarded (actual and non-monetary damages). The *Hoge Raad* held that the examination carried out by the *Gerechtshof* based on the criteria developed under *Gemeenteraadslid/ X*, in view of the guidelines of the *Hoge Raad*,[16] led to the conclusion that the restriction applied was in conformity with the "prescribed by law" requirement of article 10(2). The *Hoge Raad* applied the *Sunday Times* test, which requires case law to be adequately precise and accessible to be able to restrict freedom of expression. Subsequently, examining at which interest the interference is aimed, it concluded that the grounds of restriction were the protection of name and reputation. Finally, the *Hoge Raad* examined whether the interference, with a view to the interest to be protected, may be considered necessary in a democratic society and whether the interference is proportionate to the interest to be protected. In doing so, it considered at length the balance of interest test applied by the *Gerechtshof* against these criteria, which effectively introduced an additional criterion.[17]

7.10

---

13. See Asser-Hartkamp III, number 283, Zwolle 1994.

14. *Herrenberg/ Parool, Hoge Raad*, 8 March 1995, NJ 1995, 437.

15. See the annotation of Dommering; see also Schuijt, "Is de Hoge Raad niet meer bang voor de uitingsvrijheid?", IER/AMI 1996, number 3; de Meij, *Uitingsvrijheid*, Amsterdam 1996, at pp 45–47.

16. *Hoge Raad*, 24 June 1983, NJ 1984, 801.

17. *Cf.* the annotation by Dommering NJ 1995, 422 and Schuijt, "Is de Hoge Raad niet meer bang voor uitingsvrijheid?", IER/AMI 1996 number 3. See also de Meij, *Uitingsvrijheid*, Amsterdam 1996.

The factors given by the *Hoge Raad* in *Gemeenteraadslid/X*[18] may, but need not always be used as a checklist by the court examining the facts. *Hoge Raad* judgments are limited to an examination of questions of law and whether the judge examining the facts has taken all relevant factors into account.[19] Pursuant to a recent case,[20] the *Hoge Raad* deals with the necessity criterion as part of the questions of law and is therefore also required to pay attention to the facts.

In addition, an important aspect of Dutch case law is that the majority of judgments concerning defamatory media statements are rendered in *kort geding* proceedings. These are interim interlocutory proceedings, in which the judge renders a provisional injunction within fourteen days, or less if necessary. However, since the parties often do not bring another action in respect of the principal claim, the judgment in *kort geding* is often the final judgment. The *Hoge Raad*, however, has held that in respect of stating the grounds of the judgment in *kort geding*, different requirements apply than in respect of judgments in general.[21] Most importantly, *kort geding* procedures are of a very factual nature. Therefore, a judge's considerations will often be determined by his evaluation of the facts. An examination of the published case law suggests that since the majority of *kort geding* judgments often contain no more than a statement of the facts and a only a very brief statement of the grounds, many lower courts do not consider the case law of the *Hoge Raad* applicable to disputes before them.[22] Also, it has been noted that lower courts in assessing whether a publication is defamatory are not guided by principles of fundamental rights, such as the horizontal effect of the fundamental rights of expression and of name and reputation and by the collision between them. Rather the lower courts take a purely Civil Law approach, whereby the issue of truth is of crucial importance.[23]

Use of portraits

7.11   Article 21 of the *Auteurswet* (Copyright Act) and article 6:162 of the *Burgerijk Wetboek* regulate the use of portraits. A person may not only consider his privacy invaded as a result of published statements, but also

---

18. *Hoge Raad*, 24 June 1983 NJ 1984, 801.

19. *Cf. Saladin/HBU, Hoge Raad*, 19 May 1967, NJ 1967, 261.

20. *Hoge Raad*, 6 January 1995, NJ 1995, 422.

21. See *Hoge Raad*, 26 March 1965, NJ 1965, 163 as well as the *Hoge Raad*, decision in the present case: "judgments on the facts in particular *kort geding* judgments, in respect of which no further stating of the grounds is necessary"; *Cf.* also annotations by Brunner and *Hoge Raad*, 27 January 1984, NJ 1984, 803.

22. *Cf.* Lebesque, *Droit de response als luizenpoeder?*, Lelystad 1986, at pp 43 *et seq.*

23. Kistenkas, "Onrechtmatige Perspublicaties: de bevrijding van de grondrechten", *Mediaforum* 1996, pp 2 *et seq.*

as a result of published photographs. Mostly this concerns publication by photographers and magazines or newspapers of portraits that have not been commissioned and for publication without consent. Pursuant to article 21 of the Copyright Act, such a publication is not allowed insofar as it violates the legitimate interest of the person portrayed. According to the case law, this interest can be of a moral or a financial nature. It follows from a *Hoge Raad* judgment concerning the publication of a photograph of a nudist[24] that article 21 of the Copyright Act protects against the invasion of personal life. The picture was made at a nudist campsite without permission and accordingly published on the back of a publicly available travel guide.

The leading *Hoge Raad* judgment in this respect is *E/Uitgeverij Spaarnestad.*[25] *E* was convicted by the *Gerechtshof* Amsterdam for 20 years imprisonment and involuntary psychiatric treatment for the murder of G.J. Heijn, a very rich owner of a supermarket chain. In the weekly magazine *Panorama*, published by Spaarnestad BV, pictures were published of *E* at the time of the reconstruction of the murder. *Panorama* published one of these photographs because the photographer had won an important prize with it. *E* protested against publication and brought an action for damages in respect of the invasion of his privacy.

The *Hoge Raad* held that article 21 offers the person portrayed protection in particular against infringements of his personal life. It also held that this right has no "absolute weight" overriding the right to freedom of expression, as argued by Spaarnestad. The *Hoge Raad* considered that the case concerned two freedoms, which are essential to individual development as well as to a democratic society as such and that there was no reason to accept a priority of one over the other. The *Hoge Raad* went on to say that when due to the publication of a portrait without consent of the person portrayed, freedom of expression conflicts with freedom of personal life, there is no legitimate reason to assess the priority of the freedoms differently than when a conflict of this nature arises because of, for example, the publication of statements.

Assuming that the *Hoge Raad* will continue to opine that the publication of portraits must be judged in the same way as the publication of statements, also after the decision rendered in *Het Parool/ van Gasteren*,[26] it means that the *Hoge Raad* will use the following criteria in determining the lawfulness of an uncommissioned portrait submitted before it:

(1) Whether the action of the person portrayed involves one of the restrictions as mentioned under article 10 ECHR;

---

24. *Hoge Raad*, 30 October 1987, NJ 1988, 277.

25. *Hoge Raad*, 21 January 1994, NJ 1994, 473, annotated by DWFV.

26. NJ 1995, 422.

(2) If so, then on the basis of a balance of interests test, taking account of all circumstances of the case, which of the fundamental rights outweighs the other should be examined to determine whether the publication is unlawful under article 6:162 and whether the restriction of the freedom of expression is "prescribed by law" as mentioned under article 10(2); and

(3) Whether in a democratic society, the awarding of a compensation constitutes a restriction of the freedom of expression necessary for the protection of someone else's rights.

Civil code remedies

7.12 The following remedies are available to the plaintiff in respect of unlawful or defamatory statements:

(1) Declaratory judgment that the statements made by the journalist or press are unlawful;[27]

(2) Material damages;[28]

(3) *Immateriële schadevergoeding* (moral damages or damages for non-pecuniary loss);[29]

(4) An injunction to refrain from the statements or an injunction not to repeat them; or

(5) Publication of the judgment or a rectification,[30] or a rectification[31] by forfeiting a periodic penalty payment.

Material damages

7.13 As a result of media suspicions or accusations, someone may lose business[32] or experience damage to her career. The damage thus caused must be compensated. However, it is often the case that the damage caused cannot be determined precisely; the court then must determine the damage in reasonableness and fairness. In this way, the Amsterdam *Gerechtshof* in the case of the action brought by the *wethouder* (chairman of the executive) of the town of Bergen op Zoom against the weekly magazine *Nieuw Revue* and the television company Veronica, awarded

---

27. Article 6:162 BW and 3:302 BW.

28. Article 6:162 BW and 6:96 BW.

29. Article 6:162 BW and article 106 BW.

30. In pursuance of article 6:162 BW or article 6:103 BW.

31. Article 6:167 BW.

32. *Gerechtshof* Amsterdam in *Hoge Raad*, 22 June 1979, NJ 1979, 516.

DFL 75,000 in damages as a result of loss of income.[33] Reparation for damages — or for an advance thereof — may be demanded not only in the primary claim, but also in *kort geding*.[34] In case the medium involved goes on to publish the injured party's reaction, this may limit the damage caused, but does not take away her right to an action for damages.[35]

Reparation for moral damages

The amount of moral damages granted in the Dutch courts may seem low   **7.14** in relation to the awards granted by courts abroad. Thus, the Amsterdam Gerechtshof in the case of the *wethouder* of the town of Bergen op Zoom[36] granted DFL 125,000 in moral damages; until now, the highest sum ever to be ordered by a Dutch court in this kind of case. In *Van Gasteren/Parool*, the *Gerechtshof* granted van Gasteren DFL 50,000 in moral damages, a sum which is considered quite high by the Dutch courts.

Injunction against repetition

Basically, in *kort geding* an action may be brought for an interlocutory   **7.15** injunction to ban an intended statement, which has not yet been published, provided the content is sufficiently clear.[37] In the interest of freedom of expression, however, the President of the *Rechtbank* (District Court) is very reluctant in ordering an interlocutory injunction.[38] An injunction not to repeat the unlawful statement by no means interferes with the freedom of expression, albeit that the description of the ban must meet certain requirements.[39] According to the case law, the nature of the protected interest brings about that the wording of an effective order can hardly be anything but general. However, in such a case, the scope of the injunction must be restricted to statements, of which after serious consideration, cannot be expected, taking account of the interest on the violation of which the injunction has been granted that they will result in the

---

33. The damages claimed for loss of income amounted to DFL 300,000.

34. See for award of damages, *e.g.*, President *Rechtbank* Amsterdam, 3 September 1987, AMI 1987, p 128, annotated by Korthals Altes, Damages not awarded: President *Rechtbank* Amsterdam, 1 October 1987, *Kort Geding* (KG) 1987, 471.

35. *Hoge Raad*, 22 June, NJ 1979, 516.

36. *Gerechtshof* Amsterdam in *Hoge Raad*, 22 June 1979, NJ 1979, 516.

37. *Cf. Gerechtshof* Amsterdam, 13 September 1984, NJ 1985, 409; De Mey, *Uitingsvrijheid*, Amsterdam 1996, at pp 88–89.

38. *Cf.* President *Rechtbank* Amsterdam, 25 November 1982, *Kort Geding* 1982, 216 and President *Rechtbank* Dordrecht, 24 December 1987, KGK 1988, p 1105; *cf.* Mendel, in: *Jurist en Bedrijf*, pp 89–90.

39. Bloembergen (ed.), *Onrechtmatige Daad* IX number 51, Kluwer, looseleaf edition, Deventer.

infringements which have been banned by the court.[40] On the basis of this, an injunction not to "write or have someone else write about the plaintiff in a way similar as in the copy of . . ." was considered too wide by the *Gerechtshof* Amsterdam, whereupon this was replaced by "in the same way as . . .[41] in particular as . . .".[42] However, an injunction phrased very generally, may be justified if a prior and precise injunction did not offer the injured party the legal protection intended.[43] Sometimes the case law lays down conditions in respect of publication injunctions. Thus, a publication injunction was granted against the journalist Knoop in respect of certain details (listed in the case) concerning the suspected war criminal Menten "until the moment when in the criminal case against Menten, in a judgment of the *Rechtbank*, it is proved that those statements are factually correct".[44]

Publication of judgment or rectification

7.16   It follows from the case law that the courts, both in cases of defamation as well as in cases of unlawful statements, may order the defendant to publish the judgment rendered against him in full or in part; in certain cases, the courts may also order the defendant to publish a rectification or another announcement.[45] According to the case law and most authors, this order does not interfere with the defendant's freedom of expression.[46] There are several sources of law in respect of this order. Thus, the order may be for non-monetary compensation, in which case all the requirements of article 6:162 BW must be fulfilled. It may, however, also be an order to comply with a requirement of unwritten law, non-compliance with which would be unlawful, in which cases the fulfilment of the requirement of (imminent) unlawfulness would suffice.[47] Apart from the mentioned order against the defendant, the court may also allow the plaintiff to

---

40. *Hoge Raad*, 18 February 1966, NJ 1966 p 208; *Gerechtshof* Amsterdam, 16 December 1976, NJ 1977, p 86.

41. *Gerechtshof* Amsterdam, 16 December 1976, NJ 1977, p 86. *Cf.* also President of the *Rechtbank* Den Haag, 10 February 1970, where the injunction not to "publish anything about the plaintiff, without having determined in advance whether publication might be contrary to the facts or the truth", was held too wide.

42. See also *Gerechtshof* Den Haag, 14 November 1988, KGK 1987, 1006 following President *Rechtbank*, 6 February 1986, KG 1986, 118.

43. *Goeree/ Z Hoge Raad*, 2 February 1990, RvdW 1990, p 48 and *Gerechtshof* Amsterdam, 2 November 1977, NJ 1978, p 33 (*Willeke Alberti/ Panorama*).

44. *Gerechtshof* Amsterdam, 15 September 1977, NJ 1977, 409.

45. *Onrechtmatige Daad* II, numbers 195.1 and 2. See for rectification in particular: *Rectificatie*, Schuijt (ed.), Amsterdam, 1989.

46. *Onrechtmatige Daad* II, number 195.4. On the other hand, van Manen in *Rectificatie*, Schuijt (ed.), at p 64 considers the rectification ordered by the court to interfere with the freedom of expression.

47. Asser-Hartkamp III, number 242. *Cf.* also Schuijt, *Rectificatie*, pp 16 *et seq.*

publish the above-mentioned statements (whether or not at the defendant's expense). However, there is a difference in opinion as to whether publication of the judgment by the plaintiff without authorisation would be justified, albeit that this is considered lawful in the more recent literature.[48] The court may not grant the order or the authorisation, if publication is (no longer) of interest to the plaintiff. The case law provides many examples to this effect. If the court does grant the action then the court determines the manner of publication: thus, the court decides when and by way of which media (daily newspaper, magazine, etc.) the statement shall be published; the location and the type-face, as well as the content of statement: the judgment (in full or in part) or a statement prepared by the judge. This is entirely within the discretion of the court, so that the plaintiff's action, insofar relevant, is no more than a suggestion.[49] In particular in respect of judgments containing publication orders it can be said that: the more precise the order, the less chance there is for a enforcement dispute to arise concerning the question whether the defendant has complied with the order.[50]

Sometimes a plaintiff demands that the defendant on publication of the judgment shall withhold himself from comment. In granting such an order the court must be extremely careful so as not to unlawfully limit the defendant's fundamental right of expression.[51]

Since only statements of facts that are false or incomplete can be the subject of rectification, it is not always possible to bring an action for rectification of defamatory statements. Thus, the court cannot order a rectification of statements of opinion which are considered false and defamatory, because it is not possible to give an order to change someone's opinion or to "take back" a defamatory remark. Neither is rectification possible in respect of an unlawful invasion of someone's privacy.[52] A specification of publication of the judgment, *i.e.*, the right of rectification is laid down in article 6:167 BW. Article 6:167 in cases of false or misleading publication of factual statements due to incompleteness, allows the judge to grant an action brought by the plaintiff for publication

---

48. *Cf.* literature mentioned in *Onrechtmatige Daad* II, number 94.

49. President *Rechtbank* Amsterdam, 25 September 1986, *Kort Geding* 1986, 441: in case of rectification by the media of their own unlawful statement, there need not be a correlation in respect of location, length and lay-out between the statement and its rectification.

50. *Cf.* President *Rechtbank* Amsterdam, 25 April 1985, KG 1985, 5: placement under "letters to the editor" complies with the order of rectification at a "suitable location"; however, the layout (no framework) is not in accordance with "suitable layout". *Cf.* also *Gerechtshof* Arnhem, 7 February 1989, KG 1989,110 (*Goeree/Z*) and President *Rechtbank* Amsterdam, 28 August 1986, KG 1986, 404.

51. *Onrechtmatige Daad* II, number 195b; a generally phrased order: "without comment, discussion or consideration", infringes this right; *cf. Gerechtshof* Amsterdam, 24 January 1986, NJ 1986, 66.

52. *Cf.* van Manen, *Rectificatie,* pp 64 *et seq.*

of the judgment. Article 6:167(1) is concerned with rectification by the defendant, who as a result of his knowledge of the false or misleading statement, is liable in tort by virtue of article 6:162. Article 6:167(2) concerns rectification, following non-tortious liability, since he did not have personal knowledge. Thus, often by virtue of article 167(2) it will be possible to bring an action against the medium which published the statement. An order for rectification against the media has been considered indispensable both in cases where the author is unknown or unavailable, where he on account of insolvency could not be coerced into rectification, not even by means of a periodic penalty payment, as well as in cases where the media concerned refuse to co-operate. The courts also have a wide margin of discretion in respect of an order for rectification by virtue of article 6:167. Firstly, it has been held that a court may give an order for the publication of a rectification even if the requirements are met; the court therefore at its own discretion may refuse such an order, under the circumstances of the case. Secondly, it is entirely within the court's margin of discretion to determine in what way the original statement shall be rectified. Thirdly, article 6:167 allows the judge to apportion the costs of the procedure and the rectification to the plaintiff, fully or partly if the defendant by virtue of section 2 is not to blame. The reason for this provision is to avoid the attractiveness of bringing action against the media, without any proper cause. Finally, article 6:167 states that each party liable according to the judgment, in respect of the costs of the trial and of the rectification, has a right of recourse against anyone who is liable in respect of the damage caused by publication.

Rectification must be distinguished from the right of reply: rectification is a more powerful instrument.[53] The right of reply is a publication in which someone by way of reaction gives his opinion of the facts. There is no statutory right of reply under Dutch law. The absence of legislation, however, does not hinder the court to order the publication of a reply as a way of reparation or limitation of the damage caused. The courts are sometimes inclined to do so if in view of the facts, a rectification order is deemed too harsh a penalty. On the other hand it must be borne in mind that the publication of a reply by an editorial board, generally does not take away an injured party's right of rectification.[54]

---

53. For an extensive comment on the right of reply, see Lebesque, *Droit de Réponse als luizenpoeder*, Lelystad 1986, at pp 43 *et seq.* and van Manen, *Rectificatie*, at p 64.

54. *Onrechtmatige Daad* II, number 195.2 (rectification dismissed) and 195.3.

Privacy and publicity

There has always been a tension between privacy and publicity. Privacy   **7.17**
might even have gained its legal content in the fight against unwanted
publications. In 1890,[55] the law recognised no autonomous right to
privacy, protecting the private life from unwanted publicity. This right
would be described as the "right to be left alone". Today, the debate
about privacy continues. Technological developments make the collection and dissemination of information much easier. People are filmed
unexpectedly, in the most awkward situations, *e.g.*, in a car accident or a
police raid. The high degree of intrusion and directness sometimes go hand
in hand with a dubious degree of newsworthiness. Sometimes the victims are
only confronted with the tapes and if permission is sought, it is often only
after the filming. Even apart from the granting of permission, the people
who are filmed may experience this as an invasion of their privacy.[56] This
way of television-making presents a source of legal dispute.

In 1995, two Dutch television companies were in court accounting for
the use of hidden cameras. One had sent a Turkish family on a tour
around the most expensive hotels and restaurants in the Netherlands. At
one restaurant the Turkish family was told there was no table available,
whereas a white family was given a table. The restaurant in question sued
for libel, asked for damages and filed a complaint with the *Raad voor
Journalisitiek* (Press Council). The other television company sent an actress
with a hidden camera past a number of abortion clinics. Successfully the
clinics obtained an injunction against the television company to stop the
broadcast of the secret recordings. According to the court, the right to
privacy in case of abortion was more important than the freedom of press.
Various "reality television" programmes in the Netherlands have even
resulted in questions being asked in Parliament. These questions among
others, concerned an ambulance's team annoyance at the presence of a
camera team, but also questions whether the invasion of victims' privacy
ought not outweigh the freedom of the press.[57] A national Ombudsman
report contained recommendations for police forces on how to deal with
Reality television makers.[58] Radio uses similar methods.[59]

---

55. Warren and Brandeis, "The right to privacy", *Harvard Law Review* 1890, number 5, p 193.

56. Zaborsky van Boxtel, "Reality tv en de realiteit van het recht", *Mediaforum* 1996–1.

57. *Tweede Kamer* 1995–1996, questions 19 September 1995. See also *Privacy actueel*, Volume 2, number 16, 21 November 1995.

58. National Ombudsman, 28 August 1995.

59. Consider the hoax call to Queen Elizabeth broadcast live on the radio prior to the Independence referendum in Canada, which according to Queen Elizabeth was a confidential conversation.

Even apart from Reality television, there are sufficient examples of media publications invading a person's right to privacy. Reporters and programme makers will avow that publication serves a public interest and that the privacy interest of those involved must yield to the interest of the freedom of the press. If the question of the legality of the publication is involved, both interests are weighed. Judicial decisions that contain this balance of interest are mostly very case-oriented and therefore difficult to generalise.

This section will try to list the norms concerning the right to privacy to be taken into account by the media. An important question is how a person must demonstrate his (constitutional) right to privacy to defend himself against publication no matter through what part of the media. Several privacy aspects can be of importance when a person protests against media publication of information that he deems personal.

A publication can invade someone's personal life because:

(1) The way of observing invades the right to privacy. Publication of what has been observed may be justified by another (public) interest, but some areas of human life are so intimate that any unwanted observation constitutes an invasion of privacy; or

(2) The manner of observation does not invade privacy, but publication of what's observed does.

7.18 A person will always be confronted with the weighing of his right against the freedom of the press, which is also laid down in the Constitution. One value does not necessarily outweigh the other. A journalist who without permission makes recordings in someone else's house or in other private places is criminally liable. A person who is secretly filmed in the street can claim the right to his image, provided the victim can prove damage as a result of broadcasting. In addition, there are legal norms concerning the collecting of personal information. Finally, the Press Council should be mentioned, which in the framework of self-regulation, lays down conditions for journalists and their publications.

"Privacy" concept

7.19 The right to be left alone as formulated by Warren and Brandeis constitutes a wide definition of the term privacy. The right to privacy has no general application, but is only applicable in the area which can be described as private space or private life. Firstly, this area is mostly spatially determined. Everyone has a right to a space in which he is unobserved by others: a control-free environment in which the individual feels free to act as he pleases. Of course, this firstly includes someone's home, but also, albeit to a lesser extent, a hotel room or office. In the 1960s, in addition to being spatially defined, the term privacy was extended to include an informational dimension. The basis for the definition of "informational privacy" can be found with Westin:[60]

> "The claim of individuals, groups, or institutions to determine for themselves when, how and to what extent information about them is communicated to others."

Now that the definition of privacy has gained an informational content, **7.20** many authors distinguish between relational and informational privacy.[61] In terms of individual rights, relational privacy is defined as the right to selective contact-making. Informational privacy includes the right to selective publication of that what can be considered personal.

Korthals Altes further distinguishes between informational and publicity privacy. The latter definition is held to include: "privacy in connection with a publication by a newspaper, a television company, etc.".[62]

Privacy as norm

Constitutional protection

The Dutch Constitution, article 10 also protects private life: everyone has **7.21** the right to respect for his private life, except by or in accordance with exceptions as prescribed by law. The explanatory Memorandum only deals with the definition of private life and respect thereof in general. Included are in any event, the home, certain ways of communication, some habits, behaviour and contacts, subscriptions, memberships, as well as certain aspects of family life. Physical and moral integrity also fall under the privacy definition according to the explanatory memorandum. The observation, the recording and the publication of personal information finally, may constitute an invasion of article 10. Whether this will be the case, depends on different factors such as the nature of the intimacy as well as the way in which the information is used.[63] The constitutional protection of personal life is not only based on article 10. A number of other constitutional rights, of less recent origin, can also be regarded as

---

60. Westin, *Privacy and Freedom*, New York 1967.

61. Holvast, *naar een risicoloze maatschappy?* Academic Press, Den Haag 1985.

62. Korthals Altes, "Valt schending van privacy te rectificeren?" in: Schujt (ed.), *Rectificatie, Beschouwingen over rechtzettingen in het recht en in de praktijk*, Cramwinckel Amsterdam 1989, pp 54–62.

63. *Tweede Kamer* 1978–1979, 15463, number 2, pp 7 *et seq.*; *Tweede Kamer* 1979–1980, 16086, number 3, pp 4, 5.

privacy rights: the right to a home (article 12), privacy of correspondence (article 13) and physical integrity (article 11). The most important international privacy provision is article 8 of the European Convention of Human Rights (ECHR). In addition to private life generally, it explicitly protects family life, the home and correspondence.

The constitutional right that appeals most to journalists is the freedom of speech, a constitutional right which has been provided for under many national Constitutions and Treaties. Article 10 of the ECHR sets out the freedom of expression to include the freedom to hold opinions and to receive and impart information and ideas without interference by public authority and regardless of frontiers. The provision mentions the freedom to receive and to impart and is therefore of importance to both sender and receiver. The corresponding article 19 of the United Nations Covenant on Civil and Political Rights extends the definition of freedom of expression to include the freedom of journalists to gather information and opinions. Under the Dutch Constitution, article 7 protects freedom of expression. This provision divides the right into: freedom of the press, freedom to broadcast and other freedoms of expression. In respect of the freedom of the press, prior authorisation is excluded. A television company can be subjected to a licensing system; there is, however, no prior supervision of the content of radio or television broadcasts. Often, the court in *kort geding* (preliminary injunction proceedings) has held that an injunction prior to the broadcast was a too drastic measure. In *kort geding*, a victim of confrontational journalism brought an action to ban a broadcast; the president held that the content of the broadcast was unlawful, but nevertheless held it unjustified to issue a far-reaching restraining order prohibiting publication.[64]

Freedom of expression and privacy are two constitutional rights that must be balanced.[65] Many interim injunction proceedings concern the relationship between freedom of expression and privacy. In *E/ uitgeverij Spaarnestad*[66] the *Hoge Raad* held that the right to respect for private life is not an absolute principle which outweighs the right to freedom of expression. They are two freedoms that are essential for the development of the individual as well as for a democratic society, and there is no reason to accept a priority of one over the other.

The case law shows which factors are important in deciding whether an invasion of the right to a personal life has taken place: the seriousness of the invasion of privacy; the nature and the extent of the intimacy

---

64. President *Rechtbank* Arnhem, 24 January 1995, *Mediaforum* 1995–3.

65. As for the news coverage of court proceedings, article 6 ECHR guarantees a fair trial and allows for the court to prohibit reporting from a public court room.

66. *Hoge Raad*, 21 January 1994, NJ 1994, 473.

exposed; the importance of the facts that are revealed and the person concerned. The way in which information is collected can also be important. Persistent following of a person or continuous surveillance can be considered unlawful when the invasion of privacy is challenged before a court.

Privacy legislation

The arrival of the computer has made it possible to obtain and handle   **7.22** information increasingly efficiently. A drawback of this convenience is the danger of invasions of privacy.

Until 1970, there was hardly any interest in privacy law in the Netherlands. The 1971 census turned out to be the catalyst of a widespread concern among the population. This resulted in a discussion with large political consequences. The discussion was prompted by the plans to introduce personal registration numbers. The discussion resulted in the establishment of a government Committee assigned to advise on legislation on the safeguarding of privacy. Not until 1988 was a general Act protecting personal life in relation to personal data introduced, the *Wet Persoonsregistraties* (WPR) or "Data Protection Act".

Besides the WPR there is other legislation containing privacy provisions, for instance:

(1) *De Wet justitiële documentatie* (Justice Documentation Act);
(2) *De Wet Openbaarheid van Bestuur* (Government Information (public Access Act);
(3) *De Auteurswet* (Copyright Act);
(4) *De Wet met betrekking tot de invoering van het fiscaal nummer* (The Introduction of the Fiscal Number Act);
(5) *De Wet op de Inlichtingen- en Veiligheidsdiensten* (Intelligence and Security Services Act);
(6) *De Wet Politieregisters* (Police Registers Act);
(7) *De Wet gemeentelijke basisadminstratie persoonsgegevens* (Municipal Administration of Personal Data Act);
(8) *De Wet geneeskundige behandelingsovereenkomst* (Medical Treatment Agreement Act).

Some of these Acts will be briefly dealt with to the extent that they are   **7.23** relevant to the safeguarding of privacy of individuals who come into contact with the media.

Personal registers

The WPR regulates the keeping of personal registers in general. In princi-   **7.24** ple, this Act applies to all existing personal registers, both computerised personal registers as well as manually operated registers, such as a collection of files containing personal data. Important principles of the WPR are to oblige disclosure of personal registers[67] and to impose self-regulation on controllers of personal registers. The controller of a personal register must inform any data subject whose data are recorded in a file for the first time. The data subject need not be informed if he knows or could know that data concerning him are recorded. Self-regulation under the WPR means that the norms imposed by the WPR must be developed by those involved (often the controller of the personal register). Personal registers kept in the context of press, radio and television (article 2 WPR) are exempted from the Act because another constitutional right is involved, namely the freedom of expression. Exempted personal registers may only be used for the exempted purpose, otherwise the WPR applies. Thus, a collection of files belonging to a journalist in principle do not fall within the scope of the WPR.

However, the WPR can be relevant for the disclosure of data from a personal register by the media. In collecting information, a journalist may need data about a person from a personal register. To answer whether the WPR offers any protection to the data subject, it is firstly necessary to determine whether the personal register falls under the scope of the WPR. In addition to personal registers for the benefit of the media, there are several other personal registers exempted from the WPR. These include personal registers for private use (personal diaries) and personal registers falling under the scope of other legislation such as those of the police (Police Registers Act), security services (Act on Intelligence and Security Services) and under the Municipal Administration on Personal Data Act. If one of these exemptions applies, then the individual concerned does not enjoy the protection of the WPR.

If the personal register falls under the scope of the WPR, then personal data may only be used in accordance with the purpose of the register;[68] it may only be disclosed to third parties if in accordance with the purpose of the file, required by a statutory provision or with the consent of the data subject;[69] and the processing of personal data must be tested against the requirements of article 11 WPR. If the request for disclosure does not meet these conditions, then the data cannot be disclosed.

The data subject must be informed of every disclosure of a personal register. This follows from article 32 WPR, which empowers the subject to ask the controller of the personal register what personal data have been disclosed to whom during the last year. The controller must disclose this.

---

67. Article 28 WPR.

68. Article 6 WPR.

69. Article 11 WPR.

This makes it possible for the data subject to determine the recipient and lawfulness of the disclosure. In case of unlawful disclosure of personal data, the data subject can claim under article 9 WPR both actual and non-pecuniary damages in civil proceedings. The court can also grant an injunction against the controller to refrain from the unlawful act or an order for *restitutio in integrum*. This will be of little consequence if the information has already been disclosed. Where there is a dispute between the controller and the data subject, the data subject can file a request for mediation with the *Registratiekamer* (Chamber of Registration). The Chamber is a supervisory organ established under the WPR. It can only mediate between the parties and cannot impose any sanctions. A ruling of the Chamber of Registration may influence civil court proceedings. If it concerns an unlawful disclosure by a public body, a complaint may also be lodged with the National Ombudsman.

Government Information Act

The Government Information Act (*Wet Openbaarheid Bestuur* — WOB) is **7.25** based on the government's duty to provide for passive and active open government, the transparency of governments acts. For the media, this Act can play a role in obtaining government data. A request for information directed at a public body will basically be granted by that public body on the basis of the WOB. However, under article 10 of the WOB, it is possible to withhold information. Under the WOB, there are absolute and qualified exceptions. An absolute exception (article 10(b) WOB) is that information must be withheld where the information presents a danger to the safety of the State. Qualified exceptions include the respect for personal life. In respect of the qualified exceptions, the public interest of disclosure is weighed against interests that are protected by the relative exceptions such as the an individual right to privacy. Thus, under article 10, information about civil servants regarding their appointment or promotion should be withheld. In respect of media requests for information, there are several judicial decisions, characteristic of the way in which the courts handle the WOB.[70] Forty years later a newspaper, pursuant to the WOB, demanded access to the Internal Security Service file of a person who played an important part during World War II. The Ministry of Home Affairs refused on the basis of article 10 (then article 4) of the WOB, invoking the absolute exception of State security and the qualified exception of privacy. Both exceptions were rejected because State security

---

70. For instance, by invoking article 10, it was refused to disclose the names of the applicants for the position of mayor for the town of Goes. *Afdeling Rechtspraak*, 12 March 1984, number A–1.0918 (1982).

could only be decisive if it would actually be damaged and because the privacy interest cannot be invoked to protect relatives of a deceased person.

Health sector scientific publications

7.26   Following publication of scientific research in scientific journals, patients have regularly brought actions for the invasion of privacy before the Medical Disciplinary Tribunal. For their research, medical scientists often use data from patient files, which are made as part of the medical treatment. In respect of patient data, a physician must maintain confidentiality. Under article 272 of the *Wetboek van Strafrecht* (Criminal Code — WvSR), it is an offence for anyone except for the patient himself to breach this confidentiality. From the 1990s, with researchers requesting personal patient data on a large-scale from treating physicians without patients' knowledge, physicians assumed that the medical confidentiality that applied to treating physicians also applied to researchers and that thus that personal data could simply be disclosed to medical researchers. Lawyers who opposed this disclosure emphasised the privacy interest of the patient, whereas the physicians underlined the public health interest. This privacy concern appears to have become accepted by physicians.

Since 1995, the Act on the Medical Treatment Agreement in the Netherlands, the *Wet Geneeskundige Behandelingsovereenkomst* (WGBO), incorporated in the Civil Code (7:446 *et seq.*) regulates the relationship between patient and physician under Civil Law. It contains some important privacy provisions. The treating physician must observe confidentiality in respect of patient data (7:457 BW). The physician's duty to observe confidentiality can only be waived by the patient's consent. A separate regulation is made for the disclosure of medical information for scientific research purposes (7:458 BW). The basic rule is that the disclosure of personal data for scientific research may only occur with the patient's consent. Under strict conditions, medical information may be disclosed without consent.

Article 7:459 BW protects of the patients against pryers. It provides that medical aids must carry out operations as part of a treatment outside the observation of persons other than the patient, unless the patient has agreed to this. This provision may be of great importance to the media. An example of a situation in which a patient felt his privacy invaded concerned a medical researcher who presented with great detail an anonymous case study in a scientific publication. The patient recognised himself in the publication and lodged a complaint with the Medical Disciplinary Tribunal. The Tribunal granted the complaint. The physician had not asked the patient's permission for publication. The Medical Tribunal held that the physician negligently handled the patient data that became known to him during treatment and undermined the confidence in the medical profession.[71]

Even prior to the introduction of the WGBO, the decisions of the Medical Tribunals on this topic as well as judgments rendered by the civil court have sharpened the regulations concerning the handling of patient data within the medical sector. Since coming into effect in 1988, the WPR has also had great influence on the handling of patient data within the medical sector.

European Data Protection Directive

With regard to the protection of personal data of European Union **7.27** citizens and the free movement of such data, the European Council of Ministers issued a Directive at the end of last year.[72] The obligations on the data processors concern the quality of data, technical safeguards and notification with a supervisory authority. Data subjects have the right to be informed, to have access to the data, to demand rectification and even under certain circumstances to object to data processing. The Directive has wide application particularly due to the wide definitions of personal data and the processing of personal data. For the media, it is important that the Directive in respect of the personal data definition states that it also covers processing of sound and image data relating to natural persons. This remark was included in the framework of the current developments within the information society. The definition of "processing of personal data" not only includes the collection and storage of personal data but also the use and the dissemination of such data.

As for the processing of sound and image data for journalistic, literary or artistic purposes, in particular in the audio-visual field, the principles of the Directive are to apply in a restrictive manner. Member States are required to lay down exemptions and derogations necessary for balancing fundamental rights as regards general measures on lawful data processing, the transfer of data to third countries and the powers of the supervisory authority.

In respect of journalistic activities, the Directive defers to the courts of the Member States and hence leaves the matter undecided. The Netherlands has not laid down further measures on this. Compared to the WPR discussed above, which uses stricter definitions and which does not apply

---

71. Amsterdam Medical Disciplinary Tribunal, 3 October 1983, *Staatscourant* 1983, number 248, p 9.

72. Directive 95/46/European Community of the European Parliament and the Council of 24 October 1995, concerning the protection of individuals with regard to the processing of personal data and on the free movement of such data.

to personal registers solely for the benefit of the media, the Directive offers more possibilities for regulating media behaviour for privacy reasons.

Criminal Code

7.28 The Dutch Criminal Code also contains a number of provisions concerning the protection of personal life.[73] Of importance are articles 139(b) and 441b WvSR. These provisions prohibit wire-tapping and the (secret) recording of conversations and telephone conversations in and around the house. It is a criminal offence to use a hidden camera inside the home. Section 139f(1) states that it is a criminal offence to knowingly make a picture with a technical device, inside a house or in a non-public place, where this picture damages a lawful interest. In a case which involved a prison warden being secretly filmed and photographed to reveal his corruption, the *Gerechtshof* held on the question concerning the prison warden's legitimate interest that as for the determination of his reprehensible behaviour, reasonable doubt existed whether his interest deserved protection under this provision.[74] Due to the strict interpretation of the term legitimate interest, section 139(b) offers little protection when the media try to reveal "unlawful behaviour". It is likely that secret recordings that lead to nothing remain unpublished. Successful recordings often do not violate a legitimate interest of the person filmed.[75]

Whereas 139(b)(1) offers protection against observation, sub-section 2 makes it a criminal offence to make use of an image, where the holder knows or reasonably could know that the image has been obtained in a fashion described under sub-section 1. Publication of a picture obtained under punishable circumstances also constitutes a criminal offence.

Section 441(b) WvSR makes it a criminal offence to secretly photograph persons in cafes and other public places, at least if the presence of the technical device with which the picture was made is not revealed. No criminal liability exists where the pictures are made only on the public road.

In a recent case, two journalists revealed on television parts of illegally wire-tapped telephone conversations between an *Officier van Justitie* (Public Prosecutor) and police detectives.[76] The court accepted that an offence occurred, but held that the seriousness of the offence did not outweigh the freedom of expression interest and the charges against the journalist were

---

73. *Wet van 7 April 1971 houdende enige strafbepalingen tot bescherming van de persoonlijke levenssfeer* (Act of 7 April 1971 concerning some criminal provisions for the protection of the personal life).

74. Hof Amsterdam, 18 June 1992, *Mediaforum*, Appendix [4] 1992–9, pp 67–68.

75. *Cameratoezicht, veiligheid en de wet persoonsregistraties, juridische denkoefeningen naar aanleiding van de Franse wet van 21 Januari 1995 inzake veiligheid*, de Hert and Gutwirth, *Recht en Kritiek*, Volume 21, number 3.

76. "Grenzen vrijheid journalist blijven onduidelijk", *Volkskrant*, 4 January 1996.

dismissed. It was held that by broadcasting the wire-tapped telephone conversations the Public Prosecutor's right to privacy was undoubtedly violated. However, the consequences for the Prosecutor and the police officers involved were not serious enough for the freedom of expression to yield.

In the same case, the journalist was acquitted of having published illegally tapped telephone conversations or recorded data. The journalist published the computer files belonging to the Prosecutor. Essential for the description of the offence is the illegal tapping or recording. Article 138a WvSR is important to determine the illegality of the tapping or recording. In analogy of *huisvredebreuk*, (unlawful entry into someone's home), *computervredebreuk* (unlawful entry into someone's computer) is a criminal offence under article 138 WvSR. This means illegal entry with intent into an automated work or a part thereof used for recording or processing of data, whereby any safety is broken through a technical intervention, by means of technical signals, a false key or by accepting a false identity. In this case it could not be proved that the data were obtained through unlawful entry to the computer.

Self-regulation, privacy and journalistic ethics

Self-regulation is established through consensus within a certain group   **7.29**
on the applicable norms, for example, by the Press Council.[77]

Note that the norms that according to the Council should be followed by the journalistic profession when weighing its interests against privacy interests do no coincide with legal norms. From 1960–1987 the Council published 33 rulings concerning inadequate protection of privacy.[78] That is 15 per cent of the total amount of published rulings. The norms are geared on cases submitted before it. In the beginning all privacy-rulings concerned anonymity or the recognisability of persons in press publications. The Council is of the opinion that in respect of suspects of criminal offences, the recognisability should be restricted as much as possible. However, the situation is different in respect of persons who draw attention to themselves in civil or administrative proceedings. The basic rule is that only the initials of suspects should be mentioned and that their photograph is made unrecognisable, for example, by a inserting in the photograph a black cover over the eyes. However, the publication of drawings of defendants or convicted persons are common practice in the

---

77. The organisation and the function of this council is already described in part 1.

78. Doomen, "Opinies over journalistiek gedrag", *De uitspraken van de Raad voor de Journalistiek* 1960–1987; Arnhem 1987.

Dutch press. The Council uses the principle of own-fault: people who seek publicity can expect that they will recognise themselves in the newspapers. The rule on initials is sometimes not very effective since initials do not always depersonalise. Besides, successive media publications may lift the anonymity of victims/suspects, the so-called "Jigsaw" identification.[79]

In addition to the Press Council's rulings, there are various statements drafted by and for the use of journalists. An important international code is the Code of Conduct for Journalists.[80] The Code contains nine general principles as a standard for professional behaviour of journalists. Although this Code was never formally implemented in Dutch journalistic circles, the provisions do enjoy authority. The Code does not specifically refer to the respect for privacy. However, the fourth principle states that news, photographs and documents must be obtained in a fair manner.

At the European level, there also have been initiatives towards the drafting of standards and guidelines.[81]

Note: W.J.H.T. Dupont is the author of "Protection of Name and Reputation", and C.J.M. van Berkel and E.J.M. Jeunink are the authors of "Privacy and Publicity".

---

79. Walker, *The Impact of New Technologies: the Right of the Individual And the Public Interest in Legal Proceedings.*

80. Adopted by the IFJ at the Bordeaux Convention, April 1954.

81. *Broadcasting Freedom, International Standards and Guidelines.* Selected texts prepared for participants at the Council of Europe, the European Convention on transfrontier television, Resolution 10003/1993.

New Zealand

Chapter 8
New Zealand

William Akel and Tracey J. Walker
Simpson Grierson
Auckland, New Zealand

Introduction

New Zealand is well served by all three major branches of the media. **8.1**
There are three free to air television channels. Two are operated by
Television New Zealand Limited (a state owned enterprise) and one is
privately owned. Currently one private pay network operates six channels,
and cable television is shortly to be introduced. There are several free
to air regional UHF television broadcasters. There is a significant
number of commercial radio stations and one major publicly funded
non-commercial station.[1] Considering the size of the population, New
Zealand has a high number of daily newspapers.[2] In addition, there are
several community newspapers, frequently delivered free to households
in a particular circulation area.

There is foreign ownership of large parts of television, radio and newspapers. The usual foreign influence is present, such as CNN and BBC World
Service, each available virtually 24 hours per day.

The media compete, but not with the intensity that is found in the
United Kingdom or the United States. There is little evidence of a
chequebook journalism mentality. Over the last 10 years, New Zealand
has seen a greater sense of press freedom and much more investigative
journalism. As a result, the general body of New Zealand media law is
constantly being developed and expanded. The courts have increasingly
recognised the importance of freedom of expression. There has also
been a greater realisation, and acceptance, of the role of the media in a
free and democratic society.

---

1. Estimated at 165 separate programme broadcasters as at 2 April 1994: Statistics New Zealand, *New Zealand Official Year Book* 1995, 273.

2. There are 28 daily newspapers of which eight are published in the morning and 20 in the evening: *New Zealand Official Year Book* 1995.

The fundamental right to freedom of expression is confirmed in the New Zealand Bill of Rights Act 1990.[3] Section 14 provides that everyone has the right to freedom of expression, including the freedom to seek, receive and impart information and opinions of any kind in any form. The freedom is not stated as the freedom of the press, but there is little doubt that the media has been most active invoking section 14, and it has been the right's major beneficiary. However, the legislature and the courts have attempted to maintain a balance between freedom of expression and protection of individual rights. Those individual rights are best exemplified in reputation and privacy. The right to protect reputation is well established and confirmed in the New Zealand Bill of Rights Act 1990.[4] Protection of privacy is still a developing concept in New Zealand.

The law of defamation in New Zealand has evolved from the common law. The governing act is the Defamation Act 1992. This replaced the Defamation Act 1954, which was based on the United Kingdom's Defamation Act 1952. New Zealand applies the same basic defamation concepts as exist in other common law jurisdictions. The 1992 Act has modified some of the standard defences and introduced new remedial concepts such as court recommended corrections, declarations as to liability and a statutory procedure for retraction and reply.[5]

Apart from the Privacy Act 1993, there is no similar statutory protection of privacy. The Privacy Act affects both the public and private sectors, but it is only concerned with protection against misuse of personal data that has been collected and stored by any organisation. The media are exempt from the Privacy Act in their news-gathering activities.[6] There are suggestions that the Privacy Act is invoked to obstruct media inquiries.

Television and radio are subject to broadcasting standards in relation to privacy and fairness.[7] The Broadcasting Act 1989 established a Broadcasting Standards Authority with responsibility to hear and determine complaints against broadcasters by the general public. The main grounds of complaint are breach of good taste and decency, unfair or unbalanced reporting, breach of privacy and portrayal of violence. Significantly, however, the Broadcasting Act specifically states that no broadcaster shall be under any civil liability for failure to comply with the programme standards set out

---

3. In addition, the Official Information Act 1982 and the Local Government Official Information and Meetings Act 1987 provide for freedom of access to information held by public bodies and government agencies.

4. NZBOR, s 28.

5. Defamation Act, ss 24–26.

6. The Privacy Act applies to "agencies" that are defined by s 2 to exclude any news medium in relation to its news activities. "News activity" is also defined and includes the gathering and dissemination of news. However, Radio New Zealand and Television New Zealand, which are state-owned enterprises, are bound by two of the privacy principles set out in the Act (access to personal information and correction of personal information).

7. Broadcasting Act 1989, s 4.

in the Broadcasting Act.[8] The Broadcasting Standards Authority has established seven privacy principles that broadcasters must comply with. These principles are drawn largely from United States precedents.[9] The Authority has delivered a number of decisions applying the privacy principles.

Although there is no established action for invasion of privacy or protection of privacy in New Zealand, there has been judicial recognition over the last few years of the potential for such an action. The Privacy Act, recognition of privacy in the Broadcasting Act, and the decisions of the Broadcasting Standards Authority under that Act reflect a concern in New Zealand society about unwarranted intrusion into a person's private affairs.

Newspapers are not subject to the standards in the Broadcasting Act 1989 or to the Broadcasting Standards Authority. Complaints are made to the Press Council, a voluntary body with no legislative foundation. The Press Council does not have a set of written guidelines or a written code of ethics. Although journalists obviously have their own code of ethics, there is no authority that can provide a punitive response if the code is broken. Still, editors and producers, in all branches of the media, exercise editorial judgment against publication where the circumstances clearly call for it.

The New Zealand courts have developed an indigenous body of law, but the fundamentals for any common law action in New Zealand are based on English law. Decisions of the House of Lords and the English courts are regarded as persuasive in New Zealand. The courts also look at developments in other common law jurisdictions, in particular Canada and Australia. The Privy Council is still New Zealand's highest court although the Government has introduced a bill, which if passed, will abolish appeals to the Privy Council.[10]

This chapter focuses on specific areas of civil liability of the media in New Zealand. In a publication such as this, it is not possible to provide more than a broad overview of the relevant law.[11]

Defamation

General

New Zealand defamation law is a creature of common law and statute. **8.2**
The Defamation Act 1992 has recently refined and amended the

---

8. Broadcasting Act 1989, s 4(3).

9. See Prosser and Keeton, *Prosser & Keeton on The Law of Torts* (5th ed. 1984) 851–864.

10. New Zealand Courts Structure Bill 1996.

11. For a full discussion of media law in New Zealand, reference should be made to Burrows, *News Media Law in New Zealand* (3rd ed. 1990) and Butterworths, *Laws NZ, Defamation* (1994).

law.[12] While the Defamation Act sets out the available defences and remedies, and deals with a number of procedural points, it falls short of being a code. For example, the Defamation Act does not define what constitutes defamation. Despite the effort to refine the law in the Defamation Act, defamation remains complex with subtle distinctions dependant on the particular facts of each case. Broad principles have emerged to guide parties, lawyers and the courts alike.

There is no distinction in New Zealand between libel and slander.[13] The essential elements of defamation in New Zealand remain publication to a third party of defamatory material about an identifiable person, or company. There is no general requirement to prove actual damage resulting from the publication. However, companies and corporate plaintiffs must prove specific pecuniary loss or the likelihood of specific pecuniary loss.[14] Arguably, this statutory requirement goes no further than the common law.[15]

The Defamation Act abolished criminal libel by repealing sections 211–216 of the Crimes Act 1961. It also reduced the limitation period for defamation proceedings to two years from the date of accrual of the cause of action[16] from the six year limitation period generally applicable to actions for other tortious acts. Leave to issue proceedings out of time may be granted by the court at any time within six years from accrual of the cause of action if the delay in bringing the proceedings was occasioned by mistake of fact or of law, or by any other reasonable cause. However, the court may not grant leave where the mistake was as to the meaning of the limitation period.

In New Zealand, the media do not have the degree of immunity enjoyed by their United States counterparts when criticising public figures, whether satirically or in earnest.[17] It is an open question as to whether the New Zealand courts will adopt a public figure defence as a result of developments in Australia and England.[18] The legislature did not see fit to incorporate the American approach in the Defamation Act. However, section 14 of the New Zealand Bill of Rights Act 1990 (NZBOR) arguably provides a platform for extending the common law defence of

---

12. The Act applies to any defamation proceeding commenced after 1 February 1993.

13. The distinction formerly existing was abolished by the Defamation Act in 1954. See now Defamation Act, s 4.

14. Defamation Act, s 6.

15. See *Mt Cook Group Ltd.* v *Johnstone Motors Ltd.* [1990] 2 NZLR 488.

16. Defamation Act, s 55 inserted s 4 (6A) into the Limitation Act 1950.

17. *New York Times* v *Sullivan* 376 US 254 (1964).

18. See *Theophanus* v *Herald* & *Weekly Times Ltd.* (1994) 124 ALR 1; *Stephens* v *West Australian Newspapers Ltd.* (1994) 124 ALR 80; *Derbyshire County Council* v *Herald* & *Times Newspapers Ltd.* [1993] AC 534. See also Tobin, "Defamation of Politicians, Public Bodies and Officials: Should Derbyshire and Theophanus apply in New Zealand?" [1995] *NZ Law Review* 90.

qualified privilege as relates to criticism of public figures. At the time of writing, a High Court decision on this issue is awaited.

Still, when dealing with public figures special considerations may apply. As long ago as 1911 the New Zealand courts noted the "wide limits of criticism allowable in the case of public men and public matters".[19] While such statements fall short of creating a public figure defence, they indicate that people in the public arena are expected to be sufficiently robust to accept a certain amount of satirical comment or criticism.

Recent defamation cases

A summary of recent New Zealand defamation cases indicates that the media have not fared well at the hands of jurors. The world-wide trend of high defamation awards now extends to New Zealand. In *Keith* v *Television New Zealand Ltd.*,[20] a well known art critic was the subject of a satirical television programme. The jury found that he had been defamed. Instead of awarding a sum for damages the jury awarded "all legal fees" incurred by him in pursuing his claim. The plaintiff's legal costs totalled approximately NZ $108,000. The Judge held that this was reasonable and entered judgment for this amount. Television New Zealand Ltd. (TVNZ) appealed to the Court of Appeal.[21] The Court allowed the appeal. It held that the jury's verdict meant that the defamation was proved but ordered a new trial limited to the issue of damages on the basis that an award of costs is exclusively the domain of the court and cannot be substituted for an award of damages. Subsequently an out of court settlement was effected.

In *McRae* v *Australian Consolidated Press New Zealand Ltd.*,[22] a journalist was the subject of comments in a magazine gossip column. The journalist's own column was known as "Psst". The magazine suggested the journalist was "regularly pissed." The jury held that Ms. McRae had been defamed and awarded damages of NZ $375,000. An application to set aside the judgment was made, but before it could be heard an out of court settlement was reached including payment of NZ $100,000 damages.

In 1994, a total of NZ $1.5-million in damages was awarded in a case against TVNZ, which was found to have defamed a local horse trotting club president in two broadcasts;[23] one alleging involvement in the supply of drugs for doping horses and illegal selling of performance enhancing

---

19. *Massey* v *New Zealand Times Company Ltd.* (1911) 30 NZLR 929, 952.

20. Unreported, High Court, Auckland, 3 December 1992, CP780/91 Robertson J.

21. *Television New Zealand Ltd.* v *Keith* [1994] 2 NZLR 84.

22. Unreported, High Court, Auckland, 27 April 1994, CP1161/92 Tompkins J.

23. *Quinn* v *Television New Zealand Ltd.* [1995] 3 NZLR 216.

substances; the second implication in financial irregularities concerning the club. The jury awarded NZ $400,000 in respect of the first programme and NZ $1.1-million in respect of the second. TVNZ applied to set aside the awards on the basis they were excessive. The High Court set aside the award of NZ $1.1-million and ordered a retrial on the issue of damages. It declined to set aside the award of NZ $400,000. The Court of Appeal confirmed the High Court rulings.[24] The High Court recently set the award for the second programme at NZ $250,000. The parties agreed that the decision would be final.

In *Hawkins* v *Ayers*,[25] allegations of financial and business incompetence and political corruption against a group of people including the plaintiff, a local mayor, were published in political leaflets and in a radio interview. By the time the case came to trial it was not defended and the judge awarded NZ $130,000 damages.

What is a defamatory imputation?

8.4   There is no single all embracing definition of what constitutes a defamatory statement. Perhaps the closest one can come to a definition is a statement that adversely affects a party's reputation. The courts in New Zealand look for guidance to the well recognised definitions of the English authorities.[26]

The test is not what a publisher intended to say but how the words published would be understood by a reasonable person. The courts have stressed:[27]

> "[An] analytical, lawyer-like approach should not be brought to the detailed wording of [the publication]. It is the effect on a group of people described as 'ordinary sensible readers' that matters."

8.5   A certain amount of loose thinking on the part of the ordinary sensible reader must be expected in assessing the thrust or sting of the publication.

Along the same lines, the context and style of a publication is relevant in determining whether or not it is defamatory. By way of example, a "racy and hyperbolic style" may colour the meaning that the ordinary reasonable reader would attach to any statements in an article.[28]

---

24. *Television New Zealand Ltd.* v *Quinn* [1996] 3 NZLR 24.

25. Unreported, High Court, Auckland, 6 March 1996, CP1246/92 Tompkins J.

26. See Burrows, *News Media Law in New Zealand* (3rd ed. 1990) Ch. 2 and Butterworths, *Laws NZ, Defamation* (1994) paras 40–55.

27. *Christchurch Press Co. Ltd.* v *McGaveston* [1986] 1 NZLR 610, 616.

28. *Willis* v *Katevich*, unreported, High Court, Auckland, 21 August 1989, CP547/85 Fisher J.

The plaintiff must give particulars of all the natural and ordinary meanings which the matter complained of is alleged to bear and, where innuendo meanings are relied on, must also specify the persons to whom the defamatory meaning is alleged to be known and the facts and circumstances on which the plaintiff relies.[29]

The judge must determine as a matter of law whether the words complained of are capable of being defamatory. If this threshold is passed, then it is for a jury (or judge if there is no jury) to decide whether the words do in fact bear the defamatory meaning.

Innuendo

A plaintiff may plead that the words, although innocent in their natural and ordinary sense, carry a special meaning or innuendo that would be understood by a limited number of people in possession of special knowledge. At common law, the natural and ordinary meaning of the words and the legal innuendo gave rise to two different causes of action. Under the Defamation Act, there is only one cause of action regardless of the number of different meanings alleged.[30]   **8.6**

Identification

Although the statements complained of must be published "of and concerning" the plaintiff, the plaintiff need not be expressly named.[31] Extrinsic evidence may be used to show that a publication would be understood by ordinary sensible readers with knowledge of special facts, to refer to a particular plaintiff.[32] In *Hyams* v *Peterson*, the Court of Appeal held that it was acceptable to rely on a prior report of Parliamentary proceedings (themselves protected by privilege) to show that the plaintiff was referred to in the publication sued on. In some cases, the plaintiff may even be permitted to refer to subsequent reports to connect him or her with the defamatory publication.[33]   **8.7**

---

29. Defamation Act, s 37(2) and (3).

30. Defamation Act, s 7.

31. *Christchurch Press Co. Ltd.* v *McGaveston* [1986] 1 NZLR 610, 616; *Hyams* v *Peterson* [1991] 3 NZLR 648.

32. *Ballantyne* v *Television New Zealand Ltd.* [1992] 3 NZLR 455.

33. *Hyams* v *Peterson* [1991] 3 NZLR 648, at 656.

Parties

8.8   The plaintiff must be the person actually defamed. The words must reflect on the plaintiff personally.[34] It is not possible for the executors of the estate of a dead person to continue or bring an action in defamation. A company or corporate body may bring an action but it must prove that the publication has caused, or is likely to cause pecuniary loss.[35] The New Zealand courts will likely follow the House of Lords in *Derbyshire County Council* v *Times Newspapers Ltd.*[36] and hold that a municipal corporation such as a local council may not bring proceedings for defamation. The policy reasoning, namely that the public interest requires that such bodies should be open to public scrutiny and criticism, is as important in New Zealand as in the United Kingdom. Individual members of such corporations are able to bring an action if they can prove that they personally have been defamed. Where members of an unincorporated group are defamed, they must bring individual proceedings. A member of a group may sue in defamation if the words can be understood to relate to him or her. The smaller the group, the more likely it is that a plaintiff can show the words were directed at him or her.[37] The defendant must be the person who published the allegedly defamatory matter. Every person who participates in the publication may be liable as a publisher although the Defamation Act provides a defence for any person who published the matter as a processor or distributor (or as their employee or agent) and did not know that the matter contained the allegedly defamatory material or that the matter was of a character likely to contain such material.[38] The defence is not available if the defendant's lack of knowledge is as a result of their negligence.[39]

Defences

8.9   The Defamation Act renames the common law defences of justification and fair comment as "truth" and "honest opinion".[40]

---

34. *Cf.* words which reflect only on the plaintiff's property. Such words will not support a claim for defamation. See Butterworths, *Laws NZ, Defamation* (1994), at para 51.

35. Defamation Act, s 6.

36. [1993] AC 534.

37. Burrows, *News Media Law in New Zealand* (3rd ed. 1990), at 41–42.

38. Defamation Act, s 21.

39. Butterworths, *Laws NZ, Defamation* (1994), at para 30.

40. Defamation Act, ss 8 and 9 respectively.

Truth

To plead truth successfully the defendant must prove that the substance   **8.10** of the words is true or substantially true regardless of whether the words are fact or comment.[41] If the material complained about consists of both fact and comment, the defendant must prove not only that the basic facts are true but also that the comments are true.

This is invariably a difficult and costly defence. Once the plaintiff has made the allegations of defamation the burden rests on the defendant to prove the truth of what has been said. The defendant essentially compounds or repeats the defamation when pleading truth. Failure to establish the defence to the satisfaction of the jury can aggravate damages.

There are other practical aspects that must be considered before a defence of truth is raised. The defendant must obviously prove to the court that the defamation is true. If information has come from confidential sources this may not be easy to achieve. Even when the source is not confidential there may be evidential difficulties. In *Television New Zealand Ltd.* v *Prebble*,[42] the defendants attempted to rely on statements made in Parliament to support a defence of truth. The Court of Appeal refused to permit reliance on Parliamentary statements without a waiver of privilege from Parliament and ordered a stay of proceedings pending that waiver. This result was confirmed by the Privy Council although the Privy Council overturned the order for a stay.[43]

Previously, where justification was pleaded, a defendant was not permitted to plead an alternative meaning of the alleged defamation and seek to justify that meaning.[44] This approach differed from that adopted in the English courts.[45] The position under the Defamation Act is unclear. The Defamation Act permits the defendant to allege and prove any facts contained in the whole of a publication even if the plaintiff relies on only some of the matters contained in that publication to show defamation. This removes the "pick and choose" anomaly where the plaintiff chooses to sue on only one of a number of defamatory assertions.[46] Whether, under section 8(3), a defendant can now set out an alternative version of the allegedly defamatory statement that differs materially from the

---

41. Of course, in relation to comment the defendant may also rely on the defence of honest opinion.

42. [1993] 3 NZLR 513 (CA); [1994] 3 NZLR 1 (PC).

43. *Cf. Hyams* v *Peterson* [1991] 3 NZLR 648 where the Court allowed the plaintiff to rely on a statement in Parliament to show that a subsequent defamatory statement outside the House would be understood as referring to the plaintiff.

44. *Broadcasting Corporation of New Zealand* v *Crush* [1988] 2 NZLR 234.

45. *Lucus-Box* v *News Group Newspapers Ltd.* [1986] 1 All ER 177.

46. See, for an example of this anomaly, *Templeton* v *Jones* [1984] 1 NZLR 448.

meanings pleaded in the statement of claim, and then prove the truth of the alternative meanings, has yet to be authoritatively determined.[47]

Honest Opinion

8.11 The right to express an honest opinion has been recognised as an essential element of free speech not to be "whittled down by legal refinements".[48] The common law defence of fair comment has been renamed "honest opinion" by section 9 of the Defamation Act. At common law this defence required a comment to be "fair" and concerning a matter of public interest.[49] Fairness meant whether such comment could be honestly made on the facts proved. There was no qualification of reasonableness.

The Defamation Act has made four important changes to this defence:[50]

(1) The comment need not be made on a matter of public interest;

(2) The test is expressly subjective in that the opinion expressed must be the defendant's genuine opinion and the onus is on the defendant to prove this;[51]

(3) The defence of honest opinion is not defeated by the malice of the defendant;[52] and

(4) There is no longer any distinction between opinion or comment attributing corrupt motives to the plaintiff and comment that does not.[53]

8.12 The comment or opinion must be based on facts that are proven to be true or not materially different from the truth and these must be pleaded by the defendant. It is not necessary, however, to prove every allegation of fact in the publication if the opinion is shown to be genuine opinion having regard to those facts that are proved to be true.[54]

A defence of honest opinion is only available in relation to expressions of opinion and not statements of fact. Difficulties for a defendant arise

---

47. Butterworths, *Laws NZ, Defamation* (1994), at para 76 suggests that *Broadcasting Corporation* v *Crush* is still good law.

48. *Slim* v *Daily Telegraph Ltd.* [1968] 2 QB 157, 170.

49. *Truth (NZ) Ltd.* v *Avery* [1959] NZLR 274, 278.

50. Defamation Act, ss 9–12.

51. Defamation Act, s 10(1). *Cf.* the English position set out in *Telnikoff* v *Matusevitch* [1991] 1 QB 102.

52. Defamation Act, s 10(3).

53. Defamation Act, s 12.

54. Defamation Act, s 11.

when fact and opinion are intermingled. It is a matter for the jury to decide whether a statement is one of opinion or fact — a notoriously difficult task.[55]

This defence is available even where the defendant is not the author of the opinion, for example, in cases concerning letters to the editor, contributing writers, callers on talk-back radio and live television interviews. If the author of the opinion is the defendant's employee the defendant must prove that it believed the opinion was the genuine opinion of the author and that in the circumstances the opinion did not purport to be the defendant's opinion.[56]

Where the author is not an employee or agent of the defendant, the defendant must prove that the opinion was not that of the defendant, or any employee of the defendant, and also that the defendant had no reasonable cause to believe that the opinion was not the genuine opinion of the author.[57]

If the plaintiff intends to put in issue at trial the genuineness of the defendant's opinion then a notice to that effect must be served, along with particulars of the facts and circumstances relied on by the plaintiff.[58]

Absolute privilege

Under the Defamation Act, proceedings in the House of Representatives **8.13** are protected by absolute privilege.[59] Any live media broadcast of proceedings in the House is also protected by absolute privilege.[60] All other media reports of Parliament attract qualified privilege provided the reporting is fair and accurate.

Absolute privilege applies to protect the publication, by or under the authority of the House, of any document, and the publication of a correct copy of such a document.[61] Absolute privilege also applies to the publication, by or under the authority of the House, or under the authority of any enactment, of an official or authorised record of the proceedings of the House, and to the publication of a correct copy of such a record.[62]

---

55. See *Awa* v *Independent News Auckland Ltd.* [1995] 3 NZLR 701, 705–706.

56. Defamation Act, s 10(2)(a).

57. Defamation Act, s 10(2)(b).

58. Defamation Act, s 39.

59. Defamation Act, s 13(1).

60. Defamation Act, s 13(2).

61. Defamation Act, s 13(3)(a) and (d).

62. Defamation Act, s 13(3)(c) and (d).

Qualified privilege

8.14 There are two forms of qualified privilege, statutory and common law qualified privilege. Protection for the media is provided in the form of statutory qualified privilege for reports on the specific areas of public interest listed in the First Schedule to the Defamation Act.[63]

The categories listed in Part I of the First Schedule are subject only to the conditions that the report be fair and accurate, not prohibited by law, and that the defendant was not predominantly motivated by ill-will towards the plaintiff or did not take improper advantage of the occasion of publication. Part I protection is afforded to publications such as fair and accurate reports of Parliamentary proceedings, and the publication of a fair and accurate report of the pleadings in court proceedings once those proceedings have been set down for trial.

The publications listed in Part II of the First Schedule are subject to the further restriction that the report must be on a matter of public interest, both at the time of publication and in any place in which the publication occurs.[64] The fact that it is a matter of public interest in a different forum is not sufficient. Under this category the defendant must also allow the plaintiff the opportunity to publish a reasonable letter or statement by way of contradiction or explanation.[65]

Part II publications include fair and accurate reports of inquiry proceedings, of proceedings at a public local authority meeting, and fair and accurate reports of documents circulated to shareholders by the board of directors (provided the documents are not circulated on a confidential basis).

The media also have privilege for fair and accurate reports of court proceedings.[66] Naturally, the privilege does not apply if the court prohibits publication of any report. The media are also not protected if they "jump the gun". In *R Lucas & Son (Nelson Mail) Ltd.* v *O'Brien*,[67] a local newspaper published an article based largely on a statement of claim that had been filed in court alleging unauthorised property dealings. The article was published before the case had been heard. The newspaper's attempt to claim qualified privilege on the grounds that the article was a report of court proceedings was held by the Court of Appeal to be untenable.

Common law qualified privilege is not limited by the statutory categories although in practice the First Schedule covers most circumstances in

---

63. Defamation Act, s 16–19.

64. Defamation Act, s 18(1).

65. Defamation Act, s 18(2).

66. See cls 5 and 6 of Part I of the First Schedule of the Act.

67. [1978] 2 NZLR 289.

which qualified privilege is likely to arise.[68] Qualified privilege exists at common law where the speaker has a legal, social or moral interest or duty to communicate a matter and his or her audience has a corresponding interest or duty to receive such communication.[69] Commentators have described this as a:

> ". . . reciprocal relationship between communicator and recipient which renders the communication of the information more vital than the interest of some third person in his or her reputation."[70]

If a plaintiff has publicly attacked a defendant and the defendant **8.15** responds in the same forum, qualified privilege may apply. In a recent case, this principle applied to protect allegations made on television that the plaintiff was responsible for setting fire to the defendant's property. Privilege applied because the plaintiff had made the original approach to the television reporter asking him to investigate a problem that she said she was having with the defendant. The court held that the defendant's statements were made in response to the plaintiff's claims and the reporter was acting as the plaintiff's agent.[71]

If a speaker or writer is predominately motivated by ill will towards a plaintiff or otherwise takes improper advantage of the occasion of publication, the protection afforded by qualified privilege is lost.[72]

Other defences

Proof of a plaintiff's consent to publication is a good defence to defama- **8.16** tion.[73] The Defamation Act also contains provisions protecting the innocent disseminator of a defamatory publication.[74] There are three essential elements of the defence:

(1) Lack of knowledge that the matter contained the defamatory material;
(2) Lack of knowledge that the matter was of a character likely to contain defamatory material; and
(3) That the defendant's lack of knowledge was not due to any negligence on its part.

Other common law defences include accord and satisfaction, and release. **8.17**

---

68. Defamation Act, s 16(3).

69. *Adam* v *Ward* [1917] AC 309, 334.

70. Burrows, *News Media Law in New Zealand* (3rd ed. 1990), at 58.

71. *Doyle* v *Stemson*, unreported, High Court, Hamilton, 22 August 1995, CP122/92 Tipping J.

72. Defamation Act, s 19.

73. Defamation Act, s 22.

74. Defamation Act, s 21.

Remedies

8.18   The Defamation Act creates statutory remedies that provide an alternative to monetary damages. The purpose of these remedies is to provide swift relief focusing on rectifying damage to reputation by declarations of liability and court recommended corrections. The incentive for plaintiffs is that if they pursue the alternative remedies and not damages, they are entitled to seek solicitor-client costs. While attractive in theory, in practice little use has been made of these remedies and whether or not they provide the quick remedy intended is yet to be seen.

Declarations

8.19   Plaintiffs may seek a declaration that they have been defamed.[75] To encourage plaintiffs to seek this remedy, the Defamation Act 1992 provides for the courts to award solicitor-client costs to successful applicants.[76]

Court recommended correction

8.20   The Defamation Act also provides for a plaintiff to seek a recommendation from the courts that the defendant publish a correction in relation to the alleged defamation.[77] A provision in the original Defamation Bill that would have allowed the courts to order a defendant to publish a correction — under threat of contempt — was subject to considerable objection by the media and was modified in the Defamation Act.

If a defendant publishes a correction as recommended by the court then the plaintiff is not entitled to any other relief beyond solicitor-client costs. If the defendant refuses to publish the correction, the failure to publish is taken into account when the final assessment is made of costs and damages. A recommendation to publish a correction can be made at any time during the proceedings up until judgment.

Although the legislature decided against compulsory correction orders in the Defamation Act, the Court of Appeal held in relation to proceedings under the Defamation Act 1954 that in exceptional circumstances a mandatory injunction ordering the media to broadcast a correction may be made.[78] In 1990, as part of a current affairs programme TV3 broadcast a documentary about ionisation smoke detectors containing a minute

---

75. Defamation Act, s 24.

76. Defamation Act, s 24(2).

77. Defamation Act, s 26.

78. *TV3 Network Ltd.* v *Eveready New Zealand Ltd.* [1993] 3 NZLR 435.

quantity of radioactive material. Eveready were importers and distributors in New Zealand of a range of such detectors and their products were identified on the programme. Eveready claimed that the programme contained malicious and defamatory statements about its product and sought a mandatory injunction directing the broadcasters to broadcast corrective advertising in a form similar to the original broadcast. The defendants sought to have the claim for the injunction struck out on the grounds that it was untenable. While stressing that it would be slow to grant such a remedy the Court of Appeal refused to strike out the application for the injunction. Cooke P observed that if the plaintiffs established malicious falsehood or unlawful defamation, the NZBOR might provide a basis for an order that corrective advertising be broadcast to the viewing public.[79]

Retraction or reply

The Defamation Act provides for a plaintiff to seek a retraction or reply **8.21** directly from the publisher or broadcaster concerned.[80] For this provision to apply, the person who claims to have been defamed must act within five days of becoming aware of the publication. If the person responsible for the defamation agrees to publish a retraction or reply that person must also offer to pay all costs reasonably incurred in connection with the publication of the retraction or reply, plus the defamed person's solicitor-client costs and compensation for any pecuniary loss flowing directly from the publication. If a retraction or reply is published then this is taken into account in mitigation of damages.[81]

The difficulty with this provision is that it does not provide a complete defence for the media. In practice, it is uncommon for a retraction or reply to be published without a full and final settlement being reached between the parties.

Damages

The Defamation Act states that in any defamation proceedings in which **8.22** a news medium is the defendant, the plaintiff shall not specify the amount of damages sought in the plaintiff's statement of claim.[82] Although for some people an acknowledgement that they have been defamed and an apology correcting the allegations is sufficient, in

---

79. [1993] 3 NZLR 435, 441.

80. Defamation Act, s 25.

81. Defamation Act, s 29.

82. Defamation Act, s 43(1).

practice most plaintiffs also seek monetary compensation. The damages awarded in several recent New Zealand cases have been substantial.[83]

An appellate court will not interfere with an award made by a jury unless it is grossly excessive or inadequate,[84] or the jury has been inadequately directed by the trial judge.[85] The judge's obligation at a defamation trial is to explain the law to the jury. The quantum of damages is left entirely to the jury. Traditionally, the judge has not been permitted to suggest an appropriate sum nor to advise the jury of awards made in similar circumstances.

The trend toward large damages awards in a number of recent defamation cases in England and Australia has caused the courts in those jurisdictions to change their approach.[86]

In *Rantzen* v *Mirror Group Newspapers (1986) Ltd.*,[87] the English court of Appeal held that appellate court decisions under section 8 of the Courts Legal Services Act 1990 may, over time, come to provide general guidance as to what would be a proper award.

In *John* v *MGN Ltd.*,[88] the English Court of Appeal held that comparisons might be made with personal injury awards and references by counsel and judges to their perceptions of an appropriate award or award bracket were appropriate in directing a jury as to damages.

In New South Wales, legislation now provides that the court and not the jury is to assess damages.[89] In doing so, the court is to ensure there is an appropriate relationship between the relevant harm and the damages awarded and to take into account the range of damages awarded in personal injury cases. This is in line with recent Australian decisions that accepted the principle of comparisons being made between awards for personal injury and awards for defamation.[90]

---

83. See *Television New Zealand Ltd.* v *Keith* [1994] 2 NZLR 84; *McRae* v *Australian Consolidated Press New Zealand Ltd.*, unreported, High Court, Auckland, 27 April 1994, CP1161/92; *Quinn* v *Television New Zealand Ltd.* [1995] 3 NZLR 216.

84. See rule 494 of the High Court Rules and *Quinn* v *Television New Zealand Ltd.* [1995] 3 NZLR 216, at 225–229.

85. For a full discussion on directions by a trial judge refer to the judgment of McGechan J in *TVNZ* v *Quinn* [1996] 3 NZLR 24.

86. *Rantzen* v *Mirror Group Newspapers (1986) Ltd.* [1993] 4 All ER 975; *John* v *MGN Ltd.*, unreported, Court of Appeal, England, 12 December 1995, QBENF/93/1704/C Sir Thomas Bingham MR, Neill LJ, Hirst LJ; *Australian Consolidated Press Ltd.* v *Ettinghausen*, unreported, Court of Appeal, New South Wales, 13 October 1993, CA40079/93 Gleeson CJ, Kirby P, Clarke JA.

87. [1993] 4 All ER 975.

88. *John* v *MGN Limited* [1996] 2 All ER 35.

89. Defamation Act 1974, s 7A(4)(b).

90. *Australian Consolidated Press Ltd.* v *Ettinghausen*, unreported, Court of Appeal, New South Wales, 13 October 1993; *Carson* v *John Fairfax* & *Sons Ltd.* (1993) 178 CLR 44.

New Zealand courts do not have the opportunity to make such comparisons because accident compensation legislation expressly prohibits proceedings for personal injury.[91]

In *Rantzen,* the Court considered the effect of article 10 of the European Convention for the Protection of Human Rights and Fundamental Freedoms on awards of damages for defamation. Article 10(1) provides that everyone has the right to freedom of expression and article 10(2) provides that the exercise of the right is subject to such restrictions as are prescribed by law and are necessary in a democratic society. The issue in light of article 10 was whether a reasonable jury could have thought that the level of damages awarded was necessary in a democratic society to compensate the plaintiff and to re-establish his reputation.[92]

The Court held that to grant an almost limitless discretion to the jury failed to provide a satisfactory measure for deciding what is necessary in a democratic society. It suggested that the common law, as properly understood, required the courts to subject large awards of damages to a more searching scrutiny than had been customary.

This approach has not been favoured in New Zealand. In *TVNZ* v *Quinn*[93] the Court of Appeal did not consider that there was a trend of high damages awards which inhibited freedom of speech. Lord Cooke and Gault J stated that once liability is established the reasonable limit on the award must not exceed what is sufficient to vindicate a plaintiff's reputation, assuage injured feelings and punitive damages if called for. McGechan J believed that the best approach for judges directing a jury in relation to damages for defamation was to be direct:[94]

"The risk of irrational excess is best dealt with in a direct and focused way by emphasising (and re-emphasising) to juries that they must not go beyond the rational — must not be 'extravagant' in traditional terms — and must be 'moderate' in relation to exemplary damages."

Judges should emphasise:[95]   **8.23**

". . . [t]he real world value of sums awarded, cross checked by reference to investment returns or preferably the purchase of common place items . . . [and] [t]hat punitive damages are exceptional, and are to be awarded in addition to compensatory and any aggravated damages only so far as extra is required to adequately punish and deter . . . ."

___

91. Accident Compensation and Rehabilitation Insurance Act 1992.

92. [1993] 4 All ER 975, at 994.

93. [1995] 3 NZLR 216.

94. [1995] 3 NZLR 216, at p 23.

95. [1995] 3 NZLR 216, at p 54.

8.24 Although the case was decided under the Defamation Act 1954, the court referred to provisions of the 1992 Act that discourage excessive claims. Section 43(1) provides that where a defamation action is brought against the media the plaintiff is not to specify the amount of damages sought. Section 28 provides that exemplary or punitive damages may be awarded against a defendant only where the defendant has acted in flagrant disregard of the rights of the plaintiff.

In accordance with generally understood principles, aggravated general damages may be awarded where the defendant's conduct has caused the plaintiff additional injury.

Contribution of joint tortfeasors

8.25 Where there are joint publishers of defamatory material, there can be only one judgment in the resultant action. Damages are assessed between the publishers according to the level of responsibility for the injury caused. Where proceedings are brought against one of a number of publishers the defendant may recover contributions from the other liable publishers.[96]

Jury or judge alone trial

8.26 Where the proceedings are in the High Court and the only claim is for damages exceeding NZ $3,000, either party may require trial by judge and jury.[97] Despite this election, if the court considers there are difficult questions of law to be tried or that prolonged examination of documents is required, it may order that the trial be carried out without a jury.[98]

Injunctions/prior restraint in defamation

8.27 Successful interim injunctions are rare in defamation cases. They will not be granted where there is a reasonable possibility of a successful defence and particularly where a plea of truth or honest opinion is placed on the record. The policy behind the doctrine of prior restraint is set out in *Hubbard* v *Vosper*:[99]

> "[T]he defendant, if he is right, is entitled to publish . . . and the law will not intervene to suppress freedom of speech except when it is abused."

96. Butterworths, *Laws NZ, Defamation* (1994), at para 226.

97. Judicature Act 1908, s 19A.

98. Judicature Act 1908, s 19B. See also *Television New Zealand Ltd.* v *Prebble* [1993] 3 NZLR 513 (CA), at 525 (CA).

99. [1972] 2 QB 84, 97.

In *Auckland Area Health Board* v *Television New Zealand Ltd.,*[100] the NZBOR **8.28**
was relied on to confirm the prior restraint principle:

> "That there is such a jurisdiction [to restrain the publication of defama-
> tory matter] is well established . . . . By reason of the principle of freedom
> of the media . . . it is a jurisdiction exercised only for clear and compelling
> reasons. It must be shown that defamation for which there is no reason-
> able possibility of a legal defence is likely to be published."

The court also noted that it would only rarely order production of a script **8.29**
of an intended programme prior to broadcast.

Injurious falsehood — trade libels

The action for injurious falsehood has largely been overtaken by the **8.30**
consumer protection provisions of the Fair Trading Act 1986, although it
continues to exist. It differs from defamation in that the plaintiff need
only show the publication of false (not necessarily defamatory) words,
that the words were published maliciously and that they caused special
damage or are likely to cause pecuniary loss.

A proceeding for injurious falsehood has been described as a "proceeding for damage wilfully and intentionally done without lawful occasion or
excuse."[101] In contrast to defamation, the onus is on the plaintiff to show
that the words are false in an action for injurious falsehood.[102]

Privacy

Introduction

Until recently the issue of privacy had not been considered in any depth **8.31**
in New Zealand by the legislature or the common law. In 1992, the
Broadcasting Standards Authority, a statutory tribunal responsible for
hearing complaints against broadcasters, published an advisory opinion
on privacy for television and radio broadcasters. The opinion outlined
five privacy principles that the Authority considers when adjudicating on
privacy complaints (extended to seven privacy principles in 1996).[103]

---

100. [1992] 3 NZLR 406, 407.

101. Butterworths, *Laws NZ, Defamation* (1994), at para 259.

102. *Taylor* v *Hyde* [1918] NZLR 279.

103. See text, *infra.*

In addition, some judges have now recognised a common law right of action for invasion of privacy. In 1993, a High Court Judge stated in an injunction hearing that he was prepared to accept that the tort of invasion of privacy formed part of the law of New Zealand, but he added:[104]

> "[A]t this stage of its development its extent should be regarded with caution . . . so that there is a constant need to bear in mind that the rights and concerns of the individual must be balanced against the significance in a free country of freedom of expression."

8.32 The Privacy Act 1993 is concerned with the promotion and protection of privacy in connection with personal data collection, use and disclosure in accordance with international guidelines. The Privacy Act provides an exemption for the news media in their news-gathering activities, otherwise it applies to all media operations.[105]

The Broadcasting Standards Authority

8.33 The Broadcasting Standards Authority was established by the Broadcasting Act 1989. It is responsible for considering formal complaints about radio and television programmes. Under section 4 of the Broadcasting Act, broadcasters are required, among other things, to maintain standards consistent with the privacy of the individual. The Authority has significant powers under the Broadcasting Act. It can order a broadcaster "off air" for up to 24 hours,[106] although this power has never been exercised. It also has power to impose a fine of up to NZ $5,000,[107] and to order a broadcaster to broadcast an apology.[108]

In 1992, the Broadcasting Standards Authority issued an advisory opinion for broadcasters setting out five privacy principles. A further advisory opinion was issued in May 1996 which extended the principles to seven. The principles were developed from American precedents.[109] The Authority has stressed that in some circumstances the principles may

---

104. *Bradley* v *Wingnut Films Ltd.* [1993] 1 NZLR 415, 423 per Gallen J. *Cf.* Broadcasting Act 1989, s 4(3), which states that no broadcaster shall be under any civil liability for failure to maintain programme standards consistent with the privacy of the individual as required by s 4(1)(c) of the Broadcasting Act.

105. However, the state-owned broadcasting organisations have a more limited exemption. See text, *infra.*

106. Broadcasting Act, s 13(1)(b).

107. Broadcasting Act, s 13(1)(d).

108. Broadcasting Act, s 13(1)(a).

109. In particular, *Prosser* & *Keeton on The Law of Torts* (5th ed. 1984).

require elaboration and refinement and that they are not necessarily the only privacy principles that will apply. The principles are:

(1) The protection of privacy includes protection against the public disclosure of private facts where the facts disclosed are highly offensive and objectionable to a reasonable person of ordinary sensibilities.

(2) The protection of privacy also protects against the public disclosure of some kinds of public facts. The "public" facts contemplated concern events (such as criminal behaviour) which have, in effect, become private again, for example through the passage of time. Nevertheless, the public disclosure of public facts will have to be highly offensive to a reasonable person.

(3) There is a separate ground for a complaint, in addition to a complaint for the public disclosure of private and public facts, in factual situations involving the intentional interference (in the nature of prying) with an individual's interest in solitude or seclusion. The intrusion must be offensive to the ordinary person but an individual's interest in solitude or seclusion does not provide the basis for a privacy action for an individual to complain about being observed or followed or photographed in a public place.

(4) The protection of privacy also protects against the disclosure of private facts to abuse, denigrate or ridicule personally an identifiable person. This principle is of particular relevance should a broadcaster use the airwaves to deal with a private dispute. However, the existence of a prior relationship between the broadcaster and the named individual is not an essential criterion.

(5) The protection of privacy includes the protection against the disclosure by the broadcaster, without consent, of the name and/or address and/or telephone number of an identifiable person. This principle does not apply to details which are public information, or to news and current affairs reporting, and is subject to the "public interest" defence in principle (6).

(6) Discussing the matter in the "public interest", defined as of legitimate concern or interest to the public, is a defence to an individual's claim for privacy.

(7) An individual who consents to the invasion of his or her privacy cannot later succeed in a claim for a breach of privacy.

When lodging a complaint against a broadcaster the complainant is **8.34** usually required to make a formal complaint to the broadcaster first.[110]

---

110. Broadcasting Act, ss 6–8.

However, where the complaint relates to privacy, it may be made directly to the Broadcasting Standards Authority.[111]

Broadcasting Standards Authority's decisions

8.35 The first privacy complaint considered by the Authority was *McAllister* v *Television New Zealand Ltd.*[112] A breach of privacy complaint was made about the conduct of a television film crew at the funeral of the complainant's son. Despite a request from the family of the deceased that the funeral should not be filmed, the crew filmed the graveside service from a street outside the cemetery.

The broadcaster, Television New Zealand (TVNZ), argued that it had reported and filmed the funeral because it was in the public interest. The deceased had been a "skinhead" who dressed in Nazi trappings. He had killed the son of a former prominent sportsman. The killing had been without motive, the victim chosen at random. TVNZ believed that the public was entitled to know the type of person who could carry out such a horrifying murder.

There had been little information available about the deceased. TVNZ considered that the television coverage, showing images of skinheads, tattoos, and Nazi symbols, was able to fill this gap by providing some indication as to the sort of person the deceased was and the company he kept. TVNZ also stated the deceased's brother had invited the film crew to film the scenes at the graveside at the end of the funeral service. It was these scenes on which the report focused. There were no close-up shots of other members of the deceased's family.

The Broadcasting Standards Authority found that the complainant's right to privacy had not been infringed. It pointed out that the funeral had been held in a public place, a cemetery, which was in view of another public place, a street. TVNZ's reasons for broadcasting were found to be compelling. Although recognising that it was upsetting for the family, it was impossible to describe the broadcast item as "highly offensive and objectionable to a reasonable person of ordinary sensibilities."[113]

---

111. Broadcasting Act, s 8(1)(c).

112. BSA, 3 May 1990, Decision 5/90.

113. BSA, 3 May 1990, Decision 5/90, p 12. *Cf. Kyrke-Smith* v *Television New Zealand Ltd.*, BSA, 18 March 1993, Decisions 27/93 and 28/93 where the portrayal of a funeral service in a chapel taken without the family's permission was held to be "not only offensive to the ordinary person but . . . insensitive as well".

In the course of its decision, the Broadcasting Standards Authority reviewed the law of privacy. In summary it stated:

(1) An individual's privacy cannot be protected to such an extent that it overrides the legitimate interests of other members of society;

(2) The disclosure of private or public facts about an individual may infringe the individual's privacy if the facts disclosed would be regarded as highly offensive and objectionable by a reasonable person of ordinary sensibilities; and

(3) Unreasonable intrusions on an individual's solitude or seclusion will infringe his or her privacy if the intrusion is of a nature which would be offensive or objectionable to the reasonable person.

It acknowledged that the Broadcasting Act 1989 gave no indication as to **8.36** where the balance should be struck between the competing interests of individual privacy and the public's "right to know". It looked to the development of the legal doctrine in the United States. In reaching its conclusion, the Broadcasting Standards Authority was mindful of the possibility that New Zealand law may take a stricter view than the United States of the circumstances in which public facts may be disclosed.

In *O'Neill* v *TV3 Network Services Ltd.*,[114] the complainant's son had been involved in a tragic accident in which four young women had been killed and 12 people injured. TV3 broadcast a news item about the son's court appearance for driving under the influence of alcohol and causing the accident. He had been filmed while he was in the waiting room of the Court by a camera operator standing outside the courtroom. TV3 had been asked not to film out of respect for the family's feelings. The complaint was brought by his mother on the basis that the filming amounted to an invasion of privacy. In view of the public nature of the son's conviction and sentence, the Broadcasting Standards Authority decided that Principle (1) of its advisory opinion did not apply. Further, as both the son and the camera operator had been in a public place at the time of the filming, it believed that it was not necessary to decide whether the filming amounted to prying. It added that if it had ruled that the filming amounted to prying, it would then have been necessary to consider whether the public interest exemption set out in Principle (4) was applicable. The Authority tentatively suggested that given a similar factual situation, the public interest element would outweigh the individual's interest in privacy.

In *Chambers* v *Television New Zealand Ltd.*,[115] the complainant claimed that a television broadcast stating that his company was making unwanted

---

114. BSA, 6 October 1994, Decision 93/94.

115. BSA, 14 December 1995, Decision 146/95.

computerised telemarketing calls breached his privacy. The Authority held that the broadcast did not involve the disclosure of any private facts that could be described as highly offensive and there was no evidence of intentional interference or prying. Mr. Chambers had been aware that a call had been made from the programme reporter prior to the broadcast. The Authority held further that the broadcaster's action was in the public interest.

In *Leckey* v *Television New Zealand Ltd.*,[116] the Authority considered a complaint regarding electronic eavesdropping on a private business conversation. The Authority held that although the action was offensive to an ordinary person, the public interest in exposing the questionable practices of the person concerned outweighed his privacy interests.

A number of complaints have been made as a result of the broadcast of private addresses and telephone numbers. The Authority has held that these are not private facts because they can be obtained from public records.[117] However, where the details have been broadcast in circumstances which amount to an abuse of the power of the media, the Authority has held that the broadcast breached the privacy principles.

An example of this is *Walker* v *Triple M Ltd.*[118] Dr. Walker is a prominent Maori academic and writer. His complaint arose from a radio broadcast responding to remarks he had made about crime and Maori offenders. During the programme his home address and telephone number were broadcast and listeners were encouraged to visit his home and call him to challenge his views. The Authority found that Dr. Walker's privacy had been infringed, although his telephone number and address were matters of public record. The Authority considered that the broadcaster's actions were unethical and an abuse of the power of the media. The broadcaster was ordered to pay compensation of NZ $500 to Dr. Walker.

In a more recent decision, the complainant was a caller during a 36 hour marathon talkback session.[119] During her call the host referred to her in extremely unpleasant language and broadcast her full name, address and telephone number. There had been a prior relationship between the host and the caller. In upholding the complaint, the Authority added that a broadcaster's use of the public airwaves to abuse and denigrate an identifiable person, and the disclosure of the name and address and/or telephone number of an identifiable person

---

116. BSA, 29 October 1993, Decision 138/93.

117. *Carabatakis* v *Pirate FM*, BSA, 9 May 1994, Decision 25/94.

118. BSA, 6 June 1990, Decision 6/90.

119. *L* v *Radio Liberty Network*, BSA, 18 January 1996, Decisions 1996–004–1996–006.

without consent were each a breach of privacy. The Authority ordered compensation of NZ $750 be paid to the complainant.[120]

In *MB* v *Radio New Zealand Ltd.*,[121] the first name and address of a man seen kicking a dog on the street was broadcast by a caller to a talkback radio station. The occupier of the address complained that the broadcast was a breach of privacy. The Authority held that a person's address is not usually described as a private fact. It also held that a description of the event witnessed and a case against animal abusers in general would not endanger the privacy principles. However, the description of a specific person as an animal abuser was one that would make a person of ordinary sensibilities recoil. The information about the abuse was linked to an address and as a result identified the occupier as an abuser. Although each piece of information in itself would not have contravened the requirement for privacy, the Authority concluded that the combination of the two items did amount to a breach. It did not accept Radio New Zealand's argument that the disclosure of information could be excused on public interest grounds. No order was imposed.

The Authority also found in favour of the complainant in *Clements* v *Radio New Zealand Ltd.*[122] A breakfast-session phone call from a radio station disclosed that the complainant had had a disagreement with another driver while driving home from work. During the call the station disclosed that the other driver had chased the complainant home, and that the complainant had gone into a neighbour's property to seek refuge. The address of that neighbour's property was broadcast together with the description and registration number of the complainant's car and, more significantly, his name. The complainant had gone to some effort to ensure his pursuer would not be able to discover his name as he feared further harassment of himself and his family. The Authority held that in the circumstances the disclosure was both highly offensive and objection-able to a reasonable person of ordinary sensibilities. Compensation of NZ $1,000 was awarded.[123]

---

120. *Cf. Archer* v *Pirate FM*, BSA, 26 July 1994, Decision 56/94 where the announcer made a number of derogatory references on air about his estranged wife. The Authority declined to uphold a complaint of breach of privacy. In this case there was no broadcast of an address or telephone number. The Authority did state that it was appalled that a broadcaster should abuse the airwaves to make such personal comments.

121. BSA, 21 September 1995, Decisions 99/95 and 100/95.

122. BSA, 14 May 1992, Decision 19/92.

123. *Cf. JS* v *Television New Zealand Ltd.*, BSA, 2 June 1994, Decision 36/94. TVNZ broadcast a film of the complainant filmed openly at a public meeting. The film showed his face and name. JS complained that because he had taken steps to protect his real identity from a group of people he was involved with, the programme was a breach of his privacy. The Authority concluded that in view of the number of people at the meeting JS was unable to claim an interest in seclusion and that further the broadcast of his true identity was a public fact and the privacy principles did not apply.

In *Koster* v *Radio New Zealand Ltd.*,[124] a joke call was broadcast advising a woman that tickets for her forthcoming overseas trip were not available. The woman complained to the Authority that the broadcast breached her privacy. The facts that had been broadcast included her name, that the day of the broadcast was her birthday, that she was going on an overseas trip that included Europe and Disneyland, that she had been planning the trip for six months, and her husband's name. In the Authority's view, some of these facts, including the complainant's name, were private facts. However, it concluded that it was not offensive or objectionable to reveal any of the listed facts. The Authority declined to uphold the complaint as it related to privacy.

In *Presland* v *Northland Radio Company Ltd.*,[125] the complainants' 12 year old daughter and her 13 year old friend had requested a dedication from a Northland radio station. The dedication song was "Let's Talk About Sex". At 10.15 p.m. the announcer introduced the song and, with reference to its title, said "We know your mothers do not just talk about it." In her complaint to the Authority, the complainant stated that the comment breached broadcasting standards requiring good taste and decency, the protection of children and the protection of an individual's privacy.

One of the factors the Authority considered when making its decision was that the complainants' daughter had an unusual name and that her friend had the same name. The Authority found that sufficient information was disclosed to allow listeners who knew the family circumstances to identify her. The Authority held that the broadcast disclosed private facts of no public interest and exposed the complainants' personal life to the public in a way which most people would find objectionable.[126]

In September 1995, S, a New Zealander, was raped in South Africa. Her name was given in a news item broadcast by a New Zealand radio station during an interview with a South African journalist. This was not unlawful because the incident had taken place in another jurisdiction and there was no court order in place suppressing the victim's name in South Africa or New Zealand.[127] Members of the victim's family heard the broadcast and immediately complained to the radio station. The station agreed not to broadcast the name again.

When S returned to New Zealand she made a formal complaint to the Authority on the grounds that the station had breached the privacy

---

124. BSA, 19 December 1995, Decisions 151/95 and 152/95.

125. BSA, 28 September 1992, Decision 69/92.

126. See also *P* v *TV3 Network Services Ltd.*, BSA, 28 April 1994, Decision 21/94, where the Authority held that disclosure of private facts to one person would be sufficient to contravene the privacy principles.

127. A complainant has automatic name suppression under Criminal Justice Act 1985, s 139 if the sexual violation took place in New Zealand.

standard relating to the "public disclosure of private facts where the facts disclosed are highly offensive and objectionable to a reasonable person of ordinary sensibilities".[128] The Authority acknowledged that the radio station had acted promptly in ensuring there were no further broadcasts of the name and that they had apologised to the victim. Nevertheless, the Authority ordered compensation of NZ $2,500 to be paid to S.[129]

Another complaint regarding a breach of privacy of a rape victim was upheld by the Authority in 1993.[130] R was one of two rape complainants in a trial of nine gang members. TVNZ broadcast a shot in silhouette of her entering the Court. The shot did not show her face. The victim had taken steps to keep herself safe and anonymous during the trial. The Authority held that R would have been recognised by people who had had a considerable amount of interaction with her. It also referred to the fact that a rape victim's name was automatically suppressed and therefore a private fact.

It was apparent that TVNZ's news staff were aware that broadcasting the item might not have been in the interests of the complainant. The Authority expressed its concern that a person who had been a rape victim and was prepared to give evidence had been further victimised by the broadcaster. The Authority ordered that compensation of NZ $2,500 be paid.

TV3 Network Services Ltd. v Broadcasting Standards Authority

Although the decisions of the Authority are subject to appeal to the High Court, it was not until 1994 that the High Court had the opportunity to comment on the Authority's privacy principles.[131]   **8.37**

TV3 Network Services Ltd. v *Broadcasting Standards Authority* concerned a current affairs television programme about incest. The programme focused on the case of a man who had been convicted of sexual abuse of his five daughters just prior to the programme. There had already been newspaper reports and a magazine article on the case.

The television programme included interviews with three of the daughters but their identities were disguised. A reporter approached S, the daughters' mother, at her home and spoke to her about the case. The interview with S was filmed surreptitiously from land adjoining S's property. S's face was partially hidden. Although it was not clearly identifiable, the programme showed S's house. During the interview the reporter

---

128. *S v Radio Pacific Ltd.*, BSA, 18 January 1996, Decision 1996–003.

129. To date NZ $2,500 is the highest compensation awarded by the Authority.

130. *R v Television New Zealand Ltd.*, BSA, 21 December 1993, Decision 176/93.

131. *TV3 Network Services Ltd.* v *Broadcasting Standards Authority* [1995] 2 NZLR 720. The BSA advisory opinion was referred to by the Court of Appeal in *TVNZ v R* [1996] 3 NZLR 393.

suggested that S had been aware of the abuse inflicted on her daughters by her husband. The broadcast also suggested that S had been a victim of incest herself.

S complained that the broadcast breached her privacy in two respects:

(1)　By filming without her permission; and
(2)　By revealing that she had been a victim of sexual abuse.

8.38　　The Authority upheld the complaint and the broadcaster appealed to the High Court. The High Court upheld the Authority's decision and cited with approval the privacy principles established by the Authority. In addition, it accepted the approach of the Authority in adopting American case law as a foundation for its own guidelines on privacy.

　　The Court emphasised that what was under consideration was not whether publication of such facts would constitute a tort of breach of privacy. The focus was whether there was a basis for the imposition by the Authority of standards consistent with the privacy of the individual. The Court held that the Authority was entitled to take the view that privacy should include relief for individuals being harassed by disclosure of past events that lack sufficient connection to any matter of present public interest. It noted that the principles were not set in stone, and would always require consideration in the context of the facts of each case.

　　The Court held it was open to the Authority to take the view that although the facts had become public to a limited extent, there had been minimal identification of S prior to the interview. Such identification as there had been did not allow other members of the media to exacerbate any damage by following suit. The Court considered there was a vast difference between a situation where evidence receives media publicity and where it does not. The Court held further that this distinction had been recognised by the legislature in providing for the non-publication of details of identity relating to complainants, witnesses and parties,[132] notwithstanding that anyone who had been in Court at the time the case was heard would have become aware of such information. There was also a restriction in place prohibiting the publication of the name of any person on or with whom the offences had been committed, or of any name or particulars likely to lead to the identification of such persons. Although this order did not directly relate to S, in the circumstances, it had the effect of preventing publication of her name. The Court held that although S's statement regarding the abuse had been made public her identity remained protected from media publication to protect her children. Thus, the information retained a significant degree of privacy.

---

132. Criminal Justice Act 1985, ss 139, 139A and 140 respectively.

At the end of the judgment the Court commented generally regarding the concept of privacy:[133]

> "It will be apparent that in my view, for purposes of this legislation 'privacy' is not an absolute concept. The term should receive a fair, large and liberal interpretation; and although in the first instance this is a matter for the Authority it would certainly not be wrong to adopt a similar approach to its definition of private facts. On any sensible construction the meaning of that expression cannot be restricted to facts known to the individual alone. Although information has been made known to others a degree of privacy, entitled to protection, may remain. In determining whether information has lost its 'private' character, it would be appropriate to look realistically at the nature, scale and timing of previous publications."

8.39 There have been complaints in relation to privacy that the Authority has not upheld either because the facts disclosed were not highly offensive and objectionable,[134] or because there was no intentional interference with the complainant's privacy.[135] On a number of occasions the Authority has noted that although a complaint did not fall within the privacy principles, it might well have breached the Broadcasting Code requirement that broadcasters deal fairly and justly with persons taking part in or referred to in programmes (if the complaint had in fact been made on that basis).[136]

Privacy at common law

8.40 Despite some judicial comments about the potential for a tort of invasion of privacy there is still doubt whether such a tort exists in New Zealand. To date, only four decisions have considered the tort in any detail.[137]

The High Court first considered the tort in *Tucker* v *News Media Ownership Ltd.*[138] The case involved the publication of details of a potential heart transplant patient's criminal convictions some years earlier. He was seeking public support and funds to pay for a heart transplant operation

---

133. [1995] 2 NZLR 720, at 731.

134. *McCloy* v *Classic Gold Radio*, BSA, 16 September 1993, Decision 121/93; *Brown* v *Television New Zealand Ltd.*, BSA, 23 June 1994, Decisions 45/94 and 46/94; *Earlly* v *Radio Pacific Ltd.*, BSA, 23 June 1994, Decisions 43/94 and 44/94; *Sawyers* v *Radio Pacific Ltd.*, BSA, 22 June 1995, Decision 53/95.

135. *Hansen* v *Television New Zealand Ltd.*, BSA, 19 April 1993, Decision 44/93.

136. *Hunt* v *Radio New Zealand Ltd.*, BSA, 8 September 1994, Decision 79/94; *Hetherington* v *Television New Zealand Ltd.*, BSA, 31 May 1995, Decision 44/95.

137. Note that the Court made it clear in *TV3 Network Services Ltd.* that it was not considering the tort of privacy.

138. [1986] 2 NZLR 716.

in Australia. As part of his fund-raising campaign he was interviewed on television and radio, and newspaper advertisements were published. During the campaign he was told that a weekly newspaper had received information that he had been convicted of criminal offences some time in the past. The plaintiff was obviously upset and his health suffered. His doctor pleaded for editorial restraint. The plaintiff sought and obtained an interim injunction against the publisher, News Media Ownership Ltd. He was also granted an interim injunction against another newspaper and the Broadcasting Corporation of New Zealand.

The plaintiff travelled to Australia to be assessed for the heart transplant operation. While there, one of his major sponsors withdrew its offer of funds without giving reasons. After this, a private radio station, which was not a party to the injunction proceedings, broadcast details of the convictions. Soon after, the item was broadcast by most of the independent radio network in New Zealand, and a Sydney newspaper published an article referring to the plaintiff's convictions.

News Media Ownership Ltd. subsequently sought the discharge of the interim injunctions. In determining whether there was a serious question to be tried, McGechan J considered whether the tort of privacy would apply and cited the comments of Jeffries J in the earlier applications for the interim injunctions:[139]

> "I am aware of the development in other jurisdictions of the tort of invasion of privacy and the facts of this case seem to raise such an issue in a dramatic form. A person who lives an ordinary life has a right to be left alone and to live the private aspects of his life without being subjected to unwarranted, or undesired, publicity or public disclosure."

8.41 Jeffries J had held that the right to privacy may provide the plaintiff with a valid cause of action in New Zealand. He also found that a tort of invasion of privacy seemed a natural progression of the tort of intentional infliction of emotional distress, and the common law should provide a remedy for such a wrong. He considered that the essence of the tort was unwarranted publication of intimate details of the plaintiff's private life that were outside legitimate public concern or curiosity.

McGechan J accepted Jeffries J's findings and held that there was a serious question to be tried. He then supported:

> ". . . albeit with caution and hesitation . . . the introduction into the New Zealand common law of a tort covering invasion of personal privacy at least by public disclosure of private facts."[140]

---

139. [1986] 2 NZLR 716, 731.

140. [1986] 2 NZLR 716, 733.

The concept of privacy in relation to broadcast material was considered **8.42** in *Morgan* v *Television New Zealand Ltd.*,[141] which was part of an ongoing international child custody battle. Holland J granted an injunction restraining TVNZ from transmitting a programme about the custody dispute that had already been broadcast overseas. The injunction was granted on the basis that New Zealand law recognised some right to protection of privacy, subject to limitations where the public interest might exceed that of the privacy of the individual. Holland J could see little public interest in disclosing very private matters about the child's life. Despite previous widespread publicity in New Zealand and internationally, Holland J felt that the broadcast could be socially and emotionally detrimental to the child.

In a subsequent hearing involving publication of details of the case in a newspaper, Holland J expressed regret at being unable, on the balance of convenience, to issue an injunction to restrain publication (the newspaper was in the course of distribution to retailers at the time of the hearing).[142] He stated that it was important that injunctions were not granted if they could not be properly enforced.

In *Marris* v *TV3 Network Ltd.*,[143] Neazor J considered privacy in an injunction application. The plaintiff had been subject to disciplinary action by the Medical Practitioners Disciplinary Committee for failure to make a proper diagnosis of a patient's condition. The disciplinary action had taken place some months prior to the injunction application and information about it had been published in a provincial newspaper. TV3 proposed to screen a television programme relating to the patient's condition. The plaintiff did not take issue with the defendant's right to make or broadcast a programme that referred to him. What he and his wife objected to was the manner and circumstances of the filming and recording of discussions with him for use in the proposed programme. TV3 intended to broadcast film of the plaintiffs' private house, the reporter approaching the front door of the house, and the plaintiff speaking to the reporter from an upstairs window. The voice-over was to say that the plaintiff refused to be interviewed.

Whether or not there was tort liability in respect of invasion of privacy was not really an issue. The Court accepted TV3's argument that even if the existence of the tort was arguable, it was not arguable that the tort would extend to the facts of this particular case. Neazor J held that what was in issue in *Marris* could not be put higher than upset and anger on the part of the plaintiff and his wife when faced with the actions of TV3, and

---

141. Unreported, High Court, Christchurch, 1 March 1990, CP67/90 Holland J.

142. *Re Morgan*, unreported, High Court, Christchurch, 15 March 1990, CP93/90 Holland J.

143. Unreported, High Court, Wellington, 14 October 1991, CP754/91 Neazor J.

a degree of anger and embarrassment that the disciplinary proceedings should be publicly resurrected by TV3 in the proposed broadcast. He refused to grant an injunction against TV3.

The Judge noted that there were distinct problems as to what is, or will be, protected by a tort of invasion of privacy; whether resulting damage is an ingredient of the tort; and, if so, what resulting damage is required. The issues raised, for example, include whether obtaining information without legitimate reason is sufficient to amount to an invasion of privacy, whether publication is required as well, and what is to be regarded as "without legitimate reason".[144]

Significantly, both the courts and the Broadcasting Standards Authority have referred to *Prosser & Keeton on The Law of Torts*, which sets out several distinct privacy torts including[145] a public disclosure of private facts which are highly offensive and objectionable to a reasonable person of ordinary sensibilities; and publicity which places the plaintiff in a false light in the public eye.

Bradley v *Wingnut Films Ltd.*[146] is the fullest discussion of the tort of invasion of privacy by a High Court judge to date. In the course of his judgment, Gallen J stated that he was prepared to accept that the tort of privacy formed part of the law of New Zealand but "its extent should be regarded with caution",[147] and he implicitly accepted the validity of Prosser and Keeton's formulation. He also stated that three requirements must be satisfied before the tort of privacy is made out:[148]

(1)   The disclosure of the private facts must be a public disclosure and not a private one;

(2)   The facts disclosed to the public must be private facts and not public ones; and

(3)   The matter made public must be one which would be highly offensive and objectionable to a reasonable person of ordinary sensibilities.

8.43   In support of his views, he cited the three cases discussed above.[149] However, he noted that when considering a tort of privacy it was important

---

144. Unreported, High Court, Wellington, 14 October 1991, CP754/91, p 8.

145. See also *Tucker* v *News Media Ownership Ltd.* [1986] 2 NZLR 716 and *Bradley* v *Wingnut Films Ltd.* [1993] 1 NZLR 415 and the decisions of the Broadcasting Standards Authority referred to above.

146. [1993] 1 NZLR 415.

147. [1993] 1 NZLR 415.

148. [1993] 1 NZLR 415, 424.

149. *Tucker* v *News Media Ownership Ltd.* [1986] 2 NZLR 716, *Morgan* v *Television New Zealand Ltd.*, unreported, High Court, Christchurch, 1 March 1990, CP67/90 and *Marris* v *TV3 Network Ltd.*, unreported, High Court, Wellington, 14 October 1991, CP754/91.

to bear in mind that the "rights and concerns of the individual must be balanced against the significance in a free country of freedom of expression".[150]

Gallen J declined to uphold a breach of a tort of privacy on the facts of the case. He held that to do so would:

". . . extend the boundaries of an emerging tort far beyond what is safe and would impose restrictions on the freedom of expression that would alter the balance against such freedom more than could be justified."[151]

In a case unrelated to the media, Thorp J stated:[152]   **8.44**

"There is little doubt that at least in this country the common law action for breach of privacy is still in its formative stages, and the limitations seen to be appropriate to such a right in the few decided cases which have considered the matter stand in contrast to the agreed principles set out in the Privacy Act that have been developed, in relation to this particular area, by the Health Information Privacy Codes."

Although the trend of the High Court comment has been to accept that   **8.45**
a tort of privacy may exist within New Zealand, the issue has not been addressed in detail by the Court of Appeal. Until this occurs, it is difficult to say with certainty that the tort of privacy will be completely accepted into New Zealand law, and on what terms.[153]

The Privacy Act

The Privacy Act 1993 came into force on 1 July 1993. Its aim is to promote   **8.46**
and protect an individual's personal data and privacy in accordance with international guidelines.[154] It sets out 12 privacy principles that must be complied with in relation to the collection, use and disclosure of personal information by another person or organisation, called "an agency" by the

---

150. [1993] 1 NZLR 415, 423.

151. [1993] 1 NZLR 415, 425.

152. *Hobson* v *Harding*, unreported, High Court, Auckland, 6 March 1995, CP312/94 Thorp J, p 18.

153. Although there has not been a definitive ruling by the Court of Appeal, it agreed in *Tucker* v *News Media Ownership Ltd.* that the concept of privacy was at least arguable. See the Court's comments cited in the judgment of McGechan J [1986] 2 NZLR 716, at 732. Also refer in different context, comments of Court of Appeal in *R* v *Jefferies* [1994] 1 NZLR 290; *R* v *A* [1994] 1 NZLR 429.

154. The long title of the Act.

Privacy Act. However, the privacy principles do not confer on a complainant any legal rights that the complainant can enforce in the courts.[155] Complaints must be made to a Privacy Commissioner who may refer the complaint to a Proceedings Commissioner.[156] The Proceedings Commissioner may in turn bring civil proceedings before the Complaints Review Tribunal.[157] The board principles are as follows:

(1) *The purpose of collecting personal information* — Personal information must not be collected by any agency unless it is done so for a lawful purpose connected with a function or activity of the agency and it is necessary for that purpose.

(2) *The source of personal information* — Where an agency collects personal information, the agency must collect the information directly from the individual concerned.

(3) *Collection of information from a subject* — Where an agency collects personal information directly from the individual the agency must make full explanation of the fact, purpose, intended recipients of the information, the collecting agency's name and address, the legal authority relied on, the consequences to the individual and the right of access to and correction of personal information.

(4) *The way personal information is collected* — Personal information must not be collected by any agency by unlawful means or by means that, in the circumstances of the case, are unfair or intrude, to an unreasonable extent, on the personal affairs of the individual concerned.

(5) *Storage and security of personal information* — Any agency that holds personal information must ensure it is protected by security safeguards against loss, misuse, and unauthorised access, use, modification or disclosure of the information.

(6) *Access to personal information* — An individual is entitled to obtain, from an agency, confirmation of whether or not the agency holds personal information about him/her and to have access to that information.

(7) *Correction of personal information* — An individual can request that an agency correct any personal information held about him/her. If the agency is not prepared to do this, he/she can request that a statement be attached to the information detailing the correction

---

155. Privacy Act, s 11(2), but see also s 11(1), which provides that the entitlements conferred by subclause 1 of Principle 6 are legal rights enforceable in the Courts insofar as they relate to personal information held by a public sector agency.

156. Privacy Act, ss 67(1) and 77(2).

157. Privacy Act, ss 82–83.

sought. The agency must inform each person or body or agency who has received the personal information of these steps.

(8) *Personal information must be checked* — Personal information must be checked before it is used to ensure it is accurate, up-to-date, complete, relevant and not misleading.

(9) *Keeping personal information* — Personal information is not to be kept by an agent for longer than necessary.

(10) *Limits on use of personal information* — If information is collected for one purpose it shall not be used for another purpose.

(11) *Limits on disclosure of personal information* — This principle provides limits on disclosure of personal information to any other person, body or agency. It also sets out the grounds on which disclosure can be made.

(12) *Unique identifiers* — This principle deals with a number of points where unique identifiers are used by agencies to identify individuals. One of the points is that an agency must not assign a unique identifier to an individual unless the identifier is necessary to enable the agency to carry out any one or more of its functions efficiently.

The Privacy Act 1993 sets out certain exemptions to the prohibition on **8.47** disclosure of information.[158] If one of the purposes of the initial collection of the information is eventual disclosure, then disclosure may be made. Other reasons for exemptions include:

(1) The express or implied consent to disclosure of the individual concerned;

(2) The fact that the source of the information is publicly available;

(3) The maintenance of law and order;

(4) Use of information for statistical or research purposes where the individual concerned will not be identified; and

(5) A limited exemption if disclosure is necessary to prevent a serious and imminent threat to health and public safety.

The Privacy Act 1993 creates the office of Privacy Commissioner. The **8.48** function of the Commissioner is to investigate complaints of interference with privacy and also to publicly promote, educate and explain the privacy principles.

The news media are exempt from the provisions of the Privacy Act in relation to their "news activities".[159] "News activities" is defined broadly.

---

158. Principle 11.

159. Privacy Act, s 2 defines the agencies subject to the Act to exclude any news medium in relation to its news activities.

It includes not only the gathering of news but also observations on the news and current affairs. However, state-owned broadcasting organisations are not exempt from principles (6) and (7) (relating to access to personal information and correction of that information) even if they are engaged in "news activities". All media activity not related to news activities is subject to the requirements of the Privacy Act .

An unfortunate result of the Privacy Act is the suggestion that some organisations use it to stonewall media investigations, alleging that if information is released it will breach the requirements of the Act.[160] The media need to be aware of the exemptions set out in Principle 11, in particula that the Privacy Act does not override the provisions for freedom of information in the Official Information Act 1982 and the Local Government Official Information and Meetings Act 1987.[161]

Photographs and listening devices

8.49 The focus so far has been largely on the type of material published and the unauthorised sharing of information about an individual rather than on the means of collecting information. There is no prohibition against the taking of unauthorised photographs, the use of surveillance cameras or the use of recording devices. When one is a party to the conversation.

Apart from restrictions which apply to the police in regard to the interception of private communications,[162] and to private investigators, who are not permitted to take photographs or voice recordings without consent,[163] there is no specific law to restrain a member of the public, including the media, from recording a conversation (if a party to it) or taking photographs of a person or his or her property. Naturally, if a plaintiff can base a claim on an existing cause of action such as trespass, defamation, or breach of confidence, then the offending material may be subject to an injunction or damages. If the material has been broadcast, compensation may be sought via the Broadcasting Standards Authority.[164]

If a plaintiff suspects that photographs or recordings have been made surreptitiously he or she may be able to obtain access to the material under the Privacy Act.[165] However, privately owned media are exempt

---

160. Privacy Commissioner, *Private Word*, issue number 5, May 1996.

161. Under the Official Information Act and the Local Government Official Information Act, information may be required from public agencies such as government departments, universities, state owned enterprises and local government entities.

162. Crimes Act 1961, 216B.

163. Private Investigators and Security Guards Act 1974, s 52.

164. See *TV3 Network Services Ltd.* v *Broadcasting Standards Authority* [1995] 2 NZLR 720.

165. Principle 6.

from providing access if the material has been compiled in relation to their "news activities", which includes news-gathering and preparation of articles.[166] By contrast the state-owned broadcasting media are required to provide access.[167]

The Courts have recognised that such activity is an invasion of privacy and that it is undesirable that the law does not provide an appropriate remedy. In the Court of Appeal decision *R v Menzies*, Richardson J considered whether evidence obtained by a listening device was admissible in a criminal case and stated:[168]

> "The use of a listening device planted in private property can only be regarded as an intrusion into the privacy of the home. Also, a very severe intrusion at that for the only way a person can protect himself from a hidden microphone is by not talking at all. The common law may not recognise the inviolability of conversations conducted in private . . . However, the old legal maxim 'a man's house is his castle' . . . reflects a reasonable expectation of privacy which is part of our shared heritage."

The Broadcasting Standards Authority considered issues of surreptitious **8.50** filming and recording of conversations in *S v TV3 Network Services Ltd.*,[169] and in *Leckey v Television New Zealand Ltd.*[170] In *S v TV3 Network Services Ltd.* a camera crew stationed on an adjoining property surreptitiously filmed S in her backyard. While upholding the Authority's decision that a breach of privacy had occurred, Eichelbaum CJ stated in the High Court appeal, "[O]n the authorities it is clear that no tort is committed by photographing another person's private property without consent."[171] This is in line with the English and Australian view that there is no law against spying on a person, or taking photographs of a person's property, whether it be done from a neighbour's premises, from the footpath or from an aeroplane.[172]

In *Leckey*, TVNZ secretly recorded a discussion between an immigration consultant and a Malaysian applicant who was a TVNZ "plant". When considering a breach of privacy complaint the Authority held that,

---

166. Privacy Act, s 2.

167. Privacy Act, s 2.

168. [1982] 1 NZLR 40, 52.

169. BSA, 19 January 1994, Decision 1/94.

170. BSA, 29 October 1993, Decision 138/93.

171. *TV3 Network Services Ltd.* v *Broadcasting Standards Authority* [1995] 2 NZLR 720, at 732.

172. See *Bernstein v Skyviews Ltd.* [1978] QB 479. See also *Bathurst City Council v Saban* (1985) 2 NSWLR 704 and *Victoria Park Racing and Recreation Grounds Co. Ltd. v Taylor* (1937) 58 CLR 479.

while electronic eavesdropping on a private business conversation was offensive to an ordinary person, the widespread public interest in immigration issues outweighed privacy concerns. The Authority accepted that the behaviour disclosed by the surreptitious recording was not criminal but "readily accepted that the behaviour disclosed would definitely be widely regarded as antisocial."[173]

Contempt

Criminal contempt

8.51 The law relating to contempt is as much a concern to the media in New Zealand as in other jurisdictions. Generally similar issues arise. In this part, we are not concerned with such topics as outrageous criticism of court decisions or extravagant attacks on individual judges, nor are we concerned with the privilege that attaches to reporting of court proceedings.[174]

The important daily decision editors must make relates to when discussion of a police investigation becomes *sub judice* with the result that further discussion in the media must be restricted if it poses a real risk of interference with the fairness of a trial.[175] Unlike England, New Zealand does not have legislation governing contempt. The law is judge-made.

The starting point is the decision of Davison CJ in *Solicitor-General* v *Broadcasting Corporation of New Zealand.*[176] A Member of Parliament made statements on radio implying that one or both of two persons awaiting trial on charges of murder had previous criminal convictions. The Solicitor-General issued proceedings alleging contempt of court against the Broadcasting Corporation and the Member of Parliament in that such statements were calculated to prejudice the criminal trials. A second set of proceedings was issued against a newspaper and the same Member of Parliament.

---

173. BSA, 29 October 1993, Decision 138/93, at p 6.

174. See Defamation Act 1992 s 16(1) and cls 5 and 6 of Part I of the First Schedule in relation to qualified privilege for fair and accurate reports of court proceedings.

175. *Solicitor General* v *TV3 Network Services Limited and Another,* unreported judgment of Eichelbaum CJ, 8 April 1997.

176. [1987] 2 NZLR 100.

The Court found there was no real risk of any tendency to prejudice the trials. The Court noted that the "real risk" test must be determined on the basis of practical realities, not on some hypothetical basis.[177] The Chief Justice stated:[178]

"Even though a contempt has been proved according to law, a Court may yet decide that it should not punish that contempt on grounds of public policy. The law of contempt is founded entirely on public policy and public policy requires the balancing of interests that may conflict. In the realm of contempt, there is, on the one hand, the right of an accused person to a fair trial by the Courts and not to have that trial prejudiced by interference from outside sources. On the other hand, the public's right to know, freedom of speech and the freedom of the press should not be limited to any greater extent than is necessary . . . . The public interest test has been considered by the Courts in terms that where statements deliberately made by persons or the media have a clear tendency to prejudice the fair trial of an accused then the countervailing public interest and freedom of discussion must be subordinated to the administration of justice."

The important injunction decision of the Court of Appeal in *Television* **8.52** *New Zealand Ltd.* v *Solicitor-General*[179] followed. After a homicide enquiry had commenced, the police announced that they were looking for a named suspect and his wife. The police warned the public not to approach the man. While the man was still at large, *Television New Zealand Ltd.* ("TVNZ") prepared a broadcast referring to the shooting and to the suspect. The item contained some general comments by neighbours and friends of the suspect.

The Solicitor-General obtained an *ex parte* interim injunction restraining TVNZ from broadcasting any personal information about the suspect and any other information about the events leading to the death other than those already supplied by the police. TVNZ applied to have the injunction set aside. This was refused by the High Court but granted by the Court of Appeal. Cooke P stated:[180]

"In our opinion, the law of New Zealand must recognise that in cases where the commencement of criminal proceedings is highly likely the Court has inherent jurisdiction to prevent the risk of contempt of Court by granting an injunction. However, the freedom of the press and other

---

177. [1987] 2 NZLR 100, 107. See also *Solicitor-General* v *Radio Avon Ltd.* [1978] 1 NZLR 225 and *John Fairfax & Sons Pty Ltd.* v *McRae* (1955) 93 CLR 351.

178. [1987] 2 NZLR 100, 108.

179. [1989] 1 NZLR 1.

180. [1989] 1 NZLR 1, 3.

media is not lightly to be interfered with and it must be shown that there is a real likelihood of a publication of material that will seriously prejudice the fairness of the trial."

8.53   The test of serious prejudice to a fair trial has since been considered in a series of contempt decisions in the Courts, where freedom of expression, underscored by section 14 of the New Zealand Bill of Rights Act 1990 (NZBOR), has been curtailed or at least postponed. The right to a fair trial (also a guaranteed right under the NZBOR) has taken precedence. The High Court has stated:[181]

"Adopting the general approach of the Canadian Courts modified to New Zealand conditions, there is no doubt that the objective of the law of contempt, generally and specifically in this case, is of sufficient importance to warrant the limit of the freedom of expression. Both as expressed in section 25 of the Privacy Act in declaring minimum standards of criminal procedure, and at ordinary common law, the protection of the due administration of justice, the impartiality and the freedom of deliberation of a jury, the finality of its verdict and preservation of the juror's anonymity are certainly important, substantial and pressing concerns of a free and democratic society. They are at least as fundamental as the freedom of expression . . . . The means available, by the sanction of procedures of contempt, to further and achieve this objective and to impose the limitation must, we think, be accepted to be reasonable and to be demonstrably justified. The means by which they are carried out is by another criminal or Court procedure, impartially and fairly conducted by the Court. The result in any and each case is to prevent and to punish the particular contempt that has occurred."

8.54   In *Solicitor-General* v *Radio New Zealand Ltd.*,[182] the High Court held Radio New Zealand in contempt for interviewing and broadcasting comments of jurors in a murder trial even though the trial had ended nearly a year before. When the trial took place the victims' bodies had not been recovered. The interviews with jurors were conducted when one of the bodies was found. The Court held the sanctity of jury deliberations and the privacy of the jurors outweighed freedom of expression. The Court stated:[183]

"The right to a fair and impartial trial, one in which the onus of proof is on the prosecution and the accused is presumed innocent until proved guilty, is at least as fundamental and as important as the right to freedom

---

181. *Solicitor-General* v *Radio New Zealand Ltd.* [1994] 1 NZLR 48, 64.

182. [1994] 1 NZLR 48, 64.

183. [1994] 1 NZLR 48, 64, 60.

of speech. At the heart of the criminal trial is the jury's impartiality and its freedom from any constraint from outside. The finality of the verdict, the preservation of frankness in deliberation and the privacy of jurors are all important in the due administration of justice as we have already emphasised. We think that on balance the right to freedom of expression is qualified by the necessity to preserve and protect those fundamental elements in the jury system. Freedom of expression does not authorise or permit the conduct of the defendant in this case. The right does not encompass the contempt alleged and found."

In *Solicitor-General* v *Wellington Newspapers Ltd.*,[184] the High Court consid-   **8.55**
ered the pre-trial publication of the prior convictions of an accused. The reports also referred to the accused being on bail on charges of assaulting police or prison officers and police concerns that bail had been granted. The Court noted that a fundamental assumption of the jury trial system is that any previous criminal record of the accused is kept from the jury. The Court again emphasised the preservation of an impartial and effective system of justice.

On appeal the Court of Appeal referred to the different in approach in the Canadian decision of *Dagenais* v *Canadian Broadcasting Corporation*[185] and the High Court of Australia decision in *Hinch* v *Attorney-General for the State of Victoria*[186] and held that fair trial considerations outweighed the freedom of speech interest.[187] The Court elected to follow the approach of the Australian Court in Hinch:[188]

"The common law of contempt is based on public policy. It requires the balancing of public interest factors. Freedom of the press as a vehicle for comment on public issues is basic to our democratic system. The assurance of a fair trial by an impartial Court is essential for the preservation of an effective system of justice. Both values have been affirmed by the Bill of Rights. The public interest in the functioning of the Courts invokes both these values. It calls for free expression of information and opinions as to the performance of those public responsibilities. It also calls for a determination of disputes by Courts that are free from bias which make their decision solely on the evidence judicially brought before them. Full recognition of both these indispensable elements can present difficult problems for the Courts to resolve. The issue is how best those values can be accommodated under the New Zealand Bill of Rights Act 1990."

---

184. [1995] 1 NZLR 45.
185. (1994) 94 CCC (3d) 289.
186. (1987) 164 CLR 15.
187. *Gisborne Herald Co. Ltd.* v *Solicitor-General* [1995] 3 NZLR 563.
188. [1995] 3 NZLR 563, 571.

8.56 The Court found:[189]

> "First, the complex process of balancing the values underlying free expression and fair trial rights may vary from country to country, even though there is a common and genuine commitment to international human rights norms. The balancing will be influenced by the culture and values of the particular community. The Bill of Rights accords a particular status to fair trial rights. Section 25 affirms minimum standards of criminal procedure and the right to a fair and public hearing by an independent and impartial court is a guaranteed 'minimum' right. By specifying how limitations on the rights and freedoms contained in the Bill of Rights are to be justified in particular cases, our section 5 recognises explicitly that there are limits on those rights and freedoms. Within the Bill of Rights itself, the right to freedom of expression (section 14) and the importance in the public interest of contemporaneous discussion of the subject-matter must be weighed along with other affirmed rights, which include as a minimum right the right to a fair and public hearing by an impartial court (section 25(a)) and the right to be presumed innocent until proved guilty according to law (section 25(c)) and their application in the particular circumstances. The result of the balancing process will necessarily reflect the Court's assessment of society's values . . . ."

8.57 Again, as noted by the Court there is limited New Zealand data as to the impact of media publicity on jury behaviour by which to test such matters as:

(1) The effects of media coverage of criminal events on public beliefs and attitudes and their dissipation over time;
(2) The effectiveness of judicial instructions to the assembled jury panel in eliminating prejudiced jurors; and
(3) The effectiveness of judicial directions and jury deliberations in curing any prejudice resulting from pre-trial publicity about the case.[190]

8.58 In general, the courts have accepted that where there has been a substantial lapse of time between the publicity and the trial then it is unlikely that there will be a risk of prejudice.[191] The Courts have warned that the

---

189. [1995] 3 NZLR 563, 573–575. *Cf.* the comments of Richardson J in *R v Harawira* [1989] 2 NZLR 714, 729 (CA): "Our system of justice operates in an open society where public issues are freely exposed and debated. Experience shows that juries are quite capable of understanding and carrying out their role in this environment, notwithstanding that an accused may have been the subject of widespread debate and criticism".
190. [1995] 3 NZLR 563, 573.
191. *R v Sanders* [1995] 3 NZLR 545; *R v Coghill* [1995] 3 NZLR 651.

practice of the police in supplying the media with information that could prejudice the accused creates an obvious risk that a fair trial may be impossible. The Court of Appeal has stated, "[t]actics of that kind by the police are no part of their proper functions."[192]

Civil contempt

The courts in New Zealand have adopted a more robust approach to **8.59** assessing statements about pending civil trials. In the words of one judge, an application for contempt "should not be a means of muzzling legitimate public comment".[193]

While doubt has been expressed as to whether the broad "pre-judgment test" set out in *Attorney-General* v *Times Newspapers Ltd.*[194] is "applicable in its absolute rigidity to New Zealand",[195] forms of that pre-judgment test have been applied in New Zealand recently. In *Pharmaceutical Management Agency Ltd.* v *Researched Medicines Industry Association New Zealand Inc.*,[196] McGechan J held that there were two aspects to public pre-judgment of issues. The first was conduct calculated to prejudice a fair trial by influencing the decision-making tribunal or prospective witnesses in the trial of the particular action. The second is conduct calculated to deter parties generally from resorting to the Courts to enforce their rights.

In *Pharmaceutical Management Agency Ltd.* v *Researched Medicines Industry Association, New Zealand Inc.*, the litigation was between an incorporated society formed by certain medicine companies ("the Society") and a company formed by four Regional Health Authorities which determined which pharmaceuticals were to be subsidised ("the Agency"). The Society filed proceedings alleging breach of the Commerce Act 1986 and seeking judicial review of the Agency's subsidy practices. When the proceedings were issued the Society arranged a press conference to announce the litigation, invited representatives of organisations supportive of its position and organised a follow up by the national media. The Court held that the media release could be prejudicial on the basis that it might expose the Agency to the risk of hostile publicity for defending the proceedings. Having reached this point, the Court then turned to the balance of convenience, overall justice and discretion to determine

---

192. [1995] 3 NZLR 651, 661.

193. *Duff* v *Communicado Ltd.*, [1996] 2 NZLR 89.

194. [1974] AC 273.

195. *Greenpeace New Zealand Inc.* v *Minister of Fisheries* [1995] 2 NZLR 463, 471.

196. [1996] 1 NZLR 472.

whether an interim injunction should be awarded. Injunctive relief was refused because it was not sufficiently necessary.

An article by a medical journal about the litigation was also in issue in the same case. The publication carried a clear overtone that the proceedings were considered by significant and informed sectors of the medical industry to be well founded. It conveyed a pre-judgment and as such went too far. Again, while the threshold was satisfied the Court refused to grant an injunction. There was no indication that republication was likely and the Court was content that the defendant was now well aware of the risks involved. This was considered sufficient.

Clearly when the media, which has no financial or other personal interest in litigation, comment on matters of legitimate public interest the court will be more tolerant in determining what is acceptable.[197] Conversely, a contempt will occur if a litigant publicly misrepresents the issues with a view to turning public opinion against the other side, thereby pressuring them to withdraw.

Name suppression

8.60 In New Zealand, the courts have a broad discretion under section 140 of the Criminal Justice Act 1985 to grant name suppression. The Court of Appeal considered the principles that govern the making or refusing of name suppression in *R* v *Liddell*.[198] Cooke P delivered the Court's decision and noted:[199]

> "[T]he starting point must always be the importance in a democracy of freedom of speech, open judicial proceedings, and the right of the media to report the latter fairly and accurately as 'surrogates of the public'. The basic value of freedom to receive and impart information has been re-emphasised by section 14 of the New Zealand Bill of Rights Act 1990."

Search warrants against the media

8.61 Protection of sources of information is a matter of considerable importance to the media. Forced disclosure of sources raises issues of breach of confidence together with the broader concern that the free flow of information will be halted if the media are seen as agents of the state.

---

197. *Duff* v *Communicado Ltd.* [1996] 2 NZLR 89.

198. [1995] 1 NZLR 538.

199. [1995] 1 NZLR 538, 546.

In February 1995, the two major New Zealand television networks, Television New Zealand ("TVNZ") and TV3, were subjected to search warrants issued by the police to obtain copies of videotape film of protest action. Protesters had disrupted Waitangi Day celebrations allegedly committing a number of criminal offences. Both television networks had filmed the events and the police wished to use the film to assist in identifying and prosecuting the offenders.

TVNZ sought a declaration that the search warrants were illegal because their terms were too broad.[200] It also argued that the warrants breached the freedom of speech provision in section 14 of the New Zealand Bill of Rights Act 1990 and constituted an unreasonable search and seizure in terms of section 21 of that Act.

While upholding the search warrants in the particular circumstances of the case the Court of Appeal laid down five guidelines for the future issue of warrants against the media:[201]

(1) Where the media itself has committed no offence, the intrusive procedure of a search warrant should not be used for trivial or truly minor cases;

(2) As far as practicable, a warrant should not be granted or executed so as to impair the public dissemination of news;

(3) Only in exceptional circumstances where it is truly essential in the interests of justice should a warrant be granted or executed if there is a substantial risk that it will result in the "drying-up" of confidential sources of information for the media;

(4) A warrant should be executed considerately and so as to cause the least practicable disruption to the business of the media organisation; and

(5) A warrant should only be granted when it is likely that the film will have a direct and important place in the determination of the issues before the Court.

Negligence

The principles to be applied by the New Zealand Courts in determining **8.62** the circumstances in which a duty of care exists were considered in the

---

200. *Television New Zealand Ltd.* v *Attorney-General* [1995] 2 NZLR 641.

201. [1995] 2 NZLR 641, 647–648.

leading authority in *South Pacific Manufacturing Co. Ltd.* v *New Zealand Security Consultants & Investigations Ltd.*[202] As relates to defamation, Cooke P stated:

> "[A] point telling against recognising a new common law duty of care arises when such a duty would cut across established patterns of law in special fields wherein experience has shown that certain defences, not dependent on absence of negligence, are needed; or wherein an adequate remedy is already available to a party who takes the necessary steps . . . . As to the former situation, in Bell-Booth Group Ltd. v Attorney-General this Court declined to extend negligence law to a claim that the reputation of the plaintiffs had been damaged by a television broadcast. In the field of injury to reputation, the defences of justification, privilege and fair comment, and the balance of competing interests represented thereby, would have been undermined by superimposing a right to sue in negligence. The approach was taken a degree further in this Court in Balfour v Attorney-General,[203] where it was said that the cause of action unsuccessfully alleged came 'perilously close to defamation' and that any attempt to merge defamation and negligence is to be resisted."

8.63 In *Bell-Booth Group Ltd.* v *Attorney-General*,[204] the Court of Appeal was not prepared to allow a claim in negligence as an alternative to an action in defamation. Bell-Booth Group Ltd. were manufacturers and distributors of agricultural products, including a product called "Maxicrop" which was advertised as a powerful fertiliser. After testing the product the Ministry of Agriculture and Fisheries came to the conclusion that Maxicrop did not work. The opinion of the Ministry was presented on a television programme in 1985. Bell-Booth claimed that the programme destroyed its Maxicrop business. The initial claim was against both the broadcaster and the Ministry but, after a 97-day trial, Bell-Booth elected to be non-suited against the broadcaster. Bell-Booth claimed in defamation and in negligence against the Ministry, on the basis that the Ministry was under a duty of care to disclose all the results of its trials of the product to Bell-Booth prior to publishing the results.

In the High Court, the claim for defamation failed because the statements made by the Ministry were found to be true. However, the judge

---

202. [1992] 2 NZLR 282, 294–299.

203. [1991] 1 NZLR 519, 529.

204. [1989] 3 NZLR 148.

awarded NZ $25,000 general damages for negligence. The Court of Appeal overturned this award stating:[205]

> "The important point for present purposes is that the law as to injury to reputation and freedom of speech is a field of its own. To impose the law of negligence on it by accepting that there may be common law duties of care not to publish the truth would be to introduce a distorting element . . . . The duty in defamation may be described as a duty not to defame without justification or privilege or otherwise than by way of fair comment . . . . In substance the appellant would add to these duties a duty in such a case as this to take care not to injure the plaintiff's reputation by true statements . . . . In our opinion, to accept it would be to introduce negligence law into a field for which it was not designed and is not appropriate."

In *Fleming* v *Securities Commission*,[206] a claim was made that a newspaper **8.64** had been negligent in publishing advertisements offering investment opportunities that did not comply with statutory requirements. Readers lost substantial sums of money when their investments failed. The Court of Appeal held that the action should be struck out. The Court found that to impose such a duty of care on the media would open the floodgates and inhibit the free flow of information. Cooke P stated:[207]

> "[I]n an ideal world the press might perhaps be expected to have a legal obligation to take reasonable care that what is published to its readers is accurate and lawful. However, we do not live in Utopia. I accept that in practice such a rule would cripple the media."

Cooke P referred to two American decisions that refused to find the **8.65** media negligent in relation to publications provided to information service subscribers.[208] Both cases involved mis-statements in financial news rather than advertisements but the same overriding policy considerations applied.

Richardson J found that it would be necessary to change the entire economic structure of advertising in newspapers if newspaper publishers were required to verify every advertisement printed.[209] He

---

205. [1989] 3 NZLR 148, 156.

206. [1995] 2 NZLR 514.

207. [1995] 2 NZLR 514, 520.

208. *First Equity Corporation of Florida* v *Standard* & *Poor's Corporation* 670 F Supp 115 (SDNY 1987); *Jaillet* v *Cashman* 189 NYS 743 (Sup Ct) (1921).

209. [1995] 2 NZLR 514, 532.

quoted 58 American Jurisprudence, 2d, Newspapers, Periodicals and Press Associations Paragraph 9 stating:[210]

> "[I]n weighing private and public considerations, the public policy of not subjecting newspapers to the chilling prospect of hordes of suits by disgruntled readers of inaccurate advertisements dominates."

8.66 The Court distinguished an advertisement, where an advertiser uses the newspaper as a mere conduit, and advice given by a newspaper in response to a specific enquiry in an advice column. In the latter situation, the Court was prepared to find a special relationship between the specific enquirer and the newspaper. However, it was likely that any liability for negligence would only be between the newspaper and the specific enquirer. The Court was not prepared to allow for the possibility of an indefinite liability to an indeterminate number of readers.

Casey J also cited the American cases, in particular the statement by Goettel J in *First Equity*:[211]

> "[I]n the absence of a contract, fiduciary relationship, or intent to cause injury, a newspaper publisher is not liable to a member of the public for a non-defamatory negligent mis-statement of an item of news . . . . The reason is one of practical expediency. First, it is simply impossible to attain perfection in the publishing business. Second, the potential number of persons to whom a publication might become available is without limit."

8.67 The media does not owe a duty of care to its general readers or viewers. As Casey J said:[212]

> "The fact that the newspaper may have been grossly negligent in continuing to publish the advertisement after the commission's warning and the undertaking it gave, cannot bear on the threshold question of whether it had a duty. Its conduct may only serve to demonstrate that had there been one, it had been well and truly broken."

Fair Trading Act

8.68 The Fair Trading Act 1986 prohibits misleading and deceptive conduct in trade. It is similar to the Australian Trade Practices Act 1974. The Fair Trading Act 1986 forms the basis of many civil claims for damages as well

---

210. [1995] 2 NZLR 514, 532.

211. [1995] 2 NZLR 514, 535.

212. [1995] 2 NZLR 514, 535.

as providing heavy fines for breaches. However, the principal provisions prohibiting misleading and deceptive conduct and false representations have only limited application to the news media.[213] The prohibitions on deceptive and misleading conduct set out in the Fair Trading Act do not apply to the publication or broadcast of any information by a newspaper publisher or a broadcaster unless what is published or broadcast is an advertisement or relates to the supply or promotion of goods or services by the publisher or broadcaster itself. In relation to advertisements, the Fair Trading Act provides a defence to prosecution if the publisher or broadcaster proves that its business is publishing or arranging for the publication of advertisements and that it received the advertisement, or information contained in the advertisement, in the ordinary course of business not knowing or suspecting that what was stated contravened the Act.[214]

Trespass

General

In New Zealand, representatives of the media have the same implied **8.69** licence as any other member of the public to enter private property for lawful purposes.[215] In recent years, there has been an increased use by the media of a technique known as "doorstepping" to obtain interviews. Although invariably used as a last resort to obtain a response from a potential interviewee, the media run the risk of a trespass action when they use the technique.[216]

The Australian courts have held that blatant, intentional intrusion by the media can be grounds for an injunction to restrain publication. In *Emcorp* v *Australian Broadcasting Corporation*,[217] a reporter from a public affairs television programme entered the plaintiff's business premises accompanied by a camera operator and a sound recordist. Despite protests from the plaintiff's staff and numerous requests to leave, the television crew asked questions, and filmed and read business papers and records.

The Court held that the material had been obtained "in flagrant disregard of the property rights of the plaintiffs" and that the media were

---

213. Privacy Act, s 15. Privacy Act, ss 9–14 set out the prohibition against misleading and deceptive conduct.

214. Privacy Act, s 44(4).

215. *Dehn* v *Attorney-General* [1988] 2 NZLR 564; *Robson* v *Hallett* [1967] 2 QB 939.

216. *TV3 Network Services Ltd.* v *Broadcasting Standards Authority* [1995] 2 NZLR 720; *Marris* v *TV3 Network Ltd.*, unreported, High Court, Wellington, 14 October 1991, CP754/91 Neazor J; *Lincoln Hunt Australia Pty Ltd.* v *Willesee* (1986) 4 NSWLR 457; *Emcorp* v *Australian Broadcasting Corporation* [1988] 2 Qd R 169.

217. [1988] 2 Qd R 169.

trespassing. The judge pointed out that if police officers acted in that manner during an investigation they would be acting unlawfully. He stated that if a police officer could not enter a home or office, armed with a video camera, to search for evidence of the commission of some offence, the law could not justify and protect the conduct of a news reporter in doing that.

The Court found that if the film was broadcast the result would be "devastating" for the plaintiff and that damages would not be an adequate remedy. An injunction was ordered preventing the broadcast.

In an earlier Australian case on similar facts, Young J found that the media had trespassed, but refused to grant an injunction on the basis that damages would be an adequate remedy.[218]

Complaints about doorstepping in New Zealand have been referred to both the Courts and the Broadcasting Standards Authority. The Authority, however, can only act when there has been a broadcast and where its standards have been breached. If complainants wish to stop the broadcast going ahead then application must be made to the High Court for an injunction.

In *Marris* v *TV3 Network Ltd.*,[219] the High Court considered an application for an injunction to stop the broadcast of an interview obtained by way of doorstepping. The reporter entered the plaintiff's property at eight a.m. and knocked loudly on the front door. When the plaintiff, in the middle of shaving, opened an upstairs window to see what the noise was about the reporter fired a series of questions at him. The encounter was filmed by a camera that was located on the public footpath in front of the house but hidden from the view of the occupants.

The reporter acknowledged that he knew before entering the property that the plaintiff would not be willing to be interviewed. Neazor J reviewed the Australian decisions and accepted that there was an arguable case that the reporter's actions amounted to a trespass. The reporter did not enter the property to enquire whether the plaintiff was willing to have him there, but to demonstrate that the plaintiff was unwilling to be interviewed. In the circumstances, however, the Court held that damages would be an adequate remedy and an injunction was refused.

The first opportunity the Broadcasting Standards Authority had to examine doorstepping in detail arose in 1994.[220] The Authority held that the broadcast of an interview with a doctor that had been obtained early

---

218. *Lincoln Hunt Australia Pty Ltd.* v *Willesee*, 4 NSWLR 457.

219. Unreported, High Court, Wellington, 14 October 1991, CP754/91.

220. *Smedley* v *Television New Zealand Limited*, BSA, 9 May 1994, Decisions 29/94 and 30/94. The Broadcasting Act 1989, under which the Authority is established, does not provide jurisdiction for the Authority to specifically consider complaints of trespass; however, it is able to consider doorstepping complaints under its privacy principles on the basis that such activity amounts to prying. Alternatively, complaints are considered under the Broadcasting Code of Practice which requires that people be treated justly and fairly.

one morning as the doctor was putting out his rubbish in his dressing gown, had been obtained unfairly. The cameraman had remained in a public place and filmed the reporter who entered the driveway of the doctor's property to talk to him, without prior consent.

The Authority pointed out that while doorstepping will not always be in breach of the Broadcasting Code of Practice, it is inherently unfair on the interviewee and should not be used unless every alternative, legitimate means of obtaining information has been exhausted:[221]

> "[C]aution is essential for a number of reasons not least the fact that most people have little experience in and no training for appearing on television. They can be at a distinct disadvantage when appearing on television even with prior knowledge and consent let alone when opening a door to find themselves confronted by a camera and reporter. Their inexperience and disadvantage can be contrasted with that of television journalists who not only have the skills but also the information and total preparedness to confront the person whom they wish to interview. An interview in which an interviewee is being asked to respond to accusations or allegations of other serious misbehaviour is, moreover, usually an adversarial situation. If the element of surprise is combined with unequal television experience and accusations of irresponsible or illegal behaviour, the situation becomes one where the unevenness between the parties is very marked. In other words, it is a situation which is potentially most unfair and intimidating to the interviewee . . . . The Authority is concerned not only with the degree of unfairness potentially involved but also the possibility that a broadcaster might decide to use this method for the expected visual impact of the confrontation which is likely to ensue, rather than its use as a source of considered information and constructive comment."

The Authority found that despite the unfairness of the tactics used there **8.70** had been no breach of its privacy principles because the programme did not disclose private facts that were highly offensive and objectionable to a reasonable person and because the filming did not involve use of a surreptitious method to film the incident. The Authority found, however, that the action was in breach of the Broadcasting Code of Practice in that the doorstepping was unfair to the complainant. No order was made for compensation or apology as there was little if any negative impact on the complainant.

In a later decision, *S v TV3 Network Services Ltd.*,[222] the Authority decided that the hidden filming of a discussion in which one party believed that she was only being asked to take part in an interview about a highly sensitive matter was in the nature of prying and would be

---

221. BSA, 9 May 1994, Decisions 29/94 and 30/94, pp 7–8.

222. BSA, 19 January 1994, Decision 1/94.

offensive to the ordinary person.[223] In response to TV3's argument that the filming was done from a public place, the Authority considered that the fact that S was on her own property while being filmed led to the result that the exception for filming in a public place did not apply.

The Authority's finding that TV3 had breached S's privacy was upheld on appeal in the High Court.[224] Eichelbaum CJ made it clear that no tort is committed by photographing another person's private property without consent.[225] He found that the purpose of the visit by TV3 was to obtain an interview. If it could not obtain an interview, TV3 was ready to surreptitiously film whatever encounter ensued and to record any statements that S might make. He found that S would not have agreed to the reporter coming on to the premises for that purpose and that TV3 was aware of this. In these circumstances, Eichelbaum CJ concluded that the reporter's entry onto the property did not fall within the terms of the normal implied licence to enter on land and, for the purposes of an action in tort, was a trespass from the outset.[226] The camera operator was not trespassing as he was not on the property. The Court did not consider whether an injunction would be granted to stop broadcast of the interview.

The suggestion that the media are trespassing from the outset if they enter a property with the knowledge that the occupier will not consent to their entry is consistent with Australian authority,[227] but contrary to the English Court of Appeal's approach in *Kaye* v *Robertson*.[228] Arguably, *S* v *TV3 Network Services Ltd.* is an exceptional decision turning on the fact that S, as the mother of the complainants in the incest case that TV3 was reporting, was implicitly protected from identification by law. Arguably, the media may use the doorstep technique as a last resort to obtain an interview where the matters raised are in the public interest and such protection, whether express or implied, does not arise.

Criminal trespass

8.71 Under the Trespass Act 1980 a person commits a summary offence if he or she refuses to leave a property after being told to do so by the

---

223. Compensation of NZ $750 was ordered.

224. *TV3 Network Services Ltd.* v *Broadcasting Standards Authority* [1995] 2 NZLR 720.

225. [1995] 2 NZLR 720, 732. See also *Bathurst City Council* v *Saban* (1985) 2 NSWLR 704 and *Victoria Park Racing and Recreation Grounds Co. Ltd.* v *Taylor* (1937) 58 CLR 479.

226. (1937) 58 CLR 479.

227. See *Bernstein* v *Skyviews Ltd.* [1978] QB 479. See also *Bathurst City Council* v *Saban* (1985) 2 NSWLR 704 and *Victoria Park Racing and Recreation Grounds Co. Ltd.* v *Taylor* (1937) 58 CLR 479.

228. (1991) 19 IPR 147.

occupier[229] or, having already trespassed on the property and been warned to stay off, a person returns to the property.[230] A criminal trespasser is liable to summary conviction and a fine of up to NZ $1,000 or three months imprisonment.[231]

Breach of confidence

Introduction

The lifeblood of investigative journalism is often the "whistleblower" or   **8.72** "mole" who discloses information to the media which others would rather keep out of the public eye. In such situations, the right to receive information and the desire of individuals and organisations to conduct their affairs in private conflict.[232]

The recent New Zealand case of *European Pacific Banking Corporation* v *Fourth Estate Publications*[233] illustrates this conflict. The case concerned attempts to report on legally contentious tax dealings of a Cook Islands group of companies called European Pacific. It was alleged the Group's activities had been designed to avoid or circumvent New Zealand tax laws. Confidential documents had been stolen from it and copies obtained by various newspapers and a broadcaster. The media intended to publish the contents of the documents. The Courts injuncted the media from publishing details of the tax schemes based on the stolen documents — for six months in the case of a proposed television documentary and well over a year in the case of the print media. Ultimately, events in Parliament overtook the court proceedings. As a consequence, much of the information found its way into the public arena and was no longer confidential.

The central issue for the media is the extent of protection afforded by the Courts to confidences, particularly when the information relates to matters of public interest. With confidential information the Courts are more willing to grant interim injunctive relief restraining publication. This is because the unrestricted ability to publish would effectively and permanently deprive a plaintiff of their only real form of relief and that

---

229. Trespass Act, s 3.

230. Trespass Act, s 4.

231. Trespass Act, s 11.

232. Not surprisingly there is a close parallel between actions for breach of confidence and protection of privacy. See *Stephens* v *Avery* [1988] 2 All ER 477.

233. *European Pacific Banking Corporation* v *Fourth Estate Publications* [1993] 1 NZLR 559; *European Pacific Banking Corporation* v *Television New Zealand Ltd.* [1994] 3 NZLR 43.

protection would be lost for all time.[234] Further, where the information is confidential there is *prima facie* an entitlement to protection unless the plaintiff is a government plaintiff.[235] The public interest or "iniquity rule" is merely a defence to the claim for protection. While the relief granted may be interim in name, in practical terms, it is often permanent.

The Doctrine of Breach of Confidence

8.73 Information is not confidential merely because its possessor does not want it in the public arena. Megarry J in *Coco v A N Clark (Engineers) Ltd.*[236] defined the central elements of an action for breach of confidence:[237]

> "First the information itself . . . must 'have the necessary quality of confidence about it.' Secondly that information must have been imparted in circumstances importing an obligation of confidence. Thirdly, there must be an unauthorised use of that information to the detriment of the party communicating it."

8.74 In general, "the necessary quality of confidence" requires only that the confidential information is not in the public domain.

In 1988, ex-Security Service agent Peter Wright disclosed confidential information about the Service in his book entitled "Spycatcher". The British Government successfully restrained publication of the book in Britain and prevented newspapers in England from publishing extracts from the book.

The British government also tried to prevent publication of *Spycatcher* in New Zealand. An interim injunction had been granted in the High Court against a leading newspaper, which had planned to publish extracts from the book. This was later rescinded since the contents of the book were already in the international public domain. This meant that nothing approaching irreparable damage would be caused by further publication.[238]

By and large, New Zealand law on breach of confidence is the same as the law in England. Even where information is private, it is not always of a type that attracts confidence. For example, the courts will not protect confidences in trivia or useless information.[239] There has also been a

---

234. [1993] 1 NZLR, 564.

235. *Commonwealth of Australia v John Fairfax & Sons Ltd.* (1981) 55 ALTR 45. It is likely that a government plaintiff has a more onerous burden of proof.

236. [1969] RPC 41.

237. [1969] RPC 41, 47.

238. *AG for United Kingdom v Wellington Newspapers Ltd.* [1988] 1 NZLR 129.

239. *Attorney-General v Guardian Newspapers Ltd.* (Number 2) [1988] 3 All ER 545, 659.

suggestion that information should not be regarded as confidential unless it is necessary to protect a genuine interest of the confider.[240]

The relationship between the confider and confidant is often crucial. The Courts will protect the confider where he or she entrusts the other with information on the understanding it will go no further. In some cases, parties in a contractual relationship will expressly agree that information supplied by them is confidential. In such a case, confidence is enforceable by the usual contractual remedies. In other cases, an obligation of confidence will be implied into the contractual relationship. In others, no contract is necessary and the relationship between the parties creates the obligation. Where the media in turn receive information knowing the provider is breaching an obligation of confidence then they too are bound by the confidence.[241]

Categories of relationship that may give rise to obligations of confidence include those of a professional adviser and client, domestic or personal relationships,[242] employer and employee relationships, the relationship of parties to business negotiations, the relationship of government employees to the government and reporter and source relationships.

While most obligations of confidence are based on a relationship, there are also cases where the obligation arises from the nature of the information itself; the information is so clearly sensitive on its face that it obviously was not meant to be divulged to a third party.[243] The courts will also restrain publication of confidential information despite the absence of a relationship where the information has been improperly or surreptitiously obtained.[244]

The third element of Megarry J's formulation requires unauthorised use to the detriment of the confider. However, it seems this will not always be necessary. For example, to obtain an injunction against the media all that needs to be shown is that the media used or received confidential information obtained directly or indirectly from the plaintiff and intends to publish it without the plaintiff's express or implied consent.[245] Although detriment may not be necessary to support an injunction, it will still probably be required to support a claim for damages.[246]

---

240. *Moorgate Tobacco Co. Ltd.* v *Philip Morris Ltd.* (1984) 56 ALR 193, 208.

241. *AG for United Kingdom* v *Wellington Newspapers Ltd.* [1988] 1 NZLR 129.

242. *Argyll* v *Argyll* [1967] Ch 302; *Stephens* v *Avery* [1988] 2 All ER 477.

243. *English and American Insurance Co. Ltd.* v *Herbert Smith* [1988] FSR 232.

244. *Ashburton* v *Pape* [1913] 2 Ch 469, 475.

245. *Seager* v *Copydex* [1967] 1 WLR 923; *Citicorp NZ Ltd.* v *Blomkamp*, unreported, High Court, Auckland, 4 September 1992, CP1017/92 Blanchard J.

246. *Attorney-General* v *Guardian Newspapers Ltd.* (Number 2) [1988] 3 All ER 545, at 640.

Defences

Public interest

8.75 The public interest defence is an extension of the narrow rule that the Courts will not prevent the disclosure of inequity. If the publication sought to be suppressed is shown to be in the overriding public interest, no injunction will lie. For the defence to apply, the matter must genuinely be one of public interest not merely one in which the public are interested.[247]

In *European Pacific Banking Corporation* v *Fourth Estate Publications* the Court stated:[248]

> "[I]n such cases what must be weighed is the public interest in maintaining confidentiality of information against the public interest in the receipt by the public of that information."

8.76 The public's right to receive information is underscored by section 14 of the New Zealand Bill of Rights Act 1990. As in other jurisdictions the right is subject to "such reasonable limits prescribed by law as can be demonstrably justified in a free and democratic society."[249]

The utility of the public interest defence to the media is diminished by the fact that sometimes the public interest requires only disclosure of the material to the proper authorities rather than to the public.

Prior publication

8.77 Confidentiality is lost when there has been disclosure of the previously confidential information. However, not all disclosure is sufficient to have this result. It is a question of degree. In the *Spycatcher* cases, publication overseas was sufficient to defeat confidentiality because the facts had become so well known. Tabling information in Parliament is not necessarily sufficient publication to destroy confidentiality.[250]

Protection of sources — the newspaper rule

8.78 The press have no greater legal right to publish material than individual citizens but its role as the eyes and ears of the public has been recognised

---

247. *Attorney-General for United Kingdom* v *Wellington Newspapers* [1988] 1 NZLR 129, 178.

248. [1993] 1 NZLR 559, 564.

249. New Zealand Bill of Rights Act 1990, s 5. *Refer Ministry of Transport* v *Noort* [1992] 3 NZLR 260.

250. *European Pacific Banking Corporation* v *Fourth Estate Publications* [1993] 1 NZLR 559.

judicially.[251] The "newspaper rule"[252] provides limited protection of media sources at the interlocutory stage of proceedings. This rule is firmly established in New Zealand and applies to both the print and the broadcast media.[253] The New Zealand Courts have extended the rule to actions for slander of goods.[254] In the *European Pacific*[255] cases the Court, exercising its discretionary jurisdiction, refused to order the media defendants to disclose their source. The Court recognised a legitimate public interest in protecting media sources from disclosure, although the decision was expressed as no more than a finding that the case to compel disclosure was not sufficiently strong or urgent.[256] They expressly did not rely on the "newspaper" rule.

Although once trial commences the rule no longer automatically applies in addition to the "newspaper rule", section 35 of the Evidence Amendment Act (Number 2) 1980 grants the Courts a statutory discretion to excuse a witness from answering questions or producing documents. The discretion is available when a witness would breach a confidence by giving the evidence and there is a sufficiently special relationship between the witness and the source. The Court must weigh the public interest in disclosure of the evidence against the public interest in preservation of confidences and freedom of communication. When considering applications under section 35 the Court must have regard to the significance of the evidence, the nature of the confidence, the relationship between the confidant and the witness and the effect of the disclosure on the confidant or any other person. The *European Pacific* cases suggest that the discretion may be exercised to protect media sources.[257]

Regulation of the media

Broadcasting Standards Authority

The Broadcasting Standards Authority (the Authority) was established **8.79** under the Broadcasting Act 1989 and is responsible for receiving and considering formal complaints about radio and television programmes.

---

251. *Police* v *O'Connor, BCNZ* v *Attorney-General* [1994] 3 NZLR 568.

252. The Law Commission is currently examining these issues in the context of a review of the law of evidence in New Zealand.

253. *Broadcasting Corporation of New Zealand* v *Alex Harvey Industries Ltd.* [1980] 1 NZLR 163.

254. *Broadcasting Corporation of New Zealand* v *Alex Harvey Industries Ltd.* [1980] 1 NZLR 163.

255. *Supra* at note 2.

256. *European Pacific Banking Corporation* v *Television New Zealand Ltd.* [1994] 3 NZLR 43, 48.

257. In England, the media is specifically protected by the Contempt of Court Act 1981, s 10.

The Authority consists of four members. The chairperson must be a barrister or solicitor of not less than seven years' experience as a barrister or solicitor of the High Court. The current chairperson is a former president of the New Zealand Law Society. The other members are from journalistic, legal or academic backgrounds. The Authority also has power to co-opt any person whose qualifications or experience are likely to be of assistance to it.[258]

The Act requires broadcasters to maintain standards consistent with those it sets out and with codes of practice approved under the Act. The standards are:[259]

(1) The observance of good taste and decency;

(2) The maintenance of law and order;

(3) The privacy of the individual;

(4) The principle that when controversial issues of public importance are discussed, reasonable efforts are made, or reasonable opportunities are given, to present significant points of view either in the same programme or in other programmes within the period of current interest; and

(5) Those specified in any approved code of broadcasting practice applying to the programmes.

8.80 The Act also requires the Authority to encourage broadcasters to develop codes of practice in relation to:[260]

(1) The protection of children;

(2) The portrayal of violence;

(3) Fair and accurate programmes and procedures for correcting factual errors and redressing unfairness;

(4) Safeguards against the portrayal of persons in programmes in a manner that encourages denigration of, or discrimination against, sections of the community on account of sex, race, age, disability, or occupational status or as a consequence of legitimate expression of religious, cultural, or political beliefs;

(5) Restrictions on the promotion of liquor; and

(6) Presentation of appropriate warnings in respect of programmes.

8.81 Codes have been approved by the Authority for both radio and television broadcasting. The Authority also has power to issue its own codes of

---

258. Broadcasting Act 1989, s 26.

259. Broadcasting Act 1989, s 4.

260. Broadcasting Act 1989, ss 21(1)(e) and (g) and 22.

practice and advisory opinions about broadcasting standards and ethical conduct.[261] In 1992 and 1996 the Authority issued an advisory opinion for broadcasters setting out the relevant privacy principles that it applies in its decisions.

The Authority can only consider complaints in relation to programmes that have been broadcast. It has no jurisdiction to restrain a broadcast in advance. When considering a complaint, the Authority can take into account the methods used by the broadcaster to obtain broadcast material. This is particularly relevant when a complaint alleges breach of privacy.[262]

Usually a complaint must first be made directly to the broadcaster. If the complainant is not satisfied with the response received from the broadcaster then an appeal may be made to the Authority for review of the complaint. Where the complaint concerns privacy it may be made directly to the Authority.

The Authority has significant powers. It may order a broadcaster not to broadcast at all for up to 24 hours or alternatively not to broadcast advertising for up to 24 hours.[263] It has the power to order broadcasters to broadcast an apology or statement approved by the Authority.[264] Where the complaint relates to an invasion of privacy the Authority can order a broadcaster to pay compensation of up to NZ $5000 to the complainant.[265] If a broadcaster fails to comply with orders of the Authority it can be subject to a fine of up to NZ $100,000.[266]

Decisions of the Authority may be appealed to the High Court.[267]

The Press Council

The print media are not subject to the same restrictions as broadcasters. **8.82** Complaints may be made to the Press Council. This is a voluntary body established by the Newspaper Publishers' Association and the Journalists' Association. The Press Council lacks "teeth" in dealing with complaints because it has no legislative backing and therefore no authority to enforce its decisions.

---

261. Broadcasting Act 1989, s 21(1)(f) and (h).

262. See text *supra*.

263. Broadcasting Act 1989, s 13(1)(b).

264. Broadcasting Act 1989, s 13(1)(a).

265. Broadcasting Act 1989, s 13(1)(d).

266. Broadcasting Act 1989, s 14.

267. Broadcasting Act 1989, s 18(1).

The Council does not operate on the basis of written guidelines or a code of ethics. It refers to its previous adjudications when considering complaints. The principal objects of the Council are as set out in its annual reports:

> "To preserve the established freedom of the New Zealand press; to maintain the character of the New Zealand press in accordance with the highest professional standards; to consider complaints about the conduct of the press or the conduct of persons and organisations toward the press; to deal with these complaints in whatever manner might seem practical and appropriate and to record resultant action; to keep under review developments likely to restrict the supply of information of public interest and importance."

8.83 If a complaint is upheld, the newspaper is normally required to publish the decision. The Council attempts to take a self-regulatory and common sense approach to complaints. There are relatively few complaints made to the Press Council, perhaps as a result of its relative obscurity.

Advertising Standards Authority

8.84 The Advertising Standards Authority is a self-funding body established by the advertising industry. Membership is made up of representatives of advertising agents, publishers and broadcasters. It has an established code of practice with which advertisers must comply. The code is administered by the Advertising Standards Complaints Board. The Board comprises four public representatives with no connection to media or advertising groups plus four industry representatives. It is not able to impose fines on advertisers but can order that advertisements be withdrawn from any media and not published again. This can obviously have expensive repercussions for advertisers and their agents.

In addition, if an advertisement that has been broadcast does not comply with the standards under the Broadcasting Act 1989 then a complaint may be made to the Broadcasting Standards Authority.

Note: We acknowledge the assistance of Simon Ladd, Solicitor, Simpson and Grierson, Auckland and Kay Madigan, Solicitor, Auckland, New Zealand.

Scotland

Chapter 9
Scotland

Gill Grassie and Tim J. Edward
Maclay Murray & Spens
Edinburgh, Scotland

Introduction

9.1 The media in Scotland, as in most other developed countries, have in recent years been faced with a variety of new legal issues arising from the rapidly changing technological environment in which they operate. The United Kingdom Parliament has struggled to provide legislation which addresses these issues and takes into account the separate legal traditions of its constituent parts. In some areas, the common law has simply required to adapt itself to deal with a changing environment. In this chapter on the law of Scotland relating to the civil liability of the media, areas of private international law, relating to jurisdiction and choice of law, alongside the substantive areas of defamation, verbal injury and the law of negligence will be covered, as will the law relating to privacy. The chapter will attempt to place the development of Scots law in this area in its historical context and to anticipate the future development of the law in a changing environment.

Scots law in its international context

The changing nature of communications

9.2 Scotland, although forming an integral part of the United Kingdom, has its own legal system and judiciary, and Scots law relating to defamation and other aspects of civil liability of the media, although influenced by English law, has developed in its own way. This chapter will deal with the history of this development as well as the current law in Scotland in this field. However, in the first place it is necessary to consider the issues of jurisdiction and choice of law that govern the question of whether Scots law will apply and the Scottish courts will have jurisdiction.

Jurisdiction

9.3 Questions of jurisdiction in Scots law in civil and commercial matters are largely governed by the Civil Jurisdiction and Judgments Act 1982 (the CJJA 1982), which implements in the United Kingdom the 1968 Convention on Jurisdiction and Enforcement of Judgments in Civil and Commercial Matters. The CJJA 1982 sets down rules for determination of jurisdiction in relation to disputes involving parties in other parts of the United Kingdom, in other European Union Member States and in the rest of the world. All non-contractual claims arising in Scotland from the civil liability of media organisations will be subject to the following rules.

Parties in other Member States

9.4 The fundamental jurisdiction principle is that a person (and this includes a company, partnership or association) should be sued in the courts of the place where he or she is domiciled, domicile being defined as habitual residence or in the case of companies, partnerships and associations, the place where such body was incorporated or has its central management and control, being its "seat". In other words, jurisdiction is primarily founded in the country of the defender's domicile.[1]

Alternative jurisdiction in relation to such claims can be founded in the courts of the place where the harmful event occurred.[2] The "place where the harmful event occurred" covers both the place where the damage was suffered and the place where the act which gave rise to the damage was performed.[3] The English case of *Shevill* v *Bresse Alliance SA*[4] involving a claim for defamation against proprietors of a French newspaper affirmed the principle that presumed harm is sufficient to constitute a "harmful event" and this seems to represent the position in Scotland also. This rule on jurisdiction does not apply to threatened wrongs but provision is made for an application to be made to the courts in Scotland for interim interdict (interlocutory injunction) even where domicile is founded in another Member State.[5] In practical terms this means that where a publication or broadcast gives rise to a delictual claim, jurisdiction may be founded in Scotland:

(1) Where the party being sued is domiciled in Scotland;

(2) Where the publication or broadcast originated in Scotland; or

---

1. CJJA 1982, schedule 1, art 2.

2. CJJA 1982, schedule 1, art 5.

3. *Handelskwekerij GV Bier BV* v *Mines de Botasse D'Alsace SA* [1976] ECR 1235; [1977] 1 CMLR 284.

4. [1992] 1 All ER 409.

5. 1982 Act, s 28.

(3) Where the alleged damage or loss arising from the publication or broadcast occurred in Scotland.

In the event of concurrent jurisdiction arising in two separate states, the **9.5** CJJA 1982 and the Convention provide that if proceedings are raised in separate jurisdictions involving the same cause of action, jurisdiction must be declined in proceedings in courts other than the court first seised.[6] Where related actions are raised in separate jurisdictions, courts other than the court first seised may stay proceedings pending the outcome of the original action or allow consolidation of the actions in the court first seised. This has obvious relevance in a situation where, for example, a publication or broadcast gives rise to claims in various jurisdictions on the basis of loss occurring in those jurisdictions.

Parties in other parts of the United Kingdom

The rules set out in the CJJA 1982 in relation to claims involving parties **9.6** in other Member States are essentially applied *mutatis mutandis* to claims involving parties in other parts of the United Kingdom.[7]

Parties in countries outside the European Union

Essentially the same rules as apply in relation to claims involving parties **9.7** in other European Union Member States apply in relation to claims involving parties outside the European Union. The obvious difference here is that parties in countries outside the European Union are not bound by the rules of the Convention and will simply apply their own jurisdictional rules. The result may be a contest over jurisdiction where Common Law rules of *forum non conveniens* may be applied. However, consideration of such matters is beyond the scope of this chapter.[8]

Choice of law

Even if the rules of jurisdiction provide for jurisdiction in Scotland, it **9.8** does not necessarily follow that Scots law will be applied by the Scottish courts if the action relates to a wrong occurring outside Scotland. This

---

6. Convention, art 21.

7. CJJA 1982, schedule 4.

8. See CJJA 1982, schedule 8; for a more detailed analysis of Scottish rules of jurisdiction in general, see *Anton & Beaumont on Civil Jurisdiction in Scotland.*

will depend on the choice of law rules under Scots law. In relation to defamation claims against the media, the rule of double actionability applies. In other words, it is necessary for a party pursuing the delictual claim in Scotland relating to a wrong which occurred outside Scotland to demonstrate a right of action both in Scots law, "the lex fori", and in the law of the place where the delict occurred, "the lex loci delicti".[9] However, a presumption applies that foreign law will be the same as Scots law on the issue of actionability and the onus thus rests on the defender to establish non-actionability under the *lex loci delicti*. Furthermore, quantification of damages and all other matters of procedure are questions solely for the *lex fori*.

The double actionability rule, however, does mean that the rules of prescription and limitation and general defences available, such as the defence of privilege in an action of defamation, under both the *lex fori* and the *lex loci delicti* must be considered.

This rule now provides an exception to the normal rules of choice of laws in relation to delictual claims set out in the Private International Law (Miscellaneous Provisions) Act 1995, Part 3 of which was designed to abolish the "double actionability" rule. Part 3 of the Act came into effect at the start of May 1996.

Delictual disputes other than defamation actions (defined to include actions for verbal injury) will be determined according to the "applicable law". That law will generally be the law of the country in which the events constituting the delict take place. If elements of those events take place in different countries, the country where the most significant element or elements took place is to be preferred (section 11).

This rule can, however, be put to one side if, under comparison, another country is more appropriate to be the "applicable law" country in the circumstances of the case (section 12(1)).[10]

The exclusion of defamation claims from Part 3 of the 1995 Act was the most contentious issue during the passage of the legislation. Pressure from the media against the potential impact of the new rules in encouraging "forum shopping" resulted in the exclusion of defamation claims from the scope of the rules by virtue of S13 of the Act. Under the "double actionability" rule the safeguards of Scots law will continue to apply. This may result in the further impact of the law of negligence in this area.[11]

---

9. *McElroy v McAllister* (1949) SC 110.

10. For a useful commentary on the legislation, see Blaikie, "Foreign Torts and Choice of Law Flexibility", 1995 SLT (News) 23.

11. See below.

As a result of the exclusion of defamation claims from the provisions of Part three of the Act, the Common Law rules on choice of law continue to apply to defamation claims, the normal rule being that the defamation occurs where the loss occurs[12] — which could of course be in more than one place.

Multiplicity of actions and mitigation of loss

From the fact that the delict may be deemed to have occurred in all places **9.9** where losses are incurred it follows that multiple actions arising from one publication or broadcast are possible. Only if there is duplication of the loss claimed will such actions be limited. In that instance, the principle of *res judicata* will prevent further recovery in respect of a claim that has already been resolved. This is particularly relevant in the case of liability of the media in an age of international circulation of publications and world-wide access to broadcasts.

However, the duty of mitigation of loss resting on any claimant will be taken into account by Scottish courts and the courts will be entitled to consider damages received by way of court judgments or settlements in other jurisdictions.[13]

Defamation

History and development

The law of defamation in Scotland finds its origin in the Roman law *actio* **9.10** *iniuriarum*, an action for affront to dignity. The remedy available under the *actio iniuriarum* was that of *solatium*, although patrimonial loss could also be claimed under the *lex Aquilia*. T. B. Smith in his *Short Commentary on the Law of Scotland* saw the separate Roman law actions reflected in the older Scottish practice of dealing with actions for insult in the Commissary Courts — Courts established at the time of the Reformation to deal with matrimonial and other related matters but defunct since the early 19th century — which could award *solatium*; and actions for economic loss and damage in the Sheriff Court or Court of Session. However, the modern law of defamation sees both elements, *solatium* for injured feelings and damages for patrimonial loss, absorbed into one cause of action.

---

12. *Longworth* v *Hope* (1865) 3 M 1049 and *Evans & Sons* v *Stein & Co.* (1904) 7 F 65.

13. Defamation Act 1952, s 12.

Historically, defamation also constituted a criminal offence in addition to a civil wrong. In England, defamation remains a crime in some circumstances.[14] However, in Scotland there is no evidence that the criminal offence of defamation existed beyond the early 19th century.

The current law of defamation has developed in its essentials very little from the middle of the 19th century. Apart from the Defamation Act 1952, and the Defamation Act 1996 which have introduced various statutory innovations, the law in this area is substantially determined by precedent. In this connection, it should be noted that the civil courts of first instance in Scotland are the Sheriff Courts, which have jurisdiction limited to a relatively small geographic locality but are not restricted by any financial limit on awards, and the Outer House of the Court of Session. The appellate courts are the Court of the Sheriff Principal in each of the six sheriffdoms of Scotland, the Inner House of the Court of Session and the House of Lords. The doctrine of precedent operates in Scotland as in England and other Common Law systems. English decisions are persuasive in Scotland without being binding. House of Lords decisions in Scottish cases are binding. But recent developments in Scots law owe a considerable amount to English case law.

Cases of verbal injury, covering non-defamatory malicious falsehoods, have developed separately.[15] Another aspect to the development of the law in this area is the case of *Spring* v *Guardian Assurance plc*,[16] indicating a possible move away from the law of defamation and towards remedies based on the law of negligence.[17] Although there are suggestions from some quarters that the law of defamation may tend in the future to be gradually replaced by the general law of negligence, for the present, the law remains well-characterised.

The current law of defamation

The essentials

9.11 Defamation has traditionally been and still is the most prominent area of the law of Scotland relating to civil liability of the media. The influence of Roman law and the development of Scots law in this area has already been stressed. However, in considering the essence of defamation as a cause of action, the best starting point is the Latin root of the word.

---

14. *Carter-Ruck on Libel and Slander*, 4th Edition, pp 182–195.

15. This will be dealt with below.

16. [1994] 3 All ER 129.

17. This development will be dealt with below.

Defamatus is translated as "dishonoured" and the most basic requirement for an action of defamation is a statement or communication made which is injurious in the sense of being capable of harming a person's honour or reputation. The statement must also be false and must be offensive in its nature.

Expressions such as honour and reputation have been variously interpreted and clearly their meanings have adapted to a change in social environment. However, constant elements are attributes such as honesty, moral and social standing and creditworthiness.[18]

The test of what is defamatory is perhaps best encapsulated by Lord Atkin in *Sim* v *Stretch*:[19] "Would the words tend to lower the plaintiff in the estimation of right-thinking members of society generally?" This test is specifically applied by the court in Scotland in *Muirhead* v *Geo Outram & Co.*[20]

This test will be applied with regard to the context in which the words appear and the class or section of society to which the claimant belongs.[21] In other words the character of a priest is far more readily defamed than that of a convicted thief, for example. Not only the literal meaning of words used should be considered in deciding what is defamatory. Irony and innuendo often impose very different meanings on words and it is always necessary to look at the circumstances and context of any statement in consideration of what the true meaning is. The test to be applied is perhaps best stated by Lord Shaw in *Russell* v *Stubbs Ltd.*:[22] what is "the reasonable, natural or necessary inference from the words used"?

It is impossible fully to categorise defamatory remarks as each case will entirely depend on its own circumstances, but the case law in Scotland reveals many cases based on allegations of immorality or criminal behaviour, professional incompetence or impecuniosity. Morality and particularly sexual mores, which provide a fruitful area for litigation, must be judged according to accepted standards of the age. The question of whether a statement is defamatory is essentially a question of law. If this issue is in dispute, procedures exist in Scotland to have the issue decided by the court before any evidence is heard.

The other essential element that must be established at the outset is that a statement was communicated. Unlike in England, communication to the claimant alone is sufficient and communication can cover gestures, drawings, cartoons and photographs as well as the most up-to-date technological communication such as e-mail and fax.

---

18. *Cooper on Defamation and Verbal Injury.*

19. [1936] 2 All ER 1237.

20. [1983] SLT 201.

21. Lord MacLaren in *MacLachlan* v *Orr Pollock & Co.* [1894] 22 R 38.

22. [1913] SC (HL) 14.

Parties — title and interest

9.12 Any person capable of suffering loss has title to sue for defamation and will have an interest to sue if loss is actually suffered. However, it is not possible in Scotland to defame the dead. Likewise, it is not possible for executors of a deceased person to pursue a claim arising from a defamation that took place before the death of the deceased (although an action raised by a party who subsequently dies can be continued by his or her executor).

Although a corporate body can claim damages for defamation, that right does not extend to *solatium* for hurt feelings, but only to pecuniary loss. A company may sustain damage through loss of income or loss of goodwill[23] as can a partnership or voluntary association. One important point in relation to partnerships to be borne in mind in Scotland is that a partnership forms a separate legal entity independent of the individual partners and can pursue an action in its own name.[24]

Likewise, any legal entity can be sued for defamation. In cases where it is not clear who is responsible for the defamation or where several parties are responsible, a number of parties can be sued together and as long as jurisdiction can be established against one defender, jurisdiction against the others follows from that. Liability in such a case is individual to each defender and not joint and several.[25] A defender can also take steps to bring in a third party by way of third party procedure which again will normally follow the jurisdiction of the principal action.

Trade unions fall into a difficult category, but it is thought that they are capable of suing or being sued for defamation in their own name. Local authorities and indeed central government and the police and armed forces, together with bodies emanating from central government are thought to be unable to sue for defamation.[26]

Corporate bodies and partnerships and voluntary associations can all be sued in their own name and are vicariously liable for defamation perpetrated by employees and agents in the course of their employment or agency.

Defences

Veritas

9.13 If it is established that the essential elements of defamation are present in a statement or communication, the next step is to consider the defences

---

23. *Lewis* v *Daily Telegraph* [1964] AC 234.

24. Partnership Act 1890, s 4(2).

25. *Turnbull* v *Frame* [1966] SLT 24 per Lord Fraser.

26. *Derbyshire CC* v *Times Newspapers* [1993] 1 All ER 1011 per Lord Keith.

available. The primary defence is that of *veritas*. It is well established that *veritas* or truth is a complete defence to an action of defamation. However, in relation to defamation, as opposed to verbal injury, it is for the defenders to prove the truth of the statement concerned.

In older Scottish cases, the defence of *veritas* is referred to as "justification", which is still the term used in English law. However, the defence of *veritas* has developed separately in Scotland and should not simply be presumed to be identical in all respects to the English law defence of justification.

The essence of the defence of *veritas* is that the defender must establish that the defamatory statement, or the essential core or meaning was or is true. In cases of defamatory innuendo, it will require first of all to be determined what the particular meaning conveyed is. The Defamation Act of 1952, section 5 specifically provides that it is not necessary for a defender to prove that all allegations made are true as long as the material allegations are proved to be true and "words not proved to be true do not materially injure the pursuer's reputation."

The standard of proof is the same as in civil proceedings generally in Scotland, namely on the balance of probabilities. In addition, it should be noted that *veritas* can be pled as an alternative to other defences, as indeed is often the case.

Fair Comment

Although there is no equivalent in Scots law of the United States doctrine **9.14** that public figures must accept a considerable amount of criticism to protect the constitutional right to freedom of speech,[27] there does exist a defence of fair comment designed to protect the expression of opinions on public events and public figures. This defence, which originally appears to have developed as part of the defence of qualified privilege, is an important safeguard for the media in Scotland.

The clearest expression of the nature of the defence appears in *Archer* v *Ritchie & Co.*[28] per Lord MacLaren:

"The expression of an opinion as to a state of facts truly set forth is not actionable even when the opinion is expressed in vituperative or contumelious language."

The defence of fair comment exists in English law also, but the English **9.15** doctrine differs in the important respect that proof of malice defeats the defence. Although it is thought by some that proof of malice may vitiate

---

27. *Sullivan* v *New York Times* 376 US 254 (1964).

28. [1891] 18 R 719 at 727.

the defence of fair comment in Scots law,[29] there is no substantial evidence that this question is one that the court will take into account. The real question to be considered in Scots law is the objective question of whether the opinion expressed is fair in all the circumstances.

The essentials of the defence are as follows:

(1)   The statement concerned must be a comment on fact;
(2)   The facts must be truly stated; and
(3)   The facts must concern a matter of public interest.

9.16   If these essentials are established, the onus of proof shifts to the party alleging defamation to demonstrate that the statement is unfair. Although the comment made must be based on fact, it is possible for facts to be implied within a comment or opinion. It is a matter for the court to decide in each individual case whether a statement contains comment alone or fact alone or a mixture of both.

The need to establish the truth of the facts concerned is qualified by section 5 of the Defamation Act 1952 (see above). As long as the central facts on which an opinion is based are accurate, it will not matter that incidental facts may be wrongly stated.

With regard to the definition of what amounts to matters in the public interest, the best summary of this is provided by Lord Denning:

> "Whenever a matter such as to affect people at large so that they may be legitimately interested in or concerned at what is going on; or what may happen to them or to others; then it is a matter of public interest on which everyone is entitled to make fair comment."[30]

9.17   The definition is very broad and the bounds of the public's interest are constantly being extended with the view prevailing in current society that even the private lives of public figures are matters of public interest. The matter of what amounts to legitimate public interest in what may appear to be private matters will be dealt with in the section below on privacy.

The unfairness of any comment made is for the party alleging defamation to establish. Stress has been placed in English law on the comment being honest or *bona fide*. However, there is little in Scottish case law to indicate that this applies in Scotland.[31] Rather, the courts have tended to look at whether the comment is a reasonable inference drawn from the facts stated.

---

29. See *Scots Law for Journalists*, 6th Edition.

30. *London Artists Ltd* v *Littler* [1969] 2 All ER 193, at 198.

31. Norrie, *Defamation and Related Actions in Scots Law*, pp 147–149.

Privilege

This important area of the law of defamation has undergone certain **9.18** changes in the new Defamation Act enacted on 4 July 1996.[32] There are two types of privilege that can apply to statements and communications. The first is absolute privilege, which represents a complete defence to a claim for defamation. There is a view that this defence is not presently properly constituted in Scotland, a problem that the Defamation Bill seeks to address. However, in theory absolute privilege applies to statements made in both Houses of the United Kingdom Parliament together with parliamentary committees and others acting on the authority of parliament. An exception to this is contained within section 13 of the Defamation Act 1996 which provides that where the conduct of a person in relation to proceedings in Parliament is in issue in defamation proceedings he may waive the protection of parliamentary privilege. Most actions of participants in judicial proceedings are protected by absolute privilege, including those of judges, solicitors and counsel and witnesses, and the defence is extended to most *quasi*-judicial or tribunal proceedings.[33] However, parties to a civil action are only entitled to qualified privilege.[34]

Section 14 of the Defamation Act 1996 provides that fair and accurate reports of proceedings in public before a Court, if published contemporaneously with the proceedings, are absolutely privileged. The definition of a Court is extended to include the European Court of Justice and the European Court of Human Rights together with any international criminal tribunal established by the United Nations Security Council. It should be noted, however that this does not extend to proceedings in private. An exception to this is Children's Hearings protected by qualified privilege in terms of the Social Work (Scotland) Act 1968, section 35(3).

The Parliamentary Papers Act 1840 provides that all reports, papers, votes and proceedings published under the authority of parliament are absolutely privileged as are the reports of various Ombudsmen and parliamentary commissioners.

Of more direct relevance to the liability of the media is the doctrine of qualified privilege. While in most cases, the defamatory nature of a communication justifies the court in presuming that the communication was made maliciously, in some situations the claimant must prove malice and these situations give rise to qualified privilege. All forms of privilege arise from a direct public policy interest in protecting freedom of expression. However, whereas the categories of statements and documents to

---

32. 1996 c 31.

33. *Trapp* v *Mackie* [1977] SLT 194.

34. See below.

which absolute privilege applies are closed, the extent of the defence of qualified privilege is open to development.

In determining what type of statement may be protected by qualified privilege, the dictum of Lord President Strathclyde in *James* v *Baird*[35] is important:

> "A communication honestly made on any subject in which a person has an interest, social or moral, or in reference to which he has a duty, is privileged if made to a person having a corresponding interest or duty."

9.19 A duty must be established actually to exist. It is not sufficient that a person believes that such a duty exists.

Although the categories of statements, broadcasts or publications that are subject to qualified privilege may change from time to time, the most prominent categories are specified in the Defamation Act 1996.[36] In particular, reports of parliamentary proceedings, both domestic and foreign are afforded qualified privilege as are reports of international conferences.

The other test to be applied to such reports is that of malice. Qualified privilege does not protect statements made maliciously or indeed that go beyond what is appropriate to the particular report in question.

The types of report protected by qualified privilege in terms of the Defamation Act 1996 are listed in schedule 1 to the Act and divided into two separate categories. The reports listed in Part 1 are protected by qualified privilege in the normal way and are only actionable if malice can be proved. Part 1 includes not only reports of parliamentary proceedings in any part of the world and court proceedings in any part of the world but also reports of public enquiries, legal notices and other such documents. In relation to the reports listed in Part 2, a claimant will only be able to put forward a claim where he has requested a correction to be published or broadcast and no adequate or reasonable correction has ensued.[37]

Part 2 of the schedule covers fair and accurate reports of proceedings of associations promoting the arts, science, religion or learning, trade, business, industry or professions and sports and pastimes; along with fair and accurate reports of public meetings, local authority meetings, commissions, tribunals and parliamentary committees and local inquiries.

It is provided that the provisions relating to qualified privilege shall not be construed as protecting publication of matter the publication of which is prohibited by law.[38]

---

35. [1916] SC 510, at 517.

36. Defamation Act 1996, s 15 and schedule 1.

37. Defamation Act 1996, s 15(2).

38. Defamation Act 1996, s 7(11) and s 15(4).

Malice is defined as:

". . . such animosity, illtemper, love of scandal and gossip or mere rash and thoughtless loquacity as to induce a man to forget what is due to the fair fame of his neighbour; and to use words by which his feelings and reputation may be injured".[39]

9.20 The best evidence of malice is that the party making the statement knew it to be false.[40] Otherwise, the matter is one that is invariably subjective.

Where a defender is protected by qualified privilege, one possible course of action for the pursuer is to raise proceedings in negligence. The development of this aspect of the law will be dealt with below.

Rixa and Fair Retort

9.21 The nature of the defence of *rixa* is that the defamatory words were uttered in the heat of a quarrel or argument and in circumstances where the reasonable listener would not have taken them seriously. It may be that part of the reasoning behind the defence is that the motivation for the defamatory words was anger rather than malice and thus that an essential element is absent.

This defence covers utterances of vulgar abuse and sarcasm. Lord MacLaren stated in *Cockburn* v *Reekie*: "We have never gone so far as to hold that mere unmeaning abuse, mere inspiration, will give a right of action".[41] This will include, for example, satirical lampooning.

The defence of fair retort covers responses made to provocation and the defence, if established, passes the onus to the pursuer to establish that the retort was made with malice.

Prescription and limitation

9.22 The position with regard to prescription of defamation claims is now represented by section 18A of the Prescription and Limitation (Scotland) Act 1973 as introduced by section 12 of the Law Reform Miscellaneous Provisions (Scotland) Act 1985. The section applies to claims for *solatium* and for economic loss and provides that an action for defamation or verbal injury must be brought within three years after the date when the publication or communication came to the notice of the pursuer. The position in Scotland is now different from that existing in the rest of the

---

39. *Adam* v *Allan* [1841] 3 D 1058, at 1073 per Lord Jeffrey.

40. *Mitchell* v *Smith* [1919] SC 664.

41. *Cockburn* v *Reekie* [1890] 17 R 568, at 571.

United Kingdom, where a one year limitation period is applied by sections 5 and 6 of the Defamation Act 1996.

Remedies

9.23   No legal aid is provided for defamation claims in Scotland. Although it is not unknown for legal representatives to act on a speculative basis (no win, no fee), contingency fees as a share in any award are not permitted. The system of judicial expenses in Scotland rarely provides for recovery of full expenses even in the event of success and consequently the expense involved in taking a claim to court is a severe disincentive for many potential claimants. In the last 50 years, the number of defamation cases reported in the Scottish law reports in any given year has rarely exceeded 10.[42] Although many cases settle at an early stage, the declining numbers of reported cases do seem to reflect a general decline in the popularity of the remedy itself.

Perhaps the mostly commonly invoked remedy against the media is that of a demand for an apology or a retraction. A specific statutory authority is provided by sections 2, 3 and 4 of the Defamation Act 1996, which provide for a person who has published a statement alleged to be defamatory to make amends by way of an offer in writing providing for correction, apology and compensation. The compensation falls to be assessed by the Court if not agreed.[43] Such an offer must be made before any defence is served and, even if not accepted, any correction and apology published can be founded on in relation to compensation. The Press Complaints Commission and Broadcasting Complaints Commission both also provide for a means for complaints to be put forward against the media. Reports are published periodically of the Commissions' findings.

Court actions for defamation can be raised in the Sheriff Court or the Court of Session. A jury trial is only possible in the Court of Session and is now very rare. Technically, it is necessary to show "special cause" why a jury hearing is not appropriate (*e.g.*, *Shanks* v *BBC*[44] where the complexity of the case was cited as the reason). However, jury trials are now very much the exception rather than the rule.

If the defamation is anticipated or if a repeat of the defamation is anticipated, it is possible to apply to the court for interdict and for the interim remedy of interim interdict. Interim interdict will be granted if it is established that the pursuer has a *prima facie* case in law and that the balance of convenience favours the pursuer.

---

42. Norrie, *Defamation and Related Actions in Scots law*, Appendix.

43. Defamation Act 1996, s 3(5).

44. *Shanks* v *BBC* [1993] SLT 326.

In other situations, the primary remedy is damages. Damages are normally calculated under two separate heads, patrimonial loss and *solatium* for hurt feelings. Traditionally, in Scotland, *solatium* has been assessed at modest levels. The principle for calculation of damages is that they should be compensatory and not punitive. However, all circumstances will be taken into account and even if the effect that a defamation has had on a pursuer is deemed to be extreme that may not be a good reason for limiting the damages. Patrimonial loss is assessed as loss naturally and directly flowing from the defamatory statement. A finding of malice does not aggravate damages.[45]

However, the effect of evidence of provocation by the pursuer or lack of good character on the part of the pursuer can be to mitigate of damages.[46] Section 12 of the Defamation Act 1952 provides for a statutory mitigation of loss where several actions are raised.

An assessment will also be made of remoteness of the damage suffered. If it is judged that a *novus actus interveniens* occurs which gives rise to loss, as opposed to the original act of defamation, this will exclude further damages arising from the date of that *novus actus.*[47]

Verbal injury and convicium

To be defamatory, a statement must fulfil certain strict criteria. It follows **9.24** that a statement may therefore be extremely harmful, but may yet, since it falls outwith these criteria, be non-actionable in defamation. However, Scots law may offer not one, but two possible alternative remedies to plug such gaps (other than those based on duty of care),[48] both of which are akin to defamation.

Verbal injury

More or less the equivalent to its English counterpart — malicious **9.25** falsehood — verbal injury, unlike defamation comprises a false statement designed to bring the pursuer into public hatred and contempt, thus causing patrimonial loss to him or his business. The requirements are set out in section 14 of the 1952 Act. Effectively, it is slander of business or

---

45. *Stein* v *Beaverbrook Newspapers* [1968] SC 272.

46. *McCulloch* v *Litt* [1851] 13 D 960.

47. *Slipper* v *BBC* [1991] 1 QB 283.

48. See below.

title or property or goods. The statute provides there is no need to aver or prove special damage if the words used are calculated to cause pecuniary damage. However, for an action grounded in verbal injury to succeed, the pursuer must establish that the statement was false, unlike defamation where falsity is presumed, and was maliciously made, in that there was an intention to cause patrimonial loss or at least a reckless indifference to that consequence.

Verbal injury is perhaps an underused remedy in Scotland. In one more recent case,[49] employees of the defenders (a rival business) had misrepresented to various customers of the pursuer that he was on the point of going out of business and that they should place any further orders with them. The statements were false and the defenders' employees knew this. The pursuers had suffered loss as a result. This was held to be sufficient to establish verbal injury.

Verbal injury also extends a remedy to those third parties indirectly affected by an original defamatory statement, which is not available in defamation.[50] If X alleges Y is unreliable or dishonest, and company Z was about to appoint him as its Chairman, Z might be able to rely on verbal injury for recompense — if again it could establish the statement was false and made with malicious intent to injure it and did actually do so.[51] It goes without saying that the defences to a defamation case can also be relied on in an action based on verbal injury. There are signs that it may be revitalised, since malicious falsehood has been successfully used recently in an English case on comparative advertising.[52] In conclusion, verbal injury as a subspecies of defamation should be the remedy pursued where defamation does not quite fit because the damage is commercially or professionally damaging rather than damaging to the personal reputation.

Convicium

9.26   Having its beginnings in Roman law, as its name would suggest, some doubts have been raised about whether *convicium* as a separate species of verbal injury that does not require that the statement complained of be false does form part of the law of Scotland. The essentials of *convicium* are that the statement concerned should have held the pursuer up to public hatred, ridicule and contempt and caused damage, financial or emotional. Unlike defamation, there is no need to show the statement would

---

49. *Craig* v *Inveresk Paper Merchant Limited* [1970] SLT (notes) 50.

50. Norrie, *Defamation and Related Actions in Scots Law*, p 37.

51. *North of Scotland Banking Co.* v *Duncan* (1857) 19 D 881, at 887 Lord Deas.

52. *Compaq* v *Dell* [1992] FSR 93.

lower the person's repute. For example, where the defender repeated in public a comment allegedly made by the pursuer, which demonstrated that he might be racist or classist,[53] this might be *convicium*. In that case, the complaint was that the defender, on two occasions, stated in public that the pursuer had indicated that the poorer pupils of a boarding school would contaminate those at a more middle class school if they were allowed to mix, when the pursuer had said no such thing. This could not be defamation as such, since the defender had said of the pursuer merely that he had a particular opinion. Nevertheless, it was held that there could be a remedy provided there was an intention to injure and an injurious result.

Again, unlike defamation there is no presumption that the statement is not true or that there was an intention to injure — these must be proved by the pursuer. It has never been properly judicially tested, but one commentator has suggested it exists as a separate remedy where truth is no defence.[54] However, there would appear to be no reported case that expressly supports this view and one other commentator has suggested it is no more than another name for verbal injury.[55] *Steele* v *Scottish Dairy Record and Sunday Mail Limited*[56] is a more recent example of a case that started out based on defamation and ended up founded on what was called *convicium*. The case concerned an article published which implied that a car dealer, by forcing a customer to adhere to his contract of hire purchase of a car after the customer had fallen on hard times, was unnecessarily unsympathetic. Strictly, it was not defamatory yet it was held that there could be a remedy under verbal injury or *convicium* as a species of it, had the article been capable of bringing the pursuer into public hatred and contempt.

There is therefore some debate as to whether *convicium* requires that the statement be false. The authorities prior to *Steele*[57] do not deal with the question specifically. The more persuasive view is perhaps that *convicium* in its old sense has been superseded and is now just another species of verbal injury[58] where truth is a defence.

This area obviously has great significance for the media in relation to privacy, and freedom of speech. If *convicium* remains a remedy in its purest sense, it could by default fill the gap in current Scots law, which has no delict of invasion of personal privacy. One commentator,[59] however, suggests that in the Scots Common Law, (unlike in England) there is

---

53. *Paterson* v *Welch* [1893] 20 R 744.

54. *Walker on Delict*, 2nd Edition, p 736.

55. Norrie, *Defamation and Related Actions in Scots law*, p 36.

56. [1970] SLT 53.

57. *Steele* v *Scottish Daily Record and Sunday Mail Limited* [1970] SLT 53.

58. *Thomson on Delictual Liability*, p 220.

59. Blom-Cooper "The right to be let alone" 1989 JLS 402.

already a potential remedy in *convicium* for infringement of privacy in certain cases, since there may be no need to prove that the words complained of are false. If this were the case, it might, in the writer's view, be no bad thing, but common sense would suggest that the issue of freedom of the press and the individual is one better resolved with certainty and that a solution may be better achieved by legislation, rather than by what can be a somewhat arbitary development of the Common Law.

Unintentional defamation

Defence of innocent dissemination — Defamation Act 1996

9.27   The Act seeks to increase the scope for the defence of innocent dissemination. The aim is to recognise the revolutionary technological advances in communications since 1952, in information technology and the Internet, which have given the word "published" a whole new meaning. The computer age has brought with it the potential for a huge number of innocent intermediaries and message bearers. It is they who will be relieved by the extended defence. For example, in particular, the extended defence recognises the potential difficulties of the live media interview, where there is no real control over the content of the interviewees' statements. It is not, however, available to the author, editor or commercial publisher responsible for the publication (unless they did not intend it to be published). Neither does the defence protect the negligent intermediary who should have known the defamatory nature of the message. Section 1 of the Act sets down the relevant provisions and provides that the defence is only available where the person relying on it can establish that he has taken reasonable care in relation to the publication and that he did not know and had no reason to believe he was contributing to the publication of a defamatory statement.

Reforms introduced by the Defamation Act 1996

9.28   As has been indicated, substantial changes to the law of defamation throughout the United Kingdom have been effected by the Defamation Act 1996. The Act derives its origins from the Neill Report of 1991, commissioned by Parliament, and originally sought to streamline the law in Scotland and England. However, for various reasons substantial parts of the Act, including provisions on limitation and summary procedure have not been applied to Scotland. In Scotland, the major changes introduced relate to the offer of amends procedure and the defences of innocent dissemination and privilege.

Despite the disapplication of significant parts of the Act in Scotland, the Defamation Act 1996 does represent a significant step forward in clarifying existing areas of the law and introducing the new defence of innocent dissemination. It is to be hoped that this will make the law of defamation more user friendly and stem the infiltration of the law of negligence into this area.

The law of negligence

Circumstances may arise where a statement is made which both attacks a **9.29** person's character, honour and reputation and causes him financial loss, but is made carelessly as opposed to recklessly or wilfully. Traditionally, the only remedy for the complainant in these circumstances would have been defamation and its close relations verbal injury or *convicium*. However, in the situation where qualified privilege attaches, none of these remedies would assist. It is not defamation because of qualified privilege nor is it verbal injury or *convicium*, since there malice is required which will not be present where there has merely been negligence.

It is perhaps surprising that this question remained unanswered until the decision of the House of Lords in 1994 in *Spring* v *Guardian Assurance Company plc*,[60] where the principles of Common Law negligence were extended to fill the gap. Although an English case, as a decision of the House of Lords dealing with the principles of negligence and duty of care, the decision must be regarded as highly persuasive by the Scottish courts. The facts were that Mr. Spring was dismissed from his employment with *Guardian* who had recently taken over the business of an estate agency for whom Mr. Spring had been working. He duly sought employment with *Scottish Amicable Insurance Society plc*, who asked *Guardian* for a reference which they were obliged to provide under *Lautro* rules. The reference was duly provided but was carelessly prepared on inaccurate facts and was so derogatory that it spoilt any possibility of Mr. Spring obtaining new employment in the insurance industry. Thus, Mr. Spring sued *Guardian* for damages and based his claim on malicious falsehood, negligence and breach of contract.

Mr. Spring was successful at first instance on the basis of negligence. The decision was appealed to the Court of Appeal, who found for *Guardian* on the basis that to do otherwise would circumvent the law of defamation which was where his true remedy lay. However, on appeal to the House of Lords, the decision was overruled by a majority of 4:1 on the basis of the

---

60. [1994] 3 WLR 354.

application of the case of *Hedley Byrne & Co.* v *Heller & Partners Ltd.*[61] The principle in the *Hedley Byrne* case was that an assumption of responsibility made by the defendants to the plaintiffs in respect of such a reference and reliance by the plaintiffs on the exercise by the defendants of due care and skill in respect of its preparation would give liability in negligence for pure economic loss.

The House held that there were two questions to be answered:

(1) Was there a duty of care?
(2) If there was a duty of care, should it be ignored due to policy considerations such as qualified privilege?

9.30 The majority in the House of Lords held that Mr. Spring's case could not be distinguished from the situation in *Hedley Byrne* where the reference for a customer was negligently drawn up by the defendants — a bank — and where the recipients had sued because they had relied on it to their loss. Ironically, the reference in *Hedley Byrne* was not defamatory but was of an inaccurately positive nature as to the credit-worthiness of the customer rather than his character. Nonetheless, the principles that were established in that case were that there would be a duty of care where the harm was foreseeable, where the relationship between the plaintiff and the defendant was sufficiently "proximate", where the defendant had assumed responsibility for the statement or reference made and where the plaintiff had relied on the defendant using reasonable care in providing it.

It was held that all these pre-requisites were met in the *Spring* case. The next question therefore on the House of Lords test was whether there were policy or other considerations that should cancel out such a duty. The judgments given by the House of Lords indicated that the two remedies of defamation and negligence (delict and tort) were very different ones and were based on different grounds. Defamation was based on damage to reputation, whereas negligence was based on economic loss. They questioned why it should be that what might be a defence to one legal remedy should automatically be a defence to the other. Economic loss was not a pre-requisite of defamation whereas it was of negligence. The defence of qualified privilege might therefore apply where there had been a defamatory comment made with no economic loss as a result, but that was no reason why it should apply across the board where there had been economic loss sustained as the result of a remark which would otherwise have been defamatory. As Lord Goff stated:

> "I can see no good reason why the duty to exercise due skill and care which rests on the employer should be negatived because if the plaintiff were

---

61. [1964] AC 465.

instead to bring an action for damage to his reputation, he would be met by the defence of qualified privilege which could only be defeated by proof of malice."[62]

In reaching their decision, the Lords also drew attention to the rationale   **9.31** behind the qualified privilege defence. It was originally to allow and encourage freedom to speak one's mind and to give a true view and opinion. Lord Diplock in *Horrocks* v *Lowes*[63] stated:

"The public interest that the law should provide an effective means whereby a man can vindicate his reputation against calumny has nevertheless to be accommodated to the competing public interest in permitting men to communicate frankly and freely with one another about matters with respect to which the law recognises that they have a duty to perform or an interest to protect in doing so. What is published in good faith on matters of this kind is published on a privileged occasion. It is not actionable, even though it may be defamatory and turns out to be untrue."

This rationale was not inconsistent with taking care in expressing such a   **9.32** view. Indeed, Lord Goff suggested that a finding of negligence here and thus the need to take care in providing references would not inhibit employers from giving accurate references where appropriate, but indeed would rather serve to encourage the vast majority of employers to provide careful references which were fair and just in the circumstances.

No opinion was given as to the scope of the judgments. Lord Woolf[64] indicated that the views expressed were confined to the class of case with which this was concerned and hinted that there would be an approach on a case-by-case basis in future. Although that could lead to uncertainty, he indicated that this was better than attempting to anticipate situations before they occurred. The question therefore that remains to be answered is just how far the principles of the *Spring* case can or will be extended. There is no doubt about the special position of an employee and employer relationship and the duty of care owed there. In principle, it does seem capable of extending into other situations, but the question remains how it will affect the law of defamation.

Although to establish liability under the duty of care analysis for what would otherwise be a defamatory statement, there is no need for malice, there are still strict and in some senses stricter requirements to be fulfilled than is the case for defamation. It is necessary to establish that there was foreseeable harm to be sustained as a result of a negligently-made statement; a proximity of relationship between the claimant and the maker of the

---

62. [1994] 3 WLR 151.

63. [1974] 1 AER 662, at 669.

64. [1994] 3 WLR 179.

statement; causation between the two; an acceptance of responsibility for making the inaccurate statement; and reliance on the statement by the pursuer.

It is difficult, as Lord Woolf hinted, to envisage a parallel situation to that in the *Spring* case, where all these pre-requisites would be satisfied thus allowing the principles of the law of defamation to be effectively put on one side to allow a claim under this different species of remedy. The limitations on the expansion of the *Spring* case to other situations perhaps become clearer when the possible defences to defamation are analysed in more detail. One commentator[65] suggests that absolute privilege would always be a public policy consideration which would negate a finding of negligence. More obviously *veritas* would always apply to prevent such a remedy in negligence. Similarly, the defence of fair comment, which protects the right to be able to put forward opinions in relation to the acts of public figures and such like arguably protects a more important right than those protected by qualified privilege.

With regard to other defences against defamation claims, neither rixa nor fair retort would seem to provide a defence to a negligence claim. However, innocent dissemination should provide an absolute defence in negligence.

Therefore, at first glance, the *Spring* case seemed to create a fruitful avenue for those who claim they have been defamed, but might be frustrated in their attempts to seek recompense as a result of the application of the defamation defences such as qualified privilege. The attraction of this avenue would be enhanced by the extended time period for bringing actions in negligence when compared with defamation (*i.e.*, five years) and also the possibility of obtaining legal aid for actions in negligence which is not available in respect of actions for defamation. However, on closer scrutiny it can be seen that the tests that must be met to succeed in negligence in what otherwise might be termed a defamation case are strict ones which will usually be difficult to meet. It is difficult, therefore, to foresee a huge expansion in the number of defamatory type negligence claims.

It may be indeed that the case of Spring may be regarded only as an express recognition of what has always in fact been the case. Defamation was originally designed to deal primarily with providing compensation for hurt feelings as a result of verbal attacks on character. It was not originally designed to compensate for economic losses. The primary remedy, on the other hand, to compensate economic losses is delict and tort. One must ask why then the principles applying to delict and tort should not be applied to what is in reality a form of negligent mis-statement. Hitherto, in other cases where claimants have sought recovery of damages as a result of negligence

---

65. "Defamation, Negligence and Employers' References — The Death Knell for Defamation" 1994 JLSS 418, at 419.

where the harm suffered can only be categorised as pure economic loss, the courts have been slow to recognise that a duty of care exists, as a result of the application of various strict tests set out above. There is no reason therefore to think that the *Spring* case will change that cautious approach.

Privacy

Unlike many other systems — such as in the United States where the Supreme   **9.33**
Court has determined a constitutional right to privacy — the Scottish legal system has never recognised any right of action for invasion of privacy.

This is in contrast to many of the Roman Dutch systems that recognise the basis of such a right deriving from the Roman *actio iniuriarum*, being:

> ". . . an action for outrage, insult or wanton interference with rights for any action that shows contempt for the personality of the victim and also as much as to lower him in the estimation of others."[66]

The Scottish system provides for protection of private property by way of   **9.34**
the Civil Law of trespass and a limited criminal remedy for trespass under the Criminal Justice and Public Order Act 1994, and protection of the person by way of the criminal offence of assault and related civil rights of damages. However, there is still no general protection for the privacy of the personal affairs of the individual.

The issue is one that has generated much interest and activity in recent years, with the protection of the privacy of individuals and the public interest competing for consideration. Although no specific action exists directed against infringement of privacy, for many years the Press Council and more recently the Press Complaints Commission and the Broadcasting Complaints Commission have defended the individual's right of privacy.

The issue has been considered by various committees, from the Royal Commission on the Press in 1949 to the Younger Committee on Privacy in 1972 and more recently the Committee on Privacy and Related Matters chaired by Sir David Calcutt QC, which issued an initial report in 1990 followed by a further Report in 1992. The appointment of the Calcutt Committee arose from general public concern at increasingly intrusive methods used by the media.

The first Calcutt Report recommended the introduction of various criminal offences in England for the worst cases of physical intrusion by the media, such as the use of long-range cameras and bugging devices. However, in relation to Scotland, the committee recommended simply that further consideration should be given to the extent to which the criminal law

---

66. Justinian's Institutes.

needed to be modified, in view of the perceived existing Common Law rights. No legislation ensued either in England or in Scotland.

One positive step that did emerge from the first Calcutt Report was the replacement of the press council with the Press Complaints Commission, which consists of press and lay members. The functions of the Press Complaints Commission are wide-ranging, but the Calcutt report specifically provided that the Commission should offer a means of seeking to prevent publication of intrusive material. A code of practice for the press was drawn up which formed the basis of the ultimate Code of Practice framed by the newspaper industry itself and ratified by the Press Complaints Commission in April 1994. On the subject of privacy, the Code contains provisions militating against intrusions by way of long-lens cameras and listening devices, against harassment generally, against intrusions into grief and shock and against approaches to innocent relatives and friends of people accused or convicted of a crime.

A further Report carried out by Sir David Calcutt in 1992 concluded that the press had failed to demonstrate that they are capable of self-regulation. This report recommended that various offences should be created in England and Wales, although as previously it was suggested that this might not be necessary in Scotland. In 1993, a Consultation Paper was published by the Lord Chancellor's Department and the Scottish Office entitled Infringement of Privacy, which recommended the creation of a general civil remedy for breach of privacy that would extend beyond simply the press. The terms of the proposed legislation would provide for a remedy for infringement of privacy causing substantial distress, provided that the distress would also have been suffered by a person of ordinary sensibilities in the circumstances of the complaint. A person's privacy would be taken to include matters concerning health, personal communications, family and personal relationships together with a general right to be free from harassment and molestation. The Consultation Paper makes reference to the right created in article 8(1) of European Convention and Human Rights to respect for family life, home and correspondence. To some extent the proposed new remedy can be seen as an extension of this right.

Defences proposed in the Consultation Paper are those of consent, lawful authority, absolute and qualified privilege and public interest.

With regard to remedies, the Consultation Paper proposes that the normal rules should apply in relation to interdict and interim interdict (see above) and that level of damages should be comparable to awards for mental distress in sex and race discrimination cases, *i.e.*, between £2,000 and £5,000 in most cases.

However, although the issue is one that continues to give rise to public concern, no legislation has yet resulted from the consultation (and the latest information is that the matter has been shelved), and for the present the extent to which the courts in Scotland will provide protection for the privacy of the individual remains ill-defined.

Spain

Chapter 10
Spain

Javier Cremades
López Lozano, Cremades & Sánchez Pintado
Madrid, Spain

Introduction

Media is faced by numerous restrictions and potential liabilities. This **10.1** chapter discusses the constitutional framework for freedom of expression, protection of personality and privacy in Spain as well as the civil law remedies for abuses and violations of these rights.

Legal bases and their development

Freedom of expression is guaranteed by article 20 of the Spanish **10.2** Constitution. Consideration of the development of this norm helps to understand the scope and significance of the freedoms guaranteed by article 20.

The written draft of the Constitution initially regulated freedom of expression in article 23. Except for a few minor changes, the wording of article 20 of the Spanish Constitution was taken from the draft. Although the preliminary draft spoke both of rights and freedoms, the framers of the Constitution decided in the final wording of article 20 to treat the distribution of information and opinions as rights. The article begins by confirming that these rights are recognised and protected. This formulation shows that the rights are understood to exist before their incorporation in the Constitution and that they are not conferred but recognised and thus protected by the constitutional order.

The basic right to freedom of expression

The wording of article 20 of the Spanish Constitution reflects a certain **10.3** complexity. The text is remarkably open in allowing various possible interpretations. Beside classic aspects of the freedom of expression, new aspects such as confidentiality of sources and professional secrecy are also addressed. In addition to freedom of expression as a right to actively inform, it also covers the right to receive information freely and untainted via any technically feasible medium.

The individual also has the right not to receive information. The recipient must be able to decide directly for or against receipt of the communication. Subconscious transmission of communications is illegal. The State must restrict itself to respecting the freedom of the citizen, within the constitutional limits, to receive information or not. It must also remove obstacles, whether of private or public nature, to the exercise of this right.

Article 20, as part of Chapter 2 of Title I, which is dedicated to fundamental rights and duties, encompasses a complex network of obligations and the possibilities for their limitation. Most of these rights and freedoms form what today is commonly known as freedom of expression. In part this covers freedoms of an intellectual content, and partly freedom of expression.

Freedom of expression on the basis of article 20 of the Spanish Constitution can be systematically presented as follows:

(1) Active and passive freedom of information;
(2) Freedom of expression in various forms:
　　(a) Generally: the freedom to express and disseminate thoughts through any medium whatsoever;
　　(b) Specifically:
　　　　(i) The freedom of literary, artistic, scientific and technical creation;
　　　　(ii) The freedom of instruction (the freedom to instruct);
(3) As a guarantee for the freedom of information:
　　(a) The right to professional secrecy;
　　(b) The right to invoke personal conscience;
　　(c) As the rights of reply belonging to citizens generally and to the public administration *vis-à-vis* the media (not directly taken up in the Spanish Constitution);
(4) As guarantees for the media *vis-à-vis* public authority, which like professional secrecy is subjective in character:
　　(a) Prohibition of censorship;
　　(b) The necessity of a court order for the confiscation of any medium;
(5) The right to establish media institutions.

10.4 The Judgment of the Spanish Constitutional Court 77/1982 of 20 December 1982 makes clear that neither the exercise of freedom of expression, nor realisation of the right to issue communications are conditioned on express or formal recognition by the administration. They are derived directly from article 20 of the Spanish Constitution.

The Spanish Constitutional Court held in Judgment 6/1988 of 21 January 1988 that thoughts, ideas and opinions are also covered by this freedom, and that this freedom should be interpreted broadly to include conscience and subjective value judgments. It held that the precise contents of these freedoms cannot be defined because of the abstract character of the rights. The freedom of expression covers not only the dissemination of thoughts and ideas but also their expression and formulation.

The rights to honour and privacy as limitations on freedom of expression

None of the rights in article 20 of the Spanish Constitution are absolute. **10.5** According to the Constitutional Court, basic rights are an essential part of the national community's system of values. However, their regulation reveals limitations so that they may be balanced with other freedoms. This represents the net sum of an individual's rights, or the precise legally necessary balancing of rights that have come into conflict.

According to article 20(4), the freedom of expression is limited by the maintenance of the other basic rights of Title I, and in particular the rights to honour, to privacy, to protect one's own image and many others.

Protection of honour

Article 18 of the Spanish Constitution protects honour but fails to define **10.6** it. This constitutional law norm was further elaborated by the *Ley Orgánica* 1/1982 of 5 May 1982, the Law for the Civil Law Protection of the Rights to Honour, to Privacy, to an Intimate Sphere and of the Right to One's Own Image.

Its article 7 does not define these rights positively, but describes what conduct is impermissible in this context.

Still two elements of honour become clear, one subjective, the other objective. Honour is composed of both one's self-assessment (subjective element) and of the right that others render one's person the same appreciation as any other person's (objective element). Subjectively, honour is understood as a sense of dignity or self-confidence and self-respect, *i.e.*, respect for one's own achievement, values and capabilities. Objectively, it is the evaluation of one's peers, compatriots-citizens, related to the individual's moral qualities and social value, *i.e.*, good name and reputation in the individual's surroundings.

The *Ley Orgánica* 1/1982 lacks further details as to whether, for example, it is necessary that the perpetrator acted intentionally or culpably, whether opinions and facts are of the same rank and whether the defamation is accomplished when true facts are disseminated and whether there are exceptions. The absence of precise regulation means that concrete determinations of a violation of honour depend on each case. In some cases, whether the claimants are holders of the basic right of honour is at issue.

Honour as an autonomous basic right

10.7   In the preparation of the *Ley Orgánica* 1/1982, it was never considered that the rights to honour, to privacy and to an intimate sphere and the right to one's own image were only facets of a single superordinated right. Each of these is thought of as an independent right, even though this complicated the regulation of this field.

Honour of public persons

10.8   The nature of honour of public persons does not differ from that of any other person. No person's honour is identical to that of any other person. There are always subjective and objective differences. Still, persons of public life, who occupy public office or are involved in events of public interests, must accept that their honour may be affected by the expression and dissemination of opinions or by the distribution of information of general interest. This is required by pluralism and the spirit of transparency necessary in a democratic society.

The Constitutional Court[1] has compared a private person's honour with that of public figures and determined that because the latter freely assume such a position they have also accepted a certain risk of violation of their honour. It also confirmed[2] that honour of public figures enjoys limited protection due to the need to protect freedom of expression. The Supreme Court[3] rejected the action of Mrs. Carmen Martinez Bordiu, who as the legal representative of her son, Don Luis Alfonso de Borbon, claimed against an article in the magazine *Tiempo*, which according to her ridiculed her son. That judgment stated that the public figures

---

1. Judgment 165/87 of 27 October 1987.

2. Judgment 107/1988 of 8 June 1988.

3. Judgment 944/88 of 13 December 1989.

freely accept the risk that their personality rights may be affected by information distributed in the context of public interest.

Honour of juridical persons

In principle, the right to honour is tailored to natural persons. The courts reveal different views of this problem.

Aside from this issue, it is clear that a juridical person, although it lacks any expressly regulated right to honour, may be injured in its name and reputation; the violation of these rights is comparable to the violation of such rights of a natural person. The juridical person can claim a violation of article 38 of the Civil Code (*Código Civil*) in such a case and demand compensation.

That an honour of juridical persons exists is supported by article 18 of the Spanish Constitution's differentiation of "the right to honour" — without distinguishing between the personal and the familiar — and the generally referred to right to one's own image. To restrict the right to honour to natural persons, *Ley Orgánica* 1/1982 would have had to do this expressly.

The Spanish Supreme Court has confirmed that honour of a juridical person may be the object of a complaint.[4]

The Constitutional Court has taken two contradictory positions. It has held that the right to honour guaranteed by article 18 of the Spanish Constitution is attached to a person and that this is not to be confused with dignity and moral authority, such as enjoyed by state institutions. According to this Constitutional Court judgment, one cannot speak of the honour of juridical persons. This view was justified on the basis that for constitutional law's position it would be better to use terms like dignity, esteem and moral authority, which are values protected by criminal law, but are not congruent with the right to honour, which the Spanish Constitution protects as a basic right.

Juridical persons accordingly are the holders of a certain social dignity and can claim against injuries to their esteem and authority. These rights enjoy appropriate legal protection. This protection is, however, weaker than that given to the right to honour of natural persons is.

However, the Constitutional Court has also held[5] that juridical persons also have the right to honour. The Supreme Court[6] has decided that the personal significance of honour derived out of the Constitution does not

---

4. Judgment of 5 April 1973.

5. Judgment 391/94 of 9 December 1993.

6. Judgment of 6 March 1995.

mean that violations thereof may only occur against a natural person. This would make imprecise violations of honour lawful if they were not directed specifically at a concrete person.

The Constitutional Court again decided[7] that juridical persons may be the holders of rights to honour. The underlying judgment of 9 December 1993 involved an article in the magazine *Interviú*[8] accusing officers of the *Guardia Civil* in the Canary Islands of corruption. It stated that the investigating commission had investigated the company "Lopesan Asfaltos y Construcciones, SA" and suggested that further dismissals and restructurings might occur in the *Guardia Civil*. The company then successfully claimed against the publisher in this context.

The publisher appealed against this, but the Constitutional Court again held that there had been a violation of the honour of the named company, a juridical person. The judgment is reasoned on the basis that juridical persons can also fulfil the condition of individualisation, because natural persons are behind every company and these natural persons are holders of the basic right to honour. Accordingly, individualisation may occur. This judgment did not violate article 18 or article 20 of the Spanish Constitution in finding that juridical persons can also be holders of the rights to honour because this does not disrupt the balance between freedom of expression and the right to honour.

Honour of the deceased

10.10 According to article 32 of the Civil Code, a person's personality extinguishes on death. Legal personality is the basis for all basic rights, including the right to honour. Thus, some scholars hold that the deceased has no rights and so cannot be defamed.

A large number of scholars argues that the personality values that deserve protection survive the individual's death. Even a deceased person's honour may not be violated. That person's descendants are entitled to claim accordingly. Closer examination of the legislative intent shows that this interpretation is intended. That they deserve protection can also be inferred from articles 4, 5 and 6 of the *Ley Orgánica*. Based on this principle, one must distinguish various cases.

If honour was violated after the person died then the testamentary executor can defend the deceased's honour. If there is no testament then the spouse, descendants, parents or siblings may bring an action.

---

7. Judgment 139/1995 of 26 September 1995.

8. Issue Number 611, 27 January–2 February 1988, pp 22–28.

If the violation occurred while the person was alive and it is proven that she could not defend herself, same applies as above.[9]

If the defamed person chose not to defend herself, then the rights may not be enforced by anyone else.

If the injury occurred during the deceased's lifetime and she died while an action was pending then the action may be continued by the persons named above.[10]

A very complicated case in this context involved the rights to honour and privacy of a pilot who died in a plane crash in Bilbao in 1985. After his death a series of articles apperared in *El Pais* and in *Diario 16* (major national daily newspapers) attacking his character. His children claimed successfully. The Supreme Court held[11] that the memory of the pilot warranted an extension of his personality and thus of their violated rights as well.

Private sphere

The right to privacy and a private sphere is a right limiting the freedoms **10.11** expressed in article 20 of the Spanish Constitution. Private sphere may be described as follows: each individual dedicates a part of his or her person, time and existence to personal matters and family life, and another part to life in society. By the same token each person has the right to decide whether and how his or her thoughts, feelings and emotions should be communicated to others. The right to privacy and a private sphere and the freedom of expression must be made compatible on the basis of a difficult distinction between public activities falling in the realm of the freedom of information and private life. The freedom and will of each individual must be decisive. Spanish legislation recognises the importance of individual will in this context, so that the Civil Law protection of personal privacy and private sphere is founded on this expression of will and takes account of the area that each person claims for his or her family or self.

True and not insulting information may not amount to an arbitrary interference in the private life of another and must respect the right to privacy and private sphere. The violation of this right of a person is not justified by the truthfulness of the statement.

Only the overwhelming significance of the object of the statement for the public may justify the interference in certain cases; this protects the public's

---

9. *Ley Orgánica*, article 6.1.

10. *Ley Orgánica*, article 6.2.

11. Judgment 519/88 of 7 March 1988.

right to receive news, opinions and thoughts. The preeminence of the right to information makes the distribution of information lawful even if the privacy and private sphere of an individual is affected when the information is of superior historical, scientific, cultural, political or social interest.

Eaves-dropping devices, photography and film equipment to overcome the barrier to the private sphere; distribution of an individual's mail or unsent writing; disclosure of private personal or family data; violating official confidentiality, etc. are all acts violating this right.

Article 7 of *Ley Orgánica* 1/1982 deals with this conduct. It is not unlawful with the consent of the rightholder or if it is necessary for national security, avoiding the commission of a crime or with judicial authorisation. Consent must be given expressly and may be withdrawn at any time (irrespective of a claim for compensation for damage caused by its withdrawal). Ignoring the will of the holder of the right when infringing that person's private sphere amounts to the infraction known as disregard of one's will.

One must bear in mind that certain situations make it impossible for the individual to delimit privacy and private sphere in the way they normally would be able to. Examples are the lives of persons in hospital, penitentiaries or military barracks; they continue to enjoy the right to privacy, but it is necessarily restricted. The welfare state as such represents a certain potential limitation to the right to privacy and private sphere.

In any case the right to privacy and private sphere is the right which most strongly counteracts the primacy of the right to information, which thus must bow to the former in the case of arbitrary invasions of private life. Veracity or lack of malice with respect to the intimate family and private data are no justifications.

Regarding the protection of the private sphere of juridical persons, of public figures and the deceased, the same considerations apply as discussed with respect to the right to honour.

Civil law requirements for liability

10.12 Below, the concrete conditions that must be met for civil law liability to arise are discussed.

Publication

10.13 Publication[12] occurs if the defamatory statements reach a third party. The means of dissemination are irrelevant, whether by spoken or written

---

12. As required by articles 7.3 and 7.7 of *Ley Orgánica* 1/1982.

words, printed material, photos, films or audio-visual means; these are only relevant to the degree of the injury. Writing, for example, as opposed to verbal defamation, is decisive for the court in granting compensation because this means that it may continue in existence. Every repetition of a defamatory statement is a new publication. Defamatory statements made repeatedly in a single article do not constitute new publications.

Ley Orgánica 1/1982 does not make clear who is deemed to have caused the publication. The journalist directly causes publication, but the editor or publisher responsible for that journalist may also be made responsible. In no case may the seller or printer be made responsible.

Dissemination of opinion or factual statement

Ley Orgánica 1/1982 does not further distinguish between fact and opin- **10.14** ion, but it assumes a difference in that article 7.3 talks of dissemination of facts and article 7.7 of the dissemination of statements or facts. The Constitution is clearer: to balance article 18 (honour and private sphere) and article 20.1.a) (freedom of expression), article 16 (freedom of belief) is used, which supports the idea that one is not to be made responsible (in defamation) for (expressing) one's beliefs. Article 20.1.d) of the Spanish Constitution also distinguishes information, facts, opinions and ideas. Interpreting the Constitution, defamation only occurs when false facts are disseminated, but not when opinions are disseminated; the latter are always only subjective evaluation of facts.

The differentiation between facts and opinions is extremely important in a free society for the plurality of thought. The laws thus only protect citizens from false statements, but not from opinions.

Exaggeration

Defamation occurs if certain untrue facts are disseminated, but not if **10.15** ideas are spread because these can be distinguished from reality. Equally general statements, such as "you have broken the law", do not constitute defamation because it is not clear what law has been broken, how or when. In the same way, exaggeration is treated as it has no information value save the intention to insult someone.

Defamation also does not occur when the speaker is talking nonsense or employs rhetorical devices.

Accusations are not to be promoted, but it is not for the Civil Law judges to protect persons about whom a negative opinion is expressed or who is caricatured. The aim is not to help comedians or irate persons to condemn others through negative opinions, but to show that irate opinions or poor jokes are not always credible and that they reflect more on their makers than their subjects.

Degradation

10.16 A person is defamed if his or her good reputation or name is violated by the disclosure of untrue factual information. This also constitutes a criminal infraction. A violation must always occur in the context of a community. If such a community did not exist there would be no good reputation to be violated. The essence of defamation is accordingly in the diminution and alienation *vis-à-vis* others. It remains open what violates a good reputation in an open and pluralistic society. It also remains to be clarified whether the diminution must occur *vis-à-vis* the community at large, a defined respectable group or persons with whom the injured party has a special relationship or on whom he or she depends.

An aspect could be to deny defamation *vis-à-vis* groups that are radical or marginalised according to moral or ideological criteria. But this would be incompatible with the protection of every citizen against attacks on his or her private sphere. The law should not be a rule of the majorities.

Defamation may occur if an individual's reputation is reduced before a group of persons with whom that person has direct contact (*e.g.*, neighbours, clients).

Article 9.3 of *Ley Orgánica* 1/1982 requires for compensation of an injury that the damage can be proven. In "Common Law" jurisdictions this is not always necessary. But it is hardly convincing to distinguish forms of defamation in this way. It may be useful to distinguish between permanent and ephemeral means of defamation for establishing its severity.

Defamation *per se*, which involves a statement that has a defamatory meaning without any further background, and defamation where the statement itself is not defamatory[13] and only becomes such with the knowledge of external factors[14] that give it a defamatory imputation, can be distinguished.

The latter case requires great care. That the defendant intended defamation, knowing the external facts, is not enough; the facts and the damage must have been evident. Then, the intent to defame can be assumed, which increases the extent of liability. Contrary to this, Civil Law generally assumes good faith.

---

13. "X burned his barn down."
14. "X's barn was insured against fire."

How to proceed when there is no damage because the injured no longer has a reputation is unclear. The interest in unearthing the truth confronts the avoidance of unnecessary proceedings here.

Untrue statements

In principle, defamation is the violation of reputation through the **10.17** allegation of untruths or erroneous information, but not correction of facts by putting things in the proper light. The judicial correction of an allegation is regulated by a higher law; *Ley Orgánica* 1/1982only prohibits defamation, while the Constitution protects the right to honour and not an unfounded existing good reputation.

Absolute truth cannot be expected, only an adequate approximation thereof. Persons should not be made liable for minor imprecisions in their statements. Imprecisions should be irrelevant if the dissemination does intend to deceive the recipient of the information (*criterio de la diligencia profesional*).

Scope of civil law liability

In Spain, civil law protects honour since the Supreme Court judgments **10.18** of 14 May 1861 and 5 October 1866. The right to honour is protected by article 1902 of the Civil Code since the Judgment of 6 December 1912 holding that immaterial losses are compensable. Neither the right to the protection of private sphere nor the right to one's own image are protected by the civil law to the extent that the right to honour is.

Article 18 of the Spanish Constitution calls these basic rights, while *Ley Orgánica* 1/1982 develops the protection of these rights through the civil law. Civil law protection of honour has been received positively in society because of its greater effectiveness than criminal law protection. Doctrine has also affirmed this development, noting the prevalence of the civil law remedy due to possibility of remedying the moral injury.

Civil law protection is unaffected by the right to reply regulated by *Ley Orgánica* 2/1984. The Supreme Court has distinguished the right to reply from the protection of the right to honour: reply is not necessary because the right to reply is only one of many possibilities to defend oneself. The injured party is free to choose the means of defence.

The civil law liability for unlawful acts in the context of the right to honour or the private sphere does not involve a responsibility in the usual sense, but a duty resulting from the unlawful act.

Non-contractual civil liability was introduced by article 1902 of the Civil Code: ". . . whoever, injures another through an act or omission, whether through fault or negligence, is obliged to compensate this".

Article 1903 complements this by making a person liable for the acts of another person if the former is responsible for the latter (*e.g.*, parents, teachers, employers).

Articles 9.2 and 9.3 of *Ley Orgánica* 1/1982 regulate the concrete liability for violations of the right to honour. This is an objective responsibility. Article 1902 of the Civil Code requires fault or negligence. The case law assumes that if damage has occurred someone must be at fault.

Article 9.2 of *Ley Orgánica* 1/1982 envisages ordering the defendant to pay damages. Damage is assumed if the unlawful act is proven. This removed an obstacle often lamented by the Supreme Court that the damage had to be proved. This interpretation approximates the concept of a civil law infraction. Judgment 594/90 of the Spanish Supreme Court of 16 March 1990 uses this expression.

Article 9.3 of the *Ley Orgánica* assumes damage and there are few means of legally proving that such a violation has caused no damage. Material and immaterial damage must be distinguished. Material damage requires that quantity be proven. It is determined by existing material damage and lost earnings. The first is patrimonial loss; the second represents a patrimonial interest that does not yet exist. The judge may not estimate the quantity. The parties must demonstrate the composition of these sums.

Immaterial damage creates certain problems. Reducing interests such as honour to a sum of money is unappealing. The case law has adhered to the duty, relying on the principles of article of the 1902 of the Civil Code, to compensate immaterial damage caused by violation of the right to honour. The quantification of the immaterial damage remains difficult. Article 9.3 of the *Ley Orgánica* provides three valuation criteria:

(1) Circumstances of the case;
(2) Severity of the violation; and
(3) The wrongdoer's gain from the violation.

Circumstances of the case

10.19 This criterion is ambiguous. The judgment finding the unlawful act must take account of all circumstances of the case to set the immaterial compensation. Still, a regulation by law is necessary.

Severity of the violation

Severity of the violation may be a derivative of the previous criterion. A **10.20** circumstance of the case is always the severity of the violation. The degree is the degree of infringement of the right to honour or privacy. This is subjective in that everyone will assess the violation of his or her own rights differently, but it may also be determined objectively by leaving aside the influence of emotions in the determination. A subordinate criterion here would be the means of disseminating the injury to honour, whether it reached more people through the media, or occurred only verbally in a smaller circle.

The wrongdoer's gain from the violation

This gives the impression that the compensation of immaterial damage is **10.21** also of an economic nature, which has led to criticism of this criterion. Unjustified enrichment through the compensation must be avoided. The criterion serves only to better assess the damage. If the wrongdoer gained from the violation then it is unlawful in any case.

Challenging quantification

It is unclear if quantification of damages judgments can be challenged. **10.22** The *Ley Orgánica* makes no indication. The case law is contradictory.[15] It may be that this results from the Supreme Court's unwillingness to clearly allow or disallow review generally. It has left itself the option of permitting review in individual cases. The lack of consistent case law means that it is not clear that courts will even admit review of the quantification of damages in this context and even where they do one cannot count on the award being revised.

Critical observations as to the law

The Ley Orgánica

The *Ley Orgánica* reveals several deficiencies: **10.23**

(1) It fails to indicate what should be regarded as culpable in a concrete case;
(2) It fails to distinguish between statements of fact and statements of opinion;

---

15. See Judgment 144/87 of the Supreme Court, Supreme Court Judgment 359/87 of 23 March 1987, Judgment 166/90 of 27 October 1989 and Judgment 640/87 of 11 April 1987.

(3)   It fails to distinguish legal consequences for factual statements that are true and those that are untrue. It fails to set down the role of truth in attacks on honour;

(4)   The *Ley Orgánica* avoids dealing directly with issues as to the honour of persons who are not only figures of public life but where also a greater public dimension is involved;

(5)   The press is not adequately considered. The press is a part of a state based on the rule of law, an instrument for the exercise of a basic right and an institutional guarantee for public opinion;

(6)   The *Ley Orgánica* has not succeeded in synchronising criminal law and civil law in the protection of honour; and

(7)   The undifferentiated treatment of the rights to honour and to private sphere and of the right to one's own image is incorrect. These are three similar, but distinct rights. All have the same constitutional rank but the right to honour is a supreme value in human dignity. The law was developed to protect the right to a private sphere.

Article 1902 of the Civil Code

10.24   Article 1902 of the Civil Code also reveals deficiencies:

(1)   Article 1902 requires the proof of damage, which is difficult with respect to non-patrimonial loss;

(2)   It only foresees the payment of damages, which is not always the most appropriate remedy;

(3)   The concept of "moral damage" is so abstract that a more precise definition that develops civil law protection of the personality rights is required; and

(4)   As a general law provision it is subject to normal civil procedure, whose formalities may risk undue delay in achieving satisfactory protection.

Note: I would like to express my appreciation to Carlota Hansen for her assistance in preparing this chapter.

United States

Chapter 11
United States

Dieter Huber
Constitutional Service of the Federal Chancellery
Vienna, Austria

Introduction

The vast expansion in communications has brought with it a proliferation **11.1**
of actions that could have a devastating effect on the financial viability of
the media and a chilling effect on the presentation of public issues. The
present chapter addresses civil liability issues relating to libel, infliction
of emotional distress, violations of privacy and rights of publicity. It also
faces criminal liabilities, such as for incitement. Clearly, the media are
exposed to other liabilities arising out of their activities, such as copyright
and product liability, but these cannot be dealt with here.

Libel

Libel law is a very sensitive area of law as it attempts to strike a balance **11.2**
between reputation and freedom of expression.[1] Despite this important
position, libel law is often unclear and invites litigation.[2] The Restatement
of Torts defines a defamatory communication as a communication which
tends to harm a person's reputation as to lower him in the estimation
of the community or to deter third persons from associating or dealing
with him.[3]

---

1. "Congress shall make no law . . . abridging the freedom of speech, or of the press". United States
Constitution, Amendment 1.

2. For an overview over the law of defamation, see *Prosser and Keeton on the Law of Torts* 771 (5th ed. 1984).

3. *Restatement* (2d) *of Torts* 559 (1976 Main Vol.).

Initially, libel law was meant to offer an institutionalised process for an individual who sought to avenge his damaged reputation. However, the libel tort has changed from an action to compensate for damage to reputation to an action to impose penalty on media for general publication in an irresponsible manner of an injurious and false statement about an individual or entity.[4] Injury to an individual is premised on the logical consequences of the false fact, not on community-based perception of reputation and harm. Irresponsibility is based on judicial-created standards of journalistic process and editorial judgment.[5] To summarise, a damage judgment in a libel case is aimed at compensation,[6] punishment, deterrence, and also helps to restore the plaintiff's damaged reputation. Libel law is essentially state law, and the Common Law tort remains mainly untouched by constitutional privileges in the private libel setting. Outside this limited publication setting, if mass communication is involved, the constitutional privileges apply in full force.[7]

Plaintiffs sometimes file lawsuits mainly to intimidate or harass the media. Even though such actions may be meritless, they bind media's resources and cause high defence costs. Some courts[8] have reacted to this problem and try to resolve free speech litigation expeditiously whenever possible. They use summary judgment procedures in cases involving the valid assertion of the fair report privilege or any other constitutional privilege.[9]

Although, technically, the law distinguishes between written (libel) and oral (slander) defamation and the law varies from state to state, defamation by any form of communication that has the potentially harmful qualities characteristic of written words is to be treated as libel. A libel suit can be brought by any living person. Some states have enacted "survival statutes" that allow representatives of the estate to continue the suit.[10] Defamation of the dead does not afford a civil action. Legal persons such

---

4. Bezanson, "The Libel Tort Today", 45 Wash. & Lee L. Rev. 535, 536 (1988).

5. Bezanson concludes that today's libel law "underprotects" the community-based interest in reputation, and overprotects the interests in truth.

6. Defamation is not concerned with the plaintiff's own humiliation. *Prosser and Keeton on the Law of Torts* 771 (5th ed. 1984). "The legitimate state interest underlying the law of libel is the compensation of individuals for the harm inflicted on them by defamatory falsehood." *Gertz* v *Robert Welch, Inc.*, 418 US 323, 341 (1974).

7. For media and non-media defendants, different sets of rules regarding fault and falsity exist.

8. *Cp.*, *e.g.*, the New Jersey Supreme Court in *Maressa* v *New Jersey Monthly*, 445 A2d 376, *certiorari* denied, 459 US 907 (1982).

9. Privilege defences tend to be raised immediately and are substantially adjudicated prior to trial. Bezanson, 551. "Existence and breadth of the privilege concerning reports of official or judicial proceedings are matters of law appropriate for summary disposition." *Williams* v *WCAU-TV*, 555 F.Supp. 198 (EDPa.1983).

10. *E.g.*, under the New Jersey survival statute, the deceased plaintiff's libel claim was saved from abatement. *MacDonald* v *Time, Inc.*, 554 F.Supp. 1053 (1983).

as business enterprises as well as non-profit corporations can also bring an action for libel. Courts are divided on the question whether unincorporated associations such as labour unions can sue for libel. Municipalities[11] as well as cities[12] and states are not persons for purposes of a defamation action and cannot be defamed.

Elements of libel

To successfully sue mass-media for libel, the following elements must be **11.3** established:

(1) Publication;
(2) Identification;
(3) Defamation;
(4) Falsity; and
(5) Fault.[13]

Publication

To be actionable under libel law, a statement must be made to at least one **11.4** third person in addition to the publisher and the person who is defamed. If a statement was published in a newspaper or broadcast over television, it is presumed that a third party saw it. One who republishes a libel, *e.g.*, someone who prints or broadcasts a statement, generally is subject to liability just as the author, even though he attributes the libellous statement to the original author, and even though he expressly disavows the truth of the statement.[14] However, the fair report privilege immunises the media if they publish fair and accurate accounts of official actions.[15] If media rely on reports received from news services, they are not regarded to act negligently and do not expose themselves to potential liability.[16] If media act as distributors of a product rather than as publishers, they cannot be held liable unless they knowingly distribute defamatory material. Therefore,

---

11. *Mayor of Manchester* v *Williams*, [1891] 1 QB 94.

12. *City of Chicago* v *Tribune Co.*, 139 NE 86 (SCt.Ill. 1923).

13. As mentioned already, the principal focus in litigation is on the falsity of the offending statement and the publisher's fault. Once the defendant raised a privilege defence, the plaintiff bears the burden of proof with respect to the plaintiff's status, defendant's fault, and falsity of the statement.

14. *Cianci* v *New Times Publishing Company*, 639 F.2d 54, 60 (1980).

15. *Cp.* "Qualified privileged communications" below.

16. For a discussion of the negligent standard and under which circumstances it suffices for a plaintiff to prove negligence, see chapter "Fault".

local television stations that transmit defamatory material in their function as affiliates of a network cannot be held liable.[17] Similarly, in *CompuServe*, the court held that a computer service company that provided its subscribers with access to its electronic library of news publications put together by independent third parties and loaded onto the company's computer banks was a mere "distributor" of information. It could not be held liable for defamatory statements made in news publications absent the showing that it knew or had reason to know of the defamatory character of the statements.[18] On the other hand, Prodigy was responsible for the information transmitted on one of the network's bulletin boards.[19] The court reasoned that Prodigy was more "publisher" or editor than just distributor, because in the past Prodigy had screened offensive material.

Identification

11.5 To constitute an actionable defamatory statement, such statement must be "of and concerning the plaintiff".[20] Identification can occur by making reference to the plaintiff by name and physical description or describing certain circumstances that make it clear who the statement refers to. Fictionalisation of someone in a novel can also lead to an action if the plaintiff is sufficiently identified.[21]

Careless reporting can expose the publisher to liability, *e.g.*, if a statement about person "A" includes a typographical error changing the name of the person to "B". While the statement may have been true regarding "A", it now identifies "B" and may be wrong as to "B". Some cases involve a statement that is true of one of two persons of the same name but not as to the other.[22]

Special problems arise if a statement generally condemns a group of people. The issue is whether the statement can be regarded as referring to each member of the group. Three types of cases can be distinguished:

(1) Members of a small group, *e.g.*, "some" of 11 employees of a firm: In such cases courts often examine the circumstances to determine whether the statement could reasonably affect the reputation

---

17. *Auvil* v *CBS* "60 Minutes", 800 F.Supp. 928 (ED Wash. 1992) (Washington law).

18. *Cubby, Inc.* v *CompuServe, Inc.*, 776 F.Supp. 135 (SDNY 1991).

19. *Stratton Oakmont, Inc.* v *Prodigy Services*, 23 MLR 1794 (1995).

20. *Blatty* v *New York Times*, 728 P.2d 1177 (1987), *certiorari* denied 485 US 934 (1988).

21. See *Geisler* v *Petrocelli*, 616 F.2d 636 (2 Cir. 1980), indicating that it is sufficient if those who knew the plaintiff can make out that the plaintiff was the person meant in the novel.

22. It is not clear whether in such cases the defendant is strictly liable. In light of the development of libel law, it can be assumed that a showing of at least negligence or recklessness on the part of the publisher will be required.

of a single member of the group.[23] Today statements concerning
small groups are likely to be actionable;

(2) Members of large groups (*e.g.*, "all lawyers"): A disparaging statement about members of a large group most often raises the problem that it cannot reasonably be regarded as referring to each
member of the group. Therefore, in general, such statements are
not actionable by individual members of that group;[24] and

(3) Members of a "mid-size" group: In deciding whether statements
defaming members of such group are actionable by its individual
members, courts consider whether a reasonable person would
conclude that the statement in question is probably applicable to
the plaintiff.[25] Circumstances leading to the conclusion that special
reference is made to the particular plaintiff also support the action.

Defamation

Whether or not a statement is libellous and actionable rests on state law.[26]   **11.6**
Generally, in defamation cases, all plaintiffs must prove damages. However, in many jurisdictions, it is easier for plaintiffs to establish the
existence of damages if the defamation results out of a statement containing words that can obviously damage the reputation. Such statements
which are damaging on their face include the imputations of criminal
behaviour, of a loathsome disease, or of unchastity of a woman, and
statements affecting plaintiffs in their business.

In a defamation action, the court must make a threshold determination whether the contested statements are susceptible of one or several
meanings.[27] If the statement is susceptible of more than one meaning, it is
for the jury to determine whether the words in fact convey a defamatory
meaning. If, however, the court determines that the contested statements
are reasonably susceptible of only one meaning, the court must in turn decide

---

23. The issue of reasonableness is a jury question.

24. In *Schuster* v *US News and World Report*, 602 F.2d 850, 853 (8 Cir. 1979), defamation of a large group of
persons was not actionable unless it could reasonably be understood to apply to a particular plaintiff. However,
some states have enacted criminal statutes against group defamation.

25. In *Fawcett Publications, Inc.* v *Morris*, 377 P.2d 42 (SCt. Okl. 1962), *certiorari* denied 376 US 513 (1964), the
court decided that a magazine article regarding the taking of drugs by athletes of a named university football
team libelled every member of the team because the average reader who was familiar with the team would
necessarily believe that the regular players were using the drug. The football team consisted of ca. 60 players.

26. *E.g.*, under California law, "[l]ibel is a false and unprivileged publication by writing . . . which exposes
any person to hatred, contempt, ridicule, or obloquy, or which causes him to be shunned or avoided, or which
has a tendency to injure him in his occupation." Cal.Civ.Code Ann. s 45 (West 1982).

27. *Davis* v *Ross*, 754 F.2d 80, 82 (2d Cir. 1985).

whether the statements are "reasonably susceptible of the defamatory meaning ascribed to them by plaintiff[s]."[28] This threshold determination requires the court to interpret the words naturally and in context unless the defendant can proof that they meant something different.[29]

The fact that the plaintiff finds the statement unpleasant is not sufficient. Statements reasonably susceptible of a defamatory meaning include comments about a person's sexual behaviour,[30] an allegation that a woman has been raped, comments on a person's integrity, personal habits (*e.g.*, use of drugs), and the statement that someone suffers from AIDS.[31] As mentioned already, the statement in question need not necessarily have to be defamatory in a direct way. It suffices if the statement becomes defamatory only if the recipient knows other facts in addition to the statement.[32] Making innuendoes about somebody can suffice for purposes of a libel suit.[33] Moreover, as television broadcasts add new variables to the defamation analysis,[34] courts also scrutinise the juxtaposition of the audio and video portions of a television programme. Courts often are sensitive to the possibility of subtle mixes of "opinion-like statements, adorned with orchestrated images and dramatic audio accompaniment" in self-styled "magazine" news programmes.[35] A pure opinion[36] which does not state actual facts cannot be defamatory because it cannot be proven true or false.

Another category of potentially libellous statements include reports that affect a plaintiff's business reputation.[37] These cases must be distinguished from statements criticising an actual product. The latter is called trade libel and involves disparagement of property.[38] Attributing fabricated

---

28. *Weiner* v *Doubleday & Company, Inc.*, 549 NE2d 453 (1989), *certiorari* denied 495 US 930 (1990).

29. "The words are to be construed not with the close precision expected from lawyers and judges but as they would be read and understood by the public to which they are addressed". *November* v *Time, Inc.*, 194 NE2d 126 (1963).

30. Simply stating that someone is gay does not seem to be defamatory because it only states a person's sexual preference without subjecting a person to ridicule, contempt, or disgust. *Donovan* v *Fiumara*, 114 NC. App. 524 (1994).

31. Further examples include statements that somebody refuses to pay his debts, or simply is a "rotten egg". *Prosser and Keeton on the Law of Torts* 775 (5th ed. 1984).

32. In such case it is for the plaintiff to prove the circumstantial facts and the resulting defamatory sense.

33. *Perry* v *Hearst Corp.*, 334 F.2d 800 (1964).

34. *Lasky* v *American Broadcasting Companies, Inc.*, 631 F.Supp. 962, 970 (SDNY 1986).

35. *Corporate Training Unlimited, Inc.* v *National Broadcasting Company, Inc.*, 868 F.Supp. 501 (EDNY 1994).

36. *Milkovich* v *Lorraine Journal Co.*, 110 SCt. 2695 (1991).

37. A statement was libellous if it affected a plaintiff in his "profession, trade, or business by imputing to [them] any kind of fraud, dishonesty, misconduct, incapacity, unfitness or want of any necessary qualification in the exercise thereof." *Four Star Stage Lighting, Inc.* v *Merrick*, 392 NYS2d 297 (1 Dep't 1977).

38. In disparagement of property cases a plaintiff must prove, *inter alia*, a specific monetary loss and that the defendant acted with ill will. Both are often hard to establish.

quotations to someone[39] as well as the alteration of photographs[40] can subject a defendant to liability if the remaining prerequisites are met.

Falsity

To successfully sue the media, libel plaintiffs generally must prove that **11.7** the offending statement was actually false.[41] This broad announcement is always true for so called public-person plaintiffs. However, if the plaintiff is a private person, he bears the burden of proof only if the statement involved is of "public concern".[42] The distinction between public and private persons is linked to the plaintiff's voluntary participation in the public arena, whereas the "public concern" test looks primarily to the speech itself.[43] Whether "public concern" is present must be determined on the basis of the expression's "content, form and context".[44] It has yet to be worked out whether the fact that a statement is disseminated via newspaper, television, or radio makes such statement one of "public concern" in every case.

Minor inaccuracies do not amount to falsity so long as "the substance, the gist, the sting, of the libellous charge be justified."[45] Put differently, the statement is not considered false unless it would have a different effect on the mind of the reader from that which the pleaded truth would have produced.[46] Correctly quoting someone does not necessarily mean that the statement is truthful.[47] To prove falsity, a plaintiff's evidence can include testimony that would fall within the editorial-process privilege.[48]

---

39. *Masson* v *New Yorker Magazine, Inc.*, 401 US 496 (1991). The defendant is only liable if the alteration results in a material change in the meaning conveyed by the statement and the false statement actually defames the plaintiff. Furthermore, the plaintiff must establish actual malice.

40. *Carlson* v *Hillman Periodicals, Inc.*, 163 NYS 2d 21 (1957).

41. *Philadelphia Newspapers, Inc.* v *Hepps*, 475 US 767 (1986).

42. *Philadelphia Newspapers, Inc.* v *Hepps*, 475 US 767 (1986).

43. Rodney A. Smolla, "Dun and Bradstreet, Hepps, and Liberty Lobby: A new analytic primer on the future course of defamation", 75 Geo. LJ 1519 (1987).

44. *Dun & Bradstreet* v *Greenmoss*, 472 US 749 (1985).

45. *Heuer* v *Kee*, 15 Cal.App.2d 710, 714 (1936).

46. See, *e.g.*, *Wehling* v *Columbia Broadcasting System*, 721 F.2d 506, 509 (CA5 1983).

47. Compare also the "republication" issue in chapter "Defamation".

48. As the court noted in *Herbert* v *Lando*, 781 F.2d 298 (2 Cir. 1986), *certiorari* denied 476 US 1182 (1986), it believed that inquiry into the editorial processes (depositions by the author of the defamatory article, and editors revealing the newspaper's motives in publishing the story, sources, conversations among the editors and conclusions about the impact that publishing the article would have on the subject) was not constitutionally forbidden.

Fault regarding falsity

11.8 Under Common Law, a defendant published at his peril in assessing the truth of his statement. Under these circumstances, the vast expansion in communications has brought with it a proliferation of libel actions that could have a devastating effect on the financial viability of the media and a chilling effect on the presentation of public issues. This has made the public and the courts increasingly aware of the potential harm to the public right to know caused by the Common Law of libel. Consequently, a body of constitutional law has developed limiting the potential liability of the news media. Nobody should be deterred from publishing what he believes to be the truth out of the fear that a statement could include a mistake. Therefore, courts regard certain communications as privileged.[49] Additionally, regarding the issue of fault with respect to the falsity of a statement, the Supreme Court has created a constitutional privilege based on the First Amendment.[50]

The constitutional privileges were first announced in the 1964 Supreme Court decision in *New York Times* v *Sullivan*.[51] The Supreme Court ruled that debate on public issues should be uninhibited in matters of self-government relating to "issues about which information is needed to enable the members of a society to cope with the exigencies of their period".[52] The Court acknowledged that the First Amendment requires a rule that protects some falsity to assure that taking part in public debate is neither punished nor deterred. Regarding matters of public interest and public officials, the innocent mistake should be free of liability.

Therefore, public-person defendants must establish that the defamatory statement was published with knowledge or reckless disregard of its falsity ("actual malice" standard):

> "Public officials and public figures usually enjoy significantly greater access to the channels of effective communication and hence have more realistic opportunity to counteract false statements than private individuals normally enjoy."[53]

---

49. The defendant must assert such privilege to enjoy it.

50. United States Constitution, First Amendment. Different interpretations as to the meaning and the rationales of the freedom of expression exist. Some see the value of such freedom in the protection of the rights of the speaker, others stress the public's right to know and society's right to be informed. A central value of free speech lies in checking the abuse of power by public officials. Justice Holmes saw the "market-place of competing ideas" as a possibility to determine the truth of any idea. The prospect of enlarged individual self-fulfillment is regarded as another important function of free speech. These differences regarding the perception of the freedom of expression are also reflected in different opinions when it comes to determining the scope of the protection of speech. For a discussion of the functions of the First Amendment, see *e.g.*, Nowak, Rotunda, *Constitutional Law* 991 (West 1995).

51. 376 US 254 (1964).

52. 376 US 254 (1964), at 270.

53. 376 US 254 (1964), at 270.

The Supreme Court pointed out that "the state interest in protecting **11.9** [private individuals] is greater." However, an individual who decides to seek government office must accept certain necessary consequences of that involvement in public affairs. He runs the risk of closer public scrutiny than might otherwise be the case. "Actual malice" on part of the defendant must be proved with "convincing clarity",[54] a higher standard normally applied in criminal matters. The question whether evidence in the record of a defamation case is sufficient to support a finding of actual malice is a question of law.[55] To give defendants additional security, an appellate court has the duty independently to re-examine the record in full in determining whether the record establishes "actual malice" with convincing clarity.[56]

To summarise, the status of the defamed party is a decisive factor to determine the level of protection plaintiffs and defendants are granted. Whether a defamed party is a public or private person is for the court to determine. Whether a defendant can avail himself of a fault privilege must be determined by focusing on the subjective state of mind of the publisher at the time of publication.

Public persons

Plaintiffs classified as public persons must establish that the defamatory **11.10** statement was published with knowledge of its falsity, or with reckless disregard for the truth.[57] The plaintiff must demonstrate that the author "in fact entertained serious doubts as to the truth of his publication",[58] or acted with a "high degree of awareness of . . . provable falsity"[59] at the time of publication. This kind of "actual malice" under the *New York Times* standard should not be confused with the concept of malice as an evil intent or a motive arising from spite or ill will.[60] When determining

---

54. 376 US 254 (1964), at 285. *Gertz* v *Robert Welch, Inc.*, 418 US 323, 342 (1974). *Anderson* v *Liberty Lobby, Inc.*, 477 US 242, 255–256 (1986). The "clear-and-convincing-evidence" requirement for malice must be considered by a court ruling on a motion for directed verdict; it is also relevant in ruling on a motion for summary judgment when determining a motion for summary judgment under Rule 56 of the Federal Rules of Civil Procedure in a case to which *New York Times* applies.

55. *Bose Corporation* v *Consumers Union of United States, Inc.*, 466 US 485, 510 (1984).

56. *Bose Corporation* v *Consumers Union of United States, Inc.*, 466 US 485 (1984). The reviewing court must "examine for [itself] the statements in issue and the circumstances under which they were made to see . . . whether they are of a character which the principles of the First Amendment . . . protect". *New York Times* v *Sullivan*, 376 US 254, 285 (1964).

57. *New York Times* v *Sullivan*, 376 US 254, 279 (1964).

58. *St. Amant* v *Thompson*, 390 US 727, 731 (1968).

59. *Garrison* v *Louisiana*, 379 US 64, 74 (1964).

60. *Greenbelt Cooperative Publishing Assn., Inc.* v *Bresler*, 398 US 6 (1970).

whether a defendant acted recklessly, courts sometimes consider the time-pressure media defendants may be exposed to. If the defendant had time to investigate a report further, but preferred not to do so, this may indicate recklessness.[61] On the other hand, if a story is "hot news", the source is trustworthy, and the defendant has no reason to doubt the truthworthiness of the story, he may be deemed not to have acted recklessly, even if the statement later turns out to be false and the defendant did not fully verify it.[62] The media's motives such as the increase of the newspaper's circulation, as well as mere deviation from professional standards, or ill will do not alone support a finding of "actual malice". However, courts will find that the defendant acted recklessly if he purposefully avoided the truth.[63] The fact that a plaintiff has denied the allegations before they were published does not in itself indicate the defendant's reckless behaviour.[64]

The following groups of libel plaintiffs are considered public persons:

(1)   Public officials;
(2)   All-purpose public figures;
(3)   Limited public figures; and
(4)   Private persons.

Public officials

11.11   Public officials are considered those among the government employees who have, or appear to the public to have, substantial responsibility for or control over the conduct of governmental affairs.[65] Furthermore, the position held by the person must invite public scrutiny apart from discussion originated by the particular charges in the controversy.[66] Some state courts held that a job that carries with it "duties and responsibilities affecting the lives, liberty, or property of a citizen" may confer the public official status for purposes of a libel suit.[67]

A person holding a position outlined above is considered a public person for purposes of a libel suit only if the defamatory statement involves either the person's general fitness to hold that office, or the way

---

61. *Curtis Publishing Co. v Butts*, 388 US 130 (1967).

62. *Associated Press v Walker*, 388 US 130 (1967).

63. *Harte-Hanks Communications, Inc. v Connaughton*, 491 US 657, 680 (1989).

64. *Roberts v Dover*, 525 F.Supp. 987 (1981).

65. *Rosenblatt v Baer*, 383 US 75 (1966).

66. Those charged with defamation cannot by their own statement make the plaintiff a public figure. *Hutchinson v Proxmire*, 443 US 111 (1979).

67. *Press v Verran*, 589 SW 2d 435 (1978), involving a social worker; *Soke v The Plain Dealer*, 69 Ohio St. 3d 395 (1994), involving a police officer.

such person performs his job. Statements concerning such individual's private life can fall within the purview of the "actual malice" standard only if the published facts affect the plaintiff's official responsibilities.

The Supreme Court has extended the *New York Times* requirements of "actual malice" and "convincing clarity" to persons considered "public figures".[68]

All-purpose public figures

To classify someone as an all-purpose public figure, this person must have a role of special prominence in society. This category includes people exposed to constant media attention, or well-known in the area where the defamatory statement is made.[69] Well-known celebrities may fit into this category. **11.12**

Limited public figures

To be considered a limited public figure, a private person must voluntarily[70] become involved ("thrust himself")[71] in a particular public controversy[72] to influence the resolution of an important public issue. Furthermore, the defamation must have grown out of such a public issue. The resolution of such issue must affect not only the persons caught up in the actual legal controversy.[73] **11.13**

A limited public figure must have thrust himself into the public eye. Individuals that find themselves thrust into the vortex of a public controversy[74] are not public figures for purposes of a libel suit. The Supreme Court also took a plaintiff's access to the mass media into account to determine whether this person was a private or public person.[75] Lower courts have adopted looser standards in determining the status of a libel plaintiff. The outcome of a court's analysis is sometimes hard to predict, because often a variety of different factors is taken into account. Hence, persons with a profession or way of life that exposes them to public

---

68. *Associated Press* v *Walker*, 388 US 130 (1967); *Curtis Publishing Co.* v *Butts*, 388 US 130 (1967).

69. Persons "occupying positions of such pervasive power and influence" are deemed public persons for all purposes. *Gertz* v *Robert Welch, Inc.*, 418 US 323 (1974).

70. *Wolston* v *Reader's Digest*, 443 US 157 (1979).

71. *Gertz* v *Robert Welch, Inc.*, 418 US 323 (1974).

72. *Time, Inc.* v *Firestone*, 424 US 448 (1976).

73. Therefore, divorces, etc. are not regarded issues of such paramount interest to society.

74. *Gertz* v *Robert Welch, Inc.*, 418 US 323 (1974); *Time, Inc.* v *Firestone*, 424 US 448 (1978); *Wolston* v *Reader's Digest*, 443 US 157 (1979). In this context, courts sometimes talk of the concept of "unwilling notoriety".

75. *Hutchinson* v *Proxmire*, 443 US 111 (1979).

attention may be considered limited public figures.[76] The same may be true for well-known businesses manufacturing consumer goods.[77]

Private persons

11.14   A defamed private-person party generally does not need to show "actual malice" on the part of the defendant as defined in *New York Times* v *Sullivan* to prevail in a defamation action against the mass media. However, in *Gertz* v *Robert Welch, Inc.*,[78] the Supreme Court held that compensatory damages[79] could not be awarded without some showing of fault on the part of the publisher. Furthermore, the Supreme Court pointed out that even a private-person plaintiff must show "actual malice" to recover punitive or presumed damages.[80]

Within these constitutional limits, states are free to establish their own standards of fault. In a case involving a private person suing the mass media, the plaintiff must prove a standard of fault required under the pertinent state statute to recover damages. Some states require the plaintiff to show that the media acted with a higher degree of fault than negligence when the defamatory statement was made in the context of a matter of public interest.[81] Others require the plaintiff to establish gross negligence or to show that the media acted in a "grossly irresponsible manner".[82] Generally, most states require a private-person plaintiff to prove that the media acted negligently, that is that the publication was unreasonable in light of what the publisher knew or should have known about its truth or falsity at the time of the publication.[83]

A defendant may have failed to exercise reasonable care, *e.g.*, by using an untrustworthy source, not taking into account enough sources, not examining public judicial records or verifying charges. On the other hand, the risk of harm created by the publication may not be unreasonable if the defendant investigated cautiously and the story is not one-sided.

---

76. This is often true for persons involved in the professional sports business.

77. *Snead* v *Redland Aggregates, Ltd.*, 998 F.2d 1325 (1993).

78. 418 US 323 (1974).

79. For the concepts of actual, presumed and punitive damages, see chapter "Damages" below.

80. *Gertz* v *Robert Welch, Inc.*, 418 US 323, 350 (1974). *Cp.* also *Dun & Bradstreet* v *Greenmoss Builders*, 472 US 749 (1985). In *Dun*, the Supreme Court limited *Gertz* and stated that where the situation involves a private individual and the defamatory statement does not involve a public concern, presumed and punitive damages can be awarded without adhering to the "malice" standard.

81. *Cp., e.g., Rollenhagen* v *City of Orange*, 116 Cal.App.3d 414 (1981). (In California, the plaintiff was not entitled to recover in absence of showing of lack of fair and true report or malice).

82. See, *e.g., Chapadeau* v *Utica Observer-Dispatch, Inc.*, 341 NE2d 569 (1975): New York Law.

83. *Gertz* v *Robert Welch, Inc.*, 418 US 323 (1974).

Defenses

Truth

Generally, in a libel suit against a media defendant, plaintiffs must prove **11.15**
that a statement is false. Only if the plaintiff is a private person and the
statement involved is not of "public concern",[84] does a media defendant
bear the burden of proof, that is he must show that the statement is
substantially provably true.[85] Again, the showing that the defendant quoted
someone correctly is not enough.

In most states, truth of a statement is an absolute defence. However,
some jurisdictions additionally require the defendant to show that the
defamatory statement was made for justifiable ends.[86] Those jurisdictions
maintain that even if a statement is true, it is "morally indefensible
malevolence" and needless to "kick a man when he is down".[87]

Privileged communication

Besides the constitutional privileges of negligence and malice, as well as **11.16**
the requirement that the plaintiff prove falsity, privileges exist which
reflect the social value of certain statements.[88]

Absolute privilege

In various settings, the public interest in the free flow of ideas is so **11.17**
important that any statement made is absolutely privileged.[89] Members of
Congress are immune from suits.[90] Statements in the course of legislative
or judicial proceedings, executive communications in line with the official

---

84. For an explanation of the "public concern" concept see chapter "Falsity" above.

85. *Philadelphia Newspapers, Inc.* v *Hepps*, 475 US 767 (1986).

86. *E.g.*, Maine, New Hampshire, Pennsylvania, Florida.

87. *Prosser and Keeton on the Law of Torts*, 841 (5th ed. 1984).

88. In this context, "privilege" means that conduct which otherwise would be actionable does not subject a
defendant to liability because he is acting in furtherance of some interest of social importance which grants
him "immunity".

89. An absolute privilege grants the defendant immunity without regard to his motive or reasonableness of
his conduct.

90. United States Constitution, article 1, section 6. However, the pertinent statements are only privileged
so long as they are essential to the deliberations of, *e.g.*, the Senate. *Hutchinson* v *Proxmire*, 443 US 111
(1979).

duty,[91] and political broadcasts[92] are also absolutely privileged. Consent of the defamed may give rise to absolute privilege precluding a defamation claim.[93]

Qualified privilege

11.18 The concept of qualified privilege rests on the notion that, if someone is acting in furtherance of sufficiently important social interests, he should not be deterred from publishing by the threat of liability for defamatory mistakes. This is of paramount importance for the media and is also called the privilege of the reporter. The applicability of a qualified privilege depends on how the material in question is handled.

Fair report privilege

11.19 Fair report privilege[94] permits the media to publish fair and accurate accounts of official actions or proceedings without fear of incurring liability for republishing a defamatory statement.[95] As an example, this means that, if the television news broadcasts of the defendant were fair and substantially accurate reports of the plaintiff's arrest for bank robbery, the broadcasts were covered by the fair-report privilege notwith-standing the fact that the plaintiff was released after it was determined that he was not involved in the robbery.[96]

Section 611 of the *Restatement (Second) of Torts* takes an even wider view. It also privileges the publication of a defamatory matter concerning another in a report of a meeting open to the public that deals with a matter of public concern if the report is accurate and complete or a fair

---

91. *Barr* v *Mateo*, 353 US 171 (1959).

92. In *Farmers Ed. and Co.-op. Union of America, North Dakota Division* v *WDAY, Inc.*, 360 US 525 (1959), a broadcasting station was granted federal immunity from liability for libelous statements contained in speeches broadcast by legally qualified candidates for public office. The Federal Communications Act providing that licencees shall have no power of censorship over material broadcast by a legally qualified candidate for public office bars a broadcasting station from removing defamatory statements contained in speeches broadcast. Under such circumstances, it would be unreasonable to subject broadcasting stations to liability.

93. *Hill* v *Cray Research, Inc.*, 864 F.Supp. 1070 (1991).

94. *Cp.*, *e.g.*, the codification of the fair report privilege in New York Civil Rights Law s 74 (McKinney 1992), which provides in relevant part: "A civil action cannot be maintained against any person, firm or corporation, for the publication of a fair and true report of a judicial proceeding, or for any heading of the report which is a fair and true headnote of the statement published."

95. *Schiavone Construction Co.* v *Time, Inc.*, 569 F.Supp. 614 (1983).

96. *Williams* v *WCAU-TV, WPVI-TV*, 555 F.Supp. 198 (EDPa.1983).

abridgement of the occurrence reported.[97] Two requirements must be met to qualify a potentially defamatory statement for this kind of privilege:

(1) The report must cover an official action or proceeding. Legislative proceedings, statements received by legislative bodies (*e.g.*, petitions), as well as judicial proceedings[98] are clearly within the purview of the privilege. Reports of official activities[99] are also privileged. Following the expansive view of the *Restatement*, lower courts extended the area of protected reports and apply the privilege to meetings open to the public at which matters of public concern are discussed;[100] and

(2) The report must be complete and accurate. If the statement is an abridged summary of the content of a report or of what happened during a meeting, it must be a "fair and true" report. The reporter must convey what the recipient of the information could have seen or heard, had he attended the meeting or read the report himself. Therefore, the account must not present the matter in a one-sided fashion. For a report to be characterised as "fair and true", thus immunising its publisher from a civil suit sounding in libel, it is enough that the substance of the article be substantially accurate.[101] However, the immunity may be forfeited[102] if the broadcaster "abuses the occasion" by exaggerated additions or embellishments to the account.[103]

Some jurisdictions approach the qualified privilege concept differ- **11.20** ently: If the reporter's source is reliable, an accurate report about a public

---

97. Furthermore, the *Restatement* has expressly eliminated the requirement that a publication otherwise protected by the privilege not be "made solely for the purpose of causing harm."

98. *E.g., Schuster* v *US News and World Report*, 602 F.2d 850, 853 (8 Cir.1979). Courts have been divided when it comes to determining when a report about complaint becomes privileged. In most states, it becomes privileged as soon as the complaint has been filed and a docket number has been assigned. *Cox* v *Lee Enterprise*, 723 P.2d 238 (1986).

99. *Foster* v *Turner Broadcasting*, 844 F.2d 955 (1988) (report involving official police statements). *Cp.* also, *e.g.*, a New Jersey statute granting a qualified privilege to newspaper reports of "official statements issued by police department heads and county prosecutors in investigations in progress or completed by them".

100. *Village of Grafton* v *American Broadcasting Company*, 435 NE2d 1131, 1136 (1980).

101. *Holy Spirit Ass'n for Unification of World Christianity* v *New York Times, Co.*, 399 NE2d 1185 (1979).

102. The *Restatement* (2d) *of Torts* 600 sets forth, in part that "one who on an occasion giving raise to a conditional privilege publishes false and defamatory matter concerning another abuses the privilege if he (a) knows the matter to be false, or (b) acts in reckless disregard as to its truth or falsity". The determination of whether such privilege is abused by express malice and consequently lost is a question of fact for the jury.

103. *Williams* v *WCAU–TV, WPVI–TV*, 555 F.Supp. 198 (EDPa.1983).

person can be privileged even though the reporter maintained doubts about the truth of the statement.[104]

Fair comment

11.21 The reporter's privilege protects the fair reporting of facts. Similarly, this Common Law defence of fair comment guarantees the freedom to express evaluative statements on matters of public interest or public figures as long as the statements are not made with ill will, spite, or with the intent to harm the allegedly defamed person.[105] In *Time, Inc. v Hill*,[106] the Supreme Court pointed out:

> ". . . the freedom of discussion . . . must embrace all issues about which information is needed or appropriate to enable the members of society to cope with the exigencies of the period."

11.22 To qualify for the privilege, the reporter must sufficiently set out the facts underlying the evaluation or conclusion. Due to the fact that the First Amendment and Supreme Court case law grant immunity to the transmission of opinions, the fair comment doctrine is not referred to very often any more.

Pure opinion

11.23 "Under the First Amendment there is no such thing as a false idea. However pernicious an opinion may seem, we depend for its correction not on the conscience of judges and juries but on the competition of other ideas."[107] With this rationale, under Supreme Court case law, there is constitutional immunity for transmitting "statements of opinion relating to matters of public concern that do not contain a provably false factual connotation."[108] Therefore, under the Supreme Court's test, if a statement can be proved true or false, it is not a pure opinion and can be subject to a successful libel suit.[109]

However, many courts have interpreted the First Amendment[110] or their state constitutions[111] as requiring broader protection of opinion than the *Milkovich* ruling affords and favour a test outlined in *Ollman* v

---

104. *Edwards* v *National Audubon Society, Inc.*, 556 F.2d 113 (1977); *certiorari* denied 434 US 1002 (1977).

105. *Cp., e.g., Hoeppner* v *Dunkirk Printing Co.*, 172 NE 139 (1930) (newspaper criticisms of high school football coach were not libelous, however severe, caustic, or ridiculous, unless written maliciously).

106. *Time, Inc.* v *Hill*, 385 US 374 (1967).

107. *Gertz*, 418 US 323, 339 (1974).

108. *Milkovich* v *Lorain Journal Co.*, 497 US 1, 18 (1990).

109. In *Milkovich* v *Lorain Journal Co.*, the Supreme Court refused to "create a wholesale defamation exemption for anything that might be labeled 'opinion'". 497 US 1, 18 (1990).

110. *Phantom Touring, Inc.* v *Affiliated Publications*, 953 F.2d 724 (1992).

111. *Immuno AG* v *Moor-Jankowski*, 77 NY 2d 235 (1991).

Evans.[112] This test provides also for protection of statements intended and perceived as opinions. In attempting to define as a matter of law the distinction between fact and opinion, these courts take the following parameters into account:

(1) Can the statement be proved true or false;
(2) What is the ordinary meaning of the words used;
(3) In which context is the statement made. In determining whether an assertion of fact is made or an opinion is expressed, the sum effect and the entire content of a report that contains the allegedly defamatory statement must be taken into account;[113] and
(4) What is the social setting or the medium in which the remark is made, how does the audience approach the statement.[114] If the audience expects that opinions are expressed rather than facts asserted, it is likely that they perceive the statement as an expression of a certain opinion, even though the remark might technically contain facts.

Unbelievable rhetoric and parody

Similarly to the standard announced in *Ollman*, in cases involving parody, **11.24** a statement that cannot "reasonably [be] interpreted as stating actual facts" about plaintiffs is protected.[115] The "key inquiry", therefore, is whether the statements "would reasonably appear to state or imply assertions of objective fact."[116] If this is the case, a statement may be defamatory.

A statement may also be defensible as unbelievable rhetoric. Colourful opinions, *e.g.*, in the context of a political editorial, cannot always be taken as literally verifiable fact. To determine whether a statement consists of rhetorical hyperbole, the courts look to the entire statement,

---

112. *Ollman* v *Evans*, 750 F.2d 970 (DC Cir. 1984), *certiorari* denied 471 US 1127 (1985) (Then Adjunct Justice Rehnquist dissenting). In *Ollman*, the court held that to quote an unnamed political scientist as saying that the petitioner has "no status within the profession" was constitutionally protected expressions of opinion.

113. *Cp.*, *e.g.*, *Moldea* v *New York Times Co.*, 22 F.3d 310 (1994), "courts must consider elements beyond the defamatory statement itself".

114. "Courts are obliged to consider the communication as a whole, as well as its immediate and broader social contexts, to determine whether the reasonable listener or reader [or viewer] is likely to understand the remark as an assertion of provable fact." *Gross* v *New York Times Co.*, 623 NE2d 1163, 1169 (1993).

115. *Milkovich* v *Lorain Journal Co.*, 497 US 1 (1990) (quoting *Hustler Magazine* v *Falwell*, 485 US 46, 50 (1988)).

116. In *San Francisco Bay Guardian, Inc.* v *Superior Court of San Francisco City*, 21 Cal.Rptr.2d 464 (1993), the court found that a fictional letter to the editor did not defame the alleged author because the average reader would recognize the April Fool issue of the newspaper as a parody and the letter to the editor as part of the parody.

placed in context, to determine whether the communication complained of can be construed to have the defamatory meaning ascribed to it by the complaining party.[117]

Right of reply

11.25 The concept of the right of reply is similar to the right of self-defence. It gives someone who has been defamed the right to answer a defamatory statement by using another defamatory statement to defend his own reputation.[118] However, the answer must not be overreaching. Thus, the reply would not be privileged if the respondent adds anything unconnected with the charges made against him. The right of reply also serves to protect newspapers publishing replies of defamed persons if the charges were brought using the newspaper.[119]

Damages

11.26 Punishment rather than compensation often is the dominant consideration in a libel suit. Different kinds of damages can be distinguished by looking at the level of proof required.

Actual or compensatory damages

General damages

11.27 General damages refer to losses that are to be anticipated when a person's reputation is impaired.[120] To recover actual damages, the plaintiff generally must prove injury to his reputation and resulting harm thereof. Some

---

117. *Bogash* v *Elkins*, 176 A.2d 677 (1962); *Maholick* v *WNEP–TV*, 981 F.2d 1247 (3 Cir. 1992) (television station's comment comparing a politician to Manuel Noriega was regarded as rhetoric hyperbole).

118. In this context, the right of reply is not meant to describe a right of an individual to force a newspaper to run a certain statement. This right against the newspaper to reply to editorials attacking, *e.g.*, a candidate's personal character, was held to be unconstitutional by the Supreme Court. *Miami Herold* v *Tornillo*, 418 US 241 (1974).

119. *Fowler* v *New York Herald*, 172 NYS 423 (1918) (the defendant newspaper had qualified privilege to defend editor from unjust and false charges brought by the plaintiff, even if defense revealed infirmities of the plaintiff; it was a jury question to determine whether the defendant newspaper in its publication went beyond its legal privilege).

120. In *Gertz* v *Robert Welch, Inc.*, 418 US 323, 341 (1974), the Supreme Court held that actual harm includes impairment of reputation and standing in the community, personal humiliation, and mental anguish and suffering.

types of defamatory imputations are regarded to cause damages by their nature.[121] However, in *Gertz*, the Supreme Court held that in suits involving a media defendant, the presumption of damages violated the First Amendment.

Special damages

Plaintiffs who want to successfully claim additional special damages must **11.28** show a specific monetary loss, *e.g.,* the decrease of sales, in precise terms. Furthermore, the defamatory statement must be a proximate cause of the special damage. Proof of these factors can be an insurmountable task, and plaintiffs hardly seek special damages.[122]

Punitive damages

Punitive damages are aimed at punishing the defendant. Generally, to **11.29** recover such additional damages, plaintiffs must show that the statement was made with "actual malice". However, if the statement was not of "public concern" and the plaintiff is a private person, proof of negligence is sufficient.

De facto, in public-person libel cases, the level of proof for liability (at all) and punitive damages (in addition) is the same.[123] In public-person cases, the claims are "all-or-nothing games".[124] Punitive damages have been limited[125] or barred[126] in many jurisdictions.

Damages for mental anguish

Recovery of damages for mental anxiety should be for anxiety that comes **11.30** about as a consequence of impairment or probable impairment of reputation. To recover damages for mental injury, the plaintiff's reputation must be regarded as realistically having been damaged.[127] In *Time, Inc.* v *Firestone*,[128] the Supreme Court found the false report that the plaintiff's divorce was granted on the ground of adultery a valid basis for the

---

121. *Cp.* chapter "Defamation" above. Such presumed damages may arise if the statement in question is on its face libel under the state statute. In this case, the plaintiff does not need to prove any specific damage.

122. In disparagement of property cases, plaintiffs are required to show a specific monetary loss to be able to recover at all.

123. *Gertz* v *Robert Welch, Inc.*, 418 US 323 (1974).

124. Bezanson, *The Libel Tort Today*, 546.

125. *E.g.,* Colorado, Florida.

126. *E.g.,* Louisiana, Massachusetts.

127. *Prosser and Keeton on the Law of Torts* 844 (5th ed. 1984).

128. 424 US 448 (1976).

assertion of such damages. The same standard of fault required for general damages should be required also for damages for mental anguish.

Retraction

11.31 Many jurisdictions offer media defendants an opportunity to mitigate damages expected to be awarded because of a potentially defamatory statement. These states have enacted some kind of retraction statute. Such law typically requires a prospective plaintiff to give the publisher of a defamatory statement an opportunity to correct or retract such statement. The retraction or correction must be published in the same manner as the defamatory statement was published. If the publisher complies with the stated requirements within a certain period of time, this can reduce a future damage award or exonerate him completely. The constitutionality of such retraction statutes has been called into question.[129]

Intentional infliction of emotional distress

11.32 The tort for the intentional infliction of emotional distress is the result of a relatively new development. In such action a plaintiff must show that the defendant's conduct:

(1) Is intentional or reckless;
(2) Extreme and outrageous;
(3) Is causally connected with the plaintiff's emotional distress; and
(4) Caused emotional distress that was severe.[130]

11.33 In *Hustler Magazine, Inc.* v *Falwell*[131] the court held that in public-person emotional distress claims, the same standard of proof applied as in libel cases. Besides proving that the defendant made a false statement of fact (as opposed to an opinion), a public-person plaintiff must establish "actual malice" on part of the defendant. The Supreme Court maintained its long-standing refusal to allow damages to be awarded because

---

129. In *Tornillo*, 418 US 241, 258 (1974), Justice Brennan, in his concurring opinion, indicated his doubts regarding the constitutionality of retraction statutes that afford plaintiffs able to prove defamatory falsehoods a statutory action to require publication of a retraction.

130. *Restatement* (2d) *of Torts* 46; *Womack* v *Eldridge*, 210 SE2d 145 (1974). Virginia Law substitutes the requirement of "outrageousness" by "offense to generally accepted standards of decency or morality".

131. 485 US 46 (1988).

the speech in question may have an adverse emotional impact on the audience but also mentioned that these principles are subject to limitations citing *FCC* v *Pacifica Foundation*.[132]

In *Hustler*, the Supreme Court recognised parody as a defence to a claim for damages for the tort of intentional infliction of emotional distress. Thus, the plaintiff did not succeed in proving that the publication contained a false statement of fact which was made with "actual malice".

Criminal libel — breach of peace

State criminal law has been used only in very rare instances to prosecute **11.34** someone who publishes defamatory statements. In some states criminal prosecution for libel is only possible if the defendant causes or potentially causes a breach of the peace[133] by publishing a defamatory statement. Continuing this line, in *Brandenburg* v *Ohio*,[134] the Supreme Court held that the Constitutional guarantees of free speech and free press do not permit a state to forbid advocacy of the use of force or of law violation except where such advocacy is directed to inciting or producing imminent lawless action and is likely to incite such action. In another case the Supreme Court held that the state must prove "actual malice" on the part of the defendant in such cases.[135]

Incitement

In some instances, plaintiffs seek damages on the grounds that the **11.35** viewing of a publication or film caused harm. Courts held that such publications or broadcasts allegedly causing harm do not fall within the scope of unprotected speech, unless they meet certain incitement requirements.

In *Olivia N* v *National Broadcasting Company, Inc.*,[136] the plaintiff sought damages for physical and emotional injury inflicted by assailants who had seen a television broadcast of a film drama. The assailants had viewed and

---

132. Speech that is "vulgar", "offensive", and "shocking" is "not entitled to absolute constitutional protection under all circumstances." *FCC* v *Pacifica Foundation*, 438 US 726, 747 (1978).

133. In *Chaplinsky* v *New Hampshire*, 315 US 568, 571 (1942) the Supreme Court held that a state could lawfully punish an individual for the use of insulting "'fighting' words — those which by their very utterance inflict injury or tend to incite an immediate breach of the peace".

134. *Brandenburg* v *Ohio*, 395 US 444 (1969).

135. *Garrison* v *Louisiana*, 379 US 64 (1964).

136. 178 Cal.Rptr. 888 (1981).

discussed the "artificial rape" scene in "Born Innocent", and the film allegedly caused the assailants to decide to commit a similar act on the plaintiff. She asserted civil liability premised on traditional negligence concepts. Citing *Sullivan*,[137] the court did not permit negligence actions for a television broadcast. To meet the incitement standard, the statement must be "directed to inciting or producing imminent lawless action and likely to incite or produce such action".[138] The television broadcast subject of this action did not fulfil the incitement requirements of Brandenburg. Thus, it was constitutionally protected. Similarly, in *Herzeg* v *Hustler Magazine, Inc.*[139] the court held that the imposition of civil liability for damages that resulted from the publication of a magazine article discussing the practice of "autoerotic asphyxia" and which allegedly led to a teenager's death by hanging, would violate the First Amendment because the publication could not be considered incitement to an unlawful act.

In *Olivia*, plaintiff tried to rely on *Weirum* v *RKO General, Inc.*,[140] a case involving a Los Angeles rock radio station. In *Weirum*, the California Supreme Court upheld a jury finding that the station was liable for the wrongful death of a motorist killed by two teenagers participating in a contest sponsored by the station. The court emphasised that the youthful contestants' reckless conduct was stimulated by the radio station's broadcast. Limiting its ruling, the court indicated that in other situations, there was no attempt to generate a competitive pursuit on public streets, accelerated by repeated importuning by radio to be the very first to arrive at a particular destination. Disposing of the radio station's First Amendment claim, the court pointed out that the issue was civil accountability for the foreseeable results of a broadcast that created an undue risk of harm to the decedent. The First Amendment did not sanction the infliction of physical injury merely because it was achieved by word, rather than act. Although the language utilised by the Supreme Court was broad, other courts understood it in light of the particular facts of that case. The radio station's broadcast was designed to encourage its youthful listeners to speed to announced locations. Liability was imposed on the broadcaster for urging listeners to act in an inherently dangerous manner. To summarise, it can be stated that courts distinguish "acting on the stimulus" of the broadcast from acting "in response to encouragement" of such conduct. Only the latter might subject media to civil liability for resulting harm.

---

137. "The fear of damage awards . . . may be markedly more inhibiting than the fear of prosecution under a criminal statute". *New York Times Co.* v *Sullivan*, 376 US 254, 277 (1964).

138. *Brandenburg* v *Ohio*, 395 US 444, 447 (1969).

139. 814 F.2d 1017 (5 Cir. 1987).

140. 539 P.2d 36 (1975).

Another "dangerous" setting for media is the running of phoney advertisements. In *Braun* v *Soldier of Fortune Magazine, Inc.*[141] the plaintiff sued a magazine seeking, inter alia, damages for the wrongful death of his father who had been killed by two hired murderers. One of the murderers had been contacted after he had submitted a personal service advertisement to the *Soldier of Fortune Magazine* offering a "gun for hire" and indicating that he would consider "all jobs". The Court of Appeals affirmed the compensatory and punitive damages awards granted by lower courts. The court recognised that imposing tort liability for publishing advertisements that result in injury directly implicates the First Amendment interest in commercial speech. The court then analysed a modified negligence standard, under which a magazine has no legal duty to investigate the advertisements it printed, but could be found negligent only if an advertisement "on its face" would have alerted a reasonably prudent publisher that the ad contained a clearly identifiable unreasonable risk that the offer in the ad was to commit a serious violent crime. This test satisfied the First Amendment interest in protecting commercial speech. Evidence sustained the jury's conclusion that the ad was the proximate cause of the victim's son's injuries. Therefore, the magazine had a legal duty to refrain from publishing advertisements that subjected the public to a clearly identifiable unreasonable risk of harm from violent criminal activity.

Actions were also brought against musical performers, composers, and corporations involved in the production and distribution of recorded materials for damages arising from suicides of listeners.[142] However, in McCollum, the court held that musical compositions which allegedly expressed the view that suicide was acceptable were entitled to First Amendment protection and that the suicide of listeners was not a reasonably foreseeable consequence of the distribution of recorded music.

Privacy

Although the law of privacy is nowhere mentioned in the Constitution by **11.36** name, the content of some Amendments, taken together with the Declaration

---

141. 968 F.2d 1110 (11 Cir. 1992), *certiorari* denied in 113 SCt. 1028 (1993).

142. *McCollum* v *CBS, Inc. and Ozzy Osborne*, 249 Cal.Rptr. 187 (1988); *Judas Priest* v *Second Judicial District Court of the State of Nevada*, 760 P2d 137 (1988).

of Independence's demands for the right to life, liberty and the pursuit of happiness indicate that the founders of the nation had something in mind akin to a "right to be let alone".[143] The right of privacy was proposed in a *Harvard Law Review* article in 1890.[144] Two lawyers manifested their protests against the increase of gossip in the content of daily newspapers and concluded that the "right to be let alone" should be recognised as a tort. Individuals should be able to stop unwarranted intrusions and collect damages in a court of law.[145]

The "law of privacy" was interpreted to cover more than initially envisioned. New York was the first state to recognise the law of privacy in a statute, making the commercial exploitation of an individual's name, portrait or picture without that person's consent, a misdemeanour. Two years later, the Georgia Supreme Court provided the first judicial recognition of such law.[146]

In yet another law journal article,[147] Dean Prosser analysed the kinds of actions to be included by the law of privacy and distinguished four areas of application:

(1)   Intrusion on the plaintiff's seclusion or private affairs;
(2)   Publication of private information about an individual;
(3)   Publication of material that puts an individual into a false light position; and
(4)   Appropriation of someone's personality for commercial use.

11.37   Privacy law is state law, and it is not uniform in all the states.[148] Today, most jurisdictions recognise at least some categories of acts that may constitute a violation of an individual's privacy. However, some jurisdictions do not recognise one or more of the four torts that constitute the current law of privacy.

Unlike the law of defamation, which primarily protects an individual's reputation, the aim of today's law of privacy is to protect an individual's

---

143. In *Munden v Harris*, 134 SW 1076 (1911), the court called the right of privacy "an old right with a new name. Life, liberty, and the pursuit of happiness are rights of all men".

144. Warren, Brandeis, "The Right to Privacy", 4 Harv.LRev. 193 (1890).

145. The "right to be let alone" in the sense that it is used in this context, (law of privacy) should be kept apart from the right to privacy which protects citizens against government actions. The latter right to privacy is protected in the Bill of Rights.

146. *Pavesich v New England Life Insurance Co.*, 50 SE 68 (1905).

147. Prosser, "Privacy", 48 Cal.LRev. 383 (1960).

148. Common law recognition had come in most states; some states (*e.g.*, California, New York) have passed statutes recognizing the law of privacy.

dignity.[149] In practice, plaintiffs often sue for defamation, violation of a privacy right, and infliction of emotional distress[150] on the basis of one single act.

Intrusion

One who intentionally intrudes, physically or otherwise, on the solitude **11.38** or seclusion of another or his private affairs, is subject to liability to the other for invasion of his privacy, if the intrusion would be highly offensive to a reasonable person.[151] To be actionable, in intrusion cases, the information gathered through an act of intrusion need not be published. The act itself constitutes the harm.[152]

Intrusion can occur in various ways. The most prominent cases involve cameras and hidden recording devices,[153] or simply physical intrusion. Taking photos of a person or filming someone in public does not constitute intrusion.[154] Consequently, filming from a place open to the public into a private room is lawful as long as the general public would be presented with an identical view.[155] In intrusion contexts, emphasis is put on the privacy in somebody's home. Cases involving public businesses or public officers acting in line of their duty have received less protection by the courts.[156]

---

149. This is not always true for appropriation, the fourth area. This tort involves commercial considerations and is aimed at protecting individuals' (mostly celebrities') commercial interest in their personality.

150. See, *e.g.*, the *Falwell* case, discussed under chapter "Libel" above.

151. *Restatement* (2d) *of Torts* 652B (1976 Main Vol.).

152. Consequently, journalists have not committed a tort if they merely publish material that they obtained from an intruder even if they know how that person obtained the material. *Dodd* v *Pearson*, 410 F.2d 701, 704 (DC. Cir. 1969).

153. *Dietemann* v *Time, Inc.*, 499 F.2d 245 (1971) (reporters cooperated with the district attorney and went to the plaintiff's home who was suspected to practice healing without state licence. Reporters recorded the conversation, the plaintiff sued, *inter alia*, for invasion of privacy. The court ruled that the use of hidden recording devices constituted intrusion). In some states, *e.g.*, California and Florida, the use of hidden recording devices is outlawed by state statutes. In addition, plaintiffs can have a cause of action under the Federal Wiretap Statute. *Boddie* v *ABC*, 731 F.2d 333 (6 Cir. 1984).

154. In *Galella* v *Onassis*, 487 F.2d 986 (1973), a reporter constantly followed Ms. Onassis and her children and made of himself a general nuisance. A court enjoined Galella from coming within 24 feet of Ms. Onassis. The lawsuit against Galella was based on harassment. A claim for invasion of privacy would not have been successful because taking pictures on a street does not constitute intrusion.

155. *Marks* v *KING Broadcasting*, 618 P.2d 572 (1980).

156. Later decisions have distinguished *Dietemann* on various bases: *Cassidy* v *ABC*, 377 NE 2d 126 (1978) (public officer acting in the line of duty, recording took place in public business location, no intrusion found); *McCall* v *Courier-Journal*, 623 SW2d 882 (SCt. Ky. 1981), *certiorari* denied 456 US 975 (1982) (lawyer or officer of court discussing matter with client was not in seclusion within the meaning of the law and no intrusion was found).

Disclosure of private facts

11.39 Public disclosure of private facts constitutes a violation of privacy law if such disclosure is highly offensive from an objective standpoint, and no legitimate interest by the public in the facts disclosed exists.[157] Truth is not a defence to this cause of action.[158] In such contexts, claims of invasion of privacy directly confront the constitutional freedom of speech.[159] Out of these constitutional considerations, some states do not recognise this kind of tort.

As in intrusion cases, facts visible or photos taken from public places[160] or information which is a matter of public record[161] is not considered private. However, the disclosure of a plaintiff's HIV positive status was considered illegal under California law.[162]

The publication of a rape victim's name poses serious problems. Some state statutes prohibit media from disclosing such information. If, however, the media obtain the victim's name from a public file, the information is not private. Therefore, the Supreme Court held that it was unconstitutional to prohibit the media from publishing information contained in judicial records.[163] The publishing of an individual's sexual preference does not constitute a disclosure of private facts if this fact is already well-known.[164] A person can disclose private information to news media and consent to the publication thereof. However, if consent is withdrawn prior to the act of publication, media cannot rely on the initial disclosure.[165]

Besides the fact that the information is private, the plaintiff must show that the publication thereof is highly offensive. The publication of a picture depicting the plaintiff in an embarrassing situation can violate

---

157. See *Restatement* (2d) *of Torts* 652D and, *e.g., Davis* v *Monsanto Co.*, 627 F.Supp. 418 (SD. WVa. 1986).

158. Compare the contrary rules in defamation and false light claims.

159. *Cox Broadcasting Corporation* v *Cohn*, 420 US 469 (1975).

160. "Giving further publicity to what the plaintiff himself leaves open to the public eye" does not constitute an invasion of privacy. *Restatement* (2d) *of Torts* 652D comment b (1977). *Puckett* v *American Broadcasting Company, Inc.*, 917 F.2d 1305 (6 Cir. 1990) (nude dancer shown in news magazine).

161. *Stryker* v *Republic Pictures Corp.*, 238 P.2d 670 (1951) (publication of facts that were on public record concerning former member of the marine corps depicted in a movie).

162. *Urbaniak* v *Newton*, 226 Cal.App.3d 1128, 1135 (1991) (invasion of privacy if special circumstances indicate that the information was given in a confidential communication between patient and physician).

163. *Cox Broadcasting Corporation* v *Cohn*, 420 US 469, 491 (1975). See also the holding in *The Florida Star* v *BJF*, 491 US 524 (1989), where the Supreme Court stressed the special protected nature of accurate reports of judicial proceedings.

164. *Sipple* v *Chronicle Publishing Company*, 154 Cal.App.3d 1040 (1984).

165. *Virgil* v *Time, Inc.*, 527 F.2d 1122 (9 Cir. 1975), *certiorari* denied, 425 US 998 (1976) (The voluntary disclosure of private facts to a reporter did not in itself constitute a making public of these facts).

privacy law if such picture has no news value.[166] However, privacy must give way to the interest of the public to be informed.[167] Even if the publication of private facts is highly embarrassing to the plaintiff, such publication is still not actionable if the material is of legitimate public interest.[168] Courts took a wide view of public interest and included all kinds of newsworthy matters.[169] In *Campbell* v *Seabury Press*, a court stressed the broad constitutional privilege that applies to information relating to public figures or matters of public interest and pointed out that such privilege "is not merely limited to the dissemination of news".[170]

The question whether the passing of time dims the public interest in matters that were newsworthy only a long time ago has been answered differently.[171]

False light

The publication of material that puts someone into a false light position **11.40** violates privacy law if the false light in which the plaintiff is put would be offensive to an average person and the plaintiff can prove fault on part of the publisher. Essential to this tort is the publication of false material which places the plaintiff into a false light and that the material published is highly offensive. Minor errors do not endanger the publisher. Attributing statements to the plaintiff that he did not make, using photos or film cuts with "voicing-overs" in other contexts than taken or consented to can make an individual look bad.[172]

---

166. *Daily Times Democrat* v *Graham*, 162 So.2d 474 (SCt.Ala. 1964) (publication of a picture showing plaintiff with her dress blown up as she was leaving a fun house which was operating at a county fair); "Account must be taken of the costumes and conventions of the community". *Virgil* v *Times, Inc.*, 527 F.2d 1122 (9 Cir. 1975).

167. Newsworthiness is considered in favor of the defendant.

168. *Cox Broadcasting Corporation* v *Cohn*, 420 US 469, 491 (1975). See also the holding in *The Florida Star* v *BJF*, 491 US 524 (1989), where the Supreme Court stressed the special protected nature of accurate reports of judicial proceedings (citing *Cohn*, at 492).

169. See, *e.g.*, *Virgil* v *Time, Inc.*, 527 F.2d 1122 (1975) (article containing references to "bizarre incidents" in famous surfer's life).

170. The court further noted that the privilege extends to information concerning interesting phases of human activity and embraces all issues about which information is needed or appropriate so that individuals may cope with the exigencies of their period. *Campbell* v *Seabury Press*, 614 F.2d 395, 396 (5 Cir. 1980).

171. In *Melvin* v *Reid*, 112 Cal.App. 285 (1931), the California Supreme Court found that the state Constitution protected plaintiff's privacy, citing section 1, article I: "men . . . have certain inalienable rights among which are pursuing and obtaining safety and happiness"; however, other courts found less protection for plaintiffs under these circumstances. See, *e.g.*, *Bernstein* v *NBC*, 232 F.2d 369 (1955); *Sidis* v. *F–R Publishing Co.*, 113 F.2d 806 (1940).

172. See, *e.g.*, *Leverton* v *Curtis Publishing Co.*, 192 F.2d 974 (3d Cir. 1951); *Dunacan* v *WJLA–TV, Inc.*, 106 FRD 4 (DDC 1984).

In cases involving fictionalisation, either untrue material is deliberately added to stories about actual persons or events, or the names of real persons are used in works declared as fiction. The deliberate addition of facts is actionable if it puts an individual into a false light. Using someone's name in a piece declared fiction is actionable only if the author uses the plaintiff's identity in a way that people who know the plaintiff would recognise him reading or watching the piece.[173]

Although false light claims are similar to claims for defamation,[174] it is not clear whether the standards of proof regarding the defendant's fault are the same.[175] In *Time, Inc. v Hill*,[176] the Supreme Court held, *inter alia*, that plaintiff could collect damages for false reports of matters of public interest only on showing that the defendant acted with actual malice. However, the standards of fault required in libel cases were subsequently modified.[177] Most courts still require all false-light plaintiffs to prove actual malice on the part of the defendant.[178]

Appropriation for commercial use — right of publicity

11.41 Appropriation of someone's name or likeness for commercial use is the oldest privacy tort.[179] Appropriation itself has two aspects. The difference between the two is in the nature of the plaintiff's right and the nature of

---

173. In a similar context, the makers of the hit 1993 movie "Philadelphia" acknowledged that the film was partly based on a man who was fired from the world's largest law firm, Baker & McKenzie, after developing AIDS. The admission ended a five-day trial and settled a US $10-million lawsuit brought by the family of a 33-year-old lawyer who died of AIDS.

174. "The purpose of a false light action is to protect the individual in not being made to appear before the public in an unreasonably objectionable false light and otherwise than as he is. To sustain this action, the person need not be defamed. It is sufficient that the publicity attribute to him characteristics, conduct or beliefs that are false, and that he is placed before the public in a false position." *McCall v Courier-Journal and Louisville Times Co.*, 623 SW2d 882, 888 (1981).

175. In *Cantrell v Forest City Publishing Co.*, the Supreme Court did not decide whether the standard announced in *Time, Inc. v Hill* applies to all false-light cases. 419 US 245 (1974).

176. 385 US 374 (1967). The Supreme Court applied the standard for libel suits annunciated in *New York Times v Sullivan* to a claim involving invasion of privacy.

177. *Gertz v Robert Welch*, 418 US 323 (1974). The Constitution requires only that public-person plaintiffs show "actual malice" on part of the defendant. States are free to decide that private-person plaintiffs can succeed on a showing of the defendant's negligence.

178. See, *e.g.*, *McCall v Courier-Journal and Loisville Times Co.*, 623 SW2d 882, 888 (1981).

179. In 1903, the New York legislature passed a statute making it a tort to use the name, portrait, or picture of a person for "trade purposes" without that person's consent. The protection against misappropriation is the basis of privacy law in states that have enacted privacy statutes. Other aspects of privacy law are, at most, covered by judicial interpretation of these statutes. *Cp.* also *Stephano v News Group Publications, Inc.*, 485 NYS2d 220 (1984), holding that there is no Common Law right of publicity independent of the statutory right of privacy under New York law.

the resulting injury. The first type of appropriation is the appropriation of the name and likeness that brings injury to the feelings that concern one's own peace of mind, and that is mental and subjective.[180]

The second type is based on the observation that:

". . . the reaction of the public to name and likeness, which may be fortuitous or which may be managed or planned, endows the name and likeness of the person involved with commercially exploitable opportunities."[181]

The right to be protected against such appropriations is also referred to **11.42** as the "right of publicity." Therefore, whereas the privacy part of the tort is aimed at protecting someone's right "to be left alone", the publicity right targets someone's right to control and profit from the commercial value of his or her identity.[182] It prevents the unauthorised commercial exploitation of one's name, likeness, and other aspects of identity such as a photograph, portrait, caricature, biographical facts and records of performance.[183] Another distinction between privacy and publicity rights can be made regarding the termination of the right. The privacy right is a personal right. Therefore, it terminates with the individual's life. The right of publicity is frequently seen as a property right. In many jurisdictions, it can be assigned and several states permit it to continue after an individual's death.[184]

As celebrities have a proprietary interest in the development of a marketable image, they are the principal parties who have value in their names and likenesses.[185] In advertising contexts, appropriation frequently becomes an issue. Persons who look or sound like celebrities are often used to simulate the famous persons' endorsement or connection with a product.[186] If such advertisement creates a likelihood of consumer confusion, courts are likely to regard the behaviour unlawful.

---

180. *Stilson* v *Reader's Digest Assn., Inc.*, 104 Cal.Rptr. 581 (1972).

181. *Lugosi* v *Universal Pictures*, 603 P.2d 425 (1979).

182. See, *e.g., Haelan Laboratories, Inc.* v *Topps Chewing Gum*, 202 F.2d 866 (2d. Cir. 1953) "in addition to . . . the right of privacy . . . a person has a right in the publicity value of his photograph . . . the right to grant the exclusive privilege of publishing his picture."

183. It has been argued that the right of publicity prevents or redresses unjust enrichment.

184. *Cp., e.g.,* California law or *Estate of Presley* v *Russen*, 513 F.Supp. 1339 (DNJ 1981) (protection under Common Law of New Jersey). To continue a right of publicity, some jurisdictions require the exploitation of the right during the person's lifetime.

185. "The law protects the celebrity's sole right to exploit th[e] value" of her fame. *White* v *Samsung Elec. Am., Inc.*, 971 F.2d 1395, 1399 (9 Cir. 1992).

186. Many people may assume that when a celebrity's name is used in a television commercial, the celebrity endorses the product advertised. Whether likelihood of confusion as to endorsement is present is a question for the jury. *White* v *Samsung Elec. Am., Inc.*, 971 F.2d 1395 (9 Cir. 1992).

The extent to which protection is granted varies from jurisdiction to jurisdiction. Besides imitating a celebrity's appearance (look-alikes),[187] the imitation of a person's style[188] and voice[189] can be unlawful. The mere use of a person's name[190] in a commercial context is lawful unless the name is associated with a specific person. Similarly, anything suggesting to the viewer that the plaintiff is depicted on a picture or movie is encompassed by "likeness".[191]

The fact that something is published and profit is made from such publication does not indicate that it is published for "purposes of trade" and, therefore, may not *per se* constitute a basis for a claim for appropriation.[192] On the other hand, under Common Law, appropriation of a person's identity need not be for a financial gain.[193]

Under certain circumstances, the use of a person's picture, image, etc. does not constitute appropriation. The safest way for media to proceed is to obtain a written authorisation prior to the use.[194] Whenever minors are involved, parental consent is required.[195] If material is used without written consent at all or for a specific use, courts generally maintain that even public figures did not surrender all right to privacy only because of their status in society. Damages and/or injunctions are frequently granted.[196]

---

187. *Allen* v *Men's World Outlet*, 679 F.Supp. 360 (1988); *Onassis* v *Christian Dior*, 472 NYS2d 254 (1984), aff'd, 488 NYS2d 943 (1985) "any representation, including the picture of another, which was intended to be, and did, in fact, convey the idea that it was the plaintiff." (New York law).

188. *White* v *Samsung Electronics America, Inc.*, 971 F.2d 1395 (1992) (use of a person's image by imitating her characteristics in a robot; "the key issue is appropriation of the plaintiff's identity").

189. *Midler* v *Ford Motor Company*, 849 F.2d 460 (9 Cir. 1988); *Waits* v *Frito-Lay, Inc.*, 978 F.2d 1093 (9 Cir 1992) *certiorari* denied 506 US 1080 (1993) (both California law which, in this context, differs from New York law).

190. Legal persons' names or signs are not protected under the law of privacy. In such cases copyright, trademark or competition law may apply.

191. *E.g.*, an offensive cartoon of a black boxer combined with language referring to the figure as "the Greatest" was sufficient to trigger a successful privacy claim. *Ali* v *Playgirl, Inc.*, 447 F.Supp. 723 (1978).

192. *Time, Inc.* v *Hill*, 385 US 374 (1967).

193. Use of someone's identity for some advantage, *e.g.*, political purposes, is enough. Most states which have enacted privacy statutes (*e.g.*, New York, California) require the showing of monetary advantage.

194. In states that have enacted privacy statutes, written consent is required prior to the use of the relevant material. Under Common Law, the standard is less stringent.

195. *Shields* v *Gross*, 461 NYS2d 254 (1983) (Shields unsuccessfully tried to prevent the future use in advertising and trade of nude photos of her which had been taken when she was 10 years old pursuant to a written consent granted by her mother).

196. *E.g.*, *Brinkley* v *Casablanca*, 80 AD2d 428, 438 NYS2d 1004 (1 Dept. 1981) (fashion model obtained injunction against distribution of a poster of her photograph, despite having willingly participated in the photo session, because she did not consent to this specific use in writing).

Even unauthorised use of material can be lawful if it falls within the "newsworthiness" exception.[197]

The freedom of the press restricts an individuals' privacy rights regarding matters of legitimate public interest. In *Stephano* v *News Group Publications, Inc.*,[198] the court held that the "newsworthiness" exception applied not only to reports of political happenings and social trends but also to news stories and articles of consumer interest. The media-defendant's motive to increase circulation by using certain material does not determine whether an article is newsworthy. The content of the publication is decisive, and a picture of a plaintiff illustrating an article on a matter of public interest is not necessarily considered use for the purpose of trade. Thus, such publication is protected unless it has no real relationship to the article, or the whole article is an advertisement in disguise.[199] The display of a picture of a young black man on the cover of a magazine illustrating an article about the black middle class making its way up was also justified.[200] The use of a person's name in a biography does not violate privacy law.[201]

Incidental use of a person's name or picture[202] and the republication of a person's picture in a medium are lawful.[203] Courts have been willing to take a wide view of press freedom in this context. In such situations of republication, the use of a person's identity in promotions does not constitute a violation of privacy rights so long as no false claim is made that the

---

197. *Ann-Margret* v *High Society Magazine, Inc.*, 498 F.Supp. 401 (DC 1980) (magazine included in a story in which other photos of plaintiff were included, a picture taken from a movie in which the plaintiff had appeared partially nude; the faithful reproduction was lawful). For the issue of reproduction in the advertisement context, see also *Booth* v *Curtis Publishing Co.*, 11 NYS 2d 907 (1962).

198. 485 NYS2d 220 (1984).

199. In *Eastwood* v *Superior Court of Los Angeles County*, 198 Cal. Rptr. 342 (Ct. App. 1983), the court held that "the deliberate fictionalization of Eastwood's personality constitutes a commercial exploitation, and becomes actionable when it is presented to the reader as if true with the requisite scienter". The story did not have any factual basis and was only calculated to promote the sales of a publication. No First Amendment protection was granted.

200. *Arrington* v *New York Times Co.*, 433 NYS2d 164 (1980).

201. *Cp., e.g., Estate of Hemingway* v *Random House, Inc.*, 268 NYS2d 531 (1966).

202. *Preston* v *Martin Bregman Productions, Inc.*, 765 F.Supp. 116 (1991) (pedestrian captured in a movie for some seconds).

203. *Booth* v *Curtis Publishing Co.*, 11 NYS 2d 907 (1962) (magazine used picture already used in an article, for advertisement of same magazine); *Montana* v *San Jose Mercury News, Inc.*, 40 Cal.Rptr.2d 639 (1995) (page covering newsworthy events was reproduced in poster form for purpose of showing quality and content of newspaper; newspaper had constitutional right to promote itself by reproducing its originally protected photographs) (California law). Likewise, the use of a celebrity's photo in television advertisements promoting a magazine was lawful. The photo had previously been used in the same magazine to illustrate an article.

person involved endorses the product.[204] In *Zacchini* v *Scripps-Howard Broadcasting Co.*,[205] the court reiterated that entertainment, as well as news, enjoys First Amendment protection, but held that the First Amendment did not immunise the media when they broadcast a performer's entire act without his consent.

Damages in right of publicity actions are not limited to economic injury only. The appropriation of the identity of a celebrity may induce humiliation, embarrassment, and mental distress.[206] Even punitive damages may be available when it is proven by clear and convincing evidence that the defendant has been guilty of malice.[207]

Some conclusions

11.43 The main functions of today's libel law are compensation for damages to an individual's reputation and punishment for general publication in an irresponsible manner of an injurious and false statement. Furthermore, a damage award stands as an example to the media and, thus, fulfils the function of deterrence. Retraction statutes, as well as the publication of judgments, are meant to restore the plaintiff's damaged reputation.

Sometimes meritless lawsuits are filed to intimidate or harass the media. Such suits bind the media's resources and cause high defence costs. Although some courts have reacted to this problem and try to resolve free speech litigation expeditiously whenever possible, the threat of high punitive damage awards still has a chilling effect on the freedom of expression. A developing body of constitutional law, together with other privileges, limits the potential liability of the media. As one of the principal focus points in litigation is fault, the distinction between public-person as opposed to private-person plaintiffs is of paramount importance. Plaintiffs belonging to the former category must establish that the defamatory statement in question was published with knowledge of its falsity, or with reckless disregard for the truth. Regarding

---

204. *Cher* v *Forum International*, 692 F.2d 634 (9 Cir. 1982) (Forum wrongly created the impression that Cher had given an interview directly to this magazine. Cher's name and likeness were also used for promotion).

205. 433 US 562 (1977). The court maintained that broadcasting the entire act (each performance occupied some 15 seconds) would pose a substantial threat to the economic value of that performance.

206. See, *e.g.*, *Waits* v *Frito-Lay, Inc.*, 978 F.2d 1093 (9 Cir. 1992) (California law).

207. Punitive damages were available under California law in a voice appropriation claim by a performer since the persons responsible for making the commercial were familiar with the performer's right to control the commercial use of his voice, and the defendants consciously disregarded the performer's rights. *Waits* v *Frito-Lay, Inc.*, 978 F.2d 1093 (9 Cir. 1992).

private-person plaintiffs, it is for the state legislators to determine their own standards of fault which, to be constitutional, must require the showing of at least some fault on part of the media defendant. This distinction pays tribute to one rational of the First Amendment, namely, to protect the ability of people to debate matters of public interest.

The tort for the intentional infliction of emotional distress is the result of a new development in tort law. Due to its wide scope of applicability it was regarded as a threat to the freedom of expression. However, the Supreme Court made it rather difficult for public-person plaintiffs to win such suit.

The law of privacy encompasses four different torts, not all of which are recognised in all jurisdictions. Its aim is to protect an individual's dignity, its "right to be let alone". However, today's law of privacy is not limited to cases involving intrusion or the publication of private information. It is also designed to redress the offensive publication of false material about an individual. This tort is similar to libel, and, to prevent a circumvention of the variable-fault standard announced in the area of libel law, many courts require the same showing of fault on the part of the defendant as in libel cases. Another field of application of privacy law is the appropriation of a person's name or likeness for commercial or trade purposes. A similar claim can arise out of the violation of someone's right to control the commercial value of his or her identity. Legal defences exist were legitimate public interests in a particular matter are involved.

In practice, plaintiffs often sue for defamation, violation of a privacy right, and infliction of emotional distress on the basis of one single behaviour set by a defendant. Media defendants are well advised to observe caution in cases where the scope of protection of the laws of libel and privacy is unclear. The outcome of suits brought against media defendants is sometimes hard to predict, and defence costs can be high.

Jurisdiction

In determining whether a United States court has judicial jurisdiction **11.44** over a foreigner, it is critical to distinguish between two separate requirements.[208] First, there must be a statutory authorisation granting the forum courts the power to exercise jurisdiction over the foreign defendant or its property. Second, this grant of jurisdiction must be consistent with the due process clause of the United States Constitution.[209] Only if both

---

208. Born, Westin, *International Litigation in United States Courts*, p 28 (Kluwer 2nd ed. 1992).

209. United States Constitution, 14th Amendment.

the jurisdictional statute and the due process clause are satisfied will the forum courts be competent to exercise judicial jurisdiction.

Statutory authorisation

11.45 Some state long-arm statutes provide that courts may exercise jurisdiction "on any basis not inconsistent with the constitution of this state or of the United States"[210] and, hence, simply incorporate the due process limits. Other states require the non-resident to "engage in business" in the state[211] or exhaustively detail the various circumstances in which jurisdiction can be asserted.[212]

Due process analysis

11.46 The basic principle of the due process clause is the idea of certain "minimum contacts". In judging "minimum contacts", a court focuses on the relationship among the defendant, the forum, and the litigation. Thus, generally, the victim of a libel may choose to bring suit in any forum with which the defendant located outside this forum has "minimum contacts" such that the maintenance of the suit does not offend "traditional notions of fair play and substantial justice".[213] Although the Supreme Court has sought to clarify the "minimum contacts test",[214] significant uncertainties about the due process rules exist.

In *Keeton* v *Hustler Magazine*,[215] the United States Supreme Court held that the defendant's regular circulation of magazines in New Hampshire was sufficient to support an assertion of jurisdiction in this state in a libel action against an Ohio corporation. The defendant's only contacts to New Hampshire consisted of monthly sales of about 10,000 copies of its nationally published magazine. In this suit, the plaintiff, a resident of New York, sought to recover damages suffered in all states.

---

210. *Cp.*, *e.g.*, the California long-arm statute. Cal. Code Civ. Proc. 410.10 (1973).

211. See, *e.g.*, Texas. Tex. Civ. Prac. & Rem. Code Ann. 17.042 (Vernon 1986).

212. *E.g.*, Florida. Fla. Stat. Ann. 48.193 (West 1968).

213. *International Shoe Co.* v *Washington*, 326 US 310, 316 (1945).

214. *Burnham* v *Superior Court*, 110 S.Ct. 2105 (1990); *Asahi Metal Indus.* v *Superior Court*, 107 S.Ct. 1028 (1987); *Burger King* v *Rudzewicz*, 471 US 462 (1985); *World-Wide Volkswagen Corp.* v *Woodson*, 444 US 286 (1980).

215. 65 US 770 (1984).

The tort of libel is generally held to occur wherever the offending material is circulated.[216] The fact that the plaintiff had very limited contacts with New Hampshire did not defeat jurisdiction. The Court reasoned that a state has a special interest in exercising jurisdiction over those who commit torts within their territory. This interest extends to libel actions brought by non-residents because false statements harm both the subject of the falsehood and the readers of the statement.

The court also found that New Hampshire had a substantial interest in co-operating with other states, through the "single publication rule", to provide a forum for efficiently litigating all issues and damages arising out of a libel in a unitary proceeding.[217] Regular monthly sales of thousands of magazines in the forum constituted such contacts that it was "fair" to compel the defendant to defend a multi state lawsuit in New Hampshire seeking nation-wide damages for all copies of the issue in question, even though only a small portion of those copies were distributed in New Hampshire.[218]

In *Calder* v *Jones*,[219] the Supreme Court rejected the suggestion that employees who act in their official capacity are somehow shielded from suit in their individual capacity. California courts were allowed to assume jurisdiction in a case brought by a California resident against the author of a story that was written and published in a newspaper in Florida but distributed in California. However, jurisdiction over an employee does not automatically follow from jurisdiction over the corporation which employs him. Each defendant's contacts with the forum state must be assessed individually. In *Calder*, material for the story was collected in California, and the author knowingly caused harm to the defendant's reputation in California. Therefore, defendant's contacts to the forum were sufficient to hale him into court in California. The court also rejected the suggestion that the First Amendment may defeat jurisdiction otherwise proper under the due process clause.

---

216. *Restatement* (2d) *of Torts* 577A comment a (1977).

217. In general, each communication of the same defamatory statement is a separate publication, for which a separate course of action arises. The "single publication rule" is an exception to this general rule. It provides that, as to any single publication, 1) only one action for damages can be maintained; 2) all damages suffered in all jurisdictions can be recovered in tghe one action; 3) a judgment for or against the plaintiff upon the merits of any action for damages bars any other action for damages between the same parties in all jurisdictions. *Restatement* (2d) *of Torts* 577A(4) (1977). This rule serves to protect defendants from harassment resulting from multiple suits.

218. The Court of Appeals for the First Circuit had summarized its concerns with the statement that "the New Hampshire tail is too small to wag so large an out-of-state-dog" and held that no personal jurisdiction existed. However, the Supreme Court granted *certiorari* and reversed.

219. 65 US 783 (1984).

Conflict of laws rules

11.47　The choice of law issues in libel and right of privacy actions[220] present difficult questions. The tort of libel is generally held to occur wherever the offending material is circulated. Assuming the forum's statutory requirements are met and the defendant has sufficient "minimum contacts" to the forum, any state where the defamatory material is published can assume jurisdiction.[221] This, however, still leaves the choice-of-law issue to be decided. In this respect, *Allstate Insurance Co.* v *Hague*[222] provides the guidelines for deciding whether a forum can constitutionally apply its own law. The Supreme Court held:

> ". . . for a State's substantive law to be selected in a constitutionally permissible manner, that State must have a significant contact, creating state interests, such that choice of its law is neither arbitrary nor fundamentally unfair."[223]

11.48　The regular publication in a state (as in *Keeton*) seems to provide sufficient *Allstate*-contacts for courts of this state to apply their own substantive law. Consequently, *Keeton* and *Allstate* in fact appear to enable plaintiffs to shop effectively for the forum with the law most favourable to their defamation claims.[224]

In spite of the great variety of approaches, dividing the scenarios into single state and multi state cases, one can summarise the current state of the law as follows: In cases where publication has occurred in one state only, the place of publication is a critical factor both for the assertion of jurisdiction and the choice of substantive law governing the suit.[225] Difficulties multiply because of the broad reach of media today. In defamation cases where the alleged defamatory statements were published in more than one state, the plaintiff's domicile is critical for the choice of the substantive law.[226]

---

220. The *Restatement* (2d) states that essentially the same choice-of-law rules apply to the two torts. *Restatement* (2d) *of Conflict of Laws* 152 comment d (1971).

221. Compare in this context, *Keeton* v *Hustler Magazine*, 465 US 770 (1984).

222. 49 US 302 (1981).

223. 49 US 302 (1981), at 312.

224. Pielemeier, "Constitutional Limitations on Choice of Law: The Special Case of Multistate Defamation", 133 U.Pa.L.Rev. 381 (1985).

225. *Restatement* (2d) *of Conflict of Laws* 149 and 152 (1971).

226. *McFadden* v *Burton*, 645 F.Supp. 457, 461 n. 2 (1986).

However, for the multi state scenario (*i.e.*, when publication takes place in more than one state), various sets of rules have been stated, and the current approach favouring the law of the place of the plaintiff's domicile in such cases, at least as long as it coincides with the place of publication, has been criticised. Revamping the formerly used "checkerboard set of rules" stated in *Hartmann* v *Time, Inc.*,[227] critics demand that, in multi state cases, each publication must be viewed separately for the purpose of determining the substantive laws. However, this would require courts to consider all laws of the places of publication. In order to avoid litigation involving the laws of up to 51 jurisdictions, courts invoke practical reasons, neglect the place of publication and adhere to the plaintiff's domicile.

---

227. 66 F.2d 127 (3d Cir. 1948), *certiorari* denied, 334 US 838 (1948).

Index

417